Visions of Schooling

Visions of Schooling

Conscience, Community, and Common Education

Rosemary C. Salomone

Yale University Press

New Haven and London

Set in Adobe Garamond and Stone Sans types by The Composing Room
of Michigan, Inc.
Printed in the United States of America by Sheridan Books, Chelsea, Michigan.

Library of Congress Cataloging-in Publication-Data

Salomone, Rosemary C.
    Visions of schooling: conscience, community, and common education /
Rosemary C. Salomone.
        p.   cm.
    Includes bibliographical references (p.) and index.
    ISBN 0-300-08119-7 (alk. paper)
        1. School choice–United States. 2. Community and school–United States.
    3. Education–United States–Curricula. 4. Moral education–United States.
    5. Education and state–United States. I. Title.

    LB1027.9.S26 2000
    371.19`0973–dc21
                                                                99-049202
A catalogue record for this book is available from the British Library.

The paper in this book meets the guidelines for permanence and durability
of the Committee on Production Guidelines for Book Longevity of the Council
on Library Resources.

10 9 8 7 6 5 4 3 2 1

For Andrew

Freedom to differ is not limited to things that do not matter. That would be a mere shadow of freedom. The test of substance is the right to differ as to things that touch the heart of the existing order.

—Justice Robert H. Jackson, *West Virginia Board of Education v. Barnette,* 319 U.S. 624, 642 (1943)

Contents

Preface

A decade ago I was an avowed separationist on church–state matters. I truly believed that the involvement of government in religious affairs would harm religion and fragment society. I was also a firm opponent of educational vouchers, believing that they would skim the most academically successful children and involved parents from the public schools, leaving the poor and educationally unaware in a system drained of resources and abandoned by those with political power. In the intervening years, several compelling experiences have moved me to carefully reexamine and dramatically change my views.

The first was my acquaintance with a nanny whom I had come to know through the network of caregivers when my son was a preschooler. A native of the Caribbean and a single parent, she struggled to provide a sound education within the New York City public school system for her three daughters, one of whom was severely disabled. Her persistent but largely unsuccessful efforts to obtain an appropriate education for her most needy child was my initiation into the world of parents who are trapped in the grip of a public school monopoly and who, despite their educational know-how, lack the resources to choose an alternative. Her repeated stories of phone calls unanswered and requests denied opened my eyes to the stark reality of poor families and the limitations placed upon them by an unresponsive system.

That reality came into sharper relief several years later when I was invited to meet with several Catholic school leaders in New York City to discuss the constitutional parameters of government funding for educational programs sponsored by religious schools. I warned them that government funds typically come with strings attached and could very well distort their mission. As the product of Catholic schooling through grade twelve, I was aware that such schools have had a comfortable history of compliance with government regulation. I also knew from personal experience that my own religious education had in no way impaired my ability to function later as a student and professor in secular institutions nor had it stunted my sense of civic commitment. But what I learned that day was that my perception of the Catholic school mission, at least in the inner city, was totally off the mark. When I asked various members of this group about the religious makeup of their student body, which in New York has become increasingly non-Catholic, their response startled me. They were not certain whether all of their students belonged to any organized religion, I was told. In fact, they were more immediately concerned with saving them from the crack addicts on the corner than with saving their souls. It was clear to me that these were modern-day missionaries living and working in the poorest of neighborhoods and providing not only a stable education but a sense of community and caring that the impersonal and often indifferent public school system was failing to provide. And they were doing it at half the cost.

I subsequently became acquainted with the sponsors of a privately funded scholarship program in the City. A public event in Central Park in the spring of 1997 solidified my conversion to family choice. What I encountered that day were hundreds of "working poor" families, primarily racial minorities, not only celebrating their good fortune in having been chosen at random to receive scholarships for their children to attend private schools, but also personally thanking the organizers for having offered this golden opportunity and requesting the same for their other children. This event spoke volumes on the failures of the public schools, the public service rendered by at least some religious schools, and the political shortsightedness in denying the latter public funds.

But on a more personal note, what confirmed my newly found belief in the concept of family choice was my own ability to exercise it in the selection of my son's school within the private independent sector. I had to seriously search within myself, examine my fundamental values, and question why such a committed public school advocate was opting out of public education in a suburban community known for its high quality public schools. I knew that my decision stemmed from a desire to offer my child the best educational opportunity possible, including small class size, a focused curriculum combining elements of tradition and innovation, a broad range of athletic and artistic enrichment experiences, and a track into the best colleges in the country. But as I visited various schools, I realized that academics were only part of what was driving my decision. The other, equally significant part was the institutional ethos and value structure that pervaded the formal and hidden curriculum of every institution. I was looking for a school that instilled civility and civic virtue, a sense of caring and respect for others, and a commitment to social justice. If schooling was such a powerful socializing agent, then I wanted a school that would reaffirm and reinforce in my son his family's values. I fully appreciated my ability to make this significant choice for my child. Yet at the same time I despaired in the inability of most other parents, with equally big dreams for their children and equally clear visions of the good life, to make a similar choice whether it be in the public or private, sectarian or independent sectors. For me to exercise that choice in my personal life without embracing family choice in my public life would have betrayed my commitment to equal educational opportunity.

ACKNOWLEDGMENTS

The arguments advanced here have evolved over the course of several years and several prior publications, significant portions of which I have incorporated into this work. Various chapters are drawn in part from "Common Schools, Uncommon Values," which appeared in the *Yale Law and Policy Review* 14 (1996): 169–235. Chapter 6, the case study of the Bedford school litigation, is a revised and updated version of "Struggling with the Devil: A Case Study of Values in Conflict," which originally appeared in the *Georgia Law Review* 32 (1998): 633–97. I deeply appreciate the time and interest of numerous school officials, community leaders, and parents who shared with me their hopes and fears as the legal drama in Bedford unfolded. The extensive interviews that I conducted over the course of 2½ years offered me a real-world lens for examining the political dynamics of conflicts over educational values and purposes.

In the course of developing both these earlier works and subsequently the present book, I have benefited from the generous comments and suggestions of various scholars: Stephen Arons, John Coughlin, Susan Kilbourne, Ira (Chip) Lupu, Toni Marie Massaro, Martha Minow, Jeffrey Mirel, Diane Ravitch, Albert Rosenthal, Joseph Viteritti, Philip Weinberg, and Barbara Bennett Woodhouse as well as two anonymous readers enlisted by Yale University Press. I attribute to each of them the strengths of the book while ascribing any weaknesses to myself. I also have benefited from the research of three extraordinarily capable and dedicated student assistants: Jazmine Estacio (Class of 1997), David Donohue (Class of 1998), and Stephanie Reday (Class of 1999). I wish to acknowledge the Spencer Foundation for having funded this project through several grants and St. John's University School of Law, whose Faculty Research Program provided me with summer research stipends, travel expenses to present the original concept paper at the University of Bologna in the spring of 1995, and a sabbatical leave which expedited the research. A word of thanks goes to Toni Aiello and the staff of the St. John's Law Library, who worked tirelessly to fulfill an almost endless list of ongoing requests for a vast array of interdisciplinary materials. My thanks also go to Lawrence Kenney for his skillful editing and especially to John Covell, my editor at Yale University Press, whose support and belief in this project played a pivotal role in bringing it to reality with relative ease.

Most important, I owe a world of gratitude to my husband, Joe Viteritti, for his encouragement and intellectual sustenance and to our son Andrew, who demonstrated understanding and patience well beyond his years as I raced against the clock to complete this project before I irretrievably lost his childhood.

Visions of Schooling

Chapter 1 Introduction

In recent years, reports of a national culture war have saturated the popular press and academic journals.[1] Commentators warn us that opposing forces are waging a fierce political struggle for the heart and soul of America, potentially threatening the Republic itself. Common values and ideals rooted in shared religious beliefs and nationalistic spirit have lost their resonance, we are told.[2] Admittedly some of this discussion has begun to wear thin with exaggeration. Some even sounds faintly apocalyptic. Nevertheless, the truth remains that our diverse values are shaking our national identity to the core and eroding our understanding of those values we do share. Nowhere is this struggle more volatile than in that bastion of cultural definition and reproduction that is public education.

The public school curriculum has served as the most visible target in these battles. Over the past decade, school districts from Maine to California have been caught in gridlock over value conflicts, capturing the attention of the press and the imagination of the American public. In Lake County, Florida, community members successfully fought back against a conservative Christian school board takeover and the required teaching of American culture as superior to others.[3] In New York City, a controversial multicultural curriculum and the now-infamous book *Heather Has Two Mommies* precipitated the chancellor's downfall.[4] In Pontotoc, Mississippi, a mother and her six children were harassed by teachers and students and ostracized by the community for legally challenging various prayer practices in the local public school.[5]

These stories are believable but, nevertheless, startling and troubling in view of the history, purpose, and promise of the common school as originally conceived more than a century ago. The public school was to be the crucible in which our democratic and republican roots would blend. School reformers of the mid–nineteenth century designed the common school with a view toward developing civic virtue and a national character through a shared set of values reflected in the curriculum. The common experience would create citizens who could respect each other's differences while sharing a common ethos of what it means to be an American. Mass compulsory schooling would permit individuals across the economic spectrum to both realize their own potential and support civic purposes through enhanced participation as informed citizens sharing a public philosophy. Underlying this ambitious enterprise was an unspoken assumption that Americans, old and new, could coalesce around a broad, almost all-inclusive set of values and vision of educational purpose and process on which the indoctrinative forces could build. There was a faith that education was scientifically determinate in its means and politically unified in its ends.

Social and political events over the course of the twentieth century have seemingly fractured this grand scheme so badly that some believe it may be near the breaking point. The Protestant morality that served as the bedrock of cohesion for the early common schools has given way to a secularist perspective that pervades public schooling and American popular culture. With roots in the progressive movement and the educational philosophy of John Dewey, secularism later was reinforced in the Supreme Court's prohibition in the 1960s against school prayer and Bible reading. The Court's rulings gradually but profoundly shaped the perception among the public and among educators regarding the role of religion in public education. While some communities have persistently flouted the school prayer decisions or devised ways to circumvent them, most school officials have interpreted them as an absolute ban against any hint of God or Judeo-Christian beliefs from public schools. And although numerous Americans demonstrate deep religious commitments, the expression of those commitments has been removed from the public square and from public discourse while becoming increasingly diverse with each new wave of immigration.[6]

Growth patterns among non-Judeo-Christian faiths, particularly Islam, Buddhism, and Hinduism, demand special attention. Over the past two decades, the number of Muslims in the United States has nearly quadrupled, while Buddhists and Hindus now make up sizeable religious minorities. At the same time, the nonreligious population presently constitutes between 8 and 10 percent of the population, up from 2 percent in 1952.[7]

The civil rights movement of the 1960s had an equally indelible influence on educational values. In the process of promoting equality for racial minorities, women, and other disenfranchised groups, the movement redirected the public's focus from commonalities to diversity and individual and group differences. In the process a new language of rights including the rights of children became a dominant mode of legal and political communication. Following on the heels of that movement was a cultural revolution introducing a broad range of lifestyles, worldviews, and social issues that reinforced neoprogressive ideals and gradually became reflected and addressed in the materials and practices commonly used in the schools.

Through the 1970s, the content of education underwent two main changes. Educators became increasingly uncomfortable with the concept of schooling as indoctrination. In classrooms across the country, teachers no longer taught right and wrong as moral absolutes but rather led students to define and clarify their own values, which did not necessarily reflect those of their parents. Meanwhile, a new generation of neoprogressives expanded the curriculum beyond cognitive skills and knowledge in an attempt to educate the "whole child" and to address such social issues as sexuality and drug abuse along with the psychological needs of students. Some of these programs slowly ignited a firestorm of controversy in communities around the country.

Education was no longer confined to the basics, to the proverbial three R's. Over the following two decades, visualization and relaxation techniques, sex, drug, and AIDS education, environmental and global education, decision-making programs, sensitivity toward gays and lesbians, and recognition of nontraditional roles for women and men were included among the established offerings in schools throughout the nation. These topics and perspectives became part of the established canon of public schooling and, to a large extent, private schooling as well. Major textbook companies and publishers of children's literature shaped, fostered, and reinforced the new creed.

Some Americans hardly noticed this dramatic transformation in the substance and process of schooling. Many of those who did take note, particularly members of the educational establishment, hailed the changes as reflecting diversity, tolerance, and self-awareness. It was progress. Others passively acquiesced, deferring to the expertise of professional educators. One group, however, watched carefully and with grave concern. In pockets throughout the country, conservative Christians gradually embarked upon a grassroots campaign to wrest public schooling from the secularists. This concerted effort gained momentum and national attention as the religious right began to mobilize politically in the late 1970s. As far as they were concerned, schooling had strayed from its core mission. Railing against what they perceived as a one-way street to pluralism and tolerance, they set their sights on two issues—school prayer and the curriculum. Their goals were well focused and ambitious. They wanted to reintroduce organized prayer and other forms of religious expression, to rid the schools of offensive anti-Christian ideas, and to redirect the curriculum back to the basics.

Beginning in the 1980s, efforts to promote some form of religious expression in the schools began to engage Congress and state legislatures in endless political maneuvering. By 1994, 60 to 70 percent of Americans would respond favorably to the idea of some form of school prayer, while at least twenty-five states had enacted legislation permitting a moment of silence to be observed in the schools.[8] Similar sentiments are reflected in the Religious Equality Amendments, which have been introduced in Congress repeatedly and unsuccessfully over the past decade. Variously worded, these all protect the "dictates of conscience."

In the early 1990s, religious conservative organizations expanded their efforts beyond the prayer issue into a more ambitious endeavor to reconfigure public education in a way that would reflect their traditional values and religious worldview. In doing so, they adopted the lobbying and litigation strategies and even some of the constitutional arguments developed by civil liberties groups in the 1960s. In 1995, the Christian Coalition stepped into the national spotlight with its *Contract with the American Family*. Coalition leaders described this document not as a Christian agenda but as a profamily agenda, including a provision supporting the right of parents to direct the upbringing and education of their children. According to Ralph Reed, then–executive director of the coalition, the ten provisions outlined in the *Contract* "enjoy support from 60 to 90 percent of the American people," a startling yet nonetheless compelling assertion.[9] As the 1990s wore on, religious conservatives stepped up their decades-long battle against the preeminence of evolution theory. Instead of trying to impose creation science onto the curriculum, which the Supreme Court had rejected a decade earlier, they redirected their strategy to keeping Darwin out of the class-room or ensuring that, if evolution is taught, it is presented as only one unproven theory. By the close of the decade, Georgia, New Mexico, and Nebraska had made changes to varying degrees, including disclaimers in science books noting that "evolution is not fact," while the Kansas state guidelines had deleted most references to biological evolution and big bang theory.

The educational establishment and local school officials have strongly resisted individual and organized efforts to advance this agenda. Obviously it poses a se-rious threat to public schooling as it has evolved in recent decades. In the face of local opposition, a growing number of parents have used the courts as a ve-hicle for redressing what they perceive as educational wrongs growing out of the prevailing curriculum. Relying on liberty interests, rights to religious freedom, and mandates of church/state separation founded in the federal Constitution, parents have asserted a legal right to opt their children out of certain textbooks, materials, programs, and practices, many of which are widely used in schools throughout the country and officially acknowledged by educational experts. Others have raised the specter of secular humanism and New Age philosophy to remove offensive materials and programs from the school setting, eliciting cries of censorship from the larger community.

Still others, spanning the political continuum, have abandoned institution-alized education and claimed the right to educate their children at home. Home schooling traditionally was branded a fringe activity—the domain of Bible-tot-ing parents and off-the-grid hippies. Each group rejected public schools for dif-ferent reasons—the first because it viewed the schools as undisciplined and amoral and the second because it considered them authoritarian and dehu-manizing. But now, aided by technology, the concept is inching its way into the mainstream. In recent years, a new breed of home-schooler has emerged, moti-vated less by religious beliefs and political ideology than by practical concerns, including the escalation in school violence, the decreasing quality of the aca-demic program, and increasing peer pressure and competition. In fact, in the 1995–96 school year, parents for the first time ranked dissatisfaction with the public schools above religious reasons as the most important impetus to home school their children. As *Education Week* noted in 1996, "Some see it as no less than a battle between parents and the state for the control of a child's mind."[10] By 1996–97, there were an estimated 700,000 to 1,150,000 children in grades kindergarten through twelve being schooled at home.[11] Yet, regardless of their motivational concerns, home-schoolers place high priority on family autonomy and familial bonds.[12]

At the same time, a growing number of Christian fundamentalist parents are educating their children in their own church-affiliated schools. In fact, Christian day schools have expanded at a faster rate than any other group within the private sector in recent decades. Between the 1960s and 1980s alone, eight to ten thousand such schools were established, with an estimated total enrollment of one million students.[13] Many of these are unaccredited, and some resist any form of government regulation. These typically are "total institutions" designed not as a variant or "better expression" of public schooling but rather as a closed system based on absolute beliefs, a rigid point of view, and "scriptural Truth with a capital T."[14]

Although Christian day schools conventionally have served white student populations, an increasing number of African American communities and churches are now aligning themselves with the movement and establishing schools, notably in urban areas. Since the 1970s, what has been termed black flight to the private sector has steadily increased, marking a clear departure from the historical support African American families have shown toward public education. In 1970, less than 4 percent of African American students were enrolled in nonpublic schools. That figure rose to 8.1 percent in 1987–88 and to 9.3 percent in 1993–94.[15] Coinciding with the growth in Christian schools is the revival of Catholic schooling, especially in urban areas. Often with support from private philanthropy, church leaders have maintained a commitment to educating the children of the working poor, many of them racial minorities, who are fleeing the neighborhood public school in record numbers in search of a more academically rigorous, safer, and values-focused education for their children. Between the 1992 and 1998 school years, total Catholic school enrollment nationwide increased by more than eighty-one thousand students.[16]

For most families, however, the alternative of home schooling is impractical or undesirable, while the option of private schooling lies beyond their financial or geographic reach. Others simply prefer the religiously and economically diverse student body along with the cultural enrichment and athletic programs that public schools frequently offer. Some families silently struggle to remain within public education while compromising their deeply held values and beliefs. With greater frequency they challenge the system, often at considerable emotional cost to their children. In recent decades, disaffected parents increasingly have engaged the courts in the continued struggle over educational values, both religious and secular, developing a complex body of case law that has defined the bounds of Supreme Court precedent and tested novel legal theories. In addressing these claims of parental discontent, courts have struggled to balance the interests of the state in educating for democratic citizenship and the interests of cultural and religious minorities in maintaining their identity.

But courts must operate within the confines of their legitimacy and capacity. Not only are they bound by precedent, but their remedial powers are limited even when they identify a legal wrong. Outside of such blatant and pervasive constitutional violations as legally enforced racial segregation, courts are reluctant to intrude into the daily management of schools. So despite strong dicta and favorable Supreme Court rulings in several parental rights cases dating from the 1920s through the 1970s, the ambiguities and inherent narrowness of those decisions have made federal courts less than hospitable to curricular challenges brought by parental dissenters.

While parents continue to press their claims before school officials and judges, a rising level of frustration has moved these concerns into the political arena. Advocates of parental rights, like many school prayer proponents, now pursue alternatives rooted in legislative and constitutional protections. An organized parental rights movement is now pressing for statutes and constitutional amendments that would carve into positive law the right of parents to control the education of their children. Supporters have introduced in Congress a parental rights act that would provide legal recourse to parents against governmental officials who allegedly usurp parental rights to direct their children's upbringing. A number of state legislatures have pending before them a parents' rights amendment to their respective state constitutions. These amendments would insure that the values taught in the school are not in conflict with the values taught in the home.

The political debate over values has centered, at least overtly, on the *content* of education and how to accommodate the concerns of individual parents within the current system. A related movement within the policy arena has focused on the *structure* of education and has pushed to reconfigure schooling in a way that provides parents greater discretion over the education of their children and that promotes equal educational opportunity for the economically disadvantaged. To that end, a growing number of reformers are seeking to break the state's monopoly over the operation of schooling and to use public funds to offer a variety of educational options within the public and private sectors. Whether through charter schools, which are technically public schools, or through a voucher program, these highly controversial proposals, if adequately regulated, promise to afford more voice to parents across the economic spectrum and greater opportunity for their children. The Supreme Court's apparent shift to a more accommodationist approach toward religion within certain parameters bodes well for the constitutionality of school choice programs that include religiously affiliated schools. At least one of several choice initiatives recently addressed by state courts inevitably will test the truth of that assertion.

Proposals to expand family choice along with curricular challenges are symptomatic of fundamental problems plaguing American education as we enter the twenty-first century. The surrounding debates call into question the inherently indoctrinative function of education and place under critical scrutiny the very concept of government-funded and -controlled schools. At no time since the beginning of the common school movement a century and a half ago have we witnessed such a direct challenge to the purpose, content, and structure of mass compulsory schooling or to the very premise underlying the "myth of the common school," that is, that the values promoted through public education are indeed neutral or at the very least acceptable to Americans across the political and religious spectrum.[17]

This book uses parental dissent and the litigation that it has provoked as a catalyst and context for exploring the deepest recesses of that myth. More specifically, it attempts to draw an interdisciplinary picture of the complex forces and ideas that have created and continue to fuel the contemporary movement to allow families greater voice in the education of their children. In doing so, it builds the case for a theory of educational governance that places the developmental needs of the child at the center of family autonomy, returning the discussion to its roots in what John Coons and Stephen Sugarman envisioned two decades ago in their seminal book *Education by Choice*.[18] There the authors challenged the status quo and called for the redistribution of education decision making to families regardless of economic circumstances. Here the focus is on religious conservatives, whose unswerving faith and unwillingness to compromise their core values, combined with their attack on the hegemony of certain social norms promoted in the curriculum, present the starkest of backdrops against which to dissect the issues. This in no way suggests, however, that government should accommodate extreme views, religious or otherwise, that conflict with Americans' core political commitments or that fail in other ways to prepare students for democratic participation. Indeed, in the end many but not all of the same families who challenge the public school curriculum might prove too unyielding and absolute in their religious beliefs to avail themselves of government aid under a system of structured family choice. Nevertheless, the very fact that they push to the extreme the liberal principles of autonomy, neutrality, rationality, and tolerance makes them most appropriate subjects for analyzing and testing the ideal of education in a liberal democracy.

The book attempts to move public discourse beyond the ideological and inflammatory rhetoric that too often surrounds discussion of family autonomy and beyond the rights mode in which that discussion is often cast. It also attempts to move past the skepticism that pervades contemporary works warning that the American social fabric is unraveling and to find what Arthur Schlesinger advocated a half-century ago as the "vital center" based on a democratic blueprint for creating political consensus out of conflict and discontent.[19] In doing so, it defines the underlying legal and policy issues, lays bare some of the myths surrounding the necessity of government-operated schools, and reveals how the current system privileges those of economic means while foreclosing others from meaningful voice in the education of their children. It further reaffirms the interests of children in the debate over values and choice, suggests that most but not all religious views are compatible with democratic government, and recognizes religion as an important force in preserving civil society. In the end, it defines what education for democratic citizenship means in a society that values pluralism and freedom of conscience along with civic commitment, charting a middle course for defining but not severing the relation between education and the state.

Chapter 2 The Common School: Past as Prologue

Throughout the twentieth century, the concept of government-controlled and -supported education has held worldwide appeal for its benefits to society and to the individual alike. Education is both a symbol and a practical engine for preserving national unity and identity. Nations use the educational process to develop civic virtue and a national character through a shared set of values reflected in the school curriculum and to reap the economic benefits derived from an educated citizenry. By making education compulsory, government institutionalizes its authority. By making it universal, the state affords individuals the opportunity to realize their potential to the fullest and climb as far up the economic and social ladder as their abilities and determination permit. Schools also serve as vehicles for interpreting the popular culture and managing the tensions among competing values. Such ambitious goals are achieved most effectively and smoothly in an idealized society whose members share a common core of values and beliefs. They also are best realized under a highly centralized educational system that leaves little if any room for local or regional differences. America's reality falls short of this ideal on both counts: our values have become increasingly more diverse over the past century while we have clung passionately to a school governance system built on local government control.

For more than two centuries, public officials and social reformers have taken pride in the nation's ability to cope with cultural conflict through simultaneous commitment to pluralism and consensus. *E pluribus unum* has been an American political mantra since the founding of the Republic. But this public posture and confidence mask a painful reality: the centrifugal force of an increasingly powerful *plures* is threatening to overtake the *unum* built on a civil religion or public faith. Over the past century and a half, dramatic social and demographic changes have taken place, at times more or less intense. Successive waves of immigration from all parts of the globe have rendered us more diverse in our worldviews, while industrialization has weakened family ties and church influence. As a result, these traditional mechanisms for defining our shared values, whether on a national or community level, have become marginalized against the forces of an ever expanding and centerless notion of pluralism. As Benjamin Barber tells us, "We are neither very united nor very comfortable with our diversity."[1]

The breakdown in consensus over shared values and norms becomes even more problematic in view of our abiding and profound faith in local control over education. Combined with an emphasis on local funding and the predominance of democratically elected school boards, this governance structure has made public education both highly accountable to the local electorate and highly sensitive to local politics. In the end, we expect our schools to serve as a bulwark for our national identity and ideology while at the same time reflecting the values of the local community. This is not to suggest that the federal and state governments are silent partners in the educational enterprise. All fifty state constitutions contain variously worded education clauses—some more explicitly rights-based than others—that place ultimate authority and legal responsibility for education at the state level.[2] But the state's function is largely regulatory; state statutes delegate the daily operation of schools to local communities, with funding primarily from the local property tax.

In contrast to the states, the federal Constitution makes no mention of education. Yet the federal government has played a key role in shaping educational values that ultimately affect the curriculum. Through federal statutes identifying national priorities, Congress has allocated funds for remedial education, bilingual education, the education of the disabled, and women's equity programs and has established rights and entitlements that are enforced by federal agencies, primarily the Department of Education. The federal courts in particular have played a significant role in defining policies that arguably reflect a national consensus over underlying values. The Bill of Rights and the Fourteenth Amendment to the Constitution have been a driving force in shaping this role. Supreme Court pronouncements on racial and gender equality, prohibitions against school prayer, and limitations on government support for religiously affiliated schools have directly affected the values presented in the curriculum and the organizational configuration of schooling nationwide.[3]

Looking back at the tortuous history of American schooling, we gain a sense of educational aspirations and purpose over time and the complex web of forces that have incrementally shaped present conflicts over the curriculum and educational values. Viewing education through the lens of the near and distant past sheds light on the concerns raised by modern-day parental dissenters and broadens our perspective toward redesigning an educational plan that more effectively addresses the enduring tensions and discontents. Challenges to the curriculum and the public debates they generate, while typically dismissed by courts and educators, speak volumes about who we are as a people and what we expect from our schools. These conflicts are best understood against the backdrop of the common school, its competing purposes, the demons that have haunted it over time, and the legacy left by reform efforts of the past.

EDUCATION AND REPUBLICAN IDEALS

The notion of popular education, whereby a political system trains the young to perpetuate its most cherished values, dates back to the ancient Greeks. In his *Republic,* Plato tells us that we cannot enjoy the good life without creating the good society, which in turn depends on some form of education to bring that society into being and to sustain it. For Plato, education did not mean schooling but rather all the influences within the community that shape the mind and character of the younger generation.[4] The ancient Greek *paideia,* or concept of education, joined citizenship and learning around a shared set of norms and values under the legal and moral authority of the *politeia,* or prevailing culture.[5] But for the ancient Greeks, religious life was bound up with public life, and so religious and civic values were one and the same.

This indissoluble link between education and a good society did not immediately take root on American soil. Seventeenth-century colonial schools were tied not to the state but to religious faith; unlike the Greek model, the American held church and state to be separate and distinct. In colonial America, schools served to affirm religious orthodoxy in the young. The Old Deluder Satan Act enacted by the Massachusetts legislature in 1647 is a clear example of how education was designed to serve the interests of religion. Among the earliest American laws on education, the act's purpose was to assure that children learned to read and understand the meaning of the Scriptures. Its preamble began as follows: "It being one of the chief projects of that old deluder Satan to keep men from the knowledge of the Scriptures" by means of the "false glosses of saint-seeming deceivers," education is necessary so that "learning may not be buried in the grave of our fathers in the church and commonwealth."[6] The act also contained the seeds of local financial commitment, requiring that every town of at least fifty households appoint a schoolmaster whose salary would be paid by the parents or by the inhabitants in general and who would teach the children to read and write. Towns of more than one hundred households would establish a grammar school to prepare young people for the university.

The connection between education and the political needs of secular society initially emerged in the latter part of the eighteenth century with Thomas Jefferson, who attempted to institutionalize Plato's views and tie schooling to citizenship. Jefferson fervently believed that republican government demanded citizens of virtue and intelligence. He perceived education as an instrument for meeting that end but also for realizing democracy and advancing social reform (although not in the universal sense as we know it today). He promoted free public education for all poor whites in the elementary grades and secondary education for the wealthy and talented poor. The system of government-operated schools that he proposed for Virginia in 1779 would have offered three years of free education to all regardless of wealth. Only an exceptionally gifted few would be selected for leadership from among the masses and would advance to residential grammar schools. An even more select group subsequently would enroll in the College of William and Mary along with those whose families could pay tuition.[7] His plan admittedly was democratic for its day, although it clearly failed to address the inequalities of wealth that lay at the heart of political power. The proposal also was radical in the sense that it departed dramatically from the educational paradigm of the past by omitting religion from the prescribed curriculum. For Jefferson, a nominal Episcopalian, a deist, and an exemplar of Enlightenment rationality and individualism, the most fundamental American ideal was the preservation of liberty.

Jefferson's plan for locally controlled and locally supported schools never garnered sufficient support among Virginia's propertied class. Nevertheless, the connection he drew between an educated citizenry and a republican form of government gradually attracted broader acceptance. The Northwest Ordinance, enacted by Congress under the Articles of Confederation and reenacted by the

First Congress, directed that "Religion, Morality, and Knowledge being necessary to good government and the happiness of mankind, Schools and the means
of education shall forever be encouraged." Under the ordinance, the federal government granted land for the maintenance of schools to new state governments
formed out of the territories west of the Appalachians.[8] A number of subsequent
state constitutions, including those of Kentucky and New Mexico, also incorporated in their original form a clause supporting the purposes of public education.[9] This inextricable link among education, republicanism, and virtue res-
onated throughout the common school movement of the mid-1800s, gaining
renewed appeal in the face of massive immigration and increasing religious diversity.

COMMON SCHOOLING AND THE SEEDS
OF DISCONTENT

The American architects of the common school were influenced by the works
of nineteenth-century educators, particularly the Swiss Johann Heinrich
Pestalozzi. Pestalozzi proposed a practical education for teaching the masses love
of God and country which would avoid threatening the power elite. The common school reformers, however, replaced Pestalozzi's emphasis on the whole
child with one grounded more specifically in societal purpose.[10] These two competing visions of education, one child centered and the other society centered,
would dominate educational dialogue throughout the coming century.

Horace Mann, a leading figure behind the common school movement and
the first secretary of the Massachusetts Board of Education, firmly believed that
schooling was necessary to preserve republican institutions and to create a political community out of a "maze of conflicting cultural traditions."[11] The
school was to prepare children of all religions, classes, and ethnic backgrounds,
the foreign born above all, for the intelligent and responsible exercise of citizenship. For Mann and his fellow reformers, universal education was in part a
mechanism for social control. The communal isolation of newly arrived immigrants, their low economic status, and their high rates of illiteracy posed a threat
to the vitality of the Republic. The school would teach the newcomers the proper
attitudes and values of American democracy and foster an understanding and
appreciation of American social institutions.[12] It would be common in the sense
that it would be open to all free of charge, and it would inculcate a common core
of values that would serve as the bedrock of an American public philosophy in-

termingling religion, politics, and economics in a vision of a "redeemer nation."[13]

The concept of universal common schooling appealed especially to the emerging Protestant middle class. This group saw public education as a way to affirm their values and pattern of life against the forces of continued immigration and the shift from an agrarian to an industrialized economy. Only through public control could the public define a public philosophy and avoid the dangers of partisanship.[14] The goals of the common school included moral training, discipline, patriotism, mutual understanding, formal equality, and assimilation.[15] The values reflected in the curriculum were essentially those of mainstream Protestantism. In his now-famous "Twelfth Annual Report" to the Massachusetts Board of Education in 1848, Mann advised teachers to teach the "principles of piety, justice, and sacred regard to truth, love of country, humanity and universal benevolence, sobriety, industry, frugality, chastity, moderation, and temperance, and those other virtues which are the ornament of human society, and the basis upon which a republican constitution is founded." Mann followed this list with the rhetorical question, "Are not these virtues and graces part and parcel of Christianity?" In other words, "Can there be Christianity without them?"[16]

But Mann failed either to recognize or to publicly admit that his belief in "human goodness and the centrality of morality to religion" itself represented an alternative faith steeped in his own Unitarian commitment to "a liberal religion of moral duty and enlightenment." Mann was not a secularist; he merely opposed what he considered to be sectarian religion in the schools.[17] For Mann and his fellow school reformers in Massachusetts, the apparent enemy was traditional revealed religion, which they considered to be dangerous and socially divisive.[18] And so they struck what they believed to be a nonsectarian compromise grounded in a core of what they considered widely accepted religious truths.[19] In this way they felt confident that they could protect the institution of the common school from sectarian controversy while at the same time teaching some form of political/religious values.[20] They would soon learn that their confidence was ill-founded.

This Protestant-republican ideology echoed throughout the *McGuffey Readers*. First published in 1836, the readers were used by some two hundred million schoolchildren between 1900 and 1940. They were clearly moralistic, propounding honesty and industry as leading values closely followed by courage, kindness, obedience, and courtesy.[21] They also had a decidedly religious slant, presenting life as "God-conscious and God-centered" and directing students to "live for salvation."[22] Nineteenth-century elementary school textbooks reveal a similarly pervasive religious orientation. From geography to history and science, they contained repeated references to God and his goodness. These commonly used texts were "guardians of tradition," teaching by rote and as moral absolutes such values as love of country, love of God, and duty to parents. But they also were vehicles for promoting laissez-faire capitalism, exhorting children to develop habits of thrift, honesty, and hard work as means to accumulate property.[23]

The allegedly nondenominational but decidedly Christian ethic of the common school was joined with Bible readings "without comment." These were readings that relied on individual interpretation, a marked contrast with the Catholic practice of looking to the church for understanding the Scriptures. Together they provided the necessary moral grounding. At the same time, the schools avoided controversial topics that might prove emotionally and intellectually divisive. Mann himself warned, "If a teacher . . . arrives at a controverted text, he is either to read it without comment or remark; or, at most, he is only to say that the passage is the subject of disputation." Mann made clear that "political proselytism is no function of the school."[24]

The common school continued to avoid controversy or present alternatives to its neatly defined moral world throughout the mid–twentieth century. Even at that point in time, most tax-supported schools still presented a standard uncontroversial moral education. As the historian Carl Kaestle notes, "The strategy was to be inclusive by being uncontroversial. . . . Yet [this strategy] contained the seeds of major discontent." It alienated those who believed that school morality should be more securely grounded in a distinctive religious view while never escaping its roots in white, middle-class Anglo-American Protestant tradition.[25]

Mid-nineteenth-century common school crusaders recognized the inherent threat in homogeneity and the political limits of transposing any form of state-imposed ideology onto an individualistic American culture that profoundly distrusted powerful central governments. To avoid transgressing those limits, they established a two-tiered governance structure that incorporated state oversight with local control over the operation and financing of education. This dual system struck a tolerable balance between individual and collective goals while quietly addressing the reformers' nationalistic objectives. By 1850 the majority of state legislatures had established the office of state superintendent of education. But as late as 1890, the average state department of education was composed of only two individuals, including the superintendent. Initially performing a minimal regulatory function, the office would gradually become more significant throughout the twentieth century in establishing and enforcing minimum educational standards and assuring equal educational opportunity as state governments assumed an increasing share of school funding.

As a guard against state encroachment on individual rights and liberties, the reformers attempted to inculcate a sense of community that would function not as a deterrent to individualism but as a setting within which individuality might be preserved.[26] This governance structure would maintain the transmission of political, economic, and social knowledge in the hands of each community. As David Tyack explains, the common school movement initially was a "grassroots phenomenon" wherein local citizens consciously embraced the concept and directly determined what their children learned.[27] But as the century wore on, conservative reformers began to use the state to impose their ideas of political and moral orthodoxy, particularly among the burgeoning population of poor immigrants.

Common schooling soon developed a dark side, at least from the perspective of some of its beneficiaries. It offered the poor more than mere cultural transformation and assimilation: it created communal and intergenerational alienation. For children of the disadvantaged and the foreign-born in particular, mass public schooling was designed to wipe out differences and assure conformity to rules defined by the majority culture. In the process, it disengaged students from communities grounded in emotional bonds, religious beliefs, ethnic ties, and common expression. As Jane Addams observed in the late nineteenth century, urban schools, in trying to present to immigrant children a standard of how "normal" Americans and their families looked and acted, in the end merely served to confirm rather than challenge children's feelings of marginality. Aside from the psychological dissonance and personal impact engendered, the common school also denied families any choice in deciding where their children would attend school. If, as Mann stated, the common school would be "the great [economic] equalizer of the conditions of men—the balance-wheel of the social machinery,"[28] it also would reduce diversity to the least common denominator.

It is debatable whether the common school was intended to complement or replace the family and the church as the primary socializing force in the life of the child. Nevertheless, the net effect was to fill in the gaps left by traditional institutions weighted down by social and economic pressures and dramatic changes in society. Some families on the social margins quietly acquiesced in what could be viewed in hindsight as the state's usurping of their authority. Many children simply did not attend public schooling for a variety of reasons, including cultural alienation, and faded into the shadows of the poor. A study of attendance levels in New York State counties in 1845 reveals a strong negative relation between school attendance and the percentage of foreign-born population.[29] In Boston, 90 percent of truants in 1849 had foreign-born parents.[30]

But it would not take long for organized religious opposition to mount against the common school in theory and in practice. On the one hand, religiously conservative Protestants, from Norwegian Lutherans in Minnesota to orthodox Congregationalists in New England, railed against the supposed godlessness of the common school. To their mind, the schools were not sufficiently religious. On the other hand, Catholics and Jews strongly objected to religious exercises in the schools, voicing loud opposition to the practice of Bible reading. For Catholics, the key point of contention was the state's unwillingness to fund separate church-run schools. They opposed a system that forced them to pay taxes for what they viewed as Protestant schooling while they were denied access to local funds to pay for their own schools.

In colonial times, it had not been uncommon for religious denominations to operate schools with tax revenues. Through the mid-1800s, many charity schools for the poor run by religious groups continued to receive government funds. Although this phenomenon may seem startling given modern-day interpretations of church–state separation, Methodists, Catholics, Episcopalians, and other denominations operated such schools in cities nationwide—in New York City until 1825, in Lowell, Massachusetts, through the 1830s and 1840s, in Milwaukee, Wisconsin, through the 1840s, and in Hartford, Connecticut, as late as the 1860s.[31] But as the common school movement took hold in the mid–nineteenth century, it gained a monopoly over public funds for education and abolished the concept of direct government support for private schooling. As the numbers of Catholics migrating to the United States surged throughout the 1830s and 1840s, the divergence in viewpoints on education between Protestants and Catholics in particular became manifest and fueled the fires of anti-Catholic sentiment.[32]

In the 1840s, riots erupted in Philadelphia when the school board announced that Catholic students could use the Douay (Catholic) instead of the King James (Protestant) version of the Bible. At about the same time, the Catholic clergy in New York were rebuffed in their attempt to obtain a portion of the common school fund for the maintenance of a separate system of Catholic schools. In the late 1860s, a coalition of Jews, Catholics, freethinkers, and some independent-thinking Protestants, despite serious opposition from mainstream Protestants, moved the Cincinnati Board of Education to exclude Bible reading, religious instruction, and hymn singing from the public schools. The board's decision did not go unchallenged but was upheld subsequently by the Ohio Supreme Court.[33] These conflicts represented a direct and visible threat to the pan-Protestant hegemony over American culture.

A glance at school leadership across the country through the mid to late nineteenth century underscores the depths of Protestant dominance. Protestant clergy, in fact, were major players in the formation of the common school. In Massachusetts, five of the eight members of the state board of education under Horace Mann's leadership were ministers. Mann's successor as secretary of the board was the Reverend Barnas Sears, president of the Newton Theological Institution. Protestant ministers served as school superintendents throughout the country. In Kentucky, of the first eleven superintendents during the period from 1838 to 1879, all but one were Protestant clergymen. In the West, the school and church were so intertwined that classes were often held in church buildings and church services were held in school buildings.[34]

The New York experience sheds light on the deep conflicts between Catholic and Protestant perspectives and the undeniably indoctrinative function of schooling. Catholic leaders there argued that the nonsectarian or common religion taught in the public schools was actually "sectarianism in disguise."[35] Merely purging books of "missionary Protestantism" masked as general morality would not suffice. They believed that ultimately the pro-Protestant hidden curriculum would surface in the attitudes of teachers and peers.[36] But Catholic objections ran even deeper. Textbooks commonly used in the schools, at least prior to 1870, were pervasively anti-Catholic, denouncing Catholicism as a false religion and even as a danger to the state. These books left the reader with the distinct impression that the Catholic clergy were greedy for money and that Catholicism bred ignorance and indolence.[37]

It became increasingly apparent to Catholic leaders that differences between the church and the pan-Protestant public schools were irreconcilable. The only alternative was to press for a share of public funds to operate their own schools. The most outspoken separatists among them, including Archbishop John Hughes of New York, challenged the very premise underlying the common school movement—that moral education could be separated from religious beliefs.[38] "Mere secular knowledge," they argued, was not enough; schools must cultivate religious and moral understanding in order to mold enlightened and virtuous citizens. In their final petition to city officials, church leaders denounced public education as harmful to children's morality. The Catholics' rights of conscience were at stake here.[39] But opposition carried beyond the religious to the political. Catholics aligned themselves with other localists in arguing that the common school infringed on parental responsibility and was an "inefficient and improper monopoly."[40] These nineteenth-century arguments affirming parental authority in education, the right to freedom of conscience, and the salutary effects of competition have been echoed in recent decades by reformers and religionists from the political left to the political right.

Catholic efforts in New York to obtain public funding for an alternative system of Catholic schools failed in the face of strident opposition from a rising nativist movement that had become linked with the common school enterprise during the 1830s and 1840s. Organized efforts to keep America American demonstrated a chauvinistic spirit and specifically an anti-Catholic hatred which culminated in the Know-Nothing campaigns of the 1850s and the organization of the Native American Party, whose membership was limited to those with at least two generations of white Protestant American ancestry. These political events represented more than an "intense opposition to an internal minority on the ground of its foreign (i.e., 'un-American') connections."[41] They evidenced deep fears of the Catholic Church's authoritarian organization as irreconcilable with the American concept of political liberty. The depth of that hatred and fear surfaced in the mainstream Protestant press. The following statement from the Baptist weekly the *Watchman* captures their sentiments: "If the children of Papists are really in danger of being corrupted in the Protestant schools of enlightened, free and happy America, it may be well of these conscientious parents and still more conscientious priests, to return them to the privileges of their ancestral homes, among the half-tamed boors of Germany."[42]

The raging controversy between Catholics and Protestants in New York ended in a state law passed in 1842 that expressly prohibited the granting of public funds to any school in which "any religious sectarian doctrine or tenet shall be taught, inculcated, or practiced." Following this outright prohibition, the school funding issue temporarily receded from political view, only to reemerge in 1894 with the adoption of a state constitutional amendment that prohibited public aid to any school "wholly or in part under the control or direction of any religious denomination or in which any denominational tenet or doctrine is taught."[43] But New York was not alone in its overt hostility toward state aid to religious schools. By 1917, twenty-nine states had adopted similar restrictions on the use of public funds for sectarian purposes. A similar proposed amendment to the federal Constitution, prohibiting the use of public funds to support sectarian education had failed by just several votes in Congress in 1875. Known as the Blaine Amendment, the proposal prohibited tax support of any school or institution "under the control of any religious or anti-religious sect, organization, or denomination, or wherein the particular creed or tenets of any religious or anti-religious sect, organization, or denomination shall be taught." That same year, President Ulysses S. Grant himself urged that "every child in the land [be given] a common school education unmixed with atheistic, pagan, or sectarian teaching."[44]

With the failure of their project becoming carved into state constitutional stone, dissenters of the time decided to opt out of the public schools entirely rather than compromise their most fundamental beliefs. In 1884 the Third Plenary Council of Baltimore decreed that "near every Church, where it does not exist, a parochial school is to be erected within two years . . . and it is to be maintained in perpetuum" unless the bishop should grant a postponement. The council further decreed that Catholic parents were "bound to send their children to the parish school" unless alternative means of education were approved by the bishop.[45] Separate schools thus became a matter of church policy.

For the next century, the issue of government aid to religiously affiliated schools quietly percolated beneath the surface of political debate with mild and intermittent eruptions in state legislatures and federal courts depending on the elemental forces of politics. The "cosmopolitan solution" based on a common Anglo-American Protestant culture, combined with the splintering off of dissident religious groups, apparently had warded off any direct challenges to the common school.[46] By 1920, nearly six thousand parochial Catholic schools were educating 1,700,000 students; more than a thousand Lutheran schools, six hundred Seventh-Day Adventist schools, and hundreds of other sectarian schools representing various denominations were educating hundreds of thousands more.[47]

Unlike modern-day religious dissenters, those earlier protesters who rejected the public schools in New York did not object specifically on moral grounds. They essentially shared the mainstream Protestant values promoted in the public schools. Their objections instead were grounded in the common school's blatant bias against them and in fundamental differences in theological perspective that were unrelated to the morals question per se. Their argument, however, lacked internal coherence. They maintained that moral education could not be separated from religious beliefs. Yet at the same time they avowed that they were willing to support schools that exhibited a "perfect neutrality of influence on the subject of religion."[48] The tension between these two opposing positions would become manifest a century later with religious schools struggling to preserve their distinct mission while trying to separate their secular from sectarian activities in order to maintain eligibility for government funds.

In fact, the New York experience has much to offer the contemporary debate over public and private schooling despite distinct sources of discontent, one based in theology and the other in morality. As the historian Diane Ravitch describes it, school struggles of this nature generally are framed in the context of majority rule versus minority interests. But they also represent a tension between competing visions of the common school that has played itself out repeatedly over the years, particularly in litigation. On the one hand there is a vision of schooling in which the public school belongs to the surrounding community, whose majority can determine the purpose and content of education—including sectarianism. That was the view the Catholic Church apparently espoused during the New York City common school struggle, its affirmations of neutrality notwithstanding. On the other hand, there is the vision espoused by Horace Mann and the common school reformers whereby the public school belongs to the state. Here the role of the school is to encourage inquiry and not to impose any specific interpretations. The school must avoid promoting any distinct religious or political view, and instead teach commonly held values.[49] Mann's view of the school as the agent of the state would largely prevail throughout the following century, while his faith in shared values would lose ground in the wake of rising secularism and individualism.

By the late 1800s, the notion of government-operated common schools had captured the American faith in education. It had also attracted increased financial support as immigration swelled the school-age population. By 1890, government expenditures for public schools had escalated to $147 million, up from about $7 million in 1850.[50] At the same time, the religious content of the common school curriculum declined under pressure not only from religionists but from avowed secularists, who publicly urged that moral instruction be grounded in secular rather than religious values. Liberal journals such as the *Index,* published by the Free Religious Association founded in 1867 by Ralph Waldo Emerson and other secularists, called for eliminating Bible reading from the schools. They insisted that the reading of the King James version was "just as much a symbol of the Protestant faith as saying mass or making the sign of the cross is a symbol of the Catholic faith."[51]

This trend in popular thinking was reflected in the *McGuffey Readers*. The percentage of religious content in the *Fourth Reader,* for example, declined from 30 percent in 1844 to only 3 percent in the 1901 edition, whereas the emphasis on morals had increased to 40 percent of the total content by the 1879 edition.[52] The theistic worldview of salvation and piety which dominated the 1836 edition had slowly disappeared by 1879, replaced with the spirit of self-reliance, individualism, and competition.[53] The driving force behind this gradual secularization of the curriculum was not legal but political. The primary concern of school reformers, then as now, was the continued stability and survival of the common school. As the school population became more heterogeneous following a large influx of Catholics and Jews into the public schools (many Catholic families did not follow the dictates of the church leadership), the pressure to minimize sources of religious disagreement increased.[54] It thus became clear that it was more important to Americanize than to Protestantize.

THE INDELIBLE MARK OF THE PROGRESSIVES

From the turn of the century through the mid-1900s, the secularization of the common school continued under the influence of a new wave of philosophical thought whose diverse and at times conflicting strands emphasized in varying degrees a child-centered and revisionist view of education. Originating in the first quarter century prior to World War I and tied to broader currents of social and political progressivism, what became known as progressive education blended the romantic emphasis on the needs of the child embraced by Jean-Jacques Rousseau and Pestalozzi with a democratic faith in the common school inherited from Jefferson and Mann.[55] Progressives embraced Mann's messianic role for education, believing that the common school could mitigate social conflict and the effects of economic inequalities.[56] While progressive ideas as applied to schooling varied over time and with different leaders of the movement, they are popularly ascribed to the pragmatist John Dewey, under whose influence the common school continued to shift from education based in the family and church to the public school. But here the school assumed even wider functions formerly served by these and other institutions. At times in their zeal to educate the whole child in the sense of developing an integrated person, the progressives seemed confused with the child's whole education well beyond traditional notions of schooling.

More fundamentally, progressivism redefined the purposes of schooling. Gradually the religious function of the common school evolved into the patriotic, and the goal of achieving moral goodness into the nurturing of good citizens. The Pledge of Allegiance and other patriotic exercises turned into common practices. In effect, the religion of the public schools became the religion of democracy. As Robert Michaelsen notes, in the wake of religious warfare between Catholics and Protestants, "what seemed to be needed was a 'common faith' which would emerge from the democratic community itself and which would have little or nothing to do with church religion or even with the supernaturalism of Enlightenment deism."[57]

The push toward patriotism reached an almost frenetic pace in the aftermath of World War I, when a number of states enacted legislation prescribing patriotic instruction in various forms, including mandated courses in U.S. history and citizenship, flag displays, salutes, and patriotic assemblies. At the same time, a rash of heightened nativism and postwar hysteria drove a number of states to reverse laws or customs permitting ethnic communities, primarily the Germans in the Midwest, to operate public schools in which a foreign language was used for instruction for at least part of the day.[58] By the close of 1919, the number of states that restricted the teaching of foreign languages had risen to thirty-seven, many of the restrictions applying to private as well as public schools.[59] Out of a disparate group of immigrant children, the schools would forge loyal American citizens prepared to participate in democratic government.

Dewey considered the school to be a social and transformative institution—an organ of social mobility and a mechanism for redressing social inequities. "Through education," he maintained, "society [could] formulate for its own purposes [and] organize its own means and resources."[60] Unlike the common school reformers for whom education would produce a static culture through the teaching of morals, Dewey's followers believed that education would bring about "cultural revision."[61] In their view, the moral was synonymous with the social and could be learned by doing rather than by direct instruction. Experience was at the heart of progressive education. Dewey believed that "all which the school can or need do for pupils . . . is develop their ability to think," and for him the initial stage of thinking was experience.[62] He rejected the prevailing view of the school as "a place where certain information is given, where certain lessons are to be learned, or where certain habits are formed." That approach, he maintained, neglects the "fundamental principle of the school as a form of community life" grounded in the present experiences of the child and not in some "remote future."[63] He challenged the dominant consensus represented in the *Committee of Ten Report* (1893) that education "should be directed [overtly] toward training the powers of observation, memory, expression, and reasoning" and embraced in its place the *Cardinal Principles of Secondary Edu-*

cation (1918), which promoted "health, command of fundamental processes, worthy home-membership, vocation, citizenship, worthy use of leisure, and ethical character."[64]

The progressives firmly believed that the common faith developed through the common experience of the school would transcend individual and group differences without negating the latter. Schooling would promote a sense of community awareness and further community progress while still fostering a sense of national identity and faith in democracy. In spite of the nativistic atmosphere that pervaded politics in the decade following World War I, progressives incorporated into this notion of community a recognition of cultural differences, including language, literature, cultural ideals, moral and spiritual outlook, and religion, although Dewey sharply disagreed with efforts to infuse religion per se into the public school.[65] In his view, the source of morality was not religion but the rational study of human relations and human progress.[66]

Driven by Enlightenment devotion to reason and empiricism, Dewey believed that science would liberate individuals from "the servile acceptance of imposed dogma" at the hands of the clergy. He repudiated the mainstream religions of his day as outmoded and maintained that society should guide itself instead by "new ethics derived from scientific doctrine in both the biological and physical sciences." In his essay "Religion in Our Schools," Dewey breathed into this new religion several basic elements that would gradually infiltrate the educational mainstream and permeate, a half-century later, the heated debate over the curriculum and educational values. In the gospel according to John Dewey, "Right and wrong reside only in consequences; there is no cosmic guarantee of meaning; and 'value processing' is the most wholesome way to proceed through life."[67]

Throughout the first half of the century, progressive education, while controversial, became the conventional wisdom among professional educators. At the same time, it survived continual onslaughts from the political right and left, ranging from those who believed that its underlying philosophy smacked of moral relativism to those who attacked it for acquiescing to the status quo. It also endured assaults from within its own ranks. One of the most vocal opponents of progressive child-centeredness was George Counts, who as a student at the University of Chicago had become engrossed in the theories of Dewey, among others. He fervently believed in the common school as a reformative institution that could shape the course of cultural evolution.

In a speech before the Progressive Education Association in 1932, Counts challenged educators to face up to their social responsibilities and shook the association to its core. Although progressive education had achieved some good in focusing on the child, he argued, its view of education was too narrow. "The weakness of Progressive Education" he maintained, "thus lies in the fact that it has elaborated no theory of social welfare, unless it be that of anarchy or extreme individualism. In this of course, it is but reflecting the viewpoint of the members of the liberal-minded upper middle class who send their children to the Progressive schools." Of the ten fallacies he identified in the child-centered schools, one uniquely resonates in contemporary conflicts over the curriculum: "that the school should be impartial in its emphases, that no bias should be given instruction." Counts challenged educators to "become less frightened . . . at the bogies of *imposition* and *indoctrination,*" which are not only inevitable but desirable.[68] Similar to religious conservatives today who believe that schools are promoting secular humanism or multiculturalists who view the schools as bastions of Eurocentrism, Counts essentially saw the schools as battlefields of ideas and indoctrination, although to his mind it was appropriate for professional educators to "select some things and reject others." Parental preferences played no part in his discussion.

In *The Troubled Crusade,* Ravitch describes the innovative programs reported in school systems across the country by the early 1940s:

> Their common features were: centering the curriculum around basic areas of human activity, instead of traditional subject matter; incorporating subject matter only insofar as it was useful in everyday situations; stressing functional values, such as behavior, attitudes, skills, know-how, rather than "bookish" or abstract knowledge; reorienting studies to the immediate needs and interests of students; using community resources; introducing nontraditional materials (for example audiovisual equipment or magazines) and nontraditional activities (panel discussions, dramatizations, and work projects) in addition to or instead of direct instruction and textbooks.[69]

In the post–World War II years, progressive education shifted focus from the elementary to the secondary school and introduced what came to be known as life adjustment education. This broad-based approach consisted of "guidance and education in citizenship, home and family life, use of leisure, health, tools of learning, work experience, and occupational adjustment."[70] Related to life adjustment was the concept of the core curriculum that would reflect students' needs and interests. Further related to adjustment as an educational goal was a direct concern for the psychological well-being of students, introducing a new cadre of mental health personnel into the schools. By way of example, the number of psychologists and psychiatrists employed in the public schools of New

York State rose from 92.5 (full-time equivalent) in 1944–45 to 353 a decade later.[71] This addition to the schools' staff brought with it a more open attitude toward psychological assessment and eventually other techniques, practices, and programs that would prove controversial in the decades to come.

From the postwar period also emerged what has become popularized in recent years as global education. In the shadow of world conflict and the atomic age, the progressive reform agenda adopted the notion that educating the next generation of citizens for international understanding could serve as a preventive measure against future wars. This view, clearly in accord with Dewey's belief in "education as a lever of social reform," would also meet later opposition from both political and religious conservatives.

Through the second half of the twentieth century, progressive education fell into cyclical favor and disfavor, alternating with more traditional approaches to education. Depending on the political climate, progressivism became a target for critics decrying the academic failures of the public school, but it also inspired structural and curricular reforms in the name of children's needs. The first shift took place in the late 1940s and early 1950s with the publication of numerous articles attacking or defending progressive education along with several scathing critiques of its philosophy and practices. In 1949, Bernard Iddings Bell's sweeping indictment of mass education, *Crisis in Education,* could have come directly out of the parental rights movement of the 1990s. As restated by the historian Lawrence Cremin, Bell, an ordained Episcopal bishop, claimed that "from kindergarten through the university, the school system suffered from misplaced emphases: it had taken over domestic functions that were properly parental, and it had excluded religion, without which education could have no ultimate purpose." Bell proposed "drastic reforms" to remedy the situation, including giving religion "a central place in the curriculum, in publicly supported denominational schools if necessary."[72]

Behind Bell's invective was an apparent religious and anti–public education agenda. Other critics presented a more dispassionate perspective. The following year, Albert Lynd's *Quackery in the Public Schools* challenged the "educationist" monopoly of public education. In doing so, he raised significant questions: "To whom do the public schools belong? Who has the right to select the social aims of education? The community or the educators?" A half century later, these issues continue to simmer beneath the surface of local conflicts over schooling and educational values. Robert Hutchins, in his book *The Conflict in Education in a Democratic Society* (1953), criticized the progressive "doctrine of social reform" for having turned schools into "propaganda machines for current political fashions."[73] The year 1953 also witnessed the publication of *Educational Wastelands* by the historian Arthur Bestor, one of the most influential critics of progressive education of that time. Bestor attacked the educationists for having failed to recognize that the purpose of schools is "the deliberate cultivation of the ability to think." He denounced vocational and "life adjustment" programs as breeding "servile independence"; as preparation for life, these were poor substitutes for liberal education in the basic disciplines. But he placed the blame for the system's failure not on progressive education as originally espoused by Dewey but on what he called "regressive education."[74]

By 1958, a year after Sputnik had set the United States in feverish competition with the former Soviet Union, *Time* magazine reported that "progressive education has failed the American people." There was a new mood sweeping America's schools, one emphasizing "not the social but the intellectual in education." Economists began to talk about education as investment in human capital for the good of society, a pitch reluctantly made by Horace Mann a century earlier for purely pragmatic reasons, namely, to garner support for the common school from business interests. By 1961, Cremin noted the "abrupt and rather dismal" end of progressive education, which had captured influential segments of the American public for a half century. A decade later, Samuel Bowles and Herbert Gintis suggested that Dewey's project had failed because the movement lacked the "ideological unity and fusion of educational theory and practice of the common school revival." Progressivism had perpetuated the common school's major defect—its intolerance of pluralism—while it had abandoned its strength—a coherent purpose.[75]

In spite of the deluge of criticism throughout the 1950s, there was little visible evidence that the progressive movement had dramatically transformed American schooling outside of specific innovative schools and systems. Truly progressive schools were few and far between. In 1953, the American Association of School Administrators reported that the "subject curriculum," the most traditional pattern of curriculum organization, was still the most widely used in American schools, while the most radical pattern, the "activity curriculum," based "solely on . . . pupils' needs and interests," was "more of a theoretical pattern of organization than an actual one . . . more talked about than practiced."[76] Most American public schools reflected philosophical remnants of Mann's common moral vision built on pan-Protestantism combined with threads of Dewey's emphasis on the whole child and his common faith in democracy. Prayer and Bible reading continued unabated, above all in southern schools, along with the daily salute to the flag and other patriotic exercises practiced throughout the country. In fact, until the 1970s, most American classrooms defied the progressive belief in both the child as the central focus of education and the importance of learning through experience. Charles Silberman's investigation of American schooling, *Crisis in the Classroom* (1970), paints a grim portrait of rigidly organized classes, children sitting passively bored, with learning reduced to memorization and mechanical tasks—what he called "education for docility."[77]

Progressivism indeed may have failed to radically reform the structure of and interaction within the American classroom. Nevertheless, its philosophical approach and especially its emphasis on life adjustment made an indelible mark on American schools through the introduction of numerous educational practices, some of which have since fallen into disrepute or undergone serious revision. Included among progressive initiatives were the comprehensive high school, vocational education, home economics, school guidance programs, high school athletics, educational testing, tracking and sorting of students, and the organizational dominance of professionals and experts.[78] But perhaps the most lasting and pervasive progressive contribution was the differentiated and, in effect, academically stratified curriculum which has continued into recent decades. This was exemplified in the alternative school movement of the 1960s and 1970s and the belief, now coming under serious scrutiny, that equal educational opportunity means access to a broad range of curriculum options as contrasted with the concept (currently gaining renewed favor) of a rigorous core academic curriculum offered to all students whether college bound or not.[79]

In hindsight, academicians and scholars were too quick to bury progressivism. Cremin himself ended his comprehensive analysis *The Transformation of the School* with the prescient thought that the "authentic progressive vision . . . [p]erhaps . . . only awaited the reformulation and resuscitation that would ultimately derive from a larger resurgence of reform in American life and thought."[80] The resurgence came in the late 1960s as a neoprogressive wave swept over education with renewed vigor. At that time, the civil rights, antiwar, and women's movements together with the War on Poverty were challenging traditional assumptions of life and society. School reformers turned a critical eye toward the apparent competitiveness, achievement orientation, and narrow focus on math and science skills that had crept into schooling in the previous decade.[81] Neoprogressives argued that education was a means of gaining personal fulfillment and of reconstituting society. Their recommendations for reform centered on the dynamics of the classroom and on the curriculum. The purpose of education was "to create understanding, feeling human beings." The concept of the open classroom, borrowed from the British, gained a new foothold, and the notion of student rights, constitutionalized by the Supreme Court, weakened school discipline, gave students a voice in school governance, and profoundly altered the curriculum.

This new generation of progressives had almost limitless expectations of what the schools could deliver and accomplish, carrying Dewey's call to educate the whole child to the extreme. They attacked the compartmentalization of the individual disciplines and promoted interdisciplinary learning. They replaced academic courses with "problems courses," each focused on a specific issue of immediate social concern that would develop in students a sense of "social awareness and responsibility."[82] They set aside traditional methods that relied on substance and that taught students to absorb factual information and search for a correct answer located in some authoritative text. They replaced these with innovative approaches and programs such as the New Math and the New Social Studies, emphasizing intellectual inquiry, process, and manipulating of symbols to meet desired ends.

The social studies curriculum in particular became tied to the "values clarification" movement. The thrust of that movement was to reject fixed standards of right and wrong. The teacher functioned not as a moralizer but as a moderator whose primary task was to help students clarify their own values by presenting them with dilemmas which they had to resolve. The underlying rationale was as follows: given the various influences on students' lives—parents, teachers, the church, peer groups, the media—there is no consistency regarding what constitutes allegedly desirable values. The obvious implication was that these influences and the values that young people assimilate from them are all equally valid.[83] The school would take a neutral position, granting equal legitimacy, for example, to the values of the media as to those of the family. The approach was immensely popular; the 1972 *Values Clarification Handbook* for teachers and students sold more than six hundred thousand copies.[84]

The values clarification perspective was indeed a startling departure from the diametrically opposed notion of shared values espoused by nineteenth-century common school reformers. The *Handbook* attributes the approach to the work of Louis Raths, who, according to the *Handbook*'s authors, "built upon the thinking of John Dewey."[85] This connection seems plausible, as Dewey was philosophically a pragmatist who discounted the possibility of arriving at absolute truth even on factual issues. He believed that ideas were true only if they worked in a specific situation, grounding all knowledge, including moral knowledge, in problem-solving experiences.[86]

Whether or not values clarification was the child of an evolved form of pro-

gressivism, as Dewey's critics claim, religious conservatives and other traditionalists rejected the approach as moral relativism plain and simple. Some questions recommended for classroom discussion, they argued, were stacked against
religion, for example, "Does religion have some meaning in my life, or is it nothing more than a series of outmoded traditions and customs?"[87] In certain local-
ities, religious opposition to values clarification turned hostile and ugly. In 1977,
the school board in Warsaw, Indiana, banned the *Handbook,* and the local Senior Citizens Club subsequently burned forty copies of it in a parking lot ceremony. In the aftermath, teachers were fired and the student newspaper was shut
down.[88]

In the 1970s, a second approach to moral education gained popularity in the
schools. It was based in cognitive developmental theory and was more clearly
aligned with Dewey. Developed by the psychologist and Harvard professor
Lawrence Kohlberg, the technique combined Dewey's concept of the social nature of education with the philosophical construct of duty or obligation as elaborated by Immanuel Kant.[89] Kohlberg's theory outlined six successive stages of
moral reasoning through which individuals progressed as they acquired more
adequate moral thinking. Similar to values clarification, this approach presented
students with moral dilemmas and rejected moral theorizing. The focus again
was on the *process* of moral reasoning, although the *product* was evaluated from
what were defined within the underlying theory as progressively more advanced
perspectives. Contrary to what his critics have claimed, Kohlberg rejected the
proposition that the schools could be value-neutral. In fact, he endorsed moral
education but in a form whose content would be defined in terms of the value
of justice, including respect for individual rights, and not in terms of majority
consensus. To do otherwise, he believed, would infringe on the civil rights of
parents and children.[90] Like values clarification, however, his approach differed
markedly from the list of character traits and virtues that permeated instruction
in the common school as originally envisioned and as exemplified in the moralistic lessons of the *McGuffey Readers.*

By the mid-1970s, the tide again began to turn against progressive philosophy and practices. Declining scores on standardized tests, increasing dropout
rates, drug abuse, and student violence—all the perceived ills of American education—were once more laid at Dewey's door. Critics blamed him and the neoprogressives for the permissiveness, valuelessness, and lack of academic standards reigning throughout public education. By 1981, *Newsweek* reported a
"crisis of confidence" in public schooling and warned of a phenomenon it
termed "blight flight." A private school boom, from elite independent schools

to Catholic schools to Christian academies, was skimming off the nation's most gifted and motivated students from the public schools, some fleeing disciplinary problems and declining academic rigor and others in search of a moral framework. At the same time, two controversial studies, one by the sociologist James Coleman and the other by Andrew Greeley, a sociologist and Catholic priest, presented evidence that Catholic schools were particularly effective in raising the achievement of minority students.[91] Another backlash developed, this time ushering in the Back to Basics movement and a legitimate concern that student proficiency in math and reading as measured by performance on standardized tests was on the decline. Schools needed to return to the three R's. The movement received an added boost from *A Nation at Risk* (1983), a report commissioned by the U.S. Department of Education. Compelling in its tone, the report warned of "a rising tide of mediocrity . . . threaten[ing] our very future as a Nation and as a people."[92] It gave impetus and focus to the educational debate and set off a storm of reform proposals.

The Back to Basics movement encompassed disparate groups with distinct and overlapping agendas. As Francis FitzGerald describes it, the moderates within the ranks merely wanted to "clear away some of the undergrowth of electives, mini-courses, and non-academic work from the school curriculum," while the extremists insisted that "rote work was in some metaphysical way good for children or that schoolwork should not be any more interesting than that which they themselves had endured."[93] By the early 1980s, the influence of that movement, supported by a resurgence of religious fundamentalism, became manifest in texts and curricula across the nation. Under pressure from conservative watchdog groups, publishers began to revise their biology textbooks in an effort to make statements on evolution somewhat ambiguous by calling it a theory rather than scientific fact.[94] They purged even literary anthologies of references to white racism and the evils of the Vietnam War, references that some religious conservatives found offensive. For the publishers, it was pure economics. They aimed to produce one set of texts and programs that would prove acceptable across the political/values spectrum and that would appeal to a diverse group of rural, suburban, and urban school boards in states with high student populations and statewide textbook purchasing policies. California, New York, and Texas were their chief clients.

Progressive-bashing has moved cyclically in and out of fashion for decades. The political left and right alike have castigated Dewey, the one for his naive faith in scientific progress and in the ability of schools to redress social inequities and the other for his having misguidedly extracted education from its roots in basic knowledge. Yet, as some historians maintain, the indictments leveled against Dewey may be unjust and misdirected.[95] Through the 1920s and 1930s, Dewey himself voiced doubts about what he considered "extremist or romantic oversimplifications" in the progressive movement. In an address entitled "Progressive Education and the Science of Education," he outlined the need for rigor and clarity and sharply warned against the "aimlessness and dangerous permissiveness" of extreme notions of the child-centered school with its mixture of "bohemianism, undisciplined expression in the name of individual creativity, and Freudian solicitation for avoiding inhibitions." He later criticized the many so-called progressive schools that had evaded their educational responsibility and departed from his philosophy, eliminating or minimizing rather than developing new subject matter.[96]

Eventually Dewey recognized that progressive education was a "bastard version, and in important ways, a betrayal of the new education he had called for." In 1938, in *Experience in Education*, he roundly criticized extremists within the movement for having corrupted his fundamental principles, for having proceeded "as if any form of direction and guidance by adults were an invasion of individual freedom, and for having concentrated on the present and future at the expense of the past." He warned, "It is not too much to say that educational philosophy which professes to be based on the idea of freedom may become as dogmatic as ever was the traditional education which it reacted against."[97] This admonition rings true in the hearts of modern-day religious and other dissenters who decry the unwillingness of educators to deviate from what is considered the norm within current practices and programs.

Perhaps history has treated Dewey unfairly. Succeeding generations of progressives indeed may have distorted his vision in their struggle to operationalize "the whole child" or "creative self-expression"—terms that started out, in Cremin's view, as "shibboleths" and ended up as "mere clichés."[98] But it cannot be denied that Dewey and at least two generations of his disciples, in fact, have made an indelible mark on schooling as we now know it. The progressive connection between school and society continues to pervade America's view of education. We still use the schools as instruments to redress social injustice—from dismantling racial barriers through school desegregation, to uplifting the poor through specialized programs, to promoting equality between women and men through gender-neutral policies and materials. More fundamentally, progressive education in both its original and evolved forms, along with its philosophy, its reforms, and the backlash it repeatedly has generated, has profoundly influenced contemporary educational practice, from global and environmental education to sex and AIDS education and community service, and set the stage for some of education's most bitter conflicts.

VALUES IN THE CONTEMPORARY LANDSCAPE

Mann and Dewey each espoused a distinct vision of schooling. Yet they shared the belief that education would develop a common faith, albeit through markedly different processes, one imposed by the school and the other through interaction and rational thought. For Mann, the common school would reflect the values of a static mainstream American society; students would be passive subjects for the inculcation of particular character traits or virtues. Dewey, on the other hand, believed the school should develop character not through formalized instruction but through all the instrumentalities and materials of school life. He also believed that the school should serve as the agent for social progress by instilling in students the ability to think critically and challenge the status quo. Both Mann's values inculcation and Dewey's critical thinking have become points of controversy in current debates over schooling.

Mann and Dewey drew their respective visions on a landscape that has changed over the course of the twentieth century. Throughout the hundred-year span during which they sequentially influenced educational thought and practice (Dewey was born the year Mann died), a narrow range of socially acceptable values and lifestyles placed public consensus within the realm of possibility. Governmental and other welfare institutions reflected the values of the social and intellectual elites, who used those institutions to impose traditional standards on the uneducated and the less powerful. The underclass, in turn, silently resisted educational efforts on their behalf or quietly acquiesced in their eagerness for assimilation and social acceptance.

In recent decades, however, the iconoclasm, individualism, and cultural relativism remaining from the 1960s has left us with a standard of popular culture that appears far more diffuse and ambiguous. As the sociologist Philip Selznick tells us, the achievement of self-awareness was "purchased at the price of moral disengagement. . . . No safe harbor is to be found in biblical or other unquestioned authority."[99] At the same time, social and intellectual movements from the civil rights era to postmodernism have laid bare some of our most cherished ideals while the rise of Christian fundamentalism has exerted a powerful reactive force.[100] The resulting moral indifference and confusion have spilled over into the schools, creating a moral vacuum in one sense and a moral tempest in another as the postsixties generation finally comes to terms with the fact that education is indeed inextricably bound up with values inculcation. No matter how hard educators and textbook publishers have tried to deny or undo that connection, repeated conflicts over the values reflected in the curriculum and voiced in the public school context have proven painfully sobering.

By the mid-1980s, despite the demise of moral relativism in the realm of moral education, schools continued to exert extreme efforts to avoid the controversy engendered by our diverse values. In doing so, they had ceased to provide young people with a moral compass. Pluralism had engendered paralysis. At that time, educators, scholars, and policymakers began to voice deep uneasiness over what they perceived as the valuelessness of public schooling. Critics across the political spectrum, from the sociologist James Coleman to former Secretary of Education William Bennett, pressed for a return to moral education in the schools.[101] In the critically acclaimed book *Habits of the Heart,* Robert Bellah and his colleagues presented a forgotten image of the school as one of several institutions, including the family and the church, that help create for us a morally coherent life.[102] Public discourse shifted from our increasingly diverse values to a search for our common values, from individualism to what Bellah called "our central aspirations."

At the same time, educational discourse moved away from the moral relativism of the values clarification movement of the sixties and the cognitive moral development approach of the seventies toward the direct teaching of common "core" values. By 1990, the press reported, "Despite Controversy, Consensus Grows on the Need to Teach Values in Schools."[103] Americans also began to comprehend the connection between private character and public life, that the moral problems of society reflect our personal vices.[104]

Throughout the 1990s, a marked decline in public values as evidenced by scandals from Washington to Wall Street fanned the flames of discontent with the moral state of the country. Pollsters provided hard evidence of moral decay throughout society and documented the anxieties that Americans shared over the failure of schools to create citizens of character. By mid-decade, half the country's high school students reported that drugs and violence were a serious problem in their school, while seven in ten stated unabashedly that cheating on tests and assignments was commonplace.[105] In a 1996 survey of almost twelve thousand Americans over twelve years of age, two-thirds of high school students admitted that they had cheated on an exam in the previous year, while only 33 percent strongly agreed that "honesty is the best policy."[106] More than six in ten adults noted that the failure of young people to learn such values as honesty, respect, and responsibility is a very serious problem. Close to half the American adult population voiced a similar concern that fewer families teach their children religious faith and values.[107] In communities across the country, Americans ranked character second only to basic skills in a listing of educational purposes.[108] The crisis in morals had become pandemic.

Old and young alike began to see the need for some form of values education in the schools. A 1994 survey cutting across geographic and demographic lines found that overwhelming majorities of Americans believed it was highly appropriate for public schools to teach an "inner circle of consensus values" including honesty, respect for others, and nonviolence as a means of resolving problems. Even among students, a sizeable majority (63 percent) agreed that lessons on values and principles belong in the classroom.[109] By 1996, *U.S. News and World Report* issued a headline warning: "We're at ground zero in the culture wars: how to raise decent kids when traditional ties to church, school and community are badly frayed."[110]

In response to these concerns, educators across the nation began working their way through the political and pedagogical minefields that surround values education to create programs that affect character. At all levels of government and throughout academe, the 1990s witnessed a groundswell of support for consciously developing character in the public schools, in some cases through a specific packaged curriculum and reading materials and in others through a philosophy or administrative style that pervades the life and teaching of the school. What has come to be called the character education movement is bound together by certain basic beliefs: parents are the primary moral educators of their children; despite our diverse opinions, there exist identifiable common values that are intrinsically superior to others and that define us as a nation; and public schools have an obligation to instill these personal and civic virtues that lead to responsible adulthood.

In 1992, a broad-based group representing education, labor, government, religious communities, and the media launched the Character Education Partnership, joining in a public "commitment to developing civic virtue and moral character" in young people. The group called for a return to living by "the guiding principles of our nation's framing documents" and the "core values held in our society such as honesty, fairness, integrity, and respect."[111] Other groups such as the Character Counts Coalition and the American Association of School Administrators soon endorsed similar values.[112] The association's 1996 report called for a return to the principles that Horace Mann had envisioned when he championed the cause of the American common school.[113]

In 1994, Congress enacted legislation funding character education pilot programs that incorporate civic virtue and citizenship, justice and fairness, respect, responsibility, and trustworthiness.[114] That same year, the White House hosted the first Conference on Character Building for a Democratic and Civil Society, sponsored by the Communitarian Network and George Washington University. In a speech before the 1995 conference, President Bill Clinton called for character education in the schools as "a vital part of building the kind of society that recognizes responsibilities and has a sense of community." He repeated that call in his State of the Union Address in 1996, challenging the schools "to teach values and good citizenship."[115] At about the same time, several state legislatures enacted laws mandating values education, while state education departments, including Maryland and Utah, established character education offices under federal grants.[116] As the century drew to a close, a rash of high school shootings and particularly the killings in Littleton, Colorado, prompted some educators to view character education as a means of preventing violence.

Obviously, the difficult question remains: Whose values? And even when a consensus has been reached on abstract values such as honesty and responsibility, disagreement often arises in the concrete application to specific issues or in the relative weights afforded values that conflict with each other. It is at the point of applying values that sharp differences in moral judgment often arise. A clear example is the value of tolerance, which at first glance seems indisputable. When applied to the debate over homosexual rights, however, tolerance can prove highly controversial. Does it require merely that we treat everyone with equal dignity and respect or does it mean that we accept alternative lifestyles as equally valid and socially acceptable as more conventional ones? For many if not most religious conservatives of various denominations, to accept the latter view would violate a basic tenet of their religion. The debate over abortion and reproductive rights for women is another example of conflict in the details. While values of autonomy and respect for life may have wide appeal, the balance struck between them in public discourse on abortion depends on individual religious and moral perspectives on when life begins.

Adding to the tensions over values are disagreements surrounding efforts to break what some consider to be the Eurocentric bias of the traditional curriculum. The multiculturalists argue that the curriculum must include the perspectives of formerly disenfranchised groups, including racial minorities and women. And to add just one more wrinkle to the values debate, there are those who equate both the traditional values promoted by character education proponents and the curricular objections raised by religious conservatives with certain religious beliefs. Critics on the political left oppose any suggestion of religion, religious motivation, or religious speech in the public schools, yet argue that the curriculum should reflect a broader range of secular values and perspectives, some more controversial than others. Critics on the political right contend that schools cannot teach virtue without relating moral values to a particular worldview, and that the values currently represented in the curriculum are so secular as to convey a message of hostility toward religion and, in certain cases, directly offend religious beliefs. Dissenters of various political and religious persuasions oppose the values and views imposed upon their children by the educational establishment—from community service, to reproductive freedom, to conventional dress codes, to alternative lifestyles and drug awareness.

SCHOOLING AS INDOCTRINATION

Both the character education movement and values-based challenges to the curriculum demonstrate the direct relation between education and ethics. Schooling, however, involves indoctrination that goes beyond the direct teaching of values and even beyond the curriculum as conventionally understood. Ethical or value considerations permeate the entire educational process. As George Counts laid bare before the progressives decades ago, to believe that the school is impartial is an untenable position and plainly fallacious. Of course, Counts was trying to build his case for a society-oriented school, and so he not only acknowledged the indoctrinative nature of schooling but wholeheartedly endorsed it. Nevertheless, it is undeniable that classroom instruction does in fact reflect certain judgments on the part of the school and the teacher as to what should be valued as good or important based on certain assumptions about the good society and the good life. Schools normalize a dominant ideological perspective whose "regulating power" affects both consciousness and behavior. As socializing agents, schools "classify, transmit, evaluate, and make coherent a partisan version of what knowledge is of most worth."[117]

Both the overt and the hidden curricula undeniably affect the transmission of culture as well as the formation of students' self-image, beliefs, and worldviews. Not only the textbooks and library books used, but also the governance structure of the school (hierarchical or democratic), the extracurricular activities offered (karate, hockey, chess, or ballet), the role models that teachers provide including their mode of dress and affect, the importance and substance of exams, the dress code, the layout of the classrooms (lecture or seminar style), teaching and learning styles (individual or cooperative)—all of these factors are value-laden and send subtle but powerful messages to students.[118] The very debate within progressive thinking between the child-centered and the social revisionist camps as well as the more consensual points on educational practice that they shared support the notion that schooling inevitably involves values imposition.

It is widely believed, although hotly disputed, that moral principles must be grounded in a cultural tradition and perhaps even in transcendent values. For some, in fact, the concept of what the common school reformers considered nonsectarian morality is itself an oxymoron. The real dilemma for the United States is how to adapt the concept of a common education designed to preserve democracy and republican government to a pluralist society in which the Constitution, the fundamental social contract, prohibits an established church and also protects freedom of conscience and the right to dissent. Given these critical factors, the permissible scope of the state's indoctrinative power raises several fundamental questions of political and constitutional magnitude, namely: Which values *should* or *should not* be inculcated? Which values *must* or *must not* be inculcated? Who should make these decisions and by what process? And finally, is there a constitutional remedy available when consensus over educational values cannot be achieved through the administrative and political processes?

Much of the debate over values in the schools turns on two indisputable facts: education is compulsory under state law, and the right of parents to send their children to nonpublic schools is more formal than substantive. Limited financial resources prevent most students from attending any institution other than government-operated schools. Both the compulsory nature of schooling and the state monopoly over its delivery combined obviously raise potential dangers of indoctrination and censorship.

Related to the concept of compulsory schooling is the notion that students are a captive audience. Children, unlike most adults, have not yet formed sufficiently firm beliefs to help them resist indoctrination. Most parents hand their children over to governmental authorities at five or six years of age. For at least thirteen years of their lives, these same children spend a considerable portion of their waking hours each weekday, nearly ten months out of the year, absorbing viewpoints that may or may not agree with those of their parents on a range of value-laden issues. As the legal scholar Mark Yudof has noted, "In some ways, public schools are a communications theorist's dream: the audience is captive and immature . . . the messages are labeled as educational (and not as advertising) . . . and a system of rewards and punishments is available to reinforce the messages."[119]

Legal commentators have analyzed the inculcative aspect of schooling from two diametrically opposed perspectives, one focusing on students' right to freedom of conscience, including freedom of expression, and the other focusing on school governance. Inherent in each of these views are distinct value judgments about the role of schooling and the relationship between children and parents on the one hand and between children and the state on the other. The first view, based on individual rights, looks at what public schools as governmental agencies *may not* include or exclude. Those who take this position concede that education by nature must promote some values while denying recognition to others. They maintain, however, that the state cannot indoctrinate students or establish uniform values. The formation and expression of beliefs are intertwined, they argue; governmental limits on one inevitably limit the other.[120] A broad state indoctrinative interest in using schools as the vehicle for inculcating the values of the local community and reflecting majoritarian preferences, they maintain, is inconsistent with the "constitutional ideal of citizen self-government."[121]

This view joins in a strained alliance a disparate group of proponents who agree at the philosophical core but disagree on the political margins and who ironically often find themselves in the culture wars hurling charges of censorship at each other across a wide ideological divide. Included in this camp are secularists and political liberals who oppose the censorship of ideas and the promotion of fixed political values but who also voice disagreement with religious expression in the public schools.[122] Also included are religious conservatives who believe that religious views must be protected and who strongly oppose what they consider to be the pronounced secularism and outright hostility toward religion evidenced in the conventional public school curriculum. By failing to inculcate certain ethical, moral, or religious values or to permit those values to be freely expressed, they argue, public schools have attempted to inculcate in students a secularist ideology.[123]

Depending on the particular issue, each of these camps at times does a turnabout and aligns itself with those espousing an opposing view, representing a range of deference to school decision making. Social and religious conservatives look to what schools *may* do in the name of values inculcation. Here the balance shifts in favor of school authority to inculcate values that reflect those of the local community or the larger society. One cautious approach on the political left suggests that schools may promote values considered essential to a democratic constitutional system, for example, tolerance of religious differences.[124] Commentators embracing a more comprehensive approach maintain that education is in fact a legitimate governmental presence in the "sphere of intellect and spirit,"[125] that historically we have accepted that presence, that schools are unique institutions linking the young to the local community and larger society, and that courts should uphold curricular decisions as long as they are educationally rational.[126] Some even suggest that neither students nor teachers enjoy a First Amendment presumptive right to use the schools as a forum for personal expression.[127]

The various arguments in this debate touch the very essence and inherent tensions within the common school as originally envisioned by nineteenth-century crusaders and later reenvisioned by twentieth-century progressives and neoprogressives. When raised in the political arena, these conflicting and overlapping perspectives often reach an impasse where the battle lines are drawn on irreconcilable worldviews and issues of cultural identity. Whether tied to religion and concepts of "ultimacy" or based in moral or philosophical beliefs, disputes over values center on issues about which people feel profoundly and disagree sharply. Yet compromise frequently proves elusive or fragile at best within the modern-day remnant of the state-operated common school. In the end, values-based conflicts frequently work their way into federal courts, straining the capacity and legitimacy of the judiciary to find legal solutions to what essentially are bitter political and philosophical disagreements over the aims and purposes of education. As Cremin wisely observed, unlike the political process, which tends to advance what is common in seeking a long-term solution, courts stress our differences for the short-term, affirming the right to "dissent from agreed upon policies."[128]

The right to dissent lies at the heart of curriculum challenges. In fact, the concept of rights—both children's and parents'—and their relation to each other and to the state have played a key role in the legal and political debates over educational values. The child/parent/state triad of competing interests has become the fulcrum around which the resolution of values-based claims inevitably turns in the judicial, legislative, and administrative arenas. Parents and school officials now struggle to reconcile their differences over the ambiguous legacy left by reformers whose revisionist plans reflected distinct philosophical and political perspectives on childhood and parenting that bear directly on current controversies. It is to these perspectives that I now turn in order to present a clearer sense of the issues underlying contemporary rights-based challenges to the curriculum and to begin establishing a framework for developing policies that promise a more politically stable and pedagogically sound resolution.

Chapter 3 From
Children's Rights
to Parents' Rights

Discourse on children generally revolves around two interrelated issues. The first addresses the distribution of decisional power among the child, the parent, and the state. The second involves interest balancing among the child, the parent, and either a particular segment of society or society at large. Discourse on education, on the other hand, typically reverts to a traditional liberal mode projecting a direct relation between the individual child and the state in which the interests of the child are merged with those of the parent. In recent years, however, the debate over educational values has refocused the discourse as between the parent and the state, almost totally eclipsing the child, whose present and future lie at the heart of this seemingly bipolar dispute between parents and the schools. Yet regardless of how courts, legislatures, and the media present the issues to the public, the debate over educational values undeniably involves the distinct and overlapping interests of children, their parents, and society.

As with similar policy questions affecting children and families, whether it be child custody, abuse and neglect, or reproductive freedom of minors, where the balance rests depends in large measure on how the individual interests are conceptualized and whether such factors as the child's capacity and age are considered in the process. More fundamentally, it depends on how we as a society define our overall policy objectives. Are we primarily concerned with protecting children from parental abuse, neglect, or misguidance or from overreaching by the state? Are we interested in allowing children a voice in decisions that significantly affect their lives? Are we looking to preserve stable family relationships or meet broader societal needs, such as educating future citizens for democratic participation? Or are we trying to meet a combination of these objectives? These concerns have played out differently over time in response to social movements, cultural forces, and prevailing philosophies of childhood, parenting, and the role of government. A backward glance at these competing perspectives presents a backdrop for examining the contemporary debate now cast in the language of parental rights and educational values. It also underscores the importance of making the developmental needs of the child the central focus of any project proposing alternative approaches to redistributing decisional power.

HISTORICAL CONCEPTIONS OF CHILDHOOD AND PARENTING

Over the centuries, philosophers, historians, lawyers, and more recently psychologists have attempted to explain and resolve the inherent tensions that necessarily arise from governmental decisions concerning the lives and futures of children. Philippe Ariès, in his comprehensive study of the history of childhood, noted that the concept of childhood itself is a relatively modern invention coming out of seventeenth-century Europe.[1] More recently, historians have challenged the blanket assertion that there existed absolutely no notion of childhood as a distinct stage in human development before modern times.[2] Nevertheless, Ariès' detailed description of children's changing reality over the centuries draws an inseparable connection between the concepts of childhood and family.[3]

There is evidence to suggest that during the Middle Ages, at least in western Europe, children were regarded as miniature adults with corresponding rights and responsibilities. Their specific needs or capacities were of little consequence. Medieval society had lost any sense of the ancient Greek *paideia,* which had presumed a formal education for the benefit of the state and community. Education was by apprenticeship, which began between the ages of twelve and seventeen. An arguable exception was the nobility, whose boys were sent away at the age of six or seven to be educated in the chivalric arts in the courts of lords. Some girls went to nunneries, while others were betrothed at an early age and reared in the home of their future husband. The medieval family served a narrow, pragmatic function: to transmit "life, property and names" to succeeding generations.[4]

From the Renaissance and particularly the Reformation emerged the idea of children as innocent and weak with a resulting need for discipline. To the upper and middle classes of this period, the education of children became the key to civilization, while the child's different nature and needs also demanded separation and protection from the adult world.[5] The modern concept of the family emerged during this time, taking on both a moral and spiritual function. Parents demonstrated greater concern for and connection with their children. This personalization of family ties had a negative aspect, however, subsequently evolving into more repressive child-rearing practices and a revival of the authoritarian paterfamilias. Children became the legal property of their parents, specifically, the father, who used them as "personal or family assets." At the extremes of the social scale, the poor exploited their children's labor while the rich arranged their marriages, all for the economic or social benefit of the parents.[6]

The notion of childhood as a distinct stage in life corresponds with similar advances in European intellectual thought, found most notably in the writings of John Locke, Rousseau, and John Stuart Mill. Locke, in his *Two Treaties on Government,* published in 1690, introduced the concept of parental duty. Parental authority (both fathers and mothers) over children, he tells us, derives from divine duty. Parents have an obligation to "preserve, nourish, and educate" their children "during the imperfect state of childhood."[7] Although children do not enjoy independent rights, they are not parental property. Locke assumed that parental benevolence was sufficient to protect the child's interests.

Freedom and liberty are grounded in reason, he tells us. Although children are born with the capacity for reason, they can exercise it only with age. During this period of incapacity when the child cannot yet exercise independent judgment, the parent has the duty to be its guide. For the parent to turn the child loose before the child has reason "is not allowing him the privilege of his Nature." Implicit in this parental duty of care is a corresponding limited authority over the child until the child is sufficiently mature to follow the dictates of reason. And implicit in one's freedom from arbitrary state action[8] is the right to be free from the state's arbitrary taking of one's children.[9]

By the mid–eighteenth century, the Lockean concept of parental duty had become incorporated into the English common law. Sir William Blackstone in his classic *Commentaries* reported that the power of parents (more specifically fathers since mothers were "entitled to no power, but only to reverence and re-spect") over their children derives from the parents' duty to maintain, protect, and educate their children, assigning the first two to natural law and the last to reason. But there remained remnants of the child as chattel. A child could be forced to work for the benefit of the father, could not marry without the father's permission, could be handed over to a guardian with all powers in loco paren-tis, and could be disposed of in the father's will like any other piece of property.[10]

Rousseau also called for parental authority over the child but in a natural, not arbitrary, way. The family, he tells us, is "the earliest of all societies, and the only natural one. Yet children remain attached to their father only so long as they have need of him for their preservation."[11] According to Rousseau, a child is better raised by a "wise father, however limited, than by the cleverest teacher." Rousseau recognized the unique character and needs of the child: "Childhood has a way of seeing, thinking, and feeling peculiar to itself."[13] He believed that the child would develop naturally through experience. Yet while he proclaimed the child's natural innocence, at the same time he refuted Locke's assertion that children were rational beings. "Be reasonable," he tells us, but "do not reason" [with the child]. . . . Exercise body, senses, powers, but keep the mind inactive as long as possible. Let childhood ripen in children."[12]

Rousseau's views of childhood, seen as revolutionary and even dangerous in mid-eighteenth-century France, had a definitive effect on twentieth-century ed-ucational practices, as evidenced for example by child-centered progressives, as well as on developmental psychology. Nevertheless, his apparent celebration of childhood should not be mistaken as a statement of children's rights. To the con-trary, by asserting the natural childishness of the child, in fact, he legitimized the supremacy of the adult.[14]

The writings of Mill equally influenced twentieth-century views of child-hood and children's rights which at times extended his theory beyond its origi-nal intent. Mill is best known for his ultimate value of free choice in self-re-garding acts. His basic libertarian principle, however, did not extend to children. In the spirit of paternalism reminiscent of Locke, he warned that "those who are still in a state to require being taken care of by others must be protected against their own actions as well as against external injury."[15] This admonition subse-quently would give political leverage to nineteenth-century social reformers.

Mill believed that the obligation to protect children resided not only in the state but in parents, whose "sacred duties" include giving the child "an educa-tion fitting him to perform his part well in life toward others and toward him-self." For Mill, the parents' duty to educate carried a corresponding freedom to determine the content of that education free of state interference. Although the state should require and compel education up to a certain level and provide funding for the poor, it should not take it upon itself to provide education directly. "Individuality of character" for Mill involved not just diversity of opinion but diversity of education. "A general state education," he warned, "is a mere contrivance for molding people to be exactly like one another . . . establish[ing] a despotism over the mind."[16] This dramatic assertion would inspire two distinct twentieth-century movements joined only in their suspicion of government-controlled education. The child liberationists of the 1970s would close their eyes to the age limitations of Mill's theory and extract from this oft-quoted statement a child autonomy principle. Barely two decades later, social and religious conservatives would transform it into a philosophical foundation for parental rights and educational choice.

In spite of their marked differences, Locke, Rousseau, and Mill in their general philosophical orientation held one significant point in common. They all rejected the notion of children as autonomous rights holders. All three premised rights acquisition on capacity or reason, and capacity, or at least the ability to exercise it, comes with maturity. These three thinkers would profoundly influence American perspectives on childhood, parenting, and the role of the state.

In order to understand the American experience, however, it is necessary to step back in time to colonial America, which placed a darker cast on the common law concept of parental duty. The Puritans, in sharp contrast to Rousseauian romantics who in the following centuries would consider children innately good, firmly believed in the depravity of infants and the need for moral redemption. They also considered parents to be the "natural protectors" of their children but believed that the state could intervene and remove children from parental custody when "the morals, or safety, or interests" of the children required it.[17] During this period, the doctrine of *parens patriae,* whereby the state was deemed the ultimate parent of the child, gradually took hold. Pervasive state intervention in family matters became acceptable practice, extending into morals and religion well into the eighteenth century.[18] That doctrine subsequently would serve as the guidepost for a generation of nineteenth-century reformers determined to redeem children not from the original sin of the Puritans but from their own misjudgment and from what reformers perceived to be an increasingly harmful social and family environment.

The American Revolution, imbued with the spirit of the Enlightenment, reaffirmed a commitment to the worth of the individual and the human capacity for improvement. Social thought began to focus on manipulating the environment in order to improve the lot of the underclass. With the rise of industrialization, the needs of children became more visible and compelling. As the economy expanded at the turn of the century, children as young as eight years of age were working in factories and living apart from their parents in boardinghouses or dormitories. Alexis de Tocqueville, commenting on the American family in 1839, noted that "[in] America there is, strictly speaking, no adolescence: at the close of boyhood the man appears and begins to trace out his own path."[19]

By midcentury, a massive influx of poor, marginally educated immigrants had begun to accelerate the effects of industrialization and urbanization. This confluence of forces gave rise to a host of social ills that profoundly influenced the lives of children and engaged the imagination and energies of middle- and upper-class reformers. Thus began an era of governmental paternalism that would extend into the twentieth century. The well-intentioned reforms that followed looked to the state as the arbiter of children's interests, pushing the doctrine of *parens patriae* into full gear. Succeeding generations of child advocates would vacillate between Locke's Enlightenment notions of duty and obligation and Rousseau's romantic convictions as to the innate goodness of the child.

THE AGE OF PATERNALISM

The years between the mid–nineteenth and mid–twentieth centuries actually represent several distinct periods that nevertheless share a reliance on the state to save the child through government engineering and intervention. These years witnessed an organized child-saving movement largely in response to mounting evidence of neglect, delinquency, and child abuse, particularly among newly arrived immigrants. Whatever "rights talk" entered public discourse was in the context of children's rights to assistance and care and corresponding parental failure. This unusual dialect, unlike conventional discourse on adult rights, did not emphasize autonomy and liberty but rather custody, protection, and the distinct nature of childhood. Nevertheless, the language of rights proved useful in garnering political acceptability for state intervention into the private sphere of the family.

Organized child saving drew on three basic assumptions: the child could best be understood from the perspective of modern science, not religion or other "antipositivistic" systems of thought; the child was the link from the past to the present and future; and outside institutions and agencies could intervene in the family on behalf of children.[20] Reform efforts placed primary importance on integrating children into the mainstream by socializing them in American values, echoing the sentiments of the common school reformers.

Christopher Lasch in *Haven in a Heartless World,* his seminal work on the family, tells us that educators and social reformers of this period viewed the immigrant family as "an obstacle to what they conceived as social progress—in other words, to homogenization and 'Americanization.'" The family preserved separatist religious practices, alien languages and dialects, local lore, and other traditions that retarded the growth of the political community and the national state.[21] As the public sphere rejected the family and its adult world it transformed the child into a cultural symbol with redemptive qualities. Social reform would redeem the child, while the child would redeem society—a concept carried over into the social reconstructionist views of at least some progressive educators, including John Dewey. The child was no longer the property of the parent but essentially the property of the state, in whose interests the future adult would serve. This conception of the child and the family, in fact, would continue to influence educational policy and would permeate the writings of late twentieth-century liberal philosophers despite assertions of individual rights. It would also create a backlash of conservative Christian opposition and give rise to an organized parental rights movement as that century drew to a close.

The early years of this paternalistic era focused on institutions and legislative action: the New York Children's Aid Society, established in 1853, offered vocational training and placement with farm families to get children off the streets; the New York Society for the Prevention of Cruelty to Children, founded in 1875, protected children from family abuse, neglect, and exploitation; and institutions for juvenile delinquents known as houses of refuge extended to major cities.[22] During this period, legislative enactments brought about three major policy reforms: compulsory education laws, child labor legislation, and the establishment of the juvenile court system. The first two clearly were related to each other. As mass public education took firm hold from the mid to the late 1800s, social reformers grew increasingly concerned over rising truancy, dropout, and illiteracy rates. Financial need, combined with parental disinterest in the value of education, was driving poor immigrant children to become a cheap source of labor for a burgeoning economy. At the same time, the growing population of adult immigrants competed for jobs held by children.

In an effort to improve the wages and working conditions of adults, labor interests joined with education advocates to press for both child labor and compulsory education laws at the state level. Reformers believed that schools would remove children from their family's harmful sway and place them under the "benign influence" of the state.[23] Massachusetts passed the first compulsory school attendance law in 1852. By 1890, twenty-nine states required minors within a given age range to attend school for a given number of days per year.[24] By 1920 the numbers of working children between the ages of ten and fifteen had been reduced by half.[25] With enforcement procedures remaining vague at best until the 1920s, however, a causal link between compulsory education and rising school enrollments remains unclear. An alternate theory ascribes the burgeoning school population during this period to the elimination of adolescent jobs wrought by technological change and the demand for skilled workers, the same phenomenon that spurred the movement toward vocational education in the schools.[26]

Central to both child labor reform and compulsory schooling was a reconception of childhood and parenting. No longer were children considered economic assets to their families but rather valuable resources for the future of society. Children became valued not in their present state but as potential persons. Childhood became a formative period for developing the skills and knowledge to become productive and informed adult citizens. In a speech of 1846 before the New York State Convention of Superintendents, Horace Mann concisely articulated that view. "The individual," he argued, "no longer exists as an individual merely, but as a citizen among citizens. . . . Society must be preserved; and in order to preserve it, we must look not only to what one family needs, but to what the *whole community* needs; not merely to what one generation needs, but to the wants of a succession of generations."[27] The philosophical perspectives of Locke and Mill inspired both protection for children and limits on their freedom until they acquired the capacity for reasoned judgment.[28] At the same time, parents had no personal rights over their children but only the responsibilities of a "reverent trust."[29] In the end, the greater protection afforded children prolonged the status of childhood into adolescence. The young were thrown together into one category of minority, distinctions in competency based on maturity began to fade, and the concept of adolescence and the mature minor would not resurface until the development of child psychology research well into the next century.

Along with compulsory education and the regulation of child labor came a third significant initiative. In 1899 the Illinois legislature created the first in what would become a national trend in specialized courts for juveniles. By 1928, all but two states had established courts specifically designated for minors.[30] Reformers believed that a separate juvenile court would shield juveniles from adult standards of accountability. Underlying this differential treatment were competing visions of children both as innocent victims of circumstances and as evil beings lacking moral sensibility.[31] The court frequently committed delinquents to institutions in the belief that they would more likely be reformed if removed from immoral parents and a vicious environment. But benevolent intentions sometimes produce unexpectedly harmful results. As implemented, the juvenile court system placed almost unlimited discretion in the hands of the judge and denied minors procedural protections afforded adults. The court soon became the target of severe criticism among child advocates, who continued to push for reform in the coming decades.[32]

By the early 1900s, the so-called progressive movement was making its mark on American society and politics. Here Locke gave way to Rousseau, childhood became sentimentalized, and the professional study of children through child psychology and social work was born. Child helping changed orientation from social action through voluntarism to professional specialization. During this period, John Dewey founded the laboratory school at the University of Chicago and expounded his controversial theories on education and childhood in a series of now-classic works. The federal government drew national attention to the plight of the nation's children, organizing the first White House Conference on the Care of Dependent Children in 1909 and establishing the U.S. Children's Bureau in 1912. Progressive reformers aggressively promoted the idea that the public sector must dominate the private sector if the American dream was to be realized. They firmly believed that all Americans must enter the ranks of the middle class, and they set about this task with unrelenting zeal, playing parent to the child through program after program of state intervention.[33] In the following decades, progressive ideology would infuse energy into New Deal initiatives, including the enactment of federal child labor legislation and the Aid to Dependent Children Program (ADC).

The Conference on Child Health and Protection in 1930 reflected the progressive agenda, departing radically from previous conferences. The program addressed a range of childhood and adolescent issues, attendance was up from two hundred in prior decades to three thousand, and experts dominated the proceedings, which swelled with reports prepared by pediatricians and educators and presentations by child psychologists. The growing tension between experts and parents was manifest. As President Herbert Hoover summed it up, "In a word, parental responsibility is moving outward to include community responsibility. However, . . . we must force the problem back to the spot where the child is. This primarily means, and should mean, the home."[34]

By the 1960s, the progressive assumption that the state could best define the good life began to lose ground. Reform programs—from the juvenile court, to orphanages, to compulsory education and even child labor laws—came under serious attack. Critics claimed that many of these initiatives simply lacked "moral realism." In practice, they had proven far more coercive than liberating, taking away more freedom than they had granted.[35] A new generation of child advocates and reformers, distrustful of child-saving institutions, began dismantling the progressive agenda bit by bit under the rubric of children's rights.

CHILDREN'S RIGHTS AS HUMAN RIGHTS

The Supreme Court's decision in *Brown v. Board of Education* in the mid-1950s outlawing racial segregation in the schools helped shape a new discourse on liberty and equality.[36] Here the Court introduced the rhetoric of legally enforceable children's rights, noting that "the opportunity for an education . . . , where the state has undertaken to provide it, is a right which must be made available to all on equal terms." From *Brown* emerged a public culture of "rights consciousness" as group after group drew on the analogy of race and articulated its demands as needs in arguments about constitutional rights, wrongs, and remedies.[37]

Beginning in the late 1950s, the struggle for racial equality coalesced with a growing attention to international human rights. Bridging the gap between progressive and postprogressive eras, these movements shared a commitment to individual dignity and equal respect and redefined the relation between the individual and the state. At that time, the United Nations Declaration of the Rights of the Child adopted the language of rights to establish the framework for future discussion on the lives of children throughout the world. As an international document, the declaration was significant not only for its explicit use of the term *rights*, but for its protectionist posture toward children and its reference to the child–parent relationship. Among its ten principles, the declaration provided that children are entitled to "love and understanding . . . in the care and under the responsibility of their parents whenever possible"; "free education and . . . equal opportunity to develop their individual abilities"; "protection from all forms of neglect, cruelty, and exploitation [and] . . . from any form of racial, religious, or other discrimination." The declaration identified the best interests of the child as its guiding principle and placed responsibility with parents to make that determination.[38]

Unlike *Brown,* which articulated legally enforceable rights, the declaration was a nonenforceable statement of aspirational principles based in moral claims.

The contrast between the two reveals the somewhat ambiguous relation between law and morality. It is open to question whether children, with their limited capacity for reasoning—at least at the preadolescent stage—can assert moral claims that should be legislated as legal rights. It can be argued that their dependency disempowers them from claiming rights for themselves. One can go even further and question whether the language of rights itself is appropriate in discourse on children, in view of their rational limitations and political disempowerment. Perhaps there is a more suitable theoretical framework, either within or outside of the rights tradition, for discussing child/parent/state relations.[39] These questions surfaced repeatedly in the coming decades as the idiom of rights came to dominate policy reform on children and families.

Through the 1960s, children's rights activists piggybacked on the civil rights struggle to achieve equality for racial minorities and women. They fought to include children within the category of person, that is, one who could advance legally recognizable claims and assert public entitlements. These latter-day reformers redefined the relation between the state and the child. No longer was the state merely acting in *parens patriae,* shielding the child from harm. The state had both a negative responsibility not to intrude unnecessarily into the child's life and an affirmative obligation to furnish services and benefits.[40] The movement from its very inception assumed diverse casts, owing in no small measure to the almost paradoxical nature of children's rights and the complexity of childhood and competing visions of it. For some reformers, rights meant obligations owed by the state, not necessarily in a legal sense but in the sense of fairness and justice. Within this camp, the "needs manifesto" approach became popularized, advocating that government provide children with the basic necessities of life—food, clothing, housing, education, and medical care.

The twenty-five forum recommendations, including universal child care, that emerged from the White House Conference on Children in 1970 clearly represented this position.[41] Although participants used the language of *rights* for the first time in the seven-decade history of such conferences, a symbolically and politically significant linguistic shift, they were actually referring to children's developmental, health, and educational *needs.* The final report to the president stated, "We must recognize [children's] inherent rights which, although not exclusively those established by law and enforced by the courts, are nonetheless closely related to the law." Led by social workers and other professionals, this arm of the movement invited active federal intervention. But it also took a critical turn, placing children in connection with their parents. The report urged that any programs established by the federal government include participation of and concern for the family.[42]

Another branch of the child advocacy movement expressly promoted a reconception of children as rights holders. Here proposals typically took the form of the "rights manifesto." Some were merely broad aspirational statements intended to inform society's commitment to children. These included the right to grow up free of poverty and discrimination, to be born a wanted child, to be cared for by affectionate parents, to have a meaningful voice in the community, to be educated to the limits of individual capacity.[43] Others were general principles of moral rights that certain advocates believed should be transformed into legal rights, for example, the right to be regarded as a legal person, to receive fair treatment from all in authority, to work and keep one's earnings, to obtain medical care, and to be emancipated from a broken parent–child relationship.[44]

Still more radical proposals emerged from the movement. *Moral* rights were too indeterminate for this group, whose members spoke more directly to specific *legal* rights enforceable not only against the state but also against the family. At the most ideological extreme were the liberationists, who embraced liberalism's recognition of autonomy as the most fundamental normative value. In doing so, they framed a vision of the autonomous child unfettered by state or parental restrictions. Children, they argued, should be seen in the eyes of the law not differently but on an equal basis with adults. For them, the doctrine of *parens patriae* was harmful to children. Self-determination was at the heart of the matter.

Leading the liberationist charge were the educator John Holt, best known for his advocacy of home schooling, and the psychologist Richard Farson, whose separately published works in 1974 triggered an ideological debate throughout the children's rights movement. Holt proposed that the rights, duties, and responsibilities of adults be made available to any young person, regardless of age, including the right to vote, the right to direct and manage one's education (suggesting the abolition of compulsory education), and the right to seek and choose guardians other than one's parents.[45] Farson went even further, including within his manifesto the rights to alternative home environments and to sexual freedom.[46] Many of these proposals undoubtedly required nothing less than a cultural and constitutional revolution. They challenged our most fundamental values and traditional beliefs about childhood, parenting, and the nature of family relationships. As one reviewer half-seriously observed, had the Holt-Farson project succeeded, at least it would have solved the problem of overpopulation:

"Emancipated by birth, with all of the privileges but none of the responsibilities of adulthood, what 'child' would ever exchange his status for that of a parent?"[47]

The liberationists never succeeded in directly influencing policy reform. Nevertheless, their extremism broadened the debate and effectively legitimized more centrist proposals. They also helped lay the foundation and define key issues for a continuing public discussion on children and parental rights that would extend into the coming decades. Most reformers, in fact, took a more moderate approach. They recognized that autonomy and dependency are not fixed and bipolar but fluid concepts that change over time within the course of the child's developmental life. For them, the legal approach of merely extending adult rights to children was too narrow; children, after all, are not miniature versions of adults.[48] They harnessed their energies, instead, onto governmental programs to meet children's special needs and assure them the opportunity to maximize their potential.[49]

But even among the centrists, some leaned more to the right and others to the left of the political center. In an article published in 1973 that later proved politically controversial, Hillary Rodham called on courts and legislatures to recognize independent status for children. She outlined three proposals to support that position: (1) abolish the legal status of minority and reverse the presumption of childhood incompetency; (2) grant to children involved in judicial or administrative proceedings all procedural constitutional rights guaranteed to adults; and (3) replace the presumed identity of interests between parent and child with an evaluation of the consequences for each, permitting competent children to assert their own demonstrably independent interests against their parents.[50] While the first of these proposals could in the end disserve the interests of children, the second two merit at the very least serious discussion.

From the early to mid-1970s, the children's rights movement seemed to be hitting its stride. The Children's Defense Fund was established in 1973 to address the concerns of children who, according to its director Marian Wright Edelman, were "nonpersons" without "any rights in the present system." The organization set schools and the juvenile justice system as its immediate targets.[51] By 1976 a *New York Times* study found that every one of twenty-four states surveyed had a similar legal group fighting for human rights for children. The movement had become one not of "marches, petitions and boycotts, but one of constitutional arguments and legal theories."[52]

In the vanguard of what *Time* magazine called "the latest crusade" was the U.S. Supreme Court.[53] In a series of decisions beginning in the late sixties, the

Court seemingly impugned the progressive trust in administrative discretion and recognized minors as constitutional rights holders against the state. In case after case, the Court seemed to be charting a course of procedural and substantive rights for children. With the exception of contraception and abortion cases, most of these presented parents and children on one side of the divide and the state on the other.

The Court's *Gault* decision (1967) recognizing minors as persons under the Constitution is considered by some as the highwater mark of the children's rights movement. Here the Court granted certain procedural rights to minors in juvenile court, including a right to counsel, a right against self-incrimination, a right to notice of the charges, and a right to confront and cross-examine witnesses.[54] Two years later, the Court's *Tinker* decision not only recognized that students have rights to freedom of expression under the First Amendment, but suggested even broader constitutional protections in the public school setting, noting that "students . . . do not shed their constitutional rights at the schoolhouse gate."[55] In the mid-1970s, in *Goss v. Lopez,* the Court reaffirmed constitutional rights for children, granting them certain procedural protections, including notice, reasons, and an informal opportunity to be heard before school authorities could impose even a short-term suspension from school.[56]

In the years following, the Court recognized that minors are entitled to privacy and choice rights under the Constitution. The Court struck down a state statute that required a parent or person acting in loco parentis to provide written consent to the abortion of an unmarried woman under the age of eighteen.[57] The Justices also invalidated a statute that prohibited the sale of contraceptives to children under sixteen without parental approval, although the plurality opinion suggested that a somewhat less rigorous test should apply to state restrictions on the personal choices of minors. In such cases, a "significant" state interest "not present in the case of an adult" would suffice in lieu of a "compelling justification."[58] In the late 1970s, the Court again attempted to reconcile the competing child, state, and parental interests implicit in consent requirements. Applying the concept of the "mature minor," the Court qualified the minor's privacy rights on a demonstration of maturity. Here the Court held that states could not require a minor to obtain parental consent prior to an abortion unless the statute also provided for a judicial hearing, conducted without the parents' knowledge. The hearing would give the minor the opportunity to convince the court either that she is mature enough to make the decision herself or that it is within her best interests to have the abortion.[59] These cases dramatically altered traditional views on official and parental control over the actions of older children.

As the courts continued to advance a rights-based approach grounded in constitutional law, a protective entitlement-based concept dominated legislative policy making. On the one hand, children were to be treated the same as adults as a matter of constitutional right; that is, children, like adults, were to enjoy a wide range of civil liberties: freedom of speech, equal protection of the laws, privacy, and procedural due process. On the other hand, children had distinct needs stemming from their dependency on adults and their inability to care for themselves. They were therefore entitled to certain government services and benefits: care, food, and equal educational opportunity.

The philosophical incoherencies of this bifurcated approach to children's rights, however, soon converged into an equally incoherent and loosely defined protectionist concept. While legislative efforts continued to protect children from social evils and compensate them for social inequalities, the courts protected children from themselves and increasingly deferred to the judgment of parents and the state. In fact, if the children's rights movement reached its stride by the mid-1970s, it would soon reach its peak. Just two years after the *Goss* decision, the Court refused to extend the very same due process rights to cases of corporal punishment. In other words, a child was entitled to a hearing before being suspended from school for ten days or less but not before being struck with a large wooden paddle. The case, *Ingraham v. Wright,* was a painful setback in the struggle for legal recognition of children's rights.[60] It was also a sign of things to come.

As the late seventies approached, a number of factors coalesced to dramatically transform rights talk in subsequent decades. Changing membership on the Supreme Court began to reflect a more conservative consensus among the Justices, the political pendulum was swinging closer toward the conservative pole, the religious right was politically mobilizing and becoming more visible and vocal, there was an upsurge in serious crimes committed by juveniles, and the American people were growing disenchanted with both the perceived permissiveness toward children and the growing intrusion of government into the lives of families and communities.

Supreme Court decisions became emblematic of this changing mood. An old vision of childhood, parenting, and the state began to reemerge, animated by principles of custody and dependency. Unlike many of the earlier cases, these controversies presented the Court with more sharply defined child–parent conflicts, pushing the Justices in the direction of parental discretion. Court decisions from the late seventies to the late eighties also demonstrated an apparent return to progressive reliance on the expertise of professionals combined with a renewed sense of federalism and localism. Throughout this period, the Court gradually changed the course of constitutionalism and rejoined the rights–entitlement dichotomy; what emerged was a variation of the unified protectionist concept of nineteenth-century reformers, this time recognizing not only the state's interests but also the decisional right of parents with regard to important aspects of their children's lives. This changed judicial attitude cut across the spectrum of children's interaction with the state and redefined the child/parent/state relation.

School officials could now search students based not on probable cause, as in the adult world, but merely on reasonable suspicion that the students had violated either the law or a school rule. They could remove books from the school library as long as the removal was not politically motivated, and they could censor the student press as long as their action was based on "legitimate pedagogical concerns."[61] Within the juvenile justice system, the state could exercise its *parens patriae* power to detain minors before adjudicating their delinquency because "juveniles, unlike adults, are always in some form of custody."[62]

At the same time, the Court developed a federal constitutional dimension to family law, often viewing the family as a unitary entity. Parents could commit their child to a mental institution without the child's being granted a hearing. The Justices were confident that the parents' "natural bonds of affection" would lead them to act in the child's best interest, while the admitting medical personnel would resolve any doubt as to the appropriateness of the placement.[63] And in apparent retreat from an autonomy-based theory of constitutional privacy, states could constitutionally require a physician to notify the parents of an immature and unemancipated minor of her intent to have an abortion without providing the option of a judicial bypass. It is "basic in the structure of our society," the Court noted, to recognize parents' claims to control the upbringing of their children.[64]

RELATIONAL THEORIES OF CHILDREN AND FAMILIES

By the mid 1980s, it was evident that the Court was rethinking the notion of constitutional personhood for children. Court decisions appeared to rest on three assumptions: that minors lack the capacity to make mature decisions, that parents act in the best interest of their children, and that the state can step into the place of the parent if necessary.[65] This new jurisprudence of parental authority and state discretion deeply troubled child advocates. Nevertheless, scholars and reformers, even some deeply rooted in liberal traditions who disagreed with the Court's assumptions, began to challenge the absolutism of liberation rhetoric, its vision of the autonomous child, and its apparent denial of the child–parent relationship. They recognized that the child's developing capacity for decision making and the impact of child autonomy on family structure are indeed relevant to the question of children's rights. They sounded the alarm that perhaps as a society we were "abandoning children to their rights."[66] As John Coons and Robert Mnookin aptly noted, the "argot" of both the liberationists and the child savers had a "ring of unreality." The one's assertion that age is irrelevant to legal autonomy simply defied biological and economic reality, while the other's assertion of legal claims to "love and affection" was devoid of any means of governmental monitoring or legal enforcement.[67]

Legal scholars as philosophically and politically diverse as Martha Minow and Bruce Hafen called for a renewed discourse on children and families. Although espousing distinct perspectives on childhood, autonomy, and capacity, they shared a core belief in the importance of family in meeting the psychological needs of the child. Commentators argued that, absent extreme circumstances, parents are most informed to make decisions about their children while children derive psychological benefits from the care and nurturance of the family.[68] Equal rights, they maintained, would remove the social support needed by parents to transmit self-control, enabling virtues, and moral values to their children.[69] Parental restraints benefit children, permitting them to challenge authority and explore new ideas knowing they have a parental safety net to stop them from harming themselves.[70] Children need the stability and support of the family, it was argued, to grow into healthy, autonomous adults; if we remove family authority, we may be giving the child present liberty at the cost of his or her future self-determination.[71] The family is the "haven in a heartless world," providing emotional shelter founded in intimacy, which in turn is critical to one's sense of identity.[72] As one scholar bluntly stated, "Children cannot be adequately or even sensibly protected by giving them 'rights' that state officials will enforce against parents. Children can only be protected by giving them parents."[73] Even the American Civil Liberties Union questioned whether "the state . . . is capable of acting *in loco parentis* with more wisdom or justice and less irrationality or tyranny than a child's own parents."[74]

In recent years, scholars writing primarily but not exclusively from the perspective of feminist jurisprudence have tried to reconcile this renewed sensitivity to the value of family with liberalism's commitment to individual autonomy. They maintain that the child has only an inchoate or developing interest in autonomy which draws from the child's interest in the family relationship. They reject prevailing theories of the family based in contract, community, or rights. Although such theories attempt to replace the patriarchal approach of the common law, they fail to take account of a paradoxical feature of family life whereby family members are individuals but individuals defined partially by their relationships with others.[75] They argue that an adequate conception of the family must incorporate an "ethic of care," informed by theories of caretaking and moral relationships, that values the significance of continuous attention, affection, and help among family members.[76]

Martha Minow's writing has set the groundwork for much of this discussion. Her project is less a theory of enforceable legal rights and more a theoretical framework for guiding public and legal discourse on children and families. Her child-centered approach, which charts a middle course between the ideological extremes of liberationist rhetoric and parental authoritarianism, offers a useful theoretical framework for examining the child/parent/state relation in the debate over educational values and educational choice. But the irony in this connection between feminist theory and the claims advanced primarily by religious conservatives should not go overlooked. Sometimes truth is found in the most unexpected of places.

Building on the psychologist Carol Gilligan's concept of the "feminine voice,"[77] Minow commits to a feminist concern with relationships and a vision of the self forged in connection with, not separation from, others.[78] She acknowledges the realities of children's lives and their needs of dependency while attempting to preserve the liberal commitment to individual rights of autonomy. She sees children's rights as an aspect of human rights, emphasizing dignity, respect, and freedom from arbitrary treatment.[79] Children, she tells us, are the "paradigmatic group excluded from traditional liberal rights." Children are not autonomous individuals under the law but rather stand in relationships of dependency to adults, particularly their parents. She uses these relationships as a point of entry into what she calls a "new conception of rights."[80]

Minow places the family in the communal and cultural context and talks of mutual needs and connections between children and adults rather than contrasting their respective abilities. Contrary to other needs-focused theories, however, hers does not abandon rights talk but proposes a more expansive redefinition, proposing that the goals of autonomy and affiliation be joined.[81] She suggests that children's rights can and do take several forms: rights to autonomy, rights to connection, and rights to protection, which can either intrude on the private sphere of the family (protection from parents), as in the case of child abuse and neglect, or reinforce the privacy of the family (protection from the state), as in the case of allowing Amish children to avoid compulsory education requirements.[82] In any event, rights discourse, she tells us, carries practical implications: it makes those in power listen even to those who are treated as less than equal within the community.[83]

Minow rejects the liberal position that the rights-bearing person must be autonomous, that is, capable of expressing choice and protecting personal freedom. Others have used this argument to challenge children's rights in the first instance.[84] Autonomy is not a precondition of rights, she says; relationships are a precondition for the development of autonomy.[85] Rather than limit children's rights to constraining abuses of power by the state or by parents, she presents a parallel concept in which rights promote the ability of children "to form relationships of trust, meaning, and affection with people in their daily lives and their broader communities." Children are neither totally dependent nor totally independent, she tells us; they need care and custody in some circumstances and autonomy in others. Drawing further on Gilligan's work, she develops the concept of the child's voice. In cases of child–parent conflict, she argues, the state must consider the views of the child and even suspend its usual enforcement of parental power. In this way, the state "lift[s] children from their usual dependence on and subjection to parental authority."[86]

In recent years, other scholars have reaffirmed Minow's rejection of traditional rights discourse with its emphasis on autonomy, individuality, hierarchy, and power in favor of a construct that emphasizes relationships. They build on her commitment to family interdependency and the significance in the law's validating of children's personhood by recognizing their perspective and their evolving capacity over time.[87] Some argue for legally protected positive rights for children in the care, security, and joys of childhood itself as compared with the child's interests as a future adult.[88] These arguments obviously place an unrealistic burden on the legal system to enforce rights that defy a quantifiable measure of adequacy. Just how much care and security would meet the constitutional minimal standard?

Others more reasonably refocus the discussion away from children's rights (or adult rights over children) and on to parental obligations,[89] suggesting that we complement rights talk with the language of adult responsibility and corresponding children's needs. While rights are empowering and self-affirming, responsibility appeals to our "ethical sensibilities" and our motivation to "do right."[90] Within the family relationship, responsibility places the child's developmental needs at the center of the question of parental authority. If we enlarge our understanding of developmental needs to embrace the notion of children as moral and spiritual beings and members of distinct cultural communities, a theory built on parental responsibility in fact offers much in the way of addressing values-based conflicts in the schools.[91] Still others recognize children's needs-based rights to identity and continuity but go beyond mutuality in the work of the family and look toward the community's collective responsibility for the well-being of children in the sense of welfare rights.[92] While each of these approaches varies at the margins, they all share a commitment to the child not as a lone rights bearer but as an interdependent member within a broader context founded in family and community.[93]

The jurisprudence of relationships is a soothing antidote to the libertarian rhetoric of previous years. Its repositioning of the child in the context of the family and community and its recognition of the child's voice and developing capacity with maturity have particular applicability to the debate over dissenting views and education for democratic citizenship. These child-centered arguments, however, have deeply troubled religious and political conservatives, who view parents' authority as a natural right and therefore absolute and inalienable.[94] Representative of their views is another strand of contemporary scholarship which draws on the concept of family relationships to develop a theory of parental rights and family autonomy. Advocates of this position have reconceived the family as a form of intimate association, transposing the liberal notion of individual autonomy and associational rights on to the moral claims of parents to raise their children free of state intervention.[95]

The writings of Bruce Hafen fall within this genre. He presents an authoritarian parent-centered model with a vision of the "autonomous family," which, he tells us, carries psychological value. That value cannot be maintained, he argues, absent parental authority that is "ultimately authoritative." In Hafen's view, the truly democratic family is less likely to provide "the security, the role-modeling, the leadership, the socializing, the growth, or many of the other interests" preserved by a policy of state support for parental authority. His authoritative model, however, denies the child's developing capacity to exercise reasoned judgment over time and incorporates, instead, a monolithic view of minority. For example, he explicitly denies the capacity of adolescents to make decisions that require maturity and that carry long-term consequences. Such "choice rights," he says, are not ascribable to children, falling under traditional parental control.[96] In fact, he more generally rejects rights-based analysis as potentially harmful in the family context.[97]

This perspective reflects contemporary conservative views of the family. More important, it has provided theoretical support to an organized parents' rights movement that at best has marginalized the interests of the child but that nevertheless is gaining political momentum across the country. In the abstract, that movement holds considerable appeal to parents frustrated by their relative powerlessness in directing their children's education. In the details, however, it raises serious legal and policy concerns.

PARENTAL VALUES AS PARENTAL RIGHTS

Dana Mack, the author of the controversial book *The Assault on Parenthood,* writes that "parents are on the way to creating a powerful . . . counterculture."[98] The observation may be somewhat overstated, yet it cannot be denied that in the past decade parents have asserted their political and legal rights to control the education and upbringing of their children with ever-increasing force and frequency. The debate over education and parental values has now become a major political issue, moving Congress in 1995 to hold a two-day hearing on parents, schools, and values which elicited testimony from across the political spectrum but primarily from social and religious conservatives.[99]

Religious dissenters in particular have raised their voices to a feverish pitch in seeking accommodation to their religious beliefs both inside and outside the public school system. From within, they challenge the arguably pervasive secularism of the curriculum, the inculcation of antithetical belief systems, the imposition of what they judge to be unwarranted and unauthorized psychological testing and counseling, the widespread intolerance or fear of even private religious expression on public school grounds, and the reluctance of school officials to permit parents to opt their children out of objectionable programs. From without, they join in a chorus with a growing number of inner-city minority parents to press for enhanced choice in the form of government subsidies to support alternatives to the neighborhood public school.

Parental rights advocates are fighting this battle on several fronts. A well-organized segment of the movement has coalesced around inscribing parental rights into law, focusing its energies in two converging directions: derailing U.S. ratification of the United Nations Convention on the Rights of the Child and enacting parental rights measures at the federal and state levels. These related efforts reflect a commonality of objectives and frustrations with the status quo and a commonality of purpose among religious and social conservatives to have their parental voices heard with some finality and force. They also reflect agenda items incorporated into the Christian Coalition's 1995 *Contract with the American*

Family, whose stated goal was to "legislate family values, and to ensure that Washington values families."[100]

United Nations Convention on the Rights of the Child

The United Nations Convention on the Rights of the Child grew out of the International Year of the Child in 1979, which in turn celebrated the twentieth anniversary of the Declaration of the Rights of the Child. In 1979, a working group established by the Commission on Human Rights began drafting an international treaty whose fifty-four articles were adopted by the United Nations General Assembly in 1989 after much debate and negotiation. The convention achieved the twenty ratifications necessary and came into force within nine months of its adoption—an unprecedented response by the international community to any human rights treaty. The document calls for the establishment of an elected international panel of ten experts, the Committee on the Rights of the Child, with responsibility for assessing the progress made by the signatories toward implementing the essential features of the convention (articles 43, 44, 45). It also permits nations to adopt the document with reservations as long as these are not incompatible with the object and purpose of the convention (article 51). A signatory can use reservations to limit or modify the legal effect of a provision or to alert other countries that are parties to the convention that it does not intend to comply with a specific provision.

A total of 191 countries have ratified the convention, and only 2, Somalia and the United States, have not. Since Somalia lacks the governmental capacity to ratify a treaty, the United States stands alone as the only remaining eligible nation that can ratify the convention. After much foot-dragging, the United States signed the document in February 1995 as the deathbed behest of James Grant, the former executive director of the United Nations Children's Fund (UNICEF).[101] In spite of broad-based support from more than two hundred organizations and the efforts of a working group convened by the U.S. Committee for UNICEF and Save the Children, the president still has not submitted the convention to the U.S. Senate for advice and consent to ratification.[102] Given the historical controversy over human rights treaties in general, the limitations of federalism, and the numerous objections raised particularly by religious conservatives, there is little optimism that the convention will move through the Senate in the foreseeable future.

The convention, in fact, is an ambitious effort. It goes beyond prior international documents in setting forth not just rights to care and protection for children, but also individual rights to personalty, or what some critics have called "rights of choice."[103] As compared with the 1959 Declaration of the Rights of the Child, the convention is "an amalgam of both connection and autonomy," expressly acknowledging children's perspectives and their existence as dependent members of families and communities.[104] It assigns to parents the right and duty to give direction as long as it is consistent with the child's evolving capacities (article 5). The document identifies the best interests of the child as a primary consideration in all action concerning children (article 3). It also grants to the child capable of forming his or her own views the right to express those views freely in matters affecting the child and guarantees the opportunity to be heard in judicial and administrative proceedings (article 12). It recognizes the child's broadly defined freedom of expression, including the right to receive and impart ideas orally, in writing or print, or art form (article 13), as well as freedom of thought, conscience, and religion (article 14), and the right to education (article 28).

From the global perspective of children's interests and needs, these articles offer broad universal protections. Opponents maintain, however, that from the more particular viewpoint of the United States they potentially present serious legal conflicts with existing law. They appear, for example, to grant more expansive rights than those found in the Constitution, at least as the Supreme Court has interpreted that document in recent decades. The convention's rights to freedom of expression seem more akin to the Court's 1969 *Tinker* decision (upholding broad constitutional rights of students within public schools) than with the more recent 1988 *Hazelwood* ruling (upholding the authority of school officials to limit school-sponsored speech so long as the limitations are "reasonably related to legitimate pedagogical concerns").[105] The "right to be heard" combined with a broad-scale right to freedom of conscience and religion resounds more in Justice Douglas's dissent in *Yoder* (criticizing the majority's failure to consider the wishes of the Amish children with respect to their exemption from public schooling) than in the more parent-centered majority opinion (holding that a state compulsory education law requiring the Amish to send their children to school beyond the eighth grade violated their First Amendment right to free exercise of religion).[106] Critics argue that a federal right to education runs counter to the Court's interpretation of the Fourteenth Amendment equal protection clause.[107] More significantly, they maintain that various articles pose a direct threat to parental rights.

These articles, opponents maintain, also differ linguistically from the Constitution, requiring that governments respect or assure the stated rights or mandating that the child shall have the particular right. The use of affirmative language suggests a positive duty on the part of countries signing the document to provide programs and guarantee positive rights. This departs from the federal Bill of Rights, which serves as a limit on governmental action, merely protecting individuals in a negative way from state interference in the enjoyment of rights. These distinctions have contributed to the stalemate over ratification.[108]

Such arguments represent a misreading of the convention's text as well as an incomplete perspective on the legal force of international conventions and their relation to federal and state law. To say that a particular right is not protected under the Constitution does not mean that it is prohibited by the Constitution. They also ignore the various options whereby an adopting nation may narrow the scope of its commitments through the use of reservations and declarations. Judging from past experience, the United States typically ratifies human rights treaties with two such qualifications. The first is a declaration that all substantial provisions of the treaty are deemed "not self-executing," which means they would require legislation to carry out the treaty's commitments. The second is a "federal–state clause," which modifies the effect of the treaty on the states. The apparent purpose of the federal reservation is to facilitate Senate ratification and to afford states the discretion to comply with treaty obligations regarding matters traditionally regulated by the states as they deem most appropriate.[109]

It can only be assumed that the convention, if ratified, would include both of these qualifications because so many of its provisions fall under the purview of the states and not the federal government. In fact, some do not fall under the government's authority at all but traditionally have been left to the family. With these two provisions added, however, the convention would have no effect on rights, entitlements, or government obligations in this country unless and until some affirmative act gave them legally binding force, nor would the convention intrude on those aspects of educational governance traditionally left to state and local government. Besides, the United States already is in compliance with some of the convention's provisions. For example, while the right to education does not exist in the federal Constitution under existing Supreme Court interpretation, every state constitution guarantees all children within a given age range the right to free public schooling. Compulsory attendance laws, which exist in every state, further suggest that all states recognize a right to education.

As for the distinction between positive and negative rights, the problem here seems to lie in differing cultural understandings. The notion of nonbinding economic rights, while unfamiliar to American legal culture, is commonly accepted in many Western European countries whose post– World War II constitutions supplement negative rights, that is, protections against government, with affirmative constitutional commitments. But these are what European lawyers refer to as "programmatic rights" or "statements of public goals and social aspirations whose implementation must await legislative or executive action or budgetary appropriations."[110] In a similar way, all rights agreed upon in the convention are qualified by financial resource limitations.

Finally, the issue of family autonomy needs to be addressed. Nothing in the treaty's text, drafting history, or jurisprudential interpretation from the Committee on the Rights of the Child indicates an intent to police parents. To the contrary, the intent is to establish standards for national policies. The rights afforded children, including rights to expression, religion, association, and privacy, protect them from governmental intrusion. In fact, article 5 requires participating nations to "respect the responsibilities, rights, and duties of parents . . . to provide, in a manner consistent with the evolving capacities of the child, appropriate direction and guidance in the exercise by the child of the rights recognized in the present Convention." Other provisions reaffirm the vital role of the family. For example, article 29 states that the child's education should be directed to "the development of respect for the child's parents, his or her own cultural identity, language and values." Comments of the Committee on the Rights of the Child regarding other nations and noting high rates of abortion as a method of family planning (Russia) and teenage pregnancy (Costa Rica), access to harmful media (Nicaragua), and the negative consequences of divorce and single-parent families (Great Britain and Northern Ireland) have proven supportive of the family. More fundamentally, even where the committee finds a violation of the convention's provisions, it is not empowered to conduct investigations or prosecutions against parents or guardians. Enforcement resides entirely in international and internal political pressure on state parties to voluntarily comply.

Despite such misreadings, several points raised by the opposition may indeed pose conflicts for the United States. Article 19 requires state parties to "take all appropriate . . . measures to protect children from all forms of physical or mental violence." The Committee on the Rights of the Child has interpreted this provision to require the prohibition of corporal punishment within the family. Some parents would object on privacy or religious grounds if the United States were to adopt this requirement.[111] Article 28 requires state parties to "take all appropriate measures to ensure that school discipline is administered in a manner consistent with the child's human dignity." If this language were interpreted to impose a complete ban on corporal punishment in public schools, then it would conflict with a number of state statutes, some of which permit local school boards to use corporal punishment as a disciplinary tool while others place restrictions on its use without banning it entirely.[112]

Article 29 specifically addresses social values and educational ends that are highly value laden. It requires signatories to direct education toward the teaching of "tolerance, equality of the sexes, friendship among all peoples," and "respect for the natural environment." Private schools are permitted to exist, but they must conform with these stated goals and other minimal standards established by the national government. This apparent value imposition on private, including religiously affiliated, schools may raise First Amendment problems under the free speech and free exercise clauses. Does tolerance require acceptance of other religious beliefs as equally valid? Does international friendship include multicultural education? Does respect for the environment override competing economic concerns? These are highly charged issues, especially for religious conservatives. But assuming that the convention is ratified with a not-self-executing declaration and a federal qualifying reservation, then a strong political culture of state and local control over education in this country together with Supreme Court decisions affirming the constitutional right of private schools to remain free from unreasonable regulations strongly militates against the adoption of minimum values-laden standards that would bind private schools.

In any event, treaties cannot conflict with federal constitutional guarantees. And although the convention does appear to make several incursions into autonomy and empowerment rights—a lightning rod for conservative opposition in the United States—the not-self-executing declaration prevents enforcement of these provisions absent legislative action.[113] These misgivings can also be addressed through specific reservations so long as they are compatible with the object and purposes of the convention.

Taken as a whole, the convention is a sweeping international declaration of concern for the interests of children. Even though, as noted, the United States already complies with most of its key provisions, in many countries around the world children are subjected to appalling indifference, neglect, and abuse. Here is a global confirmation that governments must take affirmative steps to protect children from the vulnerabilities of childhood, and the world's largest and most powerful democracy has failed to recognize the symbolic force of its approval or its disapproval.

In its *Contract with the American Family,* the Christian Coalition calls the convention "a terrible risk to the parental rights and freedom of U.S. citizens" and urges "concerned citizens" to make known their support for a federal Parental Rights Act by defeating the convention. In June 1995, Sen. Jesse Helms (R. N.C.) introduced a resolution "expressing the sense of the Senate . . . that, because the United Nations Convention on the Rights of the Child could undermine the rights of the family, the President should not sign and transmit it to the Senate."[114] For political and religious conservatives, the convention is just another governmental interference with the basic right of the parent to direct the upbringing of the child.[115]

In the view of parental rights advocates, however, there is a more fundamental connection here between the convention and federal or state proposals establishing legally enforceable parental rights. Under the Supremacy Clause of the Constitution, the provisions of a treaty entered into by the national government take precedence over state law. In that sense, the convention could either completely block the enactment of state parental rights measures or render them unenforceable. On the other hand, the Supremacy Clause regards treaties as being on an equal plane with federal law so that any conflict between them would be resolved in favor of the last one enacted or adopted (the "last in time" rule).[116] If the United States were to adopt the convention, it arguably could invalidate existing parental rights statutes and constitutional provisions at the state level and block any future efforts. It could also negate any prior federal parental rights legislation. In other words, unless parental rights advocates derail the convention, it potentially could derail the parental rights movement. But then again, these concerns appear overstated in view of qualifying declarations and reservations.

Parental Rights and Responsibilities Act

Religious conservatives continue to mount a steady attack on ratification of the convention. Undoubtedly, the document raises serious questions on sensitive issues over which Americans continue to struggle for consensus. For oppositionists, however, there is no room for discussion or negotiation here; it is not just the letter but the spirit of the convention that they find offensive. And so they refuse to consider the compromise option, undeniably the more reasonable route, of ratifying the convention with reservations to effectively address conflicts and controversies. At the same time, they continue to press for parental rights measures which they claim merely codify the standards set forth in *Meyer v. Nebraska* and *Pierce v. Society of Sisters.*[117] The broad dicta in these two cases from the 1920s arguably established the right of parents "to direct the upbringing and education of their children."

In addition to *Meyer* and *Pierce,* parental rights supporters have woven together dicta from more recent Supreme Court decisions affirming that "the custody, care and nurture of the child reside first in the parents," that the claim of parents to direct their children's upbringing "is basic in the structure of our society," that there exists a "private realm of family life which the state cannot enter," and that parents have an interest in "the companionship, care, custody, and management of their children."[118] Yet despite these ringing endorsements of parental rights, the Court's use of a mere reasonableness standard in *Meyer* and *Pierce* combined with its failure to explicitly identify such rights as fundamental in later parental decisions which would trigger more exacting judicial scrutiny have led lower federal courts to either avoid "fundamental" terminology altogether or uphold state action as long as it is reasonable. In either case, parents are left without a legal remedy to what they perceive as serious intrusions into family privacy.

Parental rights advocates further strengthen their legal arguments with seemingly isolated and extreme yet nonetheless compelling stories of overreaching by school officials—from sixth-grade girls undergoing physical examinations against their will, to third graders receiving psychological counseling without parental consent, to a high school AIDS awareness program featuring lewd behavior and explicit discussion of sexual techniques. As Steve Largent, one of the congressional sponsors of the federal legislation, stated in testimony before Congress, the act is needed because "the government is using its coercive force to dictate values, offend the religious and moral beliefs of families, and restrict the freedoms of families to live as they choose. . . . [The act] is about who should be responsible for your children—a bureaucrat or parents."[119]

The Parental Rights and Responsibilities Act, subtitled "A bill to protect the fundamental right of a parent to direct the upbringing of a child," was originally introduced into both houses of Congress in June 1995 with 137 cosponsors in the House and 16 cosponsors in the Senate.[120] The drafters argued that federal legislation was needed to combat the unprecedented assault by the lower courts on the rights of parents to "direct their children's education, health care decisions, and discipline despite the Supreme Court's having clearly established the right of parents to direct the upbringing of their children as fundamental under the Fourteenth Amendment."[121] Both bills provide that "No Federal, State, or local government, or any official of such a government acting under color of law, shall interfere with or usurp the right of a parent to direct the upbringing of the child of the parent." Once a parent makes such a claim, the government, whether it be a school district or some other government agency, must prove that the alleged intrusion was the "least restrictive means" to achieve a "compelling governmental interest." This standard departs from the reasonableness test now used by the courts in parental rights cases, giving parents a clear advantage over government actors. In an effort to neutralize the most problematic criticisms leveled against parental rights proposals, more recent versions exclude from coverage the right of a parent to make health care decisions that will endanger the life of the child or cause serious physical injury. The act further excludes disputes between parents. The drafters have made clear that the act would not protect the right of a parent to engage in child abuse or neglect, as these terms have "traditionally been defined and applied in State law."

The Parental Rights and Responsibilities Act has proven politically controversial, underscoring a clear dividing line between traditionally conservative and liberal groups and individuals. A letter sent in June 1996 to congressional members supporting the legislation reads like a Who's Who of conservative Christian organizations. Heading the list of signatories were many of the same groups opposing the U.N. Convention on the Rights of the Child, including Focus on the Family, the Family Research Council, the Christian Coalition, the Eagle Forum, Concerned Women for America, and the Home School Legal Defense Association followed by numerous statewide Christian educator and home education associations. On the other side of the issue has stood a coalition of more than forty education, health, women's, child advocacy, and civil liberties groups, many of them active supporters of the U.N. convention, including the National Education Association, the American Association of School Administrators, the National School Boards Association, the American Civil Liberties Union, the American Academy of Pediatrics, the National Parent Teachers Association and People for the American Way.

Conservative Christians undeniably are driving the parental rights engine. But their conscious framing of the issue as a matter of civil liberties is designed to make it appealing to a larger constituency. The arguments advanced by supporters appear compelling at first glance. Protecting families from unlawful state intervention is a worthy principle, as are the motives of those endorsing it. Nevertheless, on closer scrutiny it becomes clear that the act will produce unintended and potentially harmful consequences for both families and children. The legislation is drafted in vague terminology. For example, what the drafters consider to be a traditional level of abuse may not be acceptable to most modern-day Americans. The bill gives rights to parents but leaves the definition of *parents* to state law, potentially excluding many caretakers who are raising children, for example, grandparents and stepparents, who need the protection, while including others who do not.[122]

With regard to education specifically, although the current governmental monopoly over education demands thoughtful political reconsideration, the act is scarcely the cure for what ails American education. It would precipitously turn the concept of local control on its head and interject the federal judiciary into the daily governance of the schools. Implementation of parental rights legislation would require judges to substitute their judgment on curricular issues for the practical experience of school officials, would allow parents a veto over courses and curricula, would derail school counseling and health programs, and would open school districts to lawsuits on everything from textbooks to field trips to dress codes to after-school activities.[123] As one critic has described the situation, "Try running a high school class on Shakespeare. Romeo and Juliet? You've got teen-aged sex, children disobeying their parents and a suicide pact. Macbeth? You start with witchcraft and go from there."[124] Critics argue that a more prudent and effective approach would be to address specific concerns through state laws or local school board policies rather than federalize educational policy.

State Constitutional Amendments and Statutes

Proposals to adopt parental rights amendments to state constitutions have generated similar arguments in support and opposition. Leading the supporters' movement at the state level is an organization called Of the People Foundation, which was founded in 1994 by the conservative author Jeffrey Bell and is based in Arlington, Virginia. Allied with the American Legislative Council, a network of twenty-six hundred conservative legislators, Of the People has drafted a model amendment, revised in 1997 to address concerns with respect to child abuse and neglect. The amendment contains even broader language than the federal proposal. It states that "the right of parents to direct the upbringing and education of their children is a fundamental right" and that "the state maintains a compelling interest in investigating, prosecuting and punishing child abuse and neglect as defined in statute." According to materials distributed by the group, the amendment "will make public schools more accountable by giving parents a greater role in shaping public school curriculum, providing consistency with mainstream values, and greater access to textbooks, materials and records" and will strengthen "efforts to enact public school choice."[125]

Of the People has successfully engineered the introduction of parental rights amendments in twenty-eight state legislatures. None of these has been adopted, although bills have been defeated in Kansas, Virginia, and North Dakota. In 1996, 57 percent of the voters in Colorado rejected the group's efforts to use the initiative process in the state as a testing ground to gain political momentum and national visibility for the parental rights concept. The defeat was due in no small measure to a public education campaign mounted by a broad coalition that included the Democratic governor along with associations of teachers, churches, pediatricians, sheriffs, district attorneys, and others. The opposition arguments echoed those leveled against the federal Parental Rights and Responsibilities Act—the dangers of child abuse and neglect (addressed in the 1997 revised model amendment) and the negative impact on school curricula, materials, and health and counseling programs.

Adopting a constitutional amendment is a lengthy process. Most states require approval from both legislative houses, often by more than a simple majority vote, followed by popular ratification. In view of these procedural obstacles, some states have followed the legislative route as a more efficient and politically palatable alternative, in a few cases in the wake of a failed attempt at constitutional amendment. Since 1996, the legislatures of Indiana, Kansas, Michigan, and Texas have enacted broadly worded statutes that affirm the right of parents to direct the upbringing and education of their children, the latter three expressly recognizing this right to be fundamental, which apparently would give it greater force in the state courts. Other states, including Massachusetts, Virginia, and Oklahoma, have enacted more specific legislative or administrative measures. The Massachusetts statute requires school districts to notify parents when sexual issues will be discussed in the classroom. Parents can then request that their children "opt out" of the class. In Virginia, the State Board of Education unanimously adopted into the state's new Standards for Accreditation for public schools a provision that ends mandatory sex education throughout the state. Local boards can eliminate the program entirely or insist on an abstinence approach, depending on the preference of parents in the community. Oklahoma permits parents and guardians to preview all curriculum and materials used in connection with a sex education class or program or any test, survey, or questionnaire "whose primary purpose is to elicit responses on sexual behavior or attitudes."

These more narrowly tailored efforts to confer some measure of parental discretion on a program-by-program basis are clearly preferable to broad parental rights measures that inevitably would create an adversarial atmosphere in the schools and regularly involve the judiciary in determining curricular matters. Enacted as state statutes or administrative rulings, they allow for greater flexibility and diversity. They also preserve education as a local and state matter, avoiding the federalization of schooling that a federal measure would inevitably produce. They recognize the sensitivity of certain topics and subjects and respect differing parental values and views without carving into constitutional law, federal or state, an ambiguously worded bill of rights for parents that makes no express provision for the interests of children.

This is not to deny that school officials at times act imprudently and invade the privacy of parents and children. Neither can it be denied that at least some of the horror tales told to federal and state legislative committees hold at the least a kernel of truth.[126] But one should not lose sight that these are extreme examples presented for their shock value. These stories, in fact, mask the more subtle but pervasive incursions on parental decision making that ineluctably flow from a one-size-fits-all approach to public schooling that we are just beginning to earnestly rethink. These intrusions run throughout the system, from the values presented in the curriculum, to methods of assessing student performance and achievement, to disciplinary methods, to the dress code. Nevertheless, given the lack of empirical data supporting any one curricular approach or program, imposing a "compelling governmental interest" justification on school officials in the face of each and every parental challenge would have a chilling effect on instruction and could completely immobilize the schools.

THE CONSTRAINTS OF THE RIGHTS APPROACH

Parental rights measures and the Convention on the Rights of the Child obviously are miles apart in their goals and underlying philosophies. Nevertheless, they both have brought to the fore of public debate significant controversial issues, particularly over schooling, that are best resolved through negotiation and compromise and not through judicial process or federalization. Granting parents a legal weapon to wield at school districts is a short-term and educationally harmful solution to a serious political problem of how to recognize diverse values while preserving a shared public philosophy through compulsory education. Addressing that problem rationally and effectively demands a reconceptualization of child–parent interests as neither totally separate nor totally united but based on a combination of mutually supportive concerns and individual interests that education, however we reconfigure it, must take into account. It also demands a renewed trust in parental instincts which we never have regained from nineteenth-century child savers and progressive era professional experts. But most important, it demands serious reconsideration of the state's role in preparing children for democratic participation with an eye toward the broad developmental needs of the child and the various roads to achieving the good life.

The rights approach admittedly holds a certain appeal. It offers an institutionalized mechanism for achieving an individualized solution. However, it accomplishes at most incremental reform at the margins, while leaving the core systemic problems in place. Forcing parental concerns and preferences into the rights mode, without equal consideration for the child's interests, closes off discussion and debate that potentially could lead to a more widely acceptable political solution. Transfixing the debate with a specific position grounded in legally enforceable rights precludes examining the big policy picture and the various options for permitting parents a voice in the education of their children. The search for a political solution becomes even more compelling when set against the understandable reluctance of the judiciary to find a meaningful legal remedy to what essentially is a complex political problem.

Chapter 4 The Supreme
Court as Schoolmaster

By the close of the nineteenth century, a truce seemingly had been reached in the religious wars over schooling in America. Catholics and Lutherans had retreated into separate schools while the common school had commandeered the full share of educational tax revenues and had grown increasingly secular in focus. This multilayered political compromise would prove periodically unstable in the coming years in the face of resurging nativism and anti-Catholicism following World War I, a dramatic loosening of the public school curriculum from its moral moorings through the 1960s and 1970s, and a marked revival of Christian fundamentalism toward the close of the century. Unforeseen by the common school reformers, these and other social dramas would be played out in the federal courts and particularly in the Supreme Court, which would come to assume the role, intermittently and at times reluctantly, of schoolmaster and arbiter of child, family, and societal interests in the school setting.

Throughout this century, in fact, the Court has been a major force in shaping educational policy through constitutional interpretation. In broad rulings covering desegregation, school prayer, state school finance, student suspensions and searches, free speech, and government aid to religious schools the Court has established standards that profoundly affect the structure and substance of schooling. Repeatedly the Court has been called upon to resolve the tensions among competing constitutional values and balance the interests of individual students and their families against those of the local community and the larger society. The Court's evolving views on these issues have defined and redefined the context within which school officials, policy makers, interest groups, and lower courts have tried to fill in the details of elusive but nonetheless appealing notions of freedom of conscience and belief in the modern-day common school.

In recent decades, the Court has selectively drawn from the legacy of Horace Mann and John Dewey in attempting to reconcile the conflicting goals and expectations of public education. Yet the Court has failed to develop a coherent and stable theory of schooling, articulating instead a general view of education that has redirected its emphasis from a rights-based to a values-based ideology over time. The focus has shifted from student and parental rights based in the First and Fourteenth amendments to the authority of school officials to make curricular and administrative determinations that reflect community and societal values. This change in the Court's perspective reflects in part a changing Court membership and in part changing social pressures, anxieties, and popular attitudes.

Parental rights advocates repeatedly draw on a limited body of Supreme Court decisions, all predating the Court's ideological shift and all addressing extreme circumstances of government intrusion, to develop several legal theories that they consistently advance in the courts. The broad dicta of these cases, superimposed on rulings that are vague or narrow, give little guidance to lower courts in their attempts to flesh out the contours of educational rights within the framework of a state-controlled system of schools. A close look at the Court's rulings affords useful insights into the complex nature of educational dissent and the extent and limits of constitutionalism.

PARENTAL LIBERTY TO EDUCATE ONE'S CHILD

The modern-day parents' rights movement draws from a trilogy of Supreme Court decisions that laid the foundation for contemporary claims by parents to control the education of their children free from state intrusion. All three present compelling facts amid rhetorical flourishes and ambiguous rulings repeatedly relied upon by parents and cited broadly by the Court itself but often distinguished by lower courts. Although these decisions have proven of limited utility to claimants in recent litigation, they fail to lose their inspirational appeal to parental dissenters and organized interest groups challenging the public school monopoly. The first two decisions, dating from the 1920s, are grounded in the due process clause of the Fourteenth Amendment, which states, "No state shall . . . deprive any person of life, liberty, or property without due process of law." The term *due process* suggests procedural standards, but the Court nevertheless has also recognized a substantive element within the clause. The concept of substantive due process permits the courts to review governmental decisions regardless of the process used. Whether or not the procedures for decision making conformed to fundamental notions of fairness is of no relevance in these cases.

Substantive due process has its roots in natural law theory, which maintains that certain rights exist in every society whether through social contract or divine intervention. The state cannot intrude on these rights without a justification; the more fundamental the right, the more compelling the justification must be. The Court's aggressive use of this doctrine to overturn economic legislation through the first third of the twentieth century subsequently fell into disrepute. In the 1960s, however, the Court began slowly and tentatively to resurrect the concept in support of reproductive freedom and specifically abortion rights. Judicial efforts to breathe life into the due process concept of liberty continue to prove controversial and legally uncertain. Yet in an odd twist of politics, religious conservatives who conventionally oppose judicial activism in the realm of policy making in general and abortion rights in particular have embraced the notion of substantive due process in recent years to support the constitutional right of parents to direct the upbringing and education of their children.

The first decision in the parental rights trilogy is *Meyer v. Nebraska,* whose facts were born out of nativism, hysteria, and suspicion of foreigners during and after World War I.[1] The entry of the United States into a war of such imposing scale against a foreign nation, many of whose native-born had immigrated to America, put to the acid test the country's grand experiment in nation building through immigration. Gradually the negative feelings evoked by the war effort worked their way into governmental policies, especially those affecting the German-speaking population. German language schools operated predominantly by Lutherans throughout the Midwest became a target of hostility. These schools were not unique, but they were by far the most numerous among immigrant-based private schools that reinforced the native culture and used the language for at least some part of daily instruction.

Nativists viewed bilingual schools as a threat to progressive reform and to the acculturative purposes of the common school movement. More directly, they perceived Germans as a national security risk. Not only was Germany our arch-enemy, but German Americans had clung to their language and culture perhaps more tenaciously than other immigrant groups and were concentrated in a stretch of closely knit communities from the Middle Atlantic states through the Great Plains. Those embroiled in the frenzy of Americanization firmly believed that Germans must be forced to abandon their native language and culture in order to assure their loyalty to the United States. As the Nebraska state attorney general argued before the U.S. Supreme Court in the aftermath of the war, "We should not forget the lessons we learned when the safety of the nation hung in the balance. That conflict taught us that we must have a united people, united in ideals, language and patriotism."[2]

During 1919 alone, nineteen states enacted laws that restricted the teaching of foreign languages. Most of these statutes required that all basic subjects be taught in English. All of them, except the New Hampshire law, applied not only to public but also to private and parochial schools. In several states, prohibitions became extreme. In Iowa, for example, the governor had issued a proclamation the previous year that prescribed English not only as the sole language of instruction in public, private, and denominational schools but as the sole permissible language in public addresses and conversations in public places, on trains, and over the telephone.[3] The same legislature that enacted the Nebraska law at issue in *Meyer* had earlier in the same session come one vote short of passing even more radical legislation that would have prohibited the maintenance of private schools in the elementary grades throughout the state.

The Nebraska law invalidated in *Meyer,* known as the Siman Act, made it a criminal offense to teach a subject in a language other than English to any student attending a public or private school or to teach a language other than English to any student who had not completed the eighth grade. When the county school superintendent and the county attorney visited a school operated by the Evangelical Lutheran Zion Church in Hamilton County, Nebraska, a hotbed of anti-German sentiment, they observed a teacher named Robert Meyer offering instruction from a German Bible to a ten-year-old child. The instruction was taking place during a half-hour recess period that the school apparently had established in order to circumvent the Siman Act. Meyer was later charged and convicted of having violated the law, unlawfully teaching German to a student who had not yet completed the eighth grade.[4] The Nebraska Supreme Court upheld his conviction. The case went to the U.S. Supreme Court as one of five cases seeking to overturn state court decisions from Nebraska, Iowa, and Ohio upholding similar language statutes. The parties to these cases undoubtedly realized that the Court's decision potentially would have broad impact on similar language laws across the states. They never could have predicted, however, that the case would have lasting significance on the broad question of personal liberties and be cited repeatedly in subsequent court decisions into the close of the century.

Meyer was argued before the Supreme Court along with another case from Nebraska, *Nebraska District Evangelical Lutheran Synod et al. vs. McKelvie*.[5] In *McKelvie*, the Nebraska Supreme Court had dismissed a lower court injunction and upheld the Norval Act, the successor to the Siman Act. Unlike the facts of *Meyer*, which appeared limited to the rights of the teacher, *McKelvie* broadened the controversy to include parental rights. Attorneys for the plaintiffs apparently had decided to use a shotgun approach to the case, bringing in an intervenor, John Seidlik, whose constitutional rights to due process liberty and property, religious liberty and freedom of conscience, and even Fourteenth Amendment equal protection and privileges and immunities arguably had been violated. Seidlik was a Polish immigrant parent whose children attended a parochial school in which instruction was in English and Polish through the sixth grade. The attorneys strategically had chosen a non-German to carry the weight of the parental argument, one whose compelling story would more readily elicit sympathy from the Court. At oral argument, they stated that Seidlik's wife, like many other immigrant mothers, could not speak a word of English and that the Nebraska laws denied these women the same right enjoyed by English-speaking mothers: the right to send their children to a private school that reinforced the language and religion of the home.[6]

The State of Nebraska, on the other hand, maintained that the statute was part of a "general Americanization program." In their brief before the Court, the state attorneys expressed concern that isolated pockets of "little Germanys, little Italys and little Hungarys" were springing up across the state, rearing their children in a "foreign atmosphere and in a foreign language" which prevented them from assimilating into the American Republic. To the state, this was tantamount to parents raising their children in "physical, moral and intellectual gloom" to which they had no "inalienable right."[7]

The Court issued two separate opinions, with the facts of *Meyer* serving as the centerpiece of the primary pronouncement.[8] The Court acknowledged that "the desire of the legislature to foster a homogeneous people with American ideals prepared readily to understand current discussion of civic matters is easy to appreciate." Nevertheless, the Court concluded that "the means adopted . . . exceed the limitations upon the power of the State" and that the statute as applied was "arbitrary and without reasonable relation to any end" within the state's competency. Yet the Court was clear to note that its decision had limitations, reaffirming the power of the state "to compel attendance at some school . . . to make reasonable regulations for all schools [and] . . . to prescribe a curriculum for institutions which it supports."[9]

On its way through the state court system, *Meyer* had become transformed from a religious liberty case to one grounded in parental rights. In crafting the *Meyer* decision, the Court pieced together elements of the then highly controversial and since discredited doctrine of economic due process with a newly forged theory of personal freedom. The facts bore on economic rights in the sense that they involved the right of the teacher to pursue his occupation and the right of parents "to engage him so to instruct their children." But the legislation, according to the Court, also "attempted to materially interfere with . . . the opportunities of pupils to acquire knowledge, and with the power of parents to control the education of their own" which, the Court noted, are all encompassed within the liberty guaranteed by the Fourteenth Amendment. The Justices recognized distinct concepts of student rights to education and parental rights to direct that education, which they suggested are both fundamental rights guaranteed by the Constitution.[10]

The facts here did not present a conflict between parents' and children's rights, so the Court was able to avoid this far more complex issue. Yet the Court's extension of liberty into the realm not only of parental but also student rights, although seemingly overlooked by courts and commentators over the years, gives added texture to current controversies over parental dissent and the values represented in the school curriculum. If children have a constitutional right to acquire knowledge, who has the ultimate authority to define the substance of that knowledge—the state, the parents, or the children themselves?

Reading between the lines, one discovers that *Meyer* was more than a decision invalidating language laws: it was a decision upholding private education in a much broader sense. What produced this anomalous result was an amicus brief filed on behalf of "various religious and educational institutions." The sole objective of the brief was to prevent the Court from deciding *Meyer* in language that might have undercut a pending challenge to a compulsory public education initiative approved by the voters in Oregon the previous year. The brief's architect was William Dameron Guthrie, a prominent New York lawyer, Columbia Law School professor, devout Catholic, and ardent supporter of private schools and parental rights. His arguments contrasting the parent's "tender care for his children" with the "systematic relinquishment of children" found in Plato's *Republic* are reflected directly in the Court's opinion repudiating Plato's paternalistic theory in the interest of parental and student rights.[11] Guthrie's brief would serve as a warm-up for his arguments before the Court two years later in *Pierce v. Society of Sisters,* the second key case upholding the right of parents to direct the education of their children.[12]

In *Pierce* the Court returned to the liberty interest of substantive due process and directly addressed the question of compulsory public education. The Court's silence here on the issue of student rights is unexplainable in light of *Meyer.* Nevertheless, *Pierce* is important not only for its reaffirmation of parental rights but also for what its history reveals about underlying fears of private schooling and concerns about patriotism, egalitarianism, and the dangers of pluralism—issues that animate modern-day opposition to curricular challenges and school choice proposals.

As *Meyer* was born of nativism and anti-German sentiment, *Pierce* was a case of Americanism masking resurgent anti-Catholicism, this time overtly sponsored by the Scottish Rite Masons, the American Legion, and other groups but covertly engineered by the Ku Klux Klan. Somehow the circumstances and the effort did not add up, as they say. First of all, the Klan was an unlikely defender of the common school. Second, Oregon was an unlikely state in which to mount a campaign in defense of the public school monopoly. Only 8 percent of the state's inhabitants in 1920 were Catholic, 85 percent of the population was native-born and half of the remainder naturalized, and 93 percent of the students attended public schools. Nevertheless, as David Tyack notes, "Along with pure womanhood, white supremacy, the Constitution, uncorrupted religion, freedom of speech, and the common people, Klansmen were sworn to uphold education."[13]

The facts and events leading up to *Pierce* paint a picture of deep-seated hostility toward private schools, church-related schools being the most disfavored among them. Opponents had made unsuccessful attempts to enact legislation banning or severely limiting private education in Washington, Ohio, California, Wisconsin, and Indiana while a constitutional amendment had failed in Michigan. They finally met victory in 1922 in Oregon, where voters enacted by popular initiative a provision requiring parents to send their children between the ages of eight and sixteen to public schools unless they were physically unable, lived too far from a school, had completed the eighth grade, or were allowed by the county superintendent to have private tutoring. Parents who were found violating the law were subject to fine or imprisonment or both in the court's discretion.

The ballot measure was misleadingly titled "Compulsory Education," a curious designation given the fact that Oregon already had a statute that required all children within a given age range to attend school. Proponents of the initiative maintained that "compulsory public education was needed to ensure the assimilation and education of foreign-born citizens and their children [and] . . . that nonpublic schools exacerbated social conflict and bigotry by perpetuating religious, ethnic, and economic divisions." As the statement included in the official ballot explained, children should not "be divided into antagonistic groups" based on "money, creed or social status," as such divisions would separate the nation into "cliques, cults and factions" that would strive "for the supremacy of themselves" rather than for "the good of the whole."[14] A strikingly similar argument would resurface almost three-quarters of a century later, this time in opposition to government funding of private schooling.

The initiative was a clear example of "faith in the common school" run amok, driven entirely by fear of cultural differences. Yet unlike previous waves of anti-Catholicism or even the English-language movement in the Midwest, this effort to extinguish private elementary education had the support of neither the popular press nor of any Protestant denomination. Opponents of the bill included an odd assortment of Catholic, Protestant, and Jewish leaders, blacks, private school proprietors, and "citizens of many persuasions [who] saw the tyranny of the majority in a law that threatened religious freedom, parental duty, and constitutional rights." For Lutherans, Seventh-Day Adventists, Catholics, and other religious denominations, the primary issue at stake here was freedom to educate their children according to their religious convictions. In Tyack's words, "The state was constricting religious pluralism and establishing a civil religion of homogeneous Americanism."[15]

Representatives of private schools throughout Oregon selected the Society of the Sisters of the Holy Names of Jesus and Mary, a Catholic religious order that operated numerous schools and one orphanage in the state, and the Hill Military Academy, a private, nonsectarian school, to officially challenge the initiative in court. Their legal arguments came straight out of the Court's decision two years earlier in *Meyer v. Nebraska* centering on the liberty and property rights of the schools and of the parents.

To undergird their legal claims, the schools wove a web of policy arguments that struck at the heart of the common school and extolled the virtues of private

education. The act embodied, they argued, a "pernicious policy of state monopoly of education" whose "standardization" would "strait-jacket" the "young
minds of the Nation" so that their "diversification and individual development"
would be "dwarfed and prevented." By removing the competition of private
schools from the marketplace, the initiative would impede "experimentation,
innovation, and progress." They attacked the "regimentation and centralized
control" that characterized public schools and the way in which the initiative
would preclude "large groups of citizens from exercising . . . freedom of
choice."[16] In response, the state expressed fear for the ultimate demise of public education if the Court were to declare the law unconstitutional. "Religious
denominations," the state argued, "could potentially develop a system of educational training which [would] result in doing away with public schools."[17]
Despite the distance in time and circumstances, the terms used—*diversification,
state monopoly, competition, standardization, experimentation, choice*—as well as
the potential threat to public schooling and fears of cultural and social balkanization expressed in the ballot measure itself all echo throughout contemporary
discourse on vouchers, charter schools, and other reform proposals that embrace
alternatives to the public school.

Following its lead in *Meyer,* the Supreme Court upheld the decision of the
lower court that the initiative deprived the private schools of their property interests protected under Fourteenth Amendment substantive due process. Once
again the Court moved beyond the immediate facts and gave a ringing affirmation of parental rights. According to the Justices, the Oregon initiative interfered with "the liberty of parents and guardians to direct the upbringing and education of children under their control." In an oft-quoted statement that in
hindsight has had more rhetorical than analytic value, the Court maintained
that "the child is not the mere creature of the State; those who nurture and direct his destiny have the right, coupled with the high duty, to recognize and prepare him for additional obligations."[18]

But the Court went even further in sweeping statements that defined the parameters and purpose of compulsory education but also specified standards for
mapping the contours of the state's permissible role in determining the curriculum. With a qualified nod toward the inculcative function of schooling and
the state's interest in fostering civic virtue, the Court explicitly acknowledged
that "no question is raised concerning the power of the State reasonably to regulate all schools, to inspect, supervise and examine them, their teachers and
pupils; to require that all children of proper age attend some school, that teach-

ers shall be of good moral character and patriotic disposition, that certain studies *plainly essential* to good citizenship must be taught, and that nothing be
taught which is *manifestly inimical* to the public welfare."[19]

The details of this pronouncement seemingly have faded against the Court's
more general assertion that private schools could continue to exist as an alternative to public schooling and that parents had a right to direct their children's
education, while the state could also use its police powers to impose reasonable
regulations. Yet herein lies the legacy of *Pierce.* The standards established by the
Court could prove useful in mediating current battles over the public school curriculum as well as challenges to government regulation of nonpublic schools.
The Court's language, in fact, bears on many of the values-based concerns raised
in recent years by disaffected parents. *Pierce* leaves us with the principle of education for citizenship, that the state may reasonably require studies that are "essential" to that end while it may prohibit the teaching of anything that is "manifestly inimical" to the public welfare. The controlling question left unanswered,
however, is whether local school officials, in their discretion, may "require" studies that go beyond the state essentials. At the time of the decision, the *New Republic* commented, "Thus came to an end the effort to regiment the mental life
of Americans through coerced public school instruction."[20] But as Tyack later
observed, the *Pierce* decision ended only this chapter of coercion: "The schools
would remain a ready target for those who saw peril in pluralism."[21]

In the years following the *Meyer* and *Pierce* decisions, their significance as a
watershed in the development of personal freedom was not apparent. In recent
decades, however, the Court has repeatedly cited both decisions to support the
proposition that there is a private realm of family life that the Constitution protects from state interference. These later cases have addressed policy issues ranging from zoning regulations defining the family, through child custody disputes,
to privacy rights in the abortion context, all the way to student free speech
rights.[22] The Court has noted that matters within the private sphere of family
"involv[e] the most intimate and personal choices a person may make in a life-
time, choices central to personal dignity and autonomy" and in certain circumstances may encompass fundamental rights entitled to some level of heightened
judicial scrutiny beyond mere reasonableness.[23] And although not directly citing *Meyer* and *Pierce* but upholding their principle, the Court more recently has
affirmed the continued vitality of substantive due process in family life, stating
that "the interest of parents in their relationship with their children is sufficiently
fundamental to come within the finite class of liberty interests protected by the
Fourteenth Amendment."[24] As Laurence Tribe has stated, *Meyer* and *Pierce*

"have remained durable and fertile sources of constitutional doctrine concerning the nature of liberty, the representative rights of social institutions, and the limits of government power to homogenize the beliefs and attitudes of the populace. The cardinal principle animating the Court's decisions despite the expected bow to liberty of contract, was that the state had no power to 'standardize its children' or 'foster a homogeneous people' by completely foreclosing the opportunity of individuals and groups to heed the music of different drummers."[25]

A related case that followed on the heels of *Meyer* and *Pierce* and directly descended from them demands brief mention at this point. *Farrington v. Tokushige,* also grounded in the liberty and property interests of substantive due process, has all but vanished from the discussion on parental rights. Here the Court struck down as excessively burdensome a Hawaii statute and regulations governing foreign language schools. The schools, predominantly Japanese, were required to pay fees, submit numerous reports, establish their commitment to the "ideals of democracy," adhere to strict rules regarding the hours of daily operation, and conform to detailed regulations on textbooks and other matters. The Court concluded that enforcement of the act would "probably destroy most, if not all" of the foreign language schools (most likely the intent of the law) and "deprive parents of fair opportunity to procure for their children instruction which they think is important and we cannot say is harmful." Echoing the language of *Pierce,* the Court reaffirmed the right of Japanese parents to direct the education of their children "without unreasonable regulations."[26]

While lost in history for unknown reasons, the case is important not only for what it says about parental rights but for the limits it sets on the power of the state to regulate private schools and, perhaps by contemporary implication, other alternatives to conventional public schooling. It suggests that state regulation may not go so far as to destroy the distinct nature of such schools or force them out of business. Parental choice and educational pluralism are substantive as well as structural.

RELIGIOUS FREEDOM AND THE UNUSUAL CASE OF THE AMISH

Perhaps nowhere in constitutional history is there more dramatic evidence of a group marching to the tune of a different drummer than the Amish, whose challenge to a state compulsory education law forms the basis of the third case in the parental rights trilogy. In contrast to *Meyer* and *Pierce, Wisconsin v. Yoder* was constitutionally grounded not in substantive due process but in the free exercise clause of the First Amendment, which prohibits government from denying to any person "the free exercise of religion." This shift in legal strategy was not surprising.[27] In the years since the Court had decided the earlier parental rights cases, the constitutional landscape had changed in three important ways. Substantive due process, at least in the economic realm, had fallen into disrepute, although it seemed to be making a tentative comeback to support personal liberty.[28] The Court had begun applying the First Amendment free exercise clause to state and not just federal action. And finally, a decade earlier the Court had developed an exacting standard for the judiciary to apply when examining laws or policies that interfered with religiously motivated conduct—such laws must yield unless they promote a compelling state interest.[29] Although the Court in recent years has placed into serious question the principle that religious believers can disregard generally applicable neutral laws that conflict with the mandates of their religion, *Yoder* appears to have survived as a hybrid case based in both religious rights and parental rights to direct the education of their children.[30]

The Amish accept literally the teaching of the gospel that one must turn the other cheek and never use force to resist evil. Given this deep religiosity, one wonders what extreme circumstances compelled them to pursue their complaint all the way to the U.S. Supreme Court. The law that they challenged required children between the ages of six and seventeen to attend a public or private school or a substantial equivalent approved by the state superintendent. Jonas Yoder, Wallace Miller, and Adin Yutzy had failed to enroll their three respective children between the ages of fourteen and fifteen in any school or equivalent instruction after the children had completed the eighth grade in a local public school. The local school district administrator signed the truancy complaint against them after learning that the Amish had opened their own elementary school, which resulted in a loss of thirty-seven children and eighteen thousand dollars in state aid to the district.

Amish do not as a rule take their grievances to court. The district's action, however, was forcing them to either defend or seriously compromise their deeply held religious beliefs. They found their voice before the law in William Bentley Ball, a seasoned litigator on church–state matters and well regarded within the religious conservative network. Ball's services were enlisted through the National Committee for Amish Religious Freedom and its founder, William C. Lindholm, a young Lutheran minister from Michigan.[31] The trial court convicted the parents of having violated the state compulsory education law and fined them five dollars each. Ball appealed the decision through the Wisconsin court system, where the state Supreme Court reversed the conviction, upholding the parents' claim under the free exercise clause of the First Amendment. The court applied a broad definition of religion, holding that the free exercise clause is not restricted to formal ritualistic acts of worship common in theistic religions but includes the practice or exercise of religion that is binding in conscience.[32]

The Amish were not new to harassment at the hands of public education officials. Of the nineteen states in which they resided at the time the Wisconsin case arose, nine had subjected them to prosecution for refusal to send their children to high school. In some cases, state officials had fined them and had seized and sold their possessions. In some instances, the Amish had sold their farms and moved to other states and even to Canada and South America. In others, they had successfully negotiated administrative accommodation or legislative exemptions.[33] A little-known fact of *Yoder* but one that is essential to understanding the larger picture of parental dissent for which the case has become emblematic is that the parents' attorney had attempted to explore such a compromise prior to trial. Under the proposal, the state would have permitted the Amish to establish their own vocational training plan, similar to those instituted in other states with high concentrations of Amish, for example, Pennsylvania, Indiana, Iowa, and Kansas. In these programs, Amish children of high school age could satisfy compulsory education requirements by attending an Amish vocational school three hours a week for instruction in English, mathematics, health, and social studies by an Amish teacher. They would spend the balance of the week on farm and household duties under parental supervision.[34]

The state superintendent of public instruction had rejected the proposal, informing the Amish that the state lacked power to provide such an accommodation under existing law and that amendatory legislation would prove difficult to obtain and possibly unconstitutional.[35] As their attorney Ball would later observe, the very fact that the superintendent could offer no hope that the Amish, a minority sect, could possibly obtain legislative relief had a legal significance in terms of religious freedom that state officials most likely did not realize. In fact, that point would strengthen their case before the Supreme Court.[36]

At trial Ball argued that the parents' objection to formal education beyond the eighth grade was firmly grounded in the basic tenets of their religion. The parents maintained that they accepted compulsory elementary education because their children must have basic skills in the three R's in order to read the Bible, to become good farmers and citizens, and to interact with the outside world when necessary. They objected to high school education, however, because the values taught there undermined Amish values and the Amish way of life, because high school would expose their children to worldly influence that conflicted with their sincerely held religious beliefs, and because high school attendance takes Amish children away from their community during a crucial period in which they must develop Amish attitudes favoring manual work and the skills needed to function as an adult in Amish society.[37] The parents' key witness, Professor John Hostetler, a sociologist and anthropologist who was originally from an Amish household, captured the very essence of the case in his testimony before the trial court. In response to questioning from the state's attorney as to whether the primary purpose of education was to prepare the child to "make his place in the world," Hostetler responded, "It depends which world."[38]

When the case finally made its way to the U.S. Supreme Court, Chief Justice Warren Burger spoke for the majority. His opinion relied heavily upon the concept of community, here the religious or cultural community, not the secular political community often recognized in Burger Court decisions.[39] It also touched on the weighty issues that arise when democratic citizenship as the end and values inculcation as a means collide with distinct cultural values and religious beliefs. The Amish feared that the values taught in the high school would lead to the disintegration of their insular community. The state had set the problem up as an either/or situation with no middle ground. Either the Amish complied with a law that burdened their sincerely held religious beliefs or they would be forced to migrate to a more tolerant state or country that would accommodate those beliefs.[40]

Yoder, in fact, represented a definitive shift from the liberal individualism of *Meyer* and *Pierce*, decided against the backdrop of laissez-faire economic theory, to a republican desire to preserve from state encroachment traditional intermediate institutions such as family and church.[41] The Court indirectly addressed the first of these in the sense of parental autonomy. But the case is far more noteworthy as a decision rich in the virtues of religious pluralism almost as an end in itself. Nowhere before or since has the Court articulated such insight into the role that religious subgroups play as sources of values and control over their members that, in the end, benefit and stabilize the larger society. The Court noted that Amish education exemplified the diversity that "we profess to admire and encourage." And while the Justices acknowledged that the purpose of education was to prepare children for life, they distinguished between preparing the child for life in modern society, in which education for an additional year or two beyond eighth grade may be necessary, and preparing the child for life in the separated agrarian community as required by the Amish faith. To enforce the compulsory education law against the Amish beyond that point posed "a very real threat of undermining the Amish community and religious practice as they exist today."[42]

The majority opinion in *Yoder* is steeped in parental rights and group self-determination. Unlike *Meyer*, which spoke directly to the rights of children "to knowledge," and *Pierce*, which was silent on the question of children's rights, *Yoder* affirmatively dismissed the notion of the child's interests as distinct from those of the parent. The Court seemed to suggest, at least hypothetically, that Amish parents could "prevent . . . their minor children from attending high school despite their expressed desires to the contrary."[43] The Court implicitly rejected a key argument advanced by the state of Wisconsin, that the child has a substantive right to an elementary and secondary education. The State had relied on *Brown v. Board of Education* asserting that the denial of such a right to a basic education constituted a denial of equal protection.[44] According to the State, "the Amish child is being denied this right by the theocratic society into which he was born. Any desire for knowledge is stifled."[45] But the parents also resurrected *Brown* in their arguments before the Court, relying on the following quote that just as easily could have supported the State's case: "[Education] is a principal instrument in awakening the child to cultural values, in preparing him for later professional training, and in helping him to adjust normally to his environment."[46]

Whose cultural values, professional training, and environment—whose world—was each side talking about? Those of the religious community of Amish or those of the larger society? For the Court, at least in this case, the scales tipped in favor of cultural, that is, religious autonomy or pluralism. The Justices, therefore, not only rejected the State's argument supporting the rights of the child and the responsibility of the state to protect those rights under the doctrine of *parens patriae*, but they turned the issue into one of parental preferences within a particular cultural context. They seemed to imply that the acceptable degree to which American parents pursue the fundamental purposes of education for their children may vary according to the collective needs or lifestyle of a particular community. In other words, education for citizenship in a democracy may mean different things to different communities depending on their level of participation in the larger democratic society. The Court acknowledged, at least at first glance, that religious subgroups in particular enjoy a qualified autonomy from state intervention. But on closer examination it appears that the Court was limiting that autonomy and the respect afforded religious (and cultural) differences to those subgroups in which the specific values under consideration are fundamentally the same as those of the majority. In the case of the Amish, they would teach their children what the majority believes the public schools teach: self-sufficiency, productivity, and respect for the law.[47]

In powerful language, the Court noted that the case involved "the fundamental interest of parents, as contrasted with that of the State, to guide the religious future and education of their children. . . . This primary role of the parents in the upbringing of their children is now established beyond debate as an enduring American tradition."[48] Yet while the Court revisited *Pierce* as "a charter of the rights of parents" regarding religious child rearing, it was careful to note that only when "the interests of parenthood are combined with a free exercise claim *of the nature revealed by this record*" would the state need to show more than *merely* a "reasonable relation" to some state purpose. The state could permissibly intervene even in the face of religious claims if a parental decision would "jeopardize the health or safety of the child, or have potential for significant social burdens." But the majority made clear that only religious and not secular philosophical or personal considerations, such as those of a Thoreau, would satisfy the demands of the religion clauses.[49]

This narrow definition of religion departed from prior Court decisions, namely, those addressing the religious rights of conscientious objectors during the Vietnam War. There the Court had suggested a broader view encompassing more than theistic beliefs, having gone so far as to define the term *Supreme Being* not only as what we conventionally understand as the supernatural God, but as that to which "all else is subordinate or upon which all else is ultimately dependent."[50] This definition, which apparently ignores the content of the individual's beliefs per se, presented a sharp contrast with the Court's careful reliance on the unique religious position of the Amish.

Despite sweeping language upholding parental rights, the opinion turned on the very specific religious foundation of the case. And despite assertions that government must maintain a position of neutrality toward religion, the Court so narrowed the decisive facts that it not only privileged organized theistic religious beliefs over more idiosyncratic ones of a nontheistic nature but it privileged the Amish religion in particular over others. The Court noted that "probably few other religious groups or sects" could make such a convincing argument supporting the adequacy of their alternative mode of vocational education.[51] The Court explicitly underscored the long history of the Amish as a successful and self-sufficient society, the sincerity of their religious beliefs, the dangers presented by the statute as applied to the Amish, and the minimal difference between the state's requirements and those that the Amish already accepted. Yet, as Tribe has noted, Chief Justice Burger's "recital of the Amish's history and up-rightness . . . was irrelevant and potentially misleading."[52] And as Justice William Douglas responded in a separate opinion, "A religion is a religion irre-spective of what the misdemeanor or felony records of its members might be."[53]

The Court hinted at a vision of the Amish as "partial citizens," having cho-sen a distinct place in liberal democratic society. Involving themselves only min-imally in the public sphere and in civil society, they minimized the state's inter-est in educating their children for the full range of citizenship skills and knowledge.[54] The majority emphasized that the Amish religion was not merely a matter of voluntary individual conscience or beliefs but rather a comprehen-sive set of rules that "pervades and determines virtually their entire way of life, regulating it with the detail of the Talmudic diet through the strictly enforced rules of the church community," a committed community in which members were socialized from childhood.[55]

The social and cultural context of the Amish was undoubtedly unique, but so was the remedy they sought. Unlike many modern-day dissenters, they were not seeking accommodation or partial exemption from a distinct educational program or activity or trying to influence the educational program of other chil-dren. They were seeking a complete exemption from the state's compulsory ed-ucation law, one that was specific to themselves and of only minimal duration (for approximately two years and upon the completion of eight years of school-ing). Their request, while at first glance more draconian from the perspective of the state's interests in educating citizens, was at the same time devoid of censor-ship and less administratively burdensome to operationalize than perhaps a re-quest for exemption from a particular program or activity or for alternative in-struction within public schooling. The Court alluded to this distinction and expressed an uneasiness with judicial intervention into education policy, noting that "courts are not school boards or legislatures, and are ill-equipped to deter-mine the 'necessity' of discrete aspects of a State's program of compulsory edu-cation." The Justices warned that courts "must move with great circumspection" when addressing "religious claims for exemption from generally applicable ed-ucational requirements." They even suggested the possibility of political com-promise whereby the state might reconsider accommodating the Amish through the establishment of an Amish vocational school similar to the proposal origi-nally offered by the parents in this case and provided to Amish in the state of Pennsylvania.[56]

Given all these limitations, it is not surprising that *Yoder* has offered scant legal support to parents who raise values-based objections, religious or otherwise, to the authority of the state in shaping the education of their children. What started out potentially as a ringing endorsement of parental rights and religious tolerance ended up perhaps even giving away some of what *Meyer* and *Pierce* had promised. *Yoder* makes clear that providing public schools is a "paramount responsibility" ranking "at the very apex of the function of a State."[57] It also makes clear that parental rights, while considered a fundamental liberty interest under Fourteenth Amendment substantive due process, can be outweighed by a state regulation that merely meets the standard of reasonableness unless the claim is tied to the free exercise of religion as defined within the narrow limits of *Yoder*. Not only were the Court's standards here more demanding than the *Pierce* requirement that the parents' choice must be found "unreasonable" and "harmful," but the Court's crabbed definition of religion excluded most religious claims from *Yoder* protection. And in the end, the majority warned that courts must act cautiously when addressing even religious claims to accommodation.

Justice Burger's opinion in *Yoder* continues to generate discussion and debate among scholars. Some hail it as a model of clarity and tolerance while others sharply criticize it for its obtuseness and lack of principled reasoning. Many express ambivalence toward it, agreeing with the ultimate decision but troubled by the narrow rationale supporting it. Equally controversial has been Justice Douglas's partial dissent, which, along with Justice Byron White's concurring opinion, raises important matters that prove helpful in thinking through parental dissent and educational purposes.

Justice White's concurrence, mentioned only in passing by most commentators, differs dramatically in tone and focus from the majority opinion and, in fact, may be the most thoughtful and instructive of all the *Yoder* opinions. Less solicitous of the Amish than the Court majority, he presented a more balanced view of their group needs as compared with the individual needs of Amish children. In fact, he offered useful guidelines for weighing those needs along with the interests of the state in the context of parental claims to accommodation, rejecting parental arguments based on "idiosyncratic views of what knowledge a child needs to be a productive and happy member of society."

Justice White suggested that the state, in order to promote identified legitimate state interests, may set such minimal standards as "nurtur[ing] and develop[ing] the human potential of its children . . . expand[ing] their knowledge, broaden[ing] their sensibilities, kindl[ing] their imagination, foster[ing] a spirit of free inquiry, and increas[ing] their human understanding and tolerance." In doing so, he shifted the discussion from the rights of the parents to the developmental needs of the child, a point too often lost in the vitriolic rhetoric that typically surrounds parental rights-based claims. In his mind, the State had "a legitimate interest" in preparing children "for the lifestyle that they may later choose or at least to provide them with an option other than the life they have led in the past." He proposed vague outer bounds of parental discretion beyond which the education parents choose to offer their children would leave them "intellectually stultified or unable to acquire new academic skills" and concluded that the accommodation sought by the Amish fell within these bounds.[58] This disputable suggestion, grounded in liberal theory, that under certain circumstances schools have an interest in preparing children for a life other than the one their parents have chosen for them has met with strong opposition from parental rights advocates.

Yet despite Justice White's attempt to strike a reasoned compromise among the competing interests at stake, his concurrence has gone largely unnoticed. At the same time, Justice Douglas's partial dissent has provoked a wealth of legal commentary for its direct and pointed support of the rights of the Amish children. Technically those rights were not before the Court in what began as a criminal proceeding against their parents, although the parents had raised the free exercise rights of the children in their motion to dismiss before the trial court. Justice Douglas faulted the majority for having assumed an identity of interests between the Amish parents and their children. In his view, not only should the Court have considered the children's interests independent of those of their parents, as Justice White suggested, but it should have required that the trial court affirmatively elicit their views, as the children had no other vehicle or forum for asserting their rights. If the Court were to grant the accommodation sought by the Amish parents, he maintained, then the Court would violate the rights of the children, which, he suggested, were grounded in free exercise.[59]

For Justice Douglas, the *Yoder* children were entitled to be heard. They had the moral and intellectual maturity to testify in court as to whether attending high school would conflict with their religious beliefs. At trial, the defense had placed only one of the three Amish children, Frieda Yoder, on the witness stand as a representative of Amish young people of similar age who desired to pursue the Amish way of life and believed that attending public schooling would violate their religion. Frieda Yoder was fifteen, the age at which females in Wisconsin can marry. Justice Douglas concurred with the Court majority as to the Yoder parents and dissented as to the others, whose children had not been called to testify. In what was far from an objective and neutral assessment, he warned that "if [the child] is harnessed to the Amish way of life by those in authority over him and if his education is truncated, his entire life may be stunted and deformed" as contrasted with life in "the new and amazing world of diversity that we have today."[60]

This argument has held considerable appeal to child advocates and to those who argue that education must prepare children for rational independence. Nevertheless, it presents as narrow a view of children's developmental needs as the majority's view of parental and group interests. In fact, one has to question the wisdom of entrapping an adolescent between loyalty to and dependence on parents on the one hand and normal adolescent desires to gain autonomy from them on the other. As one commentator has wisely observed, Justice Douglas's solution "may, indeed, only harmfully intensify the psychological bind for these children by forcing them publicly either to disavow their parents or to announce their acquiescence and consequent impotence in response to parental direction."[61]

Yoder presents several interesting but nonetheless troubling paradoxes. At first glance it appears as a hallmark of religious tolerance and pluralism, yet subsequent history has proven otherwise, rendering its legal significance disappointingly more symbolic than real. In fact, the decision has been swallowed up by its exceptions. But then again, despite its limited utility to religious claimants in court, *Yoder* continues to animate political efforts on behalf of parental autonomy. Religious conservatives persistently rely on *Yoder* in tandem with *Meyer* and *Pierce* to support parental rights to direct the education of children, even though *Yoder* loses its force when stripped of the arguably unique circumstances surrounding Amish history and culture. Nevertheless, the separate opinions and the various perspectives presented to the Court raise important questions about parental autonomy, cultural pluralism from both the group and individual perspectives, and constitutional guarantees of tolerance and diversity.[62] These still-unresolved questions bear directly on modern-day discussions of educational values and school restructuring. By examining the issues raised and weighing the arguments made on both sides in an extreme case of religious burdens like *Yoder* one can better comprehend what lies behind contemporary conflicts over values in the schools.

Yoder is a transitional case in political and judicial history. On the heels of the decision came a cultural revolution already in the making, a backlash against the perceived excesses of that revolution's radical changes, and the revival and politicization of religious fundamentalism. This sequence of social trends brought parental rights to the fore of political and legal debate, testing the continued vitality of the cultural and religious pluralism and parental autonomy implicit in *Meyer, Pierce,* and *Yoder.* By the mid-1970s, the Court had already begun to shift ground from a theory of schooling based in individual rights to one founded in school governance and values inculcation.

EXPRESSION AND FORMATION OF BELIEFS

The *Meyer-Pierce-Yoder* trilogy represents one perspective on freedom of conscience and belief—the right to direct the upbringing of one's children—although it should not be forgotten that *Meyer* also suggests the right of students to "acquire knowledge." The first two cases, dating from the 1920s, reflected the prevailing political views of their day, that government should not intrude into the private lives of individuals. All three essentially addressed a conflict of cultural or religious values between those of the parents and those that the state inculcates through compulsory education. In each case, the Court set limits on the state's power to intrude on parental values while at the same time implicitly acknowledging that education does, in fact, involve indoctrination and socialization.

A second line of Court decisions that educational dissenters cite to support freedom of thought and expression was grounded in the First Amendment free speech clause. Dating from the 1940s to the 1970s, these cases more explicitly raised issues bearing on indoctrination and values inculcation. And although the interests of parents were indirectly involved in at least two of the cases, students were at the heart of the discussion. Underlying the Court's opinions during these years was a progressive child-centeredness reflecting Dewey's view that schools should be "embryonic communities," teaching students the principles of democracy through practice and example.

Educational dissenters at times argue that the indoctrinative nature of schooling poses a threat to freedom of conscience or belief protected by the First Amendment. They rely on several cases from this period to support rights that are in essence the mirror image of each other: the positive right to freely express one's thoughts and beliefs and the negative right to refrain from expressing governmentally imposed views that offend one's thoughts and beliefs—the right to speak and the right not to speak. Two Court decisions in particular support a broad right to freedom of conscience and specifically the right to be free from coerced government expression. In the first of these, *West Virginia State Board of Education v. Barnette,*[63] the Court struck down a state statute, enacted during a period of patriotic fervor, that required all public school students to salute the American flag. The law proved to be a special burden to Jehovah's Witnesses, whose literal interpretation of Exodus 20:4, "Thou shalt not make unto thee any graven image," they argued, prohibited them from saluting the flag. School officials had expelled children within the group from school and had prosecuted their parents for causing delinquency.

Here the Court acknowledged the role played by schools in preparing young people for democratic participation. The indoctrinative function of schooling provided a context for reaffirming the student's right to freedom of conscience and belief. In powerful language with perhaps more inspirational than precedential force, the Court stated, "If there is any fixed star in our constitutional constellation, it is that no official, high or petty, can prescribe what shall be orthodox in politics, nationalism, religion, or other matters of opinion or force citizens to confess by word or act their faith therein." The Court recognized both the importance of education as the vehicle for forming democratic citizenship and the necessity for "scrupulous" constitutional protection in that setting.[64] This notion of individual freedom of conscience as a precondition for democracy was clearly an expression of progressive thinking on education.

Here was a case similar to *Yoder* in which a religious minority that was not in the mainstream, a group considered odd or eccentric by many, was claiming an exemption from a neutral law of general applicability. They based their claim, however, not only in religious freedom but also in freedom of speech. The Court sidestepped the religious claim, avoiding debate over the free exercise clause along with the dangers of inquiring into the sincerity and centrality of religious views. However, it seized the opportunity to make a more inclusive and dramatic statement about freedom of conscience irrespective of religious dissent, affirming that there are constitutional limitations on the government's power to "invade the sphere of intellect and spirit which is the purpose of the First Amendment."

The Justices seemed to acknowledge the values of diversity and tolerance for the unusual, dismissing any "fear that freedom to be intellectually and spiritually diverse or even contrary will disintegrate the social organization." According to the Court, "We can have intellectual individualism and the rich cultural diversities that we owe to exceptional minds only at the price of occasional eccentricity and abnormal attitudes." In other words, by prohibiting coerced expression the First Amendment serves instrumental values that benefit society. That assertion undermines the most compelling arguments supporting the common school on the basis of social and political cohesion. In fact, the Court was mindful of the dangers inherent in government-operated schools: "That [boards of education] are educating the young for citizenship is reason for scrupulous protection of Constitutional freedoms of the individual, if we are not to strangle the free mind at its source."[65]

Several decades later, the Court extended protection beyond instrumentalism to include individual personalty itself in a case completely unrelated to education. In *Wooley v. Maynard,* the Court upheld another challenge by the Jehovah's Witnesses, this time to a New Hampshire law requiring all license plates on noncommercial vehicles to bear the state motto, "Live Free or Die," which again the Witnesses argued was a graven image. The Court affirmed the "right of individuals to hold a point of view different from the majority and to refuse to foster . . . an idea they find morally objectionable."[66] Here the Court was suggesting that when government compels individuals to speak, it deprives them of the persona that they present to the world. But compelled expression not only requires a denial of the self, it represents the "ultimate submission of the individual—submission of mind."[67]

Wooley, unlike *Barnette,* did not raise the important policy concerns that surface in the education context. Neither did the decisive facts address an exceedingly overt form of values inculcation or a publicly demonstrable form of coerced expression like the flag salute. Nevertheless, the expansive language and spirit of both cases taken together impliedly lend qualified support to arguments advanced by parents who challenge educational programs or practices on moral, philosophical, or religious objections to the values presented. Several scholars have forcefully argued this point. A brief detour into their arguments reveals the untapped potential of what unfortunately have become mere constitutional curiosities, valued more for their rhetorical force than for their practical significance.

Stephen Arons in his now-classic book *Compelling Belief* tells us that *Barnette* stands for the proposition that the First Amendment protects not only freedom of expression but the private nature of belief formation. He goes even further and suggests that had the Court been presented with a challenge to the "pervasive inculcation of values by political majorities controlling schools," the Justices "might have recognized an invasion of 'the sphere of intellect and spirit' similar to the compulsory flag salute."[68] Contrary to Arons's speculation from the vantage point of the early 1980s, the Court in fact has proven reluctant in the intervening years to enter what the Justices apparently perceive as a political thicket.

Arons suggests that values-based claims may have firmer grounding in the

First Amendment free speech clause than in Fourteenth Amendment substantive due process despite the continued appeal of *Meyer* and *Pierce.* He argues that school socialization seems more akin to free speech than to the privacy interests surrounding decisions on marriage and procreation into which substantive due process has evolved in recent decades. He maintains that compulsory socialization not only harms those families whose values are violated by public school standards, but has a broader societal impact, threatening every citizen and disrupting the entire "system of freedom of expression and the entire basis of political individualism." He notes how even the hidden curriculum is fraught with socialization and suggests that the concern raised by the Court in *Barnette* as to coerced verbalization is comparable to certain behavior that schools require or reward. He offers the example of the student who is expected to compete with other students over correct answers to math problems and is therefore "forced to confess by action a belief" in the value of competition.[69] Arons views all government-operated education as a form of manipulation of consciousness and supports the complete separation of schools from the state. One need not embrace such an extreme position, however, to recognize the connection between the expression and formation of beliefs and their relation to school socialization.

More recently Stephen Gilles has elaborated on Arons's proposition but with specific emphasis on the concept of parental rights per se. Gilles essentially abandons the legal underpinnings of *Meyer, Pierce,* and *Yoder* in view of their doctrinal limitations—the reasonableness standard of review in the first two and the narrow limits of religious beliefs in the third. He suggests that the First Amendment free speech clause offers a more workable constitutional foundation on which to build a broad-based theory of parents' rights to direct the education of their children. He maintains that freedom of speech includes "not only the right to say what one thinks true, but the right not to affirm what one thinks false." But in contrast to Arons's theory, which at its core holds that the child has a right not to be educated by the state, Gilles develops a principal/agent theory of "indirect parental educative speech." Education, he maintains, is essentially communication, and parents have the right to communicate their values to their children through the educational process by delegating the school and its teachers as their educational agents. He suggests that his and Arons's theories can be reconciled by conceiving these issues as a matter of parental educative rights when the child is young and recharacterizing them perhaps in midadolescence in terms of the child's right.[70]

Gilles carefully works through his rationale. Yet he may have carried Arons's expression-formation connection, based in *Barnette*'s right to freedom of conscience, fatally beyond the point of legal credibility and political practicality. There are just too many leaps in doctrinal language and logic between the individual parent's right to free speech and the ideas communicated by the teachers to the child. How can parents assert a constitutional right to free speech when the communicative activities would not be carried out by themselves but by school staff as their agents? How can the parameters of that right and the scope of the agency be clearly defined in every case and for every child? Against whom would the parental "right" be enforced? Against the school and teachers for having failed to carry out the terms of the agency agreement? or against the state for having denied parents the right to choose their own agent? This model turns both First Amendment free speech theory and principles of agency on their heads. Besides, the imagery of children as passive empty vessels for the receipt of parental beliefs through the instrumentality of the school must give pause to those who contemplate the child's interests. The imagery admittedly may belie the intent of the underlying theory, but it is nonetheless powerful and in need of modification to reflect children's interests in an adequate education that prepares them for citizenship while reaffirming nonconflicting core family values.

But Gilles and Arons are on the right track in relying on the First Amendment. Rather than define the right in terms of the *child's* or the *parent's* freedom of expression, however, an alternative and less complex model would position the child in the context of the *family*, at least when there is no conflict between parent and child. Here the right would be cast as the child's freedom of conscience to be educated in values that are not inimical to those of the family, provided those values are not contrary to democratic citizenship. This approach circumvents the convoluted link to principles of agency, avoids confusion as to who exactly is engaging in the expression, and more directly focuses on maintaining the family relationship. It also avoids conflating the interests of child and parent or, at the other extreme, treating those interests as totally separate and distinct. Drawing on contemporary relational theories of children's rights, this model takes into account the stress placed on the child–parent relationship and the cognitive dissonance created in the child by a school curriculum that drastically undermines the deeply held values, whether religious or secular, of the home and the community of which the child is a part. However, as they have in other attempts at legal enforcement of rights-based claims in the educational arena, the courts undoubtedly would feel constrained from intruding into the administrative decisions of local school officials, especially in matters of curriculum.

Returning to what the Supreme Court has actually stated, one finds that even the most literal reading of *Barnette* presents a broad view of education, one in which diverse, individualistic ideas are freely expressed and valued. The Court affirmed this position in the late 1960s in *Tinker v. Des Moines Independent School District* upholding the right of students to wear black armbands in protest against the Vietnam War. In *Tinker* the Court recognized that students enjoy not only constitutional rights to freedom of speech and expression in the school setting, but broader fundamental rights guaranteed under the Constitution. Here the Court implicitly endorsed Dewey's view that schools should encourage students to participate in the learning process, stating that they may not be confined to the expression of "officially approved" sentiments.[71] *Tinker*, universally considered the highwater mark of the students' rights movement from the perspective of the political left, is tenaciously clung to by anticensorship forces in spite of the Court's having severely undercut its full impact in subsequent cases. Yet in a curious twist of politics, religious conservatives, who traditionally have supported the right of school officials to limit student speech, have now embraced its core holding. In recent years, they have successfully used *Tinker*'s legal underpinnings, while rejecting its broad dicta and its underlying educational philosophy, to support the right of students to engage in religious speech on public school grounds.

THE POLITICAL VERSUS THE CULTURAL COMMUNITY

Tinker represented the Court's most forceful affirmation of progressive child-centeredness. But as Americans became increasingly disenchanted with progressive ideas and practices through the 1970s, their changing popular sentiments became articulated in the Supreme Court's views on individual rights and school governance. As the seventies rolled into the eighties and nineties, the Court shifted from a model of schooling that supports student rights, diverse views, and cultural pluralism to one firmly grounded in cultural transmission and majoritarian politics. A new paradigm of education for democratic citizenship emerged. At the same time, the Court continued on a course of secularizing the public school curriculum, purging it of overtly religious practices, symbols, and content, including school prayer, Bible reading, the posting of the Ten Commandments, moments of silence for prayer or meditation, the teaching of creation science, and school-sponsored nonsectarian graduation prayers.[72]

For more than two decades, Court decisions repeatedly have emphasized the inculcative or indoctrinative nature of schooling for a given purpose, maintaining that public schools not only *may* but *should* influence students to adopt the political majority's beliefs, attitudes, and values, which the Court assumes are neutral among religions and between religion and nonreligion.[73] While the Court continues to recognize preparation for democratic citizenship as the primary end of state-supported education, it has taken a 180-degree turn on the means to achieve that end. From developing the individual's broad intellectual freedom implicit in *Meyer, Pierce, Barnette,* and *Tinker,* the Court has moved toward constricting that freedom while supporting the collective will. That redirection has proven markedly problematic for religious minorities in the schools.

Following on the heels of *Tinker* in the early 1970s, the Court began to use the concept of local control to further community interests and implicitly community values, particularly in desegregation and school finance litigation, both of which directly raise governance issues. Here the Justices rejected interdistrict remedies to achieve greater racial balance as well as efforts to redistribute state funds to realize greater educational equity, stating that, "neighborhood school systems . . . reflect the deeply felt desires of citizens for a sense of community in their public education," that local control guarantees "the greatest participation by those most directly concerned," and that "local autonomy has long been thought essential both to the maintenance of community concern and support for public schools and to the quality of the educational purpose."[74]

These decisions, which essentially raise equality concerns, emphasize the political community in the democratic sense of the prevailing political majority. Individual families and children who share a characteristic or status such as race or poverty or residence challenge the decisions of local school officials, who arguably (although perhaps not in fact) represent the majority consensus within the community. In contrast, older decisions such as *Meyer, Pierce, Yoder,* and *Barnette* were grounded in group-based communicative rights. These cases emphasized a clearly defined cultural community joined by common language, ethnic background, or religious beliefs (with the partial exception of *Pierce*) and a shared vision of the good life that was challenging not local policy, practice, or preference, but a law enacted by state government. While the cultural and political communities may be identical theoretically, in a culturally pluralistic society like the United States, such identity has become increasingly rare, which often gives rise to conflicts.

The Court's more recent concern for the political community is evident in Court decisions from the 1980s restricting student expressive rights. Since that time, the Court progressively has shown greater deference to school officials as representatives of the local community while moving more definitively toward a values-inculcation model of schooling in the face of individual challenges to local decision making. This intertwined emphasis is evident in case after case, from the removal of books from the school library as long as not politically motivated, to disciplinary action taken against a student for indecent speech deemed to be inappropriate, to official control grounded in "legitimate pedagogical concerns" over the style and content of a school-sponsored newspaper.[75] With increasing certitude the Justices have afforded school officials broad discretion "to establish and apply their curriculum in such a way as to transmit community values" and have noted that schools must "inculcate the habits and manners of civility as . . . indispensable to the practice of self-government."[76]

At the same time, the Court repeatedly has noted that schools are "vitally important 'in the preparation of individuals for participation as citizens' and . . . for inculcating fundamental values necessary to the maintenance of a democratic political system,'" that school officials may limit speech that is contrary to Americans' "shared values," and that schools are the primary vehicle for transmitting cultural values and "the most pervasive means for promoting our common destiny."[77] The Justices have recognized that among our shared fundamental values is tolerance of diverse political and religious views, even unpopular ones.[78] They seem to suggest, however, that while the state has unfettered discretion to enforce tolerance of its own views, tolerance for the views of individuals and minority groups most often can be outweighed by the interests of society.

The notion of schools as socializing agents is not simply a postseventies phenomenon, although it has assumed an added dimension in recent decades. Both the common school reformers and later the progressives recognized and fostered the socialization function of schooling, the one focused on moral virtue and the other on democratic citizenship to meet the nationalistic goals of a developing nation. The progressives' further emphasis on student interests and participation became reflected in such cases as *Barnette* and *Tinker*. The modern-day Court, however, looks to socialization as a mechanism not only to prepare students for citizenship in the larger society, but to preserve community interests and preferences as articulated through the decisions of elected or appointed school officials. Where the Justices discuss values, they view them from two perspectives, reaffirming both the mission of schooling to promote the fundamental values of a democratic *society* and the authority of schools to uphold the values of the *community*. This distinction bears significant implications for rights-based challenges to the public school curriculum, in which dissenting parents may embrace such widely accepted democratic values as racial equality, but sharply disagree with such nonconsensual values as gender neutrality that may find acceptance with the local majority and representation in the curriculum. The concepts of cultural and political community have a common thread in that they imagine a group of individuals bound by common experiences, values, ideals, and goals. The Court's inclination to uphold the interests of one or the other, however, has yielded starkly varying results. In the student speech, school finance, and school desegregation cases, the community is defined by the local political majority, whose interests lie in self-determination and maintaining "traditional" values. Their preferences override those of a nonculturally based minority bound by liberal democratic values of individual autonomy, equality, and tolerance for diverse views. Here the Court has upheld the right of the larger political community to make choices that would constrain individual freedom. In the *Meyer* strand of cases, on the other hand, the community was defined by culturally grounded minority interests which ultimately prevailed against state government (and not the local community). In the first, it is a loosely bound group of individuals versus the political community, while in the second it was a cultural community versus the state.

In *Yoder* the Court seemed to avoid addressing the conflict between the political and cultural community altogether by carefully depicting the Amish as a religious subgroup that in fact adequately met the state's interest in educating for citizenship. All the details in the decision—their three-hundred-year-old history, their reputation as law-abiding citizens, their success in preparing children for a self-sufficient life in an agrarian society—pointed to a traditional way of life and an affirmation of traditional values. In this way the Court upheld the interests of the cultural community of Amish, which appealed to the traditional values espoused by the majority of the Justices, while not departing from its deferential position toward the state. Yet, as Justice Douglas argued, there remained a question that deserved the Court's serious consideration, namely, that accommodating the group's interests might not necessarily be in the best interests of society or of the individual children. In the end, the Court upheld the right of a religious cultural minority to make decisions that arguably limited the choices of individuals within the subgroup. It was at least open to question as to whether the Amish did in fact share a broad, meaningful range of the country's shared democratic values, yet the majority of the Justices accepted that assumption as a given fact.

Within the scope of these decisions, community (either cultural or political) weighs only on one side of the balance. In contrast, although values-based curricular challenges occasionally are brought by individual families, they typically present two communities at odds with each other—the cultural community of minority dissenters and the political community represented by local school officials. This "war of the communities" may pose a dilemma for the Supreme Court, which has avoided such cases for a variety of institutional reasons, although the lower courts almost universally have yielded to the political majority.

Underlying the Court's pattern of deference to shared democratic values are two assumptions: first, that there exists an ascertainable body of values shared throughout society and in a particular community, and second, that the school curriculum can and should be standardized according to both these broader societal values and the more particular values of the community as defined by local school officials. In recent years, these assumptions have been laid bare by dissenters from across the political spectrum but most forcefully by religious conservatives, who doggedly rely on compelling language in *Meyer, Pierce,* and *Yoder* and even *Barnette* and *Tinker* despite the Court's repeated bow to majority values and local discretion. Each of these cases offers strong language supporting a general right of freedom of conscience and belief for parents or children or both, invoking prohibitions against compelled expression and the state's imposition of values contrary to those of the family. Nevertheless, the first three in particular when viewed as a whole begin to sink under their own weight. *Yoder* undercuts *Meyer* and *Pierce,* whose constitutional underpinnings in substantive due process place them on uncertain ground, while the rhetorical flourishes of constitutional protections threaded throughout *Barnette* and *Tinker* have all but evaporated in the contemporary air of rights skepticism, governmental deference, and majoritarian democracy.

Driven by concerns over federalism, by a minimalist view of the judicial role in policy matters, and by a clear understanding of the major impact of a Supreme Court decision, the Justices have proven increasingly reluctant to mediate these claims, apparently waiting for a political resolution. In doing so, they have offered vague direction to lower courts, which continue to struggle with the tensions inherent within educational claims based in religious and philosophical values.

Chapter 5 Voices of Dissent

The Supreme Court's continued reluctance to mediate the national culture wars over values in the schools has not stemmed the tide of litigation moving through the lower courts. Parents draw upon the arsenal of rights developed in the Court's earlier decisions and pressure schools to reflect, or at a minimum to accommodate, their particular moral values and religious beliefs within the public school setting. Accommodation can mean exemption from a textbook, materials, practice, or program with or without alternative instruction. It can also mean the removal of materials or the elimination of a program or practice.

Most but not all challenges to the curriculum are brought by religious conservatives, who are least inclined to compromise their fundamental beliefs with mainstream secular values. Yet even with the backing of well-staffed, legally astute organizations, they have met limited success in court. They have largely generated a body of court decisions that implicitly or expressly uphold the authority of school officials to inculcate the shared values of both the political communities they represent and the society at large. Still, their uncompromising beliefs and the vigor with which they have defended them in court create a dramatic context for examining the question of values-based conflicts in the schools. Several of these cases have drawn national attention for their potential political impact on schooling nationwide. They have also set the ground rules for debate among legal scholars and political philosophers and provided a framework for judicial decision making.

NETWORKS OF OPPOSITION

Key to understanding the opposition of religious conservatives to public schooling is the work of Rousas J. Rushdoony, a former missionary and ordained minister in the Orthodox Presbyterian Church, whose interpretation of American educational history laid the intellectual foundation for subsequent organized efforts. Writing in the 1960s, Rushdoony decried the notion of "education as a religion" and the contemporary focus on "education in terms of utility to the state . . . as against the traditional faith in education in terms of utility to God." He traced the contemporary "messianic character" of education back to Horace Mann, John Dewey, and others, noting that sex education, counseling, and psychological testing had been added to the curriculum in the "abiding conviction that knowledge is not only power but moral virtue" from which "a new society will be created."[1]

Rushdoony developed a set of arguments that initially gave substance to what is now a well-organized, well-financed network from which parents who challenge the educational innovations of the past several decades can draw information and strategic support. Prominent among this group are Mel and Norma Gabler and their widely publicized textbook review library; Citizens for Excellence in Education, an affiliate of the National Association of Christian Educators, whose founder and president, Robert Simonds, served as a member of Ronald Reagan's task force in 1983 to implement *A Nation at Risk,* the National Commission on Excellence in Education Report; Phyllis Schlafly and the Eagle Forum, including its Legal Defense Fund; James Dobson, president of Focus on Family, whose magazine by the same name has a distribution of more than a million and a half readers; and the American Family Association. The group also includes a number of individual experts who have gained national recognition within Christian conservative circles.

This network has mounted a concerted and visible attack on specific programs and practices that its members have opposed as reflecting either a secularist ideology, New Age thinking, or witchcraft and the occult. They list an impressive collection of enemies in their civil war over family values, including the

American Civil Liberties Union (ACLU), the National Organization for Women, the National Education Association, and People for the American Way (PFAW) as well as most journalists, television and movie producers, university professors, and members of the Washington establishment.[2]

The organized efforts of religious and social conservatives have met with only marginal success in changing education nationally. Most notably, they have prevailed upon textbook publishers to avoid controversial topics and upon some state legislatures to grant parents discretion in certain curricular matters such as sex education and psychological testing. They have met less success in achieving accommodation for individual parents at the local level. With the educational establishment proving resistant and at times impervious to their criticism, values-based conflicts have taken on a legal cast. More and more disaffected parents now seek relief in the Constitution, relying on the ambiguities and rhetorical flourishes of Supreme Court precedent from *Meyer* through *Yoder*. But the costs of pursuing a judicial remedy from trial through the appeal process can prove prohibitive for most families while the complex constitutional issues raised demand expertise well beyond the capabilities of most local attorneys. Many parents, therefore, either seek or readily accept representation from pro bono attorneys acting on behalf of public interest law groups.

Organized over the past two decades to counterbalance politically liberal claims in court, these groups initially relied on the amicus curiae brief to attract the attention of the courts and the public. In more recent years, they have turned to the liberal model of case sponsorship, eager to develop a good test case that promises to move their agenda forward.[3] As a result, the most aggressively pursued and publicly visible cases have proceeded under the direction of groups with a decidedly religious or politically conservative slant. Included among these are the Center for Law and Religious Freedom, the Catholic League for Religious and Civil Rights, the Christian Legal Society, Concerned Women for America, the American Family Association Law Center, the Rutherford Institute, and Pat Robertson's American Center for Law and Justice, which has taken a lead role in a number of high-profile cases.

Drawing on a public interest law model developed by civil rights groups like the National Association for the Advancement of Colored People and the ACLU, conservative advocacy groups have adopted *planned litigation* as a vehicle for incremental social reform. Precedent building is their key strategy. Like their liberal counterparts and opponents, these organizations in the short run represent religious minorities whose interests, they argue, have received inadequate attention in the majoritarian political process. In the long run, they seek to make the public square in general and schooling in particular more hospitable toward orthodox religious views. With each case they whittle away at a public school system that they believe has proven unresponsive at best and hostile at worst to religious beliefs. In court these groups have tested several distinct legal theories to support the underlying proposition that parents, not the state, take precedence in controlling the education and upbringing of children.

Religious conservatism encompasses a range of beliefs including evangelicalism, which constitutes a branch of Protestantism, and fundamentalism, which is a subset of evangelicalism. The so-called religious right incorporates a smaller group of fundamentalists who combine religion with political action. Members of this marginally scattered group share a core belief in the literal interpretation of the Bible. The term *fundamentalism* dates from the years 1910 to 1914, when the Bible League of North America published a twelve-volume paperback anthology of the work of a broad range of conservative American and British theologians, teachers, and writers. The series was called *The Fundamentals* and emphasized "personal salvation, individualistic religion, the doctrine of biblical inerrancy, the refutation of higher biblical criticism, the rejection of modern scientific method, millenarian literalism, and attacks on 'heretical' faiths such as Roman Catholicism and Mormonism."[4]

While mainstream Protestant religions moved steadily to the left following World War I and fundamentalism became discredited in the evolution debacle of the Scopes monkey trial,[5] the years following World War II witnessed a resurgence of evangelical Protestantism, spurred on by Billy Graham, the noted evangelist preacher. Evangelicals tend to bridge the gap between fundamentalists and mainstream Protestants. Although both groups traditionally have been committed to the inerrancy of Scripture, an estimated 40 percent of evangelical theologians have abandoned this belief in recent years.[6] Religious conservatives, including fundamentalists and other evangelicals, tend to reject mainstream culture's Enlightenment emphasis on rationality and autonomy in testing cultural values and authorizing change. They rely instead on some authoritative person, text, or tradition as their guide in defining acceptable values in society.[7] Their assumptions and perspective are colored by their belief in God as the ultimate reality and in Satan as an active force in their lives.[8]

For the past one hundred years, there also has existed a conservative equivalent to fundamentalism within the Catholic Church. Traditionalists within the church also favor a "premodern, ahistorical orthodoxy" but depart from their Protestant counterparts on the interpretation of Scripture, whose certainty for Catholics comes from the pope and the church.[9] Despite their historically deep-seated suspicion of Catholicism and the papacy, Christian conservative groups in recent years have attempted, with limited success, to engage Catholic conservatives, mainly over opposition to abortion. In 1995, the Christian Coalition launched an affiliate called Catholic Alliance to "unite hundreds of thousands of pro-life, pro-family Catholics" with evangelical Protestants in an effort to form a long-term political compact with a much broader focus than the anti-abortion cause. The coalition's mailing to half a million Catholics encouraging them to work with the group on public policy issues provoked an outcry from a number of American Catholic bishops. Church leaders forcefully made clear that the group's political position on such issues as capital punishment, immigration, and welfare reform were radically opposed to the position of the U.S. Catholic Conference.[10]

For many years, Christian conservatives—fundamentalists, above all—steered clear of politics. But several flashpoints have led to their political activation. Beginning in the 1960s, religious conservatives saw the government encroaching by degrees on their way of life. The Supreme Court's outlawing of prayer and Bible reading in the public schools proved of major significance to them. The Court's decisions sent a "seismic shock" that traveled beyond the Christian conservative world, representing for many the secularization of public space. At the same time, they became increasingly disturbed over escalating government interference with the free exercise of religion. Whether it was the federal Internal Revenue Service threatening to deny tax exemptions to private schools that engage in racial discrimination or state legislatures and education officials imposing teacher certification, testing, and curriculum requirements on Christian day schools, religious conservatives railed against what they perceived to be a serious threat to the distinctiveness of the education that they had chosen for their children.[11] But it was the Court's decision in *Roe v. Wade*[12] (1973) constitutionalizing the right to abortion that sounded the definitive wake-up call to the Christian right and mobilized them for political action.

For religious Christians, *Roe* symbolized a value shift that loosened American society from its moral and religious moorings. According to Jerry Falwell, then a little-known televangelist from Lynchburg, Virginia, the Court's decision convinced him that "government was going bad." He realized that "it was, in part, because [religious conservatives] had absented [themselves] from that process." Four years later, the government took further action that shifted Christian conservatives into political high gear. At that time, the federal government proposed regulations that would have denied tax-exempt status to private schools, established or expanded in the wake of school desegregation, which had failed to enroll a specified percentage of minority students. Inspired by his success in defeating the proposal through a massive letter writing campaign, Falwell proceeded in 1979 to convert an obscure sectarian school lobby called the Christian Action Coalition into a national political advocacy organization called the Moral Majority. The new organization had four concrete objectives: to be pro-life, pro-family, pro-moral, and pro-American. The following year, Falwell announced that he and his coreligionists were optimistic that they could "turn this nation back to God." By 1982, *U.S. News and World Report* would name Jerry Falwell one of the twenty most powerful men in America.[13]

The strident political activism of the Moral Majority provoked the television producer Norman Lear in 1980 to establish PFAW as a counterweight to Falwell's organization. Since its inception, PFAW has served as a national watchdog over censorship attempts nationwide, counseling local communities and publishing until recently a widely used annual censorship report.[14] Much of its literature and solicitation mailing focuses on the religious right and the dangers it poses to public education.[15] PFAW also carries out an ambitious litigation agenda, enlisting the pro bono legal services of some of Washington's most prestigious law firms, among them Hogan and Hartson, Covington and Burling, and Wilmer and Pickering. These firms have played a key role in representing school districts and preparing amicus curiae briefs on their behalf and on behalf of parents who intervene in support of school boards. Most recently PFAW has mounted a campaign to defeat state education voucher proposals and ballot measures across the country.

The ACLU, a leader in the protection of constitutional freedoms ever since its founding in 1920, has played a somewhat distinct role from PFAW in court battles over educational values. In recent years, the ACLU appears to have focused its energies on the school prayer issue, representing parents in cases challenging efforts by school officials to introduce any form of prayer or religious exercise in the public schools, particularly religious invocations at graduation ceremonies. PFAW has maintained a peripheral involvement in this litigation. The ACLU has joined PFAW in opposition to school choice initiatives that involve religiously affiliated schools, a partnership that has drawn criticism from choice supporters who consider the group's position to be a perversion of its own calling. The very organization that has spearheaded the defense of free speech and defended the civil rights of unpopular groups, the argument goes, is now becoming the censor of family expression. Joining the ACLU in the "anti-pietist" alliance against school prayer are traditional church–state separationist groups like Americans United for Separation of Church and State as well as national Jewish organizations, including the American Jewish Congress and the Anti-Defamation League.[16]

Over the past two decades, these nationally organized opposing forces have aggressively used the federal courts to promote their respective views of American education and American democracy, the one challenging the established system to its core and the other tenaciously holding on to it. Federal judges, struggling to apply Supreme Court doctrine to the various permutations on the educational values theme, have proven reluctant participants in this tug-of-war. Nevertheless, the competing legal and policy issues raised and the legal strategies employed in these cases provide a useful framework for reconsidering the concept of freedom of conscience within the common school as it was originally conceived and as it has evolved.

FREEDOM FROM GOVERNMENT SPEECH

Religious dissenters, fully cognizant of education's indoctrinative force, specifically have asserted the *right to be free from government speech* that offends their religious beliefs. This argument has played itself out in the form of two litigation strategies, each reflecting a distinct approach to the overlapping sovereignties of church and state over the lives of religious people. The first, which carries broad educational implications, is grounded in the establishment clause of the First Amendment, which states that "Congress shall make no law that establishes a religion." The Court has extended that prohibition beyond the federal government to the states through the operation of the Fourteenth Amendment. Here the claimants attempt to co-opt the state and inject their own practice or beliefs as a universal rule or norm to govern the entire school or district. The second is based on the free exercise clause. Like the Amish in *Yoder,* claimants in these cases want to preserve their singularity and merely search for a space to practice their religious culture or belief without implicating children outside their group.[17]

As the case law demonstrates, sometimes religious dissenters expressly argue for a limited personal remedy while implicitly aiming for a schoolwide or systemwide or even nationwide response in their favor. The political debate typically generated when these claims become public often produces this broader effect, although the intended objective originally may have been local. Even if they lose in court, there is always the chance that they will win in the court of public opinion, if not this time then maybe next. But regardless of the strategy chosen, it inevitably underscores the inherent tensions within the First Amendment. A free exercise claim for exemption from an otherwise educationally valid policy or practice potentially gives rise to establishment clause issues. For a district to exempt certain students from particular programs or materials on free exercise grounds arguably conveys a message that the state is advancing a particular religion or privileging the religious claim to exemption over those of others that are not religiously based. On the other hand, if the district removes materials or programs from the curriculum in response to religious or political pressure, then it arguably violates the free speech rights of other students. Whichever way officials turn, they face the threat of litigation.

Challenging the Norm as Religion

In the early 1980s, Tim LaHaye, founder of the American Coalition for Traditional Values, published two national bestsellers, *The Battle for the Mind* and *The Battle for the Public Schools*.[18] LaHaye warned Americans of the secularist ideology pervading public schooling, linking secularism to such evils as premarital sex, drug abuse, rock music, materialism, violence, alienation, pornography, and communism.[19] He blamed the "present anti-intellectual . . . climate" of education as the root cause of grade inflation and declining SAT scores. According to LaHaye, "Secular humanism, the official doctrine of public education, has all the markings of a religion . . . [and] monopolizes the minds of our nation's 43 million public-school children."[20] Litigators have since transformed LaHaye's argument into the legal claim that public schools are teaching a religion of "secular humanism" in violation of the First Amendment establishment clause. Despite the certainty with which LaHaye spoke, however, his argument has received a cool reception in the courts. That failure is due largely to the ambiguity surrounding both the concept of religion and the concept of secular humanism.

Before a values-based establishment claim can be addressed, a threshold question is whether the school practice, program, or materials under challenge present beliefs that are religious in nature. More than three decades ago, the Court made a limited ruling on the definition of religion under the establishment clause in finding that banning school prayer and Bible reading from the public schools would not constitute teaching of a "religion of secularism."[21] More recently, several of the Justices have noted that one of the problems inherent in nonpreferentialist arguments supporting evenhanded state aid to all religions is the inability of courts to make decisions about the types of competing beliefs that qualify as religion.[22]

Courts and scholars have struggled to identify the defining features of a religion, raising questions within questions without conclusive answers.[23] Does it require a personal belief in a higher source, a transcendent being, or what we commonly know as God, along with revelation from that source with extratemporal consequences? Can it be broadened to signify a philosophy allowing not just for vertical orientation (humans looking to God) but horizontal orientation as well (individuals looking to each other and to the world)? Can we expand the definition even more broadly to embrace the concept of worldview, which is more of an overall pattern for understanding reality? The pattern can be based in science or reason or mysticism or traditional religious beliefs.[24] Does it need a discrete set of tenets and rituals or can it be more amorphous? Must it be organizationally based or can it be more idiosyncratic? Can there exist intrafaith differences among its followers? Most of these questions have arisen in the context of religious exemptions under the free exercise clause.

The Supreme Court has created much of the confusion, seemingly using the *Yoder* decision, at least with regard to constitutional claims, to reject a view that had become less theistic over time with the increasing secularization of society. This evolving approach merging religion and conscience reached its apex in the conscientious objector cases of the Vietnam War era. There the Court adopted a highly individualistic, subjective view of religion, noting that with regard to such "intensely personal" convictions, "great weight" should be given to the claimant's assertion that "his belief is an essential part of a religious faith."[25] During that period, the Court considered purely moral and ethical beliefs as religious provided they occupied "a place parallel to that filled by . . . God" in traditional religions, recognizing that "most of the great religions of today and of the past embodied the idea of a Supreme Being."[26] As Richard John Neuhaus has stated, after the conscientious objector cases religion was "no longer a matter of content but of sincerity . . . no longer a matter of communal values but of individual convictions."[27]

The Court's rationale in *Yoder* signaled a departure from this earlier position. Here the Justices attempted to objectify at least minimally the meaning of religion, stating that religious objectors had to demonstrate more than a mere subjective belief as would a Thoreau. The Court identified two factors, consistency and comprehensiveness, that would weigh on the sincerity of the religious claim, relying on evidence of "a sustained faith pervading and regulating [the Amish's] entire mode of life support."[28] Yet Thoreau's technically nonreligious philosophical beliefs may have entitled him to conscientious objector status under 1960s' Court doctrine. The result would have depended upon whether or not he personally cast his beliefs as religious despite the fact that Congress had excluded "essentially political, sociological, philosophical views, or a merely personal moral code."[29]

The conscientious objector cases turned on the interpretation of "religious training and belief" within the federal statute. *Yoder,* on the other hand, was brought as a constitutional claim under the free exercise clause in which the Amish argued that the compulsory education law burdened their sincerely held religious beliefs, although there was no dispute as to the religious nature of those beliefs. Claims of secular humanism in the schools also are constitutionally based but in the establishment clause, in which the definition of religion is central to the discussion. Here parents charge that the absence of God is as religious as the presence of God and that government is in effect establishing a religion through a particular program or practice that promotes nontheistic beliefs. The Court in *Yoder* seemed to reject the psychological/functional approach of the earlier decisions while suggesting in its stead an organizational and perhaps even a group dimension for constitutionally protected religious beliefs. Whether this apparent shift turned on the distinction between statutory and constitutional claims remains unclear.

Lower federal courts have struggled to reconcile *Yoder's* organizational approach with the functional approach of earlier cases by adopting a "definition by analogy" which is considerably closer to the functional view. In other words, the nontraditional belief or practice must confront the same concerns or serve the same purposes as traditional religions. Courts have held that a religion is characterized by certain key features: it addresses fundamental or ultimate questions having to do with deep, imponderable matters; it is comprehensive in nature, consisting of a belief system as opposed to an isolated ideology; it is recognizable by certain formal and external signs such as services, a clergy, and holidays;[30] it adheres to and promotes certain underlying theories of human nature or one's place in the universe; and it relies on more than a mere personal code.[31]

Despite the difficulties in reaching a precise definition, the Supreme Court over the years has provided several guideposts for interpreting religion under the First Amendment. The Court has held that while judges can inquire into the sincerity of religious beliefs they cannot examine the truthfulness or accuracy of those beliefs; that inconsistent beliefs among adherents of a given religion and the fact that the claimant is a recent convert to a faith are irrelevant; and that the state cannot make membership in an organized church, religious sect, or religious denomination a condition for claiming a religious exemption.[32]

Related to the definitional problem is the question of whether secular humanism constitutes a religion. Much of the argument supporting this concept is grounded in a publication of the American Humanist Association entitled *A Humanist Manifesto*, signed in 1933 by thirty-four individuals, including John Dewey, who is reputed to have been its principal author. Not only does this document use the term *religion* nine times in its fifteen affirmations, but it defines *religious humanism* as an alternative to traditional theism, based in modern man's "understanding of the universe, his scientific achievements, and his deeper appreciation of brotherhood." Among the beliefs espoused are that the universe is "self-existing and not created" and that worship and prayer are replaced by "a heightened sense of personal life and in a cooperative effort to promote social well-being." The *Humanist Manifesto II*, signed in 1973, espoused the view that "ethics is *autonomous* and *situational*, needing no theological or ideological sanction."[33]

The only judicial support for secular humanism as religion can be found in two passing references from the 1960s. In a footnote to a 1961 Court decision that advocates persistently quote but lower courts repeatedly ignore or dismiss, the Justices made reference to "those religions based on a belief in the existence of God" as well as "those religions founded on different beliefs." Among the latter, they included secular humanism along with Buddhism, Taoism, and Ethical Culture.[34] Two years later the Court warned that public schools "may not establish a 'religion of secularism' in the sense of affirmatively opposing or showing hostility to religion."[35]

Throughout the 1980s, religious conservatives repeatedly but unsuccessfully relied on the concept of secular humanism as religion to challenge the public school curriculum. One case caused grave concern within the educational establishment and captured the attention of the academic and popular press. In *Smith v. Board of School Commissioners* (1987), Christian fundamentalist parents in Alabama claimed that forty-four textbooks covering home economics, social studies, and history advanced secular humanism and inhibited their religion.[36] By the time the case reached trial, several of the defendants had been excused from the case. Gov. George Wallace had signed a consent decree stipulating that the religion of secularism should be eliminated from public school textbooks and that the omission of religion from history books discriminates against religion and violates the students' right "to receive information and ideas," a right which the Supreme Court had articulated in the context of library book removal.[37] The Mobile County school commissioners had signed a similar agreement, leaving the state Board of Education and the state commissioner of education as the only remaining defendants. Supporting them was a group of parents who had joined the case as defendant-intervenors. They challenged the attempt to remove state-approved textbooks from public schools in order to accommodate the beliefs of a particular religion. Representing the district were the ACLU and PFAW; the National Legal Foundation, an affiliate of Pat Robertson's Christian Broadcasting Network, represented the plaintiffs. Most of the witnesses at trial were experts in religion or education. One of the plaintiff's chief witnesses was a psychologist from California named William Coulson. His testimony focused on the home economics textbooks and their implicit message that some students may grow up and choose their own careers, which teaching would violate the right of their parents in guiding them in that choice.[38] Coulson would resurface a decade later as an expert witness in a similar case in Bedford, New York.

The facts presented in *Smith* struck a sensitive nerve among public school advocates and civil liberties groups. Their fears were well founded given the political climate of the time. By the mid-1980s, the religious attack on public schools had reached a feverish pitch. For the 1986–87 school year alone, PFAW documented 103 censorship attempts of school materials. This was a 20 percent increase over the previous year and a 168 percent increase since the group's first report in 1981–82. The success rate for removing, restricting, or modifying educational materials had also increased during this period from 26 to 37 percent. Just as significantly, the number of challenges supported by organized groups within a given year had increased from 22 incidents to 54, with groups such as Citizens for Excellence in Education gaining visibility and voice in local communities across the country, organizing local chapters, and running candidates in school board elections.[39]

The political picture in Washington caused added apprehensions. Religious conservative proposals for transforming the content of public education were gaining strong support from the White House and growing support within Congress. The Reagan administration was promoting vigorously the concept of a constitutional amendment to permit organized prayer in the public schools, while the movement in Congress to remove school prayer cases from the subject matter jurisdiction of the federal courts was visibly gaining momentum.[40] At the same time the Supreme Court was moving toward a more accommodationist perspective on religion, leaving establishment clause jurisprudence in a state of flux among the Justices.

Smith posed the danger that the Religious Right would infiltrate the nation's classrooms and dictate the curriculum according to their nonmainstream beliefs. It raised the specter of censorship in the minds of many educators, policy makers, and civil rights advocates. A total of twenty-six groups filed amicus curiae briefs in the circuit court of appeals countering the challenge. Included among them were the National Education Association, the New York State School Boards Association, the American Library Association, the American Jewish Congress, the American Jewish Committee, the National Association of Laity (Catholic), the Association of American Publishers, the National School Boards Association, the American Federation of Teachers, and the Council on Religious Freedom.

Their effort proved successful. But the court sidestepped the question of whether secular humanism is a religion for First Amendment purposes. Even assuming that it is, the appeals court said, none of the textbooks "conveyed a message of governmental approval of secular humanism or governmental disapproval of theism." The books merely represented an attempt by school officials to "instill . . . such values as independent thought, tolerance of diverse views, self-respect, maturity, self-reliance and logical decision-making." Schools could omit certain historical facts for nonreligious reasons without conveying "a message of governmental disapproval of theistic religions."[41]

Implicit in the court's decision are points that bear directly on the question of values inculcation in the schools. The court suggested that independent thought or critical thinking is a permissible mode of analysis and that tolerance for diverse views is a permissible value for inculcation through the public school curriculum even when these may offend the religious beliefs of some students and parents in the school. The court suggested even further that schools need not afford religious views equal time with nonreligious views in the curriculum.

The appeals court decision in *Smith,* while of limited jurisdiction, appeared to sound the death knell for secular humanism claims. The concept was judicially unmanageable and politically troublesome. From a policy perspective, for the courts to acknowledge that the absence of God is, in fact, as religious as the presence of God would immobilize school districts from infusing any content into the school curriculum in an endless effort to provide equal coverage to theistic and nontheistic beliefs. And from a political standpoint, this apparent attempt on the part of a small group of parents to attack the secular nature of public schooling on religious grounds struck at the heart of what the common school and American culture had striven so hard to achieve. Since the elimination of pan-Protestant practices under pressure from Catholics and other religious groups a century ago, public schools have prided themselves on their secular orientation, which they interpret as maintaining a neutral position toward religion.

By the close of the 1980s, religious conservatives apparently recognized the futility of pursuing secular humanism any further in court. They also perceived, however, a strategic advantage to using the establishment in lieu of the free exercise clause as a legal basis for their claims. By attacking the program or materials on the grounds that they potentially indoctrinate children in general (not just the claimant's children) with the beliefs of a particular "religion," they effectively could compel school officials to remove the materials or program entirely from the school or district, a remedy well beyond the bounds of individual exemption. More significantly, this broader-based attack holds symbolic value of wider political importance. It permits religious conservatives to interject their values into the school curriculum and thereby gradually shift the norm away from what they perceive as the progressive excesses of the ruling educational establishment and toward their own values. In this way, the system gradually becomes redefined. Of course, this strategy is not airtight. Complete removal carries the threat of censorship claims brought by majority parents under the free speech clause as the *amici* in *Smith* forcefully and persuasively argued. Litigation breeds more litigation. It also provokes more virulent, persistent, and organized opposition from the community whose values are endangered.

As religious conservatives abandoned the secular humanism argument in the wake of *Smith* and similar losses, they began to develop an alternative, second generation of establishment clause litigation in the early 1990s that presents a variation on the secular humanism theme. Here litigants have advanced the concept of a religion based in Wicca, the occult, or New Age philosophy in which they argue the presence rather than the absence of beliefs but this time based in nontraditional religions. In one line of cases, federal courts have cited *Smith* in rejecting challenges brought by fundamentalist Christian parents to the *Impressions* reading series, a program developed by the publishing house of Harcourt Brace Jovanovich in the late 1980s and widely used in school districts throughout the country. The series presented a new technique for teaching reading and language arts—the whole language approach—which has since become highly controversial in educational circles. In contrast to the traditional phonics approach, which encourages students to decode words without examining the moral of the story, whole language encourages students to develop reading skills by reading thought-provoking stories culled from original literature. The *Impressions* series contains more than eight hundred literary selections organized in fifteen readers, including works by such critically acclaimed authors as Rudyard Kipling, Dr. Seuss, Laura Ingalls Wilder, and C. S. Lewis.

In 1989, the California State Department of Education approved the series, and sixty-seven school districts within the state adopted it, setting off a storm of opposition from religious conservatives. The following year, the *Wall Street Journal* reported that religious activists and parent groups in a dozen states had brought charges claiming that the books were "nothing less than primers on witchcraft, Satanism and the occult."[42] By 1992, upwards of forty districts in California were facing similar challenges.[43] Their core contention was that the books undermined parental authority and Christian values and were excessively violent and depressing.[44] At least two federal appeals courts have held that the selections, asking children to discuss witches or pretend that they are witches in a role-play situation, have neither the purpose nor the effect of endorsing what the courts considered to be an amorphous religion called Wicca.[45]

A third variant of the establishment clause argument is now working its way through the federal courts in New York. In some communities the New Age movement has replaced secular humanism as the cause celebre of the 1990s in attempts by religious conservatives to ban books, programs, and practices from the public schools. New Age is a term used to define a spiritual movement that became popularized in the 1960s. It can best be described as a loose amalgam of psychic, spiritual, and religious beliefs and practices that recognizes all ancient and contemporary religions and promotes a number of psychic, astrological, and meditation techniques. In the late 1980s and early 1990s, a number of books decrying the dangers of New Age philosophy appeared within the growing religious conservative network. This literature targeted specific educational practices and programs as products of New Age philosophy. Included among these were outcome-based education, multiculturalism, the whole language approach to reading, cooperative learning, peer counseling, assessment testing, global education, environmental education, drug and sex education, and transpersonal education, including meditation and relaxation techniques.

One book that religious conservatives frequently cite defines the New Age movement as a "worldview or philosophy of life . . . a particular way of defining reality and living . . . a synthesis in varying degrees of many religious traditions and practices, including Hinduism, Buddhism, Taoism, spiritism, shamanism, witchcraft, and other forms of classical occult practice and philosophy."[46] Within the network, the occult is broadly defined and not limited strictly to Satanism, black magic, or witchcraft; rather, it includes any "religion, practice, or technique which promotes the goals and worldview of the occult."[47] Legal arguments grounded in New Age philosophy must overcome the same hurdles in court as secular humanism: that it constitutes a discernible religion for purposes of the establishment clause and that the programs and practices under attack promote the beliefs of that religion. At least one federal appeals court has rejected this argument, noting that "the New Age is a very flexible, amorphous, spontaneous movement. There is no national organization, no hierarchy, no clearinghouse for information. . . . A typical believer draws on . . . different interests to create his own, personal way of thinking about himself and the world around him." More specifically, this court noted that a symbol, for example, one from an ancient religion, must have current religious adherents to be regarded as religious for purposes of the First Amendment.[48]

Whether framed in the language of secular humanism, Wicca, the occult, or New Age philosophy, these cases have one feature in common: they represent attempts by parents to remove materials from the curriculum and impose their religious views on the entire school community. Such controversies place school officials in a double bind, faced with the threat of litigation whichever way they turn. Especially when curricular materials meet valid pedagogical objectives, and school officials can offer no legitimate educational reason for their removal, schools risk coming under collateral constitutional attacks from the larger school population. When a school accedes to the demands of religious dissenters it opens itself to the interpretation that it is advancing or endorsing a particular religious view and eliminating opposing views.

The Supreme Court has unambiguously warned that for the state to tailor its curriculum to satisfy the principles or prohibitions of any religion would violate the establishment clause.[49] School officials also risk charges that they are denying other students access to ideas based on a noneducational or impermissible motivation in violation of free speech rights. Merging establishment clause and free speech principles, one may reasonably conclude that when schools attempt to modify the curriculum offered to all students primarily to accommodate the religious beliefs of some students, the courts will not defer to their decisions.

Mere Exposure and Religious Burdens

The establishment clause in theory presents a broad base of relief to parents who challenge the school curriculum on religious grounds. In practice, however, the approach has proven problematic for religious conservatives because of the questionably religious nature of the programs and practices that they challenge. In view of these limitations, they have pursued an alternative course in search of a more particularized remedy in the free exercise clause. Here parents have relied on *Yoder,* seeking individualized accommodation through exemptions or partial opting out from certain aspects of the curriculum.

The concept of religious exemption from specific educational programs or practices initially developed throughout the 1970s and 1980s in the context of sex and family life education programs. During that period, school districts across the country introduced such topics into the curriculum, typically under state mandate, although the particular program and materials generally were left to local discretion. Parents attempted to use the free exercise clause as a vehicle for persuading the courts that these programs should be banned from the schools. Most state laws included an opt-out provision which granted parents the right to request that their children be exempted from participating, generally on religious grounds. That option proved an adequate remedy as far as the courts were concerned.[50] But as religious conservatives became more organized and politically vocal throughout the 1980s, school districts were faced more and more often with requests for exemptions from programs and materials spanning the curriculum. Many of these requests centered on newly introduced social programs such as those related to the AIDS crisis or programs with a psychological dimension.[51] Others followed on the tracks of the removal cases and sought exemption from materials used in such core elements of the curriculum as reading and language arts. In the face of administrative apathy and even hostility, parents began to threaten litigation, and some took their claims to court.

One case became a focal point of media attention and educational concern and a flashpoint for scholarly commentary on parental dissent and educational values. It is no exaggeration to state that for more than a decade *Mozert v. Hawkins County Board of Education*,[52] decided by the Sixth Circuit Court of Appeals just two days prior to the *Smith* decision, has shaped the legal and political landscape of discussion and debate on religious accommodation in the public schools. The district and the three appeals court opinions generated in the case each shed a distinct light on the legal nuances, competing interests, and policy implications underlying religious accommodation in the public schools.

The facts of *Mozert* follow a pattern typical of such conflicts. During the fall of 1983, several families requested that their children be given alternate reading assignments in lieu of the basic Holt, Rinehart, Winston reading series that was used in schools throughout the county. The parents maintained that the books violated their religious beliefs. All but one principal granted the request. In the face of community protests and conflicting school policies concerning the alternate programs, the school board unanimously adopted a resolution that required all students to use the Holt readers. When the parents refused to permit their children to take part in the reading program, the school board suspended the children. Represented by Concerned Women for America, the parents sued in federal district court. The parents charged that the readers depicted witchcraft and other occult activities; taught that some values are relative and situational and that man and apes evolved from a common ancestor; encouraged students to disrespect and disobey their parents; promoted various humanistic values; disparaged free enterprise; maligned hunting; and advocated gun control, feminism, and environmentalism as a moral absolute.

Stephen Bates, in his well-crafted case study of the *Mozert* litigation, *Battleground,* suggests that these parents would have preferred the forceful patriotism of early American textbooks.[53] They argued that the stories in the Holt series built upon one another and that after reading the entire series, a child might adopt the views of a "feminist, a humanist, a pacifist, an anti-Christian, a vegetarian, or an advocate of a 'one-world government.'"[54] The parents claimed that "mere exposure" to these materials was a form of values inculcation that violated their free exercise rights under the First Amendment. They could accept the presentation of some views so long as the school labeled them as incorrect with a corresponding assertion that their views were the correct ones. Other ideas, however, including evolution, false supernaturalism, and feminism, were so contrary to their beliefs that the school would have to eliminate all references to such subjects from the classroom. Their arguments raised the question as to whether and, if so, to what extent exposure affects the formation of children's "values, identities, and beliefs."[55]

One of the parents' expert witnesses was Paul Vitz, a New York University psychology professor who would later reappear, like Coulson, in the Bedford controversy over the occult. Vitz testified at trial that the Holt series either disparaged Christianity or ignored it. Of the approximately six hundred poems and stories in the series, Vitz found that not one depicted biblical Protestantism, life in the Bible Belt, or families or individuals who pray to God. In contrast, non-Christian religions and particularly Eastern and Native American religions received adequate attention.[56] His compelling testimony demonstrated that American textbooks had traveled a distant road from the *McGuffey Readers,* with a decided push from the Supreme Court's school prayer decisions of the early 1960s, after which any mention of God, even in the Pledge of Allegiance, could provoke a lawsuit. Educators and textbook publishers simply wanted to steer clear of controversy. The thrust of Vitz's argument "was not about the evils of reflection on diversity but the alleged failure to initiate such reflection in a context where the way of life which the parents and their children shared was given due respect and recognition."[57]

The district court's opinion, subsequently reversed on appeal, has generated much discussion among scholars, some of whom commend it for its sensitivity to practical realities. The opinion, in fact, presents an interesting compromise between the legitimate interests of the school district in developing literacy skills and governing the educational program without substantial disruption and the interests of the children in remaining free of the burden that forced participation had placed on their religious beliefs. The court concluded that the parents' religious beliefs mandated that their children refrain from *exposure* to the reading series and that the school board had effectively placed students in the position of either reading the offensive books or relinquishing their right to free public schooling.

The court stopped at requiring the district to provide an alternative reading program, which would have demanded additional preparation on the part of the existing teaching staffs or required the schools to hire part-time reading tutors. Instead, the court ruled that the students could opt out of the Holt reading program and be taught reading at home by their parents, subject to state achievement tests. Just as the state permits home schooling as a complete opt-out, the court stated, this alternative could work effectively for a single subject. In this way, the court permitted the students to forego the course but not the course requirements. But the court underscored the narrowness of its decision: that it applied only to these students and only to this reading program. This was not an open invitation for widespread accommodation. The court was also careful to note the limited number of students involved and the narrowness of the parents' request—only the reading series and not a "multi-subject, multi-text objection."[58] Had the facts been otherwise, the decision would have weighed on the side of the school district.

The district court opinion soon became both a symbol of parental rights and a threat to public education. For Michael Farris, the parents' attorney in court, the case affirmed that "parents, not educational bureaucrats, control the educational process." For him, the books presented "the bias of the liberal establishment. . . . We're not saying, 'Take stuff out of textbooks'—we're saying 'Put more stuff in.' When you show a Buddhist in a story, put a Protestant in as well." The decision triggered heated political debate. Stephen Arons called the ruling "eminently reasonable," explaining that "many families are offended by the values society presents in the public schools and want a different set of values, but can't afford private schools." Others saw it differently. Anthony Podesta, president of PFAW, which assisted in the school board's defense, warned that "public schools will become nothing more that supermarkets, as every sect in the country picks and chooses which part of the curriculum they will accept."[59] The *Mozert* opinion sent shock waves throughout the educational and legal communities. By the time the case reached the appeals court, six amicus curiae briefs had been filed, primarily by groups opposed to the district court ruling. Included among them were the New York State Education Department, the National Education Association, the American Jewish Committee, and the National Council for Churches of Christ in the U.S.A.

Heeding the warning of oppositionist arguments but unable to reach a clearly defined rationale, the appeals court reversed in three separate opinions, each of which presented a divergent perspective on the legal and policy issues raised in the case. Chief Judge Pierce Lively, writing for the court, maintained that *mere exposure* to offensive materials without any attempt by the school to indoctrinate the children with any specific value or religion did not place a burden on the free exercise of their religious beliefs. The children were not "required to affirm or deny a belief or engage or refrain from engaging in a practice prohibited or required" by their religion. In contrast to the Amish parents in *Yoder,* who had no choice but to abandon their beliefs or violate the law, the parents here had the option to send their children to private schools or to home school them. Besides, in *Yoder* it was impossible to reconcile the goals of public education with the Amish religious requirement that children be prepared "for life in a separated community." The *Mozert* parents, in contrast, wanted their children to acquire the full range of skills required for life in modern society while exempting them from certain ideas that their parents found offensive. And while the district court had viewed their claims of textbook bias as a matter of balance, Judge Lively dismissed their argument. Not only would it have been difficult to "cure the omissions" in the reading series, but balanced treatment would not have satisfied the parents, who, on some issues, recognized "but one acceptable view."[60] School officials would have had to declare the "errancy" of opposing ideas on religious grounds, which in turn would have created the context for an establishment clause claim.

Rather than develop his rationale under the free exercise clause more fully, however, Judge Lively shifted to *Barnette,* the 1943 flag salute case involving the Jehovah's Witnesses who had raised both free exercise and free speech claims, the latter forming the basis of the Court's decision. Here he distinguished between active participation in a government-sponsored activity which would require an individual "to communicate by word and sign his acceptance of . . . political ideas"—for example, a ritualized flag salute or "reading aloud" or "acting out," which the *Mozert* children were not required to do—and merely reading silently. He seemed to hold that the former would prove more coercive in the formation of beliefs than the latter. He also recognized the role that public schools play in inculcating values that are fundamental to democratic government, including tolerance of diverse political and religious views. He qualified that tolerance as civil and not religious, that is, it does not require individuals to accept other religions as equal to one's own but merely to recognize that in a pluralistic society, "we must 'live and let live.'"[61]

Judge Cornelia Kennedy in a separate opinion agreed that the reading program neither required nor prohibited any affirmative act that violated the religious beliefs of the students. She focused specifically on the school board's interests that justified their imposing cultural uniformity on all students: an interest in avoiding classroom disruption (the opt-out remedy would fragment the curriculum); an interest in avoiding "religious divisiveness" in the community (opting out of a core subject like reading would undermine the school's interest in "promoting cohesion among a heterogeneous democratic people"); and an interest in developing in students the skills necessary for citizenship and self-government through the improvement of critical thinking skills.[62] In essence, she espoused the progressive view that education in a democracy must give students the opportunity to form independently their own ideas and judgments on "complex and controversial social and moral issues."[63] In effect, she turned the parents' claim on its head. Rather than view indoctrination as a potential harm, which they did, she embraced it as a civic good.[64] Looking at the case from the perspective of education for republican citizenship, she concluded that the opting-out alternative would deprive the *Mozert* children of the skills they needed for the "practice of self-government in the community and the nation."[65]

Judge Danny Boggs's opinion was far more sympathetic to the concerns raised by the parents and far more instructive on some of the myths and misunderstandings surrounding parental requests for accommodation in the school curriculum. He took the court to task for having painted the parents' claims in such an extreme light. They did not object to "any exposure to any idea opposing theirs" but only to the "overall effect of the Holt series," he explained. He also disagreed with the court's conclusion that the reading series did not burden the parents' religious beliefs and offered a more subjective approach based on the perspective of the parents. He noted that the parents believed that their religion "commands, not merely suggests, their course of action" and so the court should accept their viewpoint and not interject its own.[66]

Judge Boggs challenged Judge Kennedy's emphasis on the state's interest in "critical reading" and acknowledged the parents' objection to such instruction. He further questioned the validity of the school district's claim that acceding to the demands of the parents would have proven administratively disruptive or

confusing when there was no supporting evidence from the earlier accommodation that had taken place. Indeed, he found the state's rigidity "a bit ludicrous
in this age of individualized attention to many kinds of student language and
interests."[67] But in the end, he sided with the majority based on his reading of
the record, which differed sharply from theirs, and the constraints of Supreme
Court precedent. He deduced evidence at trial that the series in fact expected
students "to use their own value systems" in responding to the materials without minimizing their own religious beliefs. At the same time, there was no evidence that this approach was any different from the type of instruction the children could have received outside the classroom, for example, in their own
homes, and which could have been assessed by the testing program mandated
of all nonpublic students in the state.

Although he rejected the court's mere exposure standard, which has come to
define the debate on the issue, he felt constrained by prior case law from finding that the "common sense" burden on the parents' religious beliefs constituted,
"in the context of a public school curriculum, a constitutional 'burden'" on
those beliefs. For him this case was about the establishment clause "limits on
school boards to prescribe a curriculum," drawing a distinction between what
school officials *must* do and what they *may* do. On the one hand, he acknowledged that the Supreme Court had not authorized federal courts to require that
school officials justify their decisions each time they fail to address students' religiously compelled objections. But on the other hand, he also noted that nothing in the Constitution precludes local authorities from voluntarily providing
accommodation. He clearly implied that although the court could not mandate
opting-out as a legal remedy, the approach presents a valid political compromise
between the cultural community of Christian parents and the political community represented by the school board. Yet in the end he had to agree reluctantly that "on the present state of constitutional law, the school board is entitled to say, 'my way or the highway.'"[68]

Taken together, the three opinions raise several complex legal issues: whether
neutral exposure constitutes indoctrination; if so, whether such indoctrination
necessarily burdens the exercise of one's religious beliefs and thereby violates free
exercise rights under the Constitution; and if such a burden is found, whether
there exist sufficiently compelling educational justifications to override free exercise interests. Put conversely, the third question asks whether the dangers of
educational fragmentation, religious divisiveness, and political instability are
more real than speculative. If real, is the opt-out remedy sufficiently narrow in
scope to override these dangers? If merely speculative, then why not offer opt-

ing-out as a compromise solution? Post-*Mozert* fixation on the mere exposure principle has precluded serious discussion of valid governmental interests and alternatives.

Many of the tensions beneath contemporary schooling in America seem to erupt in the claims and arguments advanced on both sides in *Mozert*. The case strikes at the heart of values inculcation, the political purposes of the common school, parental discretion, the tension between cultural pluralism and assimilation, and the distinction among legally mandated, legally prohibited, and legally permissible educational practices. Nevertheless, *Mozert* may not have presented the ideal fact pattern for a winning test case on religious accommodation. Bates implies that the school board might have been motivated by a certain bias against Christian fundamentalists and might have accepted the district court's opt-out remedy had the parents been members of a more mainstream religion, while the parents may have been pursuing a broader transformation in public schooling and even schooling in general than merely "alternative readers for a handful of children." The protesters initially sought to ban the books outright along with several library books. Bates speculates that if they had succeeded, their book banning effort would have expanded, and school officials may have seen this scenario taking shape on the horizon.

Bates also intimates that there may have been an even bigger agenda behind the litigation. According to his account, the parents' lawyer predicted in a letter to a potential witness that "victory in *Mozert* would constitute 'a major building block in the effort to force the public schools to remove' humanist books from the classroom." In a separate context the parents' lawyer was quoted as stating, "It is very, very dangerous to have the machinery called public schools. . . . In fact, I believe . . . that public schools are per se unconstitutional. You can't run a school system without inculcating values. . . . Since inculcation of values is inherently a religious act, what the public schools are doing is indoctrinating your children in religion, no matter what."[69]

But these facts lend themselves to more than one interpretation on motive. Perhaps Bates read more into the lawyer's words than what the parents themselves had intended. It is not inconceivable, in the world of public law litigation, that the organization representing the parents in court, Concerned Women for America, had a long-term national agenda. The *Mozert* litigation, in fact, may have offered an opportunity to test a particular legal theory toward the ultimate end of dismantling public education. At the same time, it is also conceivable that the parents had a far more limited and personal agenda, seeking merely to free themselves and their children from the burdensome yoke of the Holt readers at the least. Of course there still exists the possibility that a win in this case might have encouraged them to pursue broader and more overt censorship, as they apparently had attempted initially. But this is all a matter of mere conjecture and, as Bates suggests, should have had no bearing on the court's determination of the parents' legal rights.

Despite all the attention heaped upon the case, none of the opinions offered definitive or wholly satisfactory answers to the opting-out debate. The district court, while demonstrating a sensitivity to the religious beliefs of the parents and children, provided a narrow window of accommodation applicable only in limited circumstances—a slightly more accommodating shade of *Yoder*. The appellate court opinions showed varying degrees of sensitivity but all seem constrained by Supreme Court religion clause doctrine and dicta acknowledging the regenerative function of schools, the authority of school officials, and the limits of judicial involvement in local educational policy. The case obviously differed from *Yoder*, in which the Amish's request for complete exemption from the last two years of compulsory schooling created no administrative inconvenience for school officials. In contrast, as a general principle the partial opting-out requested by the *Mozert* parents arguably could have mushroomed into a weighty administrative burden if repeated by other groups in the community, although there was no evidence of potentially similar claims.

According to their customs the Amish embraced only partial citizenship in civil society, which justified only a minimal state interest in educating their children in basic literacy and computational skills. And they did not take a position on the potential for biblical errancy in the ideas reflected in the curriculum. The *Mozert* parents, on the other hand, were unyielding in their commitment to a worldview which they wanted school officials to declare as correct, yet they also wanted their children to remain part of mainstream society. This apparent unwillingness to tolerate opposing views coupled with their desire for full civil participation heightened the state's interest in developing in their children the knowledge and skills necessary for citizenship in a liberal democracy, including the ability to critically evaluate the material they were reading as well as tolerance for different ways of life and political and religious perspectives.[70]

Mozert has no precedential value beyond the Sixth Circuit. And the parents' intransigent and intolerant views in themselves could reasonably justify a denial of accommodation. The case nonetheless is important as lower courts continue to draw on Judge Lively's rationale that mere exposure does not, under any circumstances, rise to the level of a cognizable claim under the federal Constitution. Unless and until courts are persuaded otherwise or adopt an alternative rationale, or the Supreme Court is willing to resolve the issue which it refused in this case, parents who deviate from the limited features of the Amish yet seek exemption for their children from any curricular requirement, whether based in religious or secular beliefs, must revert to the fragile concept of parental rights under Fourteenth Amendment substantive due process.

RIGHTS TO PARENTAL AUTONOMY

This carries the discussion full circle back to *Meyer* and *Pierce* and the right of parents to control their children's education and upbringing. Oftentimes parents also draw on *Yoder* as philosophical support for the concept of parental autonomy even when the claim is not religion-based. Secular challenges to the curriculum appear to be a phenomenon of the 1990s, a manifestation no doubt of the growing parental rights movement and the judicial roadblocks placed in the path of religion-based claims in seminal cases such as *Smith* and *Mozert*. This shift from the religious to the secular also reflects the complexity of social issues that schools now address and the heightened controversy school-sponsored social programs have generated. Two issues that have produced high-profile litigation and heated public debate offer a useful context for exploring the constitutional limitations of a secular challenge to educational programs and practices. The first concerns AIDS prevention programs, including condom distribution; the second concerns community service requirements for graduation.

In the early 1990s, school systems across the country began making condoms available to secondary school students in an effort to reduce the risk of exposure to the AIDS virus among adolescents. Many of these programs included an opt-out provision whereby parents could determine that their children would not be eligible to obtain condoms from the school. Some school districts, including New York City and Falmouth, Massachusetts, denied parents that discretion and found themselves under intense public scrutiny and ultimately in court defending their program from parental attack. As schools nationwide watched the legal scenarios play out in these two highly distinct systems, the state courts of New York and Massachusetts each struck a different balance between the public health and student rights concerns raised by school officials and civil liberties groups and the equally valid autonomy and values-based issues raised by parents.

In *Alfonso v. Fernandez* a New York State appellate court, citing *Meyer, Pierce,* and *Yoder,* held that the failure of the New York City school system to allow for a parental opting-out violated the parents' liberty interest in rearing and educating their children according to their own views. The court specifically affirmed that the Constitution grants parents the right to regulate the sexual activity of their children without state interference unless the policy is essential to serving a compelling state interest. The court acknowledged that the state's interest in preventing the spread of AIDS is sufficiently compelling but also recognized that minors can obtain condoms from alternate government sources outside of schools. On the substantive due process claim, the court distinguished the facts from *Mozert,* which was decided under the free exercise clause. The court noted that the program did not merely expose students to "talk or literature on sexual behavior . . . [but] offered the means to engage in sexual activity . . . [and thereby] interfer[ed] with parental decisionmaking in a particularly sensitive area." The court's resolution of the parental rights claim in *Alfonso* turned on several factors: a heightened standard of review whereby the government policy must be *essential* to meet a *compelling* state interest as opposed to the mere reasonableness standard of *Meyer* and *Pierce;* the distinction between mere exposure to offensive ideas or a point of view and supplying the means to *engage in activity* that violates parental values; and the carving out of certain particularly *sensitive* areas of parental decision making such as sexual activity that demand a more exacting level of judicial scrutiny.

The court, however, refused to recognize the parents' free exercise claim merely because they found the program "objectionable." As in *Mozert,* there was no element of compulsion here. The program neither prohibited parents or their children from practicing their religion nor coerced them to act contrary to their religious beliefs.[71] Although *Alfonso* reaffirmed *Mozert*'s narrow window on free exercise claims, it was a decided victory for parental rights. Yet it seems to have been a judicial aberration based on thin precedent at best. Subsequent state and federal court decisions have either qualified its holding or rejected its rationale entirely.

In a case involving identical facts and constitutional claims, *Curtis v. School Committee of Falmouth,* the Massachusetts court, also citing *Meyer, Pierce,* and *Yoder,* recognized a fundamental liberty interest in rearing one's children free from governmental intrusion—but only when it involves coercion or compulsion. The court apparently transported this factor from religious claims based in the free exercise clause to secular claims grounded in substantive due process. Here the parents had failed to demonstrate that the condom distribution program had a coercive effect on their parental liberties. According to the court, participation in the program was not mandatory and there was no penalty or disciplinary action if students refused to take part. The court again applied the coercion element to the parents' free exercise claim. The parents had not established that the burden placed on their religious beliefs was sufficiently "substantial," that is, that it was either coercive or compulsory in nature.[72]

Another group of Massachusetts parents met similar legal roadblocks when they challenged a program on AIDS awareness. Here Chelmsford High School officials had hired a company called Hot, Sexy, and Safer Productions, Inc., to deliver a ninety-minute program to two mandatory assemblies. The presenter, a former actress with no medical background or formal training in AIDS education, took a comedic approach that included sexually explicit skits and references to homosexuality, condoms, and masturbation. The program also included audience participation, one boy being asked to display his "orgasm face." A school physician had screened a promotional video of segments of past performances and had recommended it to school administrators, who later admitted that the presentation had gone too far. Parents of two fifteen-year-old students, represented by the Rutherford Institute, sued the company and school district officials but soon learned that even though this routine might have been offensive and emotionally upsetting to some students, it did not violate their constitutional rights. Among the defendants in the case were the chairperson of the Parent Teacher Organization and the school physician, who were represented by the ACLU.

According to the appeals court, although Supreme Court rulings have granted parents a right to control their children's upbringing, that right does not encompass a "fundamental constitutional right to dictate individually what the schools teach their children" or to "restrict the flow of information in the school which the parents have chosen." Implicit in this statement is the assumption that the enrollment of children in the designated public school is necessarily a matter of free choice. On the first of these points, the court discussed the confused historical evolution and ambiguous state of parental rights, noting that the Supreme Court had yet to decide whether the right to rear and educate one's child is among the fundamental rights that merit heightened scrutiny. Not only were *Meyer* and *Pierce* decided before current developments in right to privacy jurisprudence, but the cases themselves used the language of "reasonableness," which indicated that the Court at that time was applying something less than a compelling interest standard. On the second point, the court distinguished this case, which implicitly involved the rights of other students, from *Meyer* and *Pierce*, in which upholding the rights of the claimants had no bearing on any other individual interests.[73] The court also reaffirmed the distinction, drawn by the New York appellate court in *Alfonso*, between action (to engage in sexual activity) that violates parental values and mere exposure to sexually explicit language or literature on the subject of sexual behavior, reaffirming the "public school's role in preparing students for participation in a world replete with complex and controversial issues."[74]

As these cases indicate, AIDS education became the hot button school issue of the early 1990s. During this time a second type of program with perhaps less social appeal and certainly fewer social consequences also began to engender controversy in school districts across the country. Mandatory community service as a requirement for graduation presented another opportunity for developing the notion of parental rights under substantive due process. As these programs began to gain popularity, they increasingly became a point of parental opposition based more in principle than in reality. Developed within a political climate that has stressed voluntarism, mandated community service programs require students to provide services to community organizations outside of school hours. Service obviously is not voluntary in the true sense. Even when students are allowed a broad choice of organizations, these programs are part of the mandated school curriculum. There is, therefore, some merit to the argument that they involve values inculcation, that is, the value of community service. Both parents and students have challenged mandatory community service in court, claiming student free speech violations under the First Amendment, involuntary servitude under the Thirteenth Amendment, and, more significantly for purposes of this discussion, violations of parental liberty interests under the Fourteenth Amendment due process clause.[75]

In a case frequently cited for the court's clear, decisive rejection of secular parental rights claims, *Immediato v. Rye Neck School District,* the federal appeals court refused, in the absence of any express statement from the Supreme Court, to declare that parental rights are fundamental rights and thereby deserve judicial scrutiny higher than a mere reasonableness standard. The court recognized a parental liberty interest in child rearing under the Fourteenth Amendment but unequivocally interpreted *Meyer* and *Pierce* as requiring nothing more than a reasonable justification for the government's action. The court was also unwilling to draw the line at the exposure/action distinction, which other courts had analogized from *Mozert.* This court considered it "somewhat chimerical," particularly in the educational context, in which learning often requires "more than a passing glance at a book." For the court, it was inappropriate to "ratchet up" the standard of review merely because the program forced the students to act in opposition to their parents' values as compared with simply exposing them to information that conflicted with those values. And while the court acknowledged that the parents' objections here were based on their morals or values as opposed to other firmly held beliefs or even some general objection to the educational wisdom of the program, this difference had no constitutional significance. Secular objections to the school program of any nature do not rise to the level of a fundamental constitutional right.[76]

The appeals court in *Immediato* cited two prior cases from other federal circuits to support a mere reasonableness standard where parents had claimed on secular grounds that state-imposed educational requirements infringed on their right to control the upbringing of their children.[77] These decisions addressed home schooling, which has not proven as broadly controversial or as locally divisive as community service programs and certainly as AIDS education but nevertheless has engaged the lower courts in defining the contemporary meaning of *Meyer* and *Pierce.* Since the 1980s, parents have chosen with increasing frequency to educate their children entirely at home and have challenged the enforcement of state compulsory education laws and state mandates such as teacher certification and high school graduation requirements. Although the most vocal and best-organized parents to choose this alternative have tended to be religious conservatives, an increasing number of home-schoolers are motivated by academic and school safety concerns rather than religious beliefs.[78] As the appeals court noted in *Immediato,* parental claims to educate their children at home have largely met the same response as other parental rights claims; absent a grounding in religious beliefs, the right of parents to direct the upbringing of their children, whether technically considered fundamental or not, is subject to reasonable regulation by the state.

Court decisions on AIDS education, community service requirements, and home schooling together underscore the confused, fragile state of parental rights under the federal Constitution. They also reveal a decided reluctance within the federal judiciary to recognize a fundamental right to challenge the public school curriculum on purely secular grounds, even when the objections support widely held moral beliefs. With the exception of the state appeals court decision in *Alfonso,* which has limited jurisdiction, these cases reveal an unmistakable trend in judicial perspective on the question of values inculcation and school governance. Outside of a narrow range of religiously based claims asserted by groups that demonstrate the almost unique characteristics of the Amish—their insularity, the severe burdens imposed on their religious beliefs by the challenged state requirement, and the limited nature of the accommodation requested— state and federal courts continue to reject attempts by parents to shape the curriculum to fit their own individualistic values. At the same time, courts repeatedly uphold the authority of school officials to make curriculum determinations that arguably reflect the values of the local community and of society. In view of the Supreme Court's consistent refusal to review lower court decisions in these cases, it is highly doubtful that the legal issues left unresolved by *Meyer* and *Pierce* will find closure in the near future. In the meantime, parental dissenters and their values-based secular claims will continue to receive a less than cordial welcome in the courts.

RELIGIOUS SPEECH AS VIEWPOINT

Although religious conservatives have been rebuffed repeatedly in their efforts to gain control over their children's public education, in recent years they seem to have turned a corner on a related issue of critical importance to them, that is, their children's right to engage in speech of a religious nature. Religious speech in the public schools can take several forms, from school-organized or student-led prayer, to religious group meetings, to the distribution of religious literature, to the expression of religious perspectives by individual students in the course of classroom activities or as part of an assignment. The litigation in this area has been grounded in two principles: that religious expression is speech protected under the First Amendment and that it demands equal treatment as compared with other forms of speech. Courts weigh these claims against the limitations of the establishment clause.

Since the beginning of the twentieth century, public schools have become more and more secularized. First it was Dewey and the progressives who viewed religion as an affront to Enlightenment reason. Then it was the Supreme Court, whose controversial rulings on school prayer and Bible reading in the 1960s laid the groundwork for purging the public schools of any hint of religious practice or discussion. In more recent years, Court decisions striking down the posting of the Ten Commandments, a required moment of silence for meditation or voluntary prayer, the required teaching of creation science, and a school-directed graduation prayer confirmed the view that public schools were off-limits to the expression of religious views.[79] Although some school districts continued to flout the prayer decisions, by the 1980s most had removed any signs of contemporary religion.[80] Lower courts validated this interpretation well into the 1990s, upholding a teacher's decision to prohibit an elementary school student from making an oral class presentation entitled "The Power of God" as an independent research project, a teacher's refusal to permit a second-grade student the right to show a videotape during show-and-tell that presented her singing a religious song, and the awarding of a grade of zero to a student paper titled "The Life of Christ."[81] Within the very same schools that embraced progressive child-centeredness, the notion of religion as a powerful cultural force in the life of the child had become completely lost.

The religious revival of the 1980s, however, generated a national discussion on prayer and other forms of religious expression in the schools. By the mid-1980s, congressional debates over school prayer legislation and constitutional amendment proposals had become so heated that in 1984 Congress enacted the Equal Access Act as a compromise measure to fend off further attempts at reintroducing organized prayer into public school classrooms.[82] The act provides that when a public secondary school receives federal funds, which essentially all public schools do, and permit student-led groups to meet on school grounds during noninstructional time, school officials cannot deny equal access to other students on the basis of the religious, political, or other content of their speech. This bipartisan congressional attempt to afford legal protection to student-initiated religious speech while avoiding the constitutional pitfalls of school-sponsored prayer opened the schoolhouse door to religious expression within specific guidelines and gave support to the concept of equal access in a more general sense.

Through the 1990s, the religious speech debate broadened beyond the school prayer issue per se with the concept of religious speech as viewpoint taking center stage. In this debate, *viewpoint* is synonymous with *perspective*. Religious perspective has come to represent a separate viewpoint on apparently secular subject matter rather than a distinct category excludable from constitutional protection as in the past. Legal strategies to develop this concept have drawn from three principles based in constitutional doctrine. The first is a principle of *viewpoint neutrality.* Government cannot prohibit speech on government property based on its religious perspective when speakers have been permitted to speak on the same subject from a nonreligious point of view. The second principle draws a distinction between government speech and private speech. According to this precept, the establishment clause does not provide a sufficiently compelling justification for restricting private religious expression merely because it is religious. As the Court has stated, "There is a crucial difference between *government* speech endorsing religion, which the Establishment Clause forbids, and *private* speech endorsing religion, which the Free Speech and Free Exercise Clauses protect."[83] A related third principle distinguishes between official promotion and mere toleration of student speech. As the Court noted in *Hazelwood,* the school newspaper case, unlike the symbolic speech upheld in

Tinker, publication of student articles required the school not merely to tolerate, but to "lend its name and resources" to the dissemination of student speech.[84] In cases in which the public might perceive school sponsorship, *Tinker*'s standard of material disruption is replaced by *Hazelwood*'s mere reasonableness.

In several closely watched cases, the Supreme Court in recent years has drawn on these principles to develop the concept of *religious viewpoint.* The Court has upheld the right of an outside religious group to use public school facilities after school hours to show a film series on family where similar speakers and subjects previously had been granted access. Here the Court concluded that school officials had denied the request based on the film's religious orientation. The Court also has held that a state university's denial of funds to a student-run newspaper with a Christian editorial slant amounted to viewpoint discrimination. The Court noted that religion may provide "a specific premise, a perspective, a standpoint from which a variety of subjects may be discussed and considered."[85]

This emerging approach differs dramatically from past constitutional understandings which firmly advocated that public education steer clear of any religious content. Of all the legal strategies used by religious conservatives to exercise their religious beliefs in the public schools, the concept of religious speech as viewpoint carries the most potential for expanding the role of religion in public education. Not only has it received support from the Supreme Court, but it has come to serve as a cautious point of consensus among groups traditionally thought to be at polar extremes in the culture wars.

BUILDING CONSENSUS

By the late 1980s, the widely publicized "textbook trials" in Alabama and Tennessee along with continued wranglings in Congress over organized school prayer illustrated the urgent need for some agreement over the role of religion and religious perspectives in the public schools. The first organized step toward a national consensus over the role of religion in American life began with the Williamsburg Charter of 1988, an agreement drafted in consultation with political leaders, scholars, and representatives from a wide range of faith communities. The purpose of the charter, which has more than one hundred signatories, was not merely to reach a truce in the culture wars over religion, but to reach a "solemn" agreement over how "we should contend with each other's deepest differences in the public sphere," to use diversity "not as a point of weakness but as a source of strength."[86] Building on that foundation, individual organizations began to elaborate guidelines while broad-based coalitions of religious leaders and educational and advocacy groups for the first time engaged in open dialogue in an effort to find common ground on the more specific role of religion and religious speech in the public schools.

In 1992, the Anti-Defamation League published a handbook of sample scenarios to assist public schools and their communities in determining the constitutional place of religion in the schools. The publication attempted to dispel some of the pervasive misunderstandings still lingering from the Supreme Court's school prayer decisions of the 1960s, covering such issues as teaching about religious holidays, including religious music or drama in school assemblies, and the distribution of religious materials on school grounds.[87] The league's handbook, nevertheless, was guarded in its support for any of these activities, explicitly reaffirming its position that religion and government should remain separate. Two years later, the Freedom Forum First Amendment Center took a far more accommodationist stand in their comprehensive guide entitled *Finding Common Ground*. Affirmatively denouncing the "avoidance of religion and exclusion of religious perspectives" as "anything but neutral or fair," the handbook not only delineated the current status of the law but suggested strategies that school districts and parents could follow to avoid and resolve conflicts over the curriculum. For example, the handbook advised parents to "work [their] way up the chain of command" and to seek an alternative assignment before attempting to have a book removed from the curriculum or the library. At the same time, it cautioned school officials to solicit input from the community before books are selected and urged them to respond to parents' concerns on the merits without labeling them "censors" or "extremists, zealots, or kooks."[88]

The Anti-Defamation League and the Freedom Forum guidelines laid the cornerstone for a more concerted effort to clarify the role of religion in public schools. In the summer of 1994, Protestant and Jewish leaders issued a four-page document on church–state issues which they presented to Vice President Al Gore in a White House ceremony. This manifesto declared a commitment to church–state separation and denounced organized prayer in the schools. However, it supported voluntary private prayer and religious expression such as Bible reading and religious discussion among students in the classroom. In other words, public schools may not promote a religious perspective, but they should acknowledge and protect the diverse religious perspectives of students.[89]

In March 1995, eighteen religious, educational, and advocacy groups adopted a statement put forth by the Freedom Forum at Vanderbilt University that presented six principles by the title of "Religious Liberty, Public Education, and the Future of American Democracy." The signatories, from PFAW to the Christian Coalition and Citizens for Excellence in Education, pledged to "soften the tone of their rhetoric and demonstrate respect for one another's views." While the group acknowledged that "conflict and debate are vital to democracy," it also recognized the critical importance of "how we debate" and not just "what we debate." Noticeably absent from the list of endorsers were certain groups that have played an active role in litigation on these issues, including the avowedly separationist ACLU, the American Jewish Congress, Americans United for Separation of Church and State, and the American Jewish Committee as well as such staunchly conservative groups as the American Family Foundation, Focus on Family, and the Rutherford Institute. Some of these organizations reportedly found the principles so noncontroversial as to be "worth little in reducing real conflicts."[90]

The following month, the American Jewish Congress, long an advocate of strict church–state separation, convened a similarly diverse group which issued a more substantive statement on the current state of the law. This document evenhandedly addressed a number of controversial issues that in recent years had generated inconsistent rulings from the courts and confusion in classrooms nationwide. In an unexpected turnaround from prevailing attitudes and practices in the schools, the statement confirmed the right of students to "express their religious beliefs in the form of reports, homework and artwork," to make "religious or anti-religious remarks in the ordinary course of classroom discussions or student presentations," and to "distribute religious literature to their classmates" on an equal basis as nonreligious literature. The statement permitted schools to teach sexual abstinence and contraception and granted students a qualified legally protected right to be excused from objectionable aspects of the curriculum. It even permitted the teaching of specific values, including "the dual virtues of moral conviction and tolerance."[91]

This document was intended as a statement of consensus not on what the law should be but rather on what the law currently is. The dialogue from which the statement emerged, however, represented a significant step toward ultimately reaching a common understanding of the role of religion in the schools. There is no doubt that the statement embodied a dramatic shift from the usual bipolar debate toward a middle ground that leaned more toward the accommodationist end than would have been politically predictable even several years previously. In fact, conciliation on this level in the past would have proven unthinkable for some of the organizations signing the document, many of which have persistently presented diametrically opposed arguments in court. In addition to the American Jewish Congress, the drafting committee encompassed groups that had not endorsed *A Shared Vision,* the statement adopted the previous month. Included among these were the ACLU and the American Jewish Committee. Organizations most closely aligned with the religious right, such as the Christian Coalition, Concerned Women for America, Focus on Family, and the American Center for Law and Justice, were marked by their absence from the negotiating table.

In an arguable attempt to outflank Republican proposals validating organized school prayer, President Clinton publicly endorsed the manifesto, calling on the secretary of education and the attorney general to draft guidelines on religion in the schools that would be sent to the nation's fifteen thousand school districts. Before the opening of school the following fall, the secretary of education, Richard Riley, sent to every school district in the nation a statement of principles addressing the permissibility of various forms of religious expression and activity. The president's memorandum, published in national newspapers, represented a stronger endorsement of religious expression in the schools—stopping short of organized prayer—than perhaps any official statement in recent history. It noted that "nothing in the First Amendment converts our public schools into religion-free zones or requires all religious expression to be left at the schoolhouse door."[92] But the message conveyed was far deeper than the words themselves; it officially declared and sanctioned America's changing attitudes toward religion. As the *Wall Street Journal* observed, "This was a large statement by a U.S. President, and it got very close to the heart of what ails the nation. . . . If Ronald Reagan had said [the same thing] about the social worth of simple religious belief in 1982, they would have laughed him off the TV screens. This is 1995, and no one's laughing anymore."[93]

While education and advocacy groups were struggling to reach a common sense of religion in the schools, religious groups returned full circle to the more general yet still unresolved concerns raised in the Williamsburg Charter over the role of religion in public life. In a document entitled *A Cry for Renewal: Let the Voices Be Heard* (1995), a group of evangelical, Protestant, Catholic, and other religious leaders denounced the politicization of religion by extreme elements within Christian churches. The statement expressed frustration with the "old political language and solutions of the Right and Left, liberal and conservative" and called for a renewed sense of politics driven by moral values rather than "partisan warfare." It summoned the Christian community to shed traditional political categories, to apply the values of faith to the pressing social and political issues of racism, sexism, and poverty, and to renew its commitment to the virtues of personal responsibility and character.[94]

These statements and pronouncements represent a pivotal step toward neutralizing some of the religious extremism of the past several decades and particularly toward dispelling some of the confusion over the proper place of religion in the schools. If schools follow the various guidelines presented, then students of faith should feel more comfortable expressing their views and school teachers and administrators should be more amenable to incorporating a range of religious perspectives in appropriate areas of the curriculum. But it would be misleading to characterize these efforts as having achieved a cease-fire in the values-based battle over schooling in America. It undoubtedly is significant that the key offensive players took no part in the most wide-reaching and substantive agreements. Besides, these guidelines, including the president's endorsement, are merely aspirational, having no legal authority or enforcement mechanism. Given the absence of a mandate, not all school districts have made honest attempts at implementing the letter or spirit of these agreements. Even for those who have incorporated them into their school policies, the issues addressed do not cover the entire landscape of those raised consistently and with deep resolve by religious conservatives in and out of court. Whether framed in the language of secular humanism, New Age philosophy, the religion of the occult, or parental privacy rights, larger intractable disputes over the values inculcated through the curriculum still plague school districts nationwide. Disaffected parents still do battle with school officials, and some continue to press the courts to find a legal resolution where the law itself offers little definitive guidance and limited capacity for relief.

Hearings held by the U.S. Commission on Civil Rights in 1998 on the free exercise rights of students reveal that while there now exists wide support for students engaging in religious expression, avoiding conflicts in the captive audience of the schools remains a challenge. According to Steven McFarland of the Center for Law and Religious Freedom, "Students across the country are given the wrong civics lesson when they can't make religious comments in a school forum that allows moral or political comments." Ronald Rissler, legal coordinator for the Rutherford Institute, cited numerous incidents in which teachers or administrators have prohibited students from selecting religious topics for class assignments or from distributing religious materials to fellow students despite the 1995 guidelines. Experts also testified that the academic treatment of religion has been abysmal. "Religion is treated as a trivial detail of history," argued Warren Nord of the University of North Carolina. "Students learn that religion is irrelevant to the search for truth." On the other hand, Elliot Mincberg, general counsel of PFAW, warned that some "Bible as history" courses are teaching faith beliefs as real events in history. "You can't teach the Resurrection like the Gettysburg Address," he stated. The panel further heard concerns raised by the growing Muslim community over the accommodation of daily prayers required by Islam. Muslims are obliged to pray five times a day, and one of the prayers occurs at midday, when children are in school. The question arises as to whether school administrators should or must affirmatively accommodate such prayers.[95]

Obviously religious conservatives embrace a different cultural paradigm from that shared by most Americans, including mainline Christians and religious liberals of all denominations. At the margins of their legal claims, however, lie parental concerns that evoke wider agreement when pressed on the larger population. As the Bedford case that follows illustrates, that agreement all too frequently gets destroyed in the crossfire of extreme rhetoric and name-calling.

Chapter 6 Struggling with Satan

Message to the Public
"Stop the Witch Hunt"

So began a full-page advertisement in local newspapers in Westchester County, New York, in November 1995. Signed by upward of nine hundred parents and residents of the Bedford Central School System, the notice was a passionate defense of the district's teachers, administrators, and curriculum: "Our teachers do not have a pro-pagan or pro-witchcraft agenda. Teaching about historical events is not promoting evil. . . . We live in a world that is much larger and more diverse than our community, and it is an important goal to educate our children with understanding. We support the Bedford Central School's vision "providing an environment which builds the foundation for lifelong learning and responsible citizenship."[1] The advertisement ended with an invitation to Bedford residents and school staff to participate in a superintendent's open forum the following week at the district's high school.

To anyone unaware of the unusual course of events that provoked this advertisement, this was a shocking and perplexing appeal. It certainly defied the average New Yorker's view of Bedford Village with its quaint town common and rolling acres of horse farms—weekend escape for New York's old wealth and more recently home to a growing cadre of Hollywood luminaries, performing artists, and other "big-buckskys," as *Vanity Fair* wryly noted in 1999. A community or cultural event can bring out the likes of Ralph Lauren, André Previn, Susan Sarandon, Christopher Reeve, Eartha Kitt, Glenn Close, and the environmentalist Robert F. Kennedy, Jr., who monitors the New York City watershed of which Bedford is the center. All of them live in Bedford proper or in the neighboring towns that make up the Bedford school district. As the *New York Times* has described it, Bedford (including Bedford Village and Pound Ridge) is "the new anti-Hamptons . . . Aspen without the fuss, Montana before Ted Turner, East Hampton without the traffic, the scene or the gossip columnists stirring things up."[2] The advertisement also defied the conventional wisdom about the Bedford public school system, one of the most well financed and academically touted in the state, where expenditures per student approach $16,000 a year,[3] at least 90 percent of the students perform at or above grade level on statewide tests in reading and math, and the district high school in 1998 received a Blue Ribbon award for excellence—one of only 166 high schools in the country to achieve that coveted honor.[4]

The advertisement conjured up images of the Salem witch trials and the Scopes monkey trial in Tennessee. A more believable setting might have been Puritan New England or the southern Bible Belt, but not Westchester County, the bedroom community of choice to sophisticated New Yorkers. One had to wonder what had brought such a sizeable segment of the Bedford school community to publicly appeal for a stop to what they perceived as a witch-hunt.[5]

IMAGES OF THE OCCULT

It all began rather innocently in January 1995 when the mother of a fourth grader at the Pound Ridge Elementary School wanted to spend more time with her nine-year-old son. He and some of his classmates shared an interest in playing the fantasy card game *Magic: The Gathering,* and so she volunteered to host a before-school *Magic* Club one day a week. The school sent a letter home to parents of fourth graders announcing the club's formation and including an agreement for the child and parent to sign. The letter identified the activity as the *Magic* Club without any description of the game but listed a series of rules such as "no card swapping" and "bring your own cards."[6] Parents who agreed to the activity were at least somewhat aware of the nature of the game and the graphic depictions on the cards.

The club met in a fourth-grade classroom at 8:10 every Wednesday morning with the mother as chaperon. The first five sessions brought in an average of twenty-two students each week, about evenly divided between boys and girls. The meetings were so successful that another series was planned. The notice sent home to the players' parents announcing the next five-week session read in part as follows: "This group of youngsters has been fantastic to work with. . . . They have made a special effort to teach this very complicated game to others and this has been a special time. They all deserve congratulations."[7] At the same time, a teacher at the Fox Lane Middle School was running a *Magic* Club after school on Fridays as part of an enrichment program. No one could foresee how what apparently was taken for a benign extracurricular activity would soon propel the Bedford schools into the national spotlight and eventually into federal court. Neither could anyone foresee how cultural violence would become linked to a rash of school violence nationwide provoking widespread debate in the years to come.

Magic: The Gathering is produced by Wizards of the Coast, based in Renton, Washington. Wizards is the brainchild of Peter Adkinson, a former Boeing computer analyst who organized the company out of his basement in the early 1990s and began marketing fantasy role-playing games. Richard Garfield, a professor of combinational mathematics with ten years' experience in designing games, tried to convince Adkinson to produce the game *RoboRally,* but Adkinson declined, perceiving instead a market for a game that could be "played quickly, with minimal equipment, a game that would go over well at conventions." Adkinson suggested the concept of a fantasy trading card game, and Garfield agreed to develop it.[8]

Thus evolved *Magic: The Gathering.* For the next year, Adkinson and Garfield tested the game in Adkinson's basement on friends and relatives, hired artists, and traded talent for stock options. Their first big order sold out in six weeks.[9] Within two years, Wizards of the Coast was transformed from an obscure publisher of esoteric games into a thriving business whose annual sales in 1995 exceeded $65 million. By that point the company had developed a following of savvy collectors who traded cards in seven languages at conventions, in game shops, and over the Internet.[10]

Magic is billed as a "game of battle" in which opponents represent sorcerers who attempt to drive one another out of the "mystical multiverse of Dominia," a Dark

Ages fantasy world. It is a "magical duel to the death."[11] Each player tries to beat the opposition by loading his or her deck with cards bearing such names as Drudge Skeletons, the Wrath of God, and the Prodigal Sorcerer, each of which carries various gradations of power. The game also features serpents, ogres, trolls, and fairies. The cards are divided into spells and lands. Players pay for spell casting with colored magic, or "manna," generated by one of five types of land—mountains (red), swamps (black), plains (white), islands (blue), and forests (green).[12]

The cards represent more than nine hundred magic spells, some of which summon fantastic creatures while others have defensive powers. A starter deck contains sixty cards, each one unique. Players can improve their deck with cards that cast stronger spells, either by purchasing booster packs or by trading with friends or on the market. Cards with strong spells are rare, which sends their values soaring. Originally designed with high school and college students in mind, *Magic* soon became popular with the elementary and middle school set. The proponents of *Magic* include Mensa, the high-I.Q. organization, which bestowed upon the game a "Mensa Top Five Mind Games" award in 1994.[13]

The game has enjoyed enormous popularity nationwide—young people's attraction to it is similar in many respects to the *Dungeons and Dragons* phenomenon of the seventies—and is promoted by its producers as "a game of mathematical relationships." In a letter to parents, Jeff Harris of Wizards of the Coast explained that "the fantasy story element is used to present the mathematical concepts . . . in an easily digestible and entertaining fashion."[14] That apparently is how the administration and staff of the Bedford schools saw the game and how a sizeable and vocal group of parents saw it. The Bedford school board president would later state publicly that she allowed her children to play *Magic,* finding it "a perfectly enriching opportunity," one that "stimulates the intellect and uses social, math and English skills."[15] The superintendent of schools shared those sentiments, assuring the community that he "would not have a problem with [his] child playing this [game]."[16] The local Presbyterian church hosted a *Magic* tournament organized by the pastor's son and his friends.

But Ceil DiNozzi, a legal secretary and mother of twins in the fourth grade at Pound Ridge Elementary School, did not share these favorable opinions of *Magic.* Neither did MaryAnn DiBari, a grandmother and pro bono criminal defense attorney raising her two granddaughters. In fact, *Magic: The Gathering* would become the first of many value-laden disagreements between Bedford school officials and these two deeply orthodox Catholic women, who saw themselves as leading a crusade against the forces of evil.

THE SEEDS OF DISSENT

When DiNozzi's sons brought home the letter announcing the game, she ignored it. But when she saw some of the *Magic* cards they had acquired at school, she became concerned. She grew even more distressed when other children began harassing her sons, who were not *Magic* players, with taunts of, "Here's the card in your face."[17] DiBari became equally alarmed. Even though her granddaughters were not playing the game, she later described how "they were exposed to it at the school bus stop, on the playground, in the lunchroom. They [other children] would put these cards in their cubbies so that they would get frightened. . . . They did not want to go to school. [Children] were swinging on ropes in the gym chanting, 'possessed,' 'sacrifice.' They really got into the role-playing aspect of this. Children on the bus were harming other children. They were using the power and shouting, 'I have power. I want that seat. Get up.' The children who were sitting there would be assaulted with the most graphic kind of imagery."[18] According to DiBari, *Magic: The Gathering* is "steeped in the hidden language, imagery, signs and rites of at least thirty satanic cults . . . a codification of the beliefs, practices and perceptions of the new Satanists of today.[19] It's black magic and mind control. . . . It uses incantations to the devil, contact from below. It is a real belief in a real bad religion."[20] The cards "come straight from hell."[21]

To DiBari and DiNozzi, the problem was larger than just the game of *Magic.* They decided to form a grassroots coalition of parents, teachers, and citizens, naming it the Association Against the Seduction of Children (AASOC). The two women took their issues to Bruce Dennis, the superintendent of schools. Dennis, a seasoned administrator who had cut his educational teeth in the New York City public schools, knew that the right thing to do administratively and legally was to hear them out, to provide them with process. He invited them to meet with him, several school board members, and several parents whose children were involved in the game, including the mother who had organized the before-school program in the elementary school. DiBari and DiNozzi were accompanied at the meeting by Victoria Altman, a parent who would later join them in litigation against the district, and George Hogben, a Westchester psychiatrist and expert in the spiritual and psychological effects of the occult.

In Hogben's opinion, the game promotes

> occult practices and really a type of religion or so-called religion. . . . It's promoting an interaction with the supernatural. . . . When you're in a state of altered consciousness, . . . you open yourself up to the influence of the devil.[22] I think it's dangerous. . . . It talks about the devil, spells and sorcery, blocking spells, witchcraft and

occult practices. When you begin to deal with the occult, you open yourself to a lot of forces.[23] Feeding that stuff into the psyche of a child has an impact on the formation of that individual's mind.[24]

Dennis and the others listened intently, and at the conclusion of the meeting the superintendent placed a thirty-day moratorium on the game to allow the district time to study the matter further. Over the following month, he consulted two psychiatrists and a psychologist, asking them to address three issues: whether the "potential impact" of the game was "so disturbing or dangerous" that it should not be played in the schools, whether the content of the cards "posed a mental health hazard of any kind," and whether there was "any need to restrict voluntary participation, with parental consent, according to the child's age or developmental stage."[25]

Judging from the language and focus of the questions, it was clear that the district had dismissed DiNozzi's and DiBari's religious objections to the cards. Board member and psychologist Herb Nieburg confirmed that observation, agreeing that whereas DiNozzi and other parents viewed *Magic* from a "theological perspective," the school district could consider only whether it was a "psychological hazard."[26] School officials could more readily resolve the administrative question through expert advice. The religion question, on the other hand, raised a serious legal problem that they could not dismiss so easily. Yet the two women could not be rebuffed, holding fast to their religious argument. They solicited an opinion from the Reverend Bernard Bush, a Jesuit priest and trained psychologist from California who was recognized as an expert in the occult. The Reverend Bush's reply addressed both the psychological dangers and the religious aspects of the game:

> The game encourages magical thinking which is not based in normal reality and as such can lead to serious mental disorder. . . . [T]he highly competitive nature of the game, which requires a player to be reduced to zero, could stir the combative and aggressive qualities of a person. . . . [T]he young . . . should instead be learning cooperation and non-violent conflict resolution—certainly not reducing an opponent to zero. . . . The images and terms used in the game are not neutral in a religious sense. . . . [T]he energy spoken of in the Magic game (mana) is referred to in our scriptures and has a religious meaning. . . . [T]he images and words of the Magic game are promoting a very religious point of view. At the very least the religion is paganism or witchcraft.[27]

DiBari forwarded a copy of the opinion to the superintendent along with an open letter addressed to him and circulated on behalf of AASOC. The letter suggested that the conflict was shifting into legal gear: "It is the position of the coalition that 'Black Magic' has a chilling effect on students' First Amendment rights to worship freely—absent intimidation."[28] This was Dennis's first hint that he was dealing with a "newly formed grassroots-coalition" and not just "a group of parents who had divergent opinions about the game '*Magic*.'"[29]

The announcement of the moratorium halting the game on school grounds set off an immediate and visceral reaction throughout the Bedford community, much of it played out in the press. One local newspaper, the *Pound Ridge Review*, recognized the religious implications of the cards and called for the game to be permanently removed from the schools. The editorial noted that "parents are more qualified to judge what activities are appropriate for their children, but the game doesn't belong in school and should be played instead in friends' houses. . . . Given the relationship of religion and schools, would the game be played if the apostles, the Star of David or other religious symbols were depicted on the cards instead? Not likely."[30]

Others in the community thought differently, expressing outrage over what they perceived as an attempt at censorship. The owner of a local shop that sold *Magic* cards contacted the ACLU, which agreed to look into the issue. The shopowner's statement to the press reached to the heart of the issue for many community members: "Envision these parents coming in and saying they have some concerns about books in the library, and they close the library doors for 30 days."[31] On a similar note, one parent fired off a blistering letter directly to the superintendent, voicing serious misgivings and deep fears that would resurface repeatedly as the controversy gained momentum over the following months and years. For him, the issue was "freedom of expression and freedom to pursue an educational opportunity without interference from religious groups and their moral agenda. . . . Should I instruct my children to be tolerant of the intolerant? Sounds to me like some misguided advice given to German Jews in the '30s as their books were being burned. It didn't work then and it didn't work in the Spanish Inquisition, nor did it work at the Salem witch trials. In fact . . . one of the most tragic themes in history is tolerance of the intolerable."[32]

Students jumped into the fray to defend their right to play the game. A group of middle school *Magic* players, including the son of the Reverend Paul Alcorn, pastor of the local Presbyterian church, decided to make their voices heard. They organized a tournament in the Bedford Presbyterian Church. They wanted school board members and concerned parents actually to see how the game was played. Players were charged a three-dollar entrance fee, the proceeds to be donated to the Midnight Run, a church program that delivered food to the homeless in Manhattan.

The superintendent and several board members attended the tournament, in which about fifty players participated. Doug Ferguson, a representative of the card manufacturer, Wizards of the Coast, flew in from Washington to reassure parents that the game was not evil. He also met with the superintendent and board members. In a statement to the local press, Ferguson extolled the academic merits of *Magic:* "It's good social activity. . . . It makes them think. There's a lot of reading. It includes Chaucer and Shakespeare quotes." He also confirmed that the company had removed what appeared to be a pentagram from the background of one card.[33]

The Reverend Alcorn soon learned that several community members, including DiNozzi and DiBari, considered his well-intentioned hosting of the tournament in his church as scandalous. Someone in the community had tipped off the broadcast media. As Alcorn put it, "All of a sudden, I was getting calls from TV news stations wondering why a church was hosting a satanic card game."[34] Yet he saw no "validity in any charge of demonism." In fact, he viewed the game "much like the religious battle between good and evil" represented in the writings of J. R. R. Tolkien and C. S. Lewis.[35]

While the media kept a close watch over the "devil in Bedford," the three mental health experts reviewed the *Magic* game and submitted their opinions to the superintendent. The first opinion, from Flemming Graae, noted "visual symbols of a vaguely religious sort, and a large amount of representation suggesting distortions of perception and laws of nature, violence, and bizarre or somewhat grotesque images of decay, dying or death." Graae warned school officials that "the violent and rather graphic images pose a potential difficulty for some children, especially those anxious or prone to poor reality testing." Yet he did not believe that *Magic* posed "a mental health problem to children over the age of 9."

The second opinion was from Christopher Bogart, whose evaluation was largely positive, noting how the game "socialized competition and controlled expression of aggression." Yet he admitted that certain cards struck him as "gruesome and explicit in detail." He offered a word of caution, warning that no game "is without any risk" and that parents should "monitor their child's participation to be certain that their child maintains an appropriate perspective." The third opinion, from Paulina Kernberg, was brief and guarded. It cautioned that "regardless of age, emphasis should be placed on who is the user of the game."

She went on to explain that "children or teenagers with emotional or behavioral disturbances may have untoward reactions in the areas of impulse control, contact with reality, and time spent."[36]

With the three opinions in hand, the superintendent took the opportunity at the next public board meeting to review the feedback he had received and to recommend an end to the moratorium. The board voted six to one in favor of reinstating the game. The one dissenting vote came from James Markowski, a lawyer whose primary reservation was the legal risk of turning the district's elementary classrooms into a "public forum" if the game continued.[37] If that occurred, other groups could claim a free speech right under the First Amendment to use school facilities for similar purposes.[38] As a secondary yet significant matter, he said he considered the cards tasteless.[39] A second board member, the psychologist Herb Nieburg, a specialist in cults, had earlier conceded that he found some of the cards disturbing.[40] Nevertheless, he believed that the school district had followed adequate procedures in assessing the merits of the game and so agreed that the ban should be lifted.[41]

The board meeting elicited mixed responses from the community. One parent saw *Magic* as merely "an extension of what children see on television."[42] Another had "no objection to parents who want their children to play the game," but he was "raising his children differently," screening "what they see on television and what they read."[43] After the meeting, Dennis sent a letter reporting the experts' findings to parents throughout the district. The letter made clear that students could not play *Magic* during "recess, lunch, or at times other than during this club activity." The mailing included a consent form for parents to sign allowing their child to play the game on school grounds.[44]

The day after the school board meeting ended the moratorium, a letter from DiBari was hand-delivered to Dennis's office. The letter roundly criticized the superintendent for not having announced the discussion and vote in advance of the meeting. As far as DiBari was concerned, Dennis had not only "misrepresented, or misconceived" the evaluations submitted by his experts, but had "rigged" the hearing by excluding the opinions of her experts, Hogben and the Reverend Bush. She urged him "to alleviate the tension dividing our community and revisit a fair hearing on the issue."[45] Dennis responded swiftly and decisively, refusing to hold a special hearing but inviting her to voice her dissatisfaction at a future board meeting.[46]

School officials seemed satisfied, believing that they had resolved the issue on secular and psychological grounds. But the two women still saw the problem differently and would not concede defeat on their religious concerns. DiNozzi flatly warned the superintendent that she would see to it that he went down as "the superintendent who promoted satanism in the schools."[47] The next round of correspondence ended with DiBari requesting the use of the high school auditorium for her own informational forum on *Magic: The Gathering* and Dennis inviting her in response to rent the auditorium for a fee.[48] In a statement to the local press, DiBari warned that she was willing to litigate to keep *Magic* off school grounds: "We're saying the school can't do any activity that promotes or inhibits religious activity."[49]

In the meantime, the Christian Coalition of Westchester County had mailed a thirteen-question survey to school board candidates countywide, asking them if they approved of students playing *Magic: The Gathering* on school property before, during, or after school hours. From the perspective of Wendy Holibaugh, chairwoman of the chapter, "It [*Magic*] does not belong in the schools. . . . The schools are in the business of educating, not accommodating games that, in essence, teach the occult."[50] And so the mere fad of a card game had turned into a litmus test for school board candidates throughout the county, while the controversy in Bedford was about to take on a far wider scope than anyone could have imagined.

As the school year drew to a close, DiBari, DiNozzi, and the Altmans requested that school officials place in their children's files a document paraphrasing the language of the federal Protection of Pupil Rights Amendment, popularly known as the Hatch Amendment.[51] Unanimously passed by Congress in 1978, the amendment gives parents the right to inspect all instructional materials used in connection with any research or program "designed to explore or develop new or unproven teaching methods or techniques." The law also requires that school districts receive parental consent in writing before administering any survey, analysis, or evaluation to students that would reveal certain personal information regarding political affiliations; mental and psychological problems; sex behavior and attitudes; illegal, antisocial, self-incriminating, and demeaning behavior; legally recognized privileged or analogous relationships; or income. Implicit in this right to prior consent is an entitlement to exemption from any "offensive" activity.

Despite enthusiastic support in Congress, the amendment remained without implementing regulations for six years. Educators and federal officials were hoping to avoid putting any teeth into what they viewed as a dangerous incursion into the management of schools. Finally, at the urging of Phyllis Schlafly, founder and head of the Eagle Forum and longtime leader of New Right causes, the Department of Education held seven regional hearings around the country and issued regulations in 1984. The hearings generated more than thirteen hundred pages of testimony from parents, teachers, and others describing what they perceived as psychological intrusions into the behavior, moral choices, religious commitment, and family relationship of the nation's public school students. The resulting regulations provide explicit procedures for parents to report violations to the secretary of education and authorize the secretary to take enforcement action against school districts and contractors who fail to comply voluntarily with the law. The secretary can go so far as to withhold or even terminate federal funds awarded to a school district found in noncompliance. But the regulations clearly state that the law applies solely to limited categories of research and experimentation programs funded through the Department of Education.

The form letter submitted by the Bedford parents was modeled after one prepared by the Maryland Coalition of Concerned Parents on Privacy Rights in Public Education and reproduced in Schlafly's book *Child Abuse in the Classroom*.[52] Commonly used by Christian fundamentalist parents and critically referred to in mainstream circles as the "stretch letter" or "stretch technique," these letters typically misinterpret the Hatch Amendment, making it appear as if the statute applied to all activities within a district despite language to the contrary in the regulations.[53] Warning of the dangers of federal "thought control" and "educator change agents," Schlafly herself urges parents to pursue a broader interpretation on the grounds that "most psychological curricula and teacher training were either developed with the use of federal funding, or appear on lists of federally approved programs, or the teachers were trained how to use them in workshops financed with federal funds." The "burden of proof," she tells parents, "is on the school to prove that any given program has *no* federal funding involved."[54]

Yet even Sen. Orrin Hatch, the chief sponsor of the amendment, speaking from the Senate floor shortly after the regulations had gone into effect, stated expressly that the statute was intended to cover only programs that directly operate under federal funds. In fact, Senator Hatch raised potential federalism implications if the amendment were interpreted more broadly. He forcefully warned Congress of the dangers of placing veto power over the curriculum in the hands of federal authority, here the secretary of education, regardless of the source of funding. "Do we want a Federal official to tell local school boards what is or what is not appropriate curriculum materials?" he asked rhetorically. "This would be the first step," he cautioned, "in the direction of a federally sanctioned national curriculum, something that is anathema to both parents and educators, and at the present time, patently illegal."[55]

The parents' letter tracked the model letter verbatim, opening with a reminder that "under U.S. legislation and federal court decisions, parents have the primary responsibility for their children's education, and pupils have certain rights which the school may not deny. Parents have the right to be assured that their children's beliefs and moral values are not undermined by the schools." They requested that their children be excluded from a lengthy list of materials and practices without their prior review and written consent. Included among these were values clarification, the use of moral dilemmas, discussion of religious or moral standards, role-playing, sensitivity training, magic-circle techniques, sociograms, death education, drug and alcohol education, discussions of witchcraft or the occult, keeping a diary or journal or logbook, discussion of nuclear war, globalism, education in human sexuality, evolution, and nonacademic personality tests—all practices commonly challenged by religious conservatives. The letter closed with a warning that federal funds could be withdrawn for violations of the act.[56]

The response came directly from the superintendent's office, noting correctly that the statute is limited to specific psychological tests, surveys, and research supported by federal funds. As one principal observed, even if the law covered non–federally funded activities, "parents couldn't object to pieces [of programs] or we wouldn't be able to run any kind of program for kids."[57] The school year ended on this ominous note.

THE BATTLE ESCALATES

For the parents, children, and teachers of Bedford, summer promised to heal the wounds of the school year's battles over *Magic*. But that promise would not be realized. Although the *Magic* club would not resume meeting in September, the game in fact proved to be just the tip of the iceberg. As Ceil DiNozzi would later describe it, "'Magic' just opened our eyes to what is going on in our school system. . . . This is a crisis situation."[58] Over that summer, she and MaryAnn DiBari moved into a crisis mode, and the conflict between good and evil escalated into a broad-based attack on the Bedford curriculum. The women immersed themselves in anti–New Age literature and wove themselves into a network of clergy and like-minded experts in psychology and the occult. In the process, they solicited written opinions on *Magic* and identified speakers for a forum discussion they would host that fall. They sent seventy-two sample cards to Linda Osborne Blood, author of *The New Satanists*. In reply Blood described "the imagery of predominantly malevolent occultism employed in the design . . . [as] so overwhelming that it effectively supersedes and negates any other 'educational' purpose claimed for the cards by the manufacturers."[59] From John Cardinal O'Connor, the Catholic archbishop of New York, came a brief response informing them that he had assigned a staff member "to investigate the 'Magic' problem." He referred them to the Catholic League for Religious and Civil Rights, a lay Catholic antidefamation organization founded in 1973 and funded by nonchurch donations.[60] They quickly acted on the referral.

In examining the women's concerns, the league's president, William Donohue, became troubled by "the surreptitious nature" of *Magic* and saw its use in schools as "smack[ing] of a satanistic approach."[61] Donohue suggested that they contact the American Catholic Lawyers Association, which ultimately represented them in litigation.[62] He also directed them to Paul Vitz, a New York University psychology professor and convert to Catholicism, who was no newcomer to the religious culture wars. Vitz was among a rare breed of academics from prestigious universities who sympathized with religious conservatives. Not only had he written extensively on the biased representation of religion and traditional values in textbooks, but he had served as an expert witness for the parents in the *Mozert* case in Tennessee in the late 1980s (see chap. 5).[63] According to Vitz, "The idea of using the game 'Magic' to teach mathematics or special kinds of rational thought seems . . . absurd. . . . It would not surprise me," he continued, "if the imagery and plot-structures of 'Magic' had a pro-witchcraft and pro-pagan agenda, and it undermined traditional worldviews (whether Christian, Jewish or Islamic) in those who used it regularly."[64]

From Monsignor Dermot Brennan, vicar of Northern Westchester and Putnam County, came a similar response: "I am appalled that parents can see educational value in such a game. . . . Most insidious of all is the obvious connection with the cult of Satan and the spirit underworld that is advanced by this so-called game."[65] The Reverend George Mather, a Lutheran pastor from California and author of *The Dictionary of Cults, Sects, Religions and the Occult* stated unqualifiedly, "The game has no redeeming qualities, and will only serve as a doorway into the occult. It will create fear because of its superstitious character, reinforce bad behavior by encouraging selfishness and it might even aid in justifying rebellion and rage toward societal norms."[66]

DiBari and DiNozzi soon delivered on their promise (or threat) to Bruce Dennis. They would hold an "informational forum" and provide a "fair hearing" on the subject of *Magic: The Gathering*. Even though the extracurricular *Magic* Club was no longer meeting on school grounds, the game constituted a starting point for the women to launch a sweeping attack on the curriculum. As DiNozzi later explained in frustration, it was "one lesson after another to desensitize the children to anything traditional."[67] She was "bombarded by her children's stories of 'guided imagery' and 'relaxation exercises' in the class" and was "offended by a curriculum that [was] obsessed with negativity and frightening themes. We know the harm associated with everything that's going on. We just feel the public needs to know."[68]

As it turned out, the forum reached well beyond the *Magic* game and proved to be a turning point in the controversy. It swept fear through an increasingly vocal segment of the Bedford school population, and in some respects made religious fundamentalism a scapegoat for trivializing and dismissing educational concerns that had little if any connection with religion or the occult.

A flyer announcing the forum went out to the Bedford school community and beyond. It read as follows:

Parents, teachers and
concerned citizens

You are invited to an
Informational Seminar on

The Rise of New Age
Occultism and
The Influence of
'Magick' on
School-Aged Children

Fox Lane High School
Thursday, Sept. 28, 1995
7:00–10:00 p.m.

Sponsored by:
Association Against the
Seduction of Children
(A not-for-profit organization dedicated
to preserving the principle of integrity
in public school education)

The event, financed largely by the two women from personal funds, drew an estimated three hundred people, many of them apparently from prayer groups and churches outside the district.[69] Wendy Holibaugh was in the audience. She later made clear that although she supported the organizers and trusted their integrity, the coalition had not helped organize or pay for the event.[70]

Magic cards enlarged on a wide screen displayed to the audience pictures of demons, enchanted sorcerers, grave robbers, and circles of protection, while six experts from across the country explained why the game is synonymous with the occult. Among the speakers were Craig Branch, a popular speaker on the New Age and public education and author of *Thieves of Innocence;* the Reverend David Brown, founder of Logos Communications Consortium and consultant on the occult to law enforcement officials; the Reverend Larry Gesy, author of *Today's Dangerous Cults and Movements* and cult consultant to the Archdiocese of Baltimore; Steve Kosser, an expert on mental imagery; the Reverend George Mather; and Steve Russo, internationally known evangelist and coauthor of *The Seduction of Our Children.*

The forum focused on the dangers of the occult. The Reverend Gesy warned the audience that "this game is a philosophy, a religion of the occult that has no place in a public school system. No place even as a game at home." The Reverend Brown reaffirmed Gesy's view: "Magic cards teach religious principles in the real occult."[71] Several speakers, however, used the opportunity to go even further, criticizing some general practices and some more specific to the Bedford schools. Several of these had provoked a particularly negative response from DiNozzi and DiBari. Portraying these as manifestations of religious or cultlike indoctrination, they pointedly attacked New Age philosophy; meditation, guided imagery, and relaxation techniques; self-esteem programs; science experiments that demonstrate owl pellets of undigested fur and bone to learn about the animal's eating habits (allegedly focusing on a cult of death); library books that emphasize death and dying; songs celebrating the forces of nature and animals (allegedly paganish); and a lesson that allegedly included making clay dolls of the Hindu god Ganesha with the teacher purportedly telling the children to pray to the god.

If the women had intended for the forum to gather community support for their concerns, they widely missed their mark. To the contrary, their meeting served to mobilize the community against what many perceived as an organized effort by the religious right to gain control of their schools. As one local news reporter later observed, "The forum angered numerous parents, students and educators, who called the claims absurdities whipped up by a handful of ultra-conservatives."[72] Many claimed the complaints were ludicrous. Matthew Freeman, research director of PFAW, placed the events in more national scope: "What you are seeing [in Bedford] is a classic tale of religious-right organized work, judging by the rhetoric and the targets."[73]

Community members bombarded the local press with letters voicing fears of censorship and intolerance. One high school student who had attended the forum wrote, "What I found myself listening to . . . was not the voices of a solicitous group of people who cared about our education, but rather a radical Christian organization which proceeded to preach to the audience throughout the night about raising children with 'wholesome Christian values,' and the sins of practicing many common activities. . . . Yes, I was scared."[74] Another resident expressed similar fears. "Last night's presentation," he wrote, "was a classic example of the manipulation the radical Christian right is capable of. . . Hinduism and Buddhism were lumped together with Satanism, and everyone tolerant of the game, or indeed, tolerant of free speech, was painted as an enemy of family values. . . . Be afraid. The Middle Ages are returning, and, courtesy of Pat Robertson, the witch hunt is on!"[75]

One local newspaper published a blistering editorial excoriating the attackers and summoning the community to action:

> Aided by outside groups that have no business criticizing schools they virtually know nothing about, a small group of parents are trying to conjure up something ugly from a kids' card game, science experiments and a lesson about another people's culture. That's magic designed to create fear and hate—and it shouldn't be tolerated in [this] northern Westchester school district. But it shouldn't be ignored, either. [District residents] who support the separation of church and state guaranteed to Americans have a responsibility to speak out against last week's unwarranted attack on their schools. Not doing so is inviting conservative Christians to wrest control of the curriculum.[76]

School officials denounced the group and their accusations, some of which they argued were distortions of the truth. "These are the most bizarre accusations I've ever heard," said Superintendent Dennis. "This was never about *Magic Cards*, it was just a convenient way to start a campaign of censorship and control." But Dennis went even further in his assessment of the situation. "This is part of a much larger agenda," he said with certitude. "I think I would have to be blind not to see it."[77]

More immediately, the forum had a chilling effect on Bedford's classrooms. Teachers were confused, apprehensive, and plagued with uncertainty. They turned to school administrators to clarify whether they should continue with particular lessons and materials. Included among their list of concerns were a Newbury-award winning book that mentioned the Bible and different cultures, writing assignments that could be interpreted as too personal, and even class-room Halloween parties.[78] One teacher sought advice from the National Coalition Against Censorship.[79]

Dennis quickly moved to ease the fears and insecurities voiced by the professional staff, but he also wanted to make clear that he appreciated the seriousness of the charges against the district. He circulated an internal memorandum among the teachers, acknowledging that several of them "had been placed on the defensive" by "a very small number of parents." The memo went on to state, "While I believe, as educators, that we need to demonstrate sensitivity to the diverse values and beliefs held by all residents of this school district, I consider it of critical importance that we be aware of the efforts by a very small handful of people to substitute their judgment about appropriate materials and teaching for that of our well-trained and highly able professional staff. Further, I regard their seeming agenda as inconsistent with the wishes of the vast majority of the community. . . . There is much at stake."[80]

Dennis undoubtedly realized that although there appeared to be a strong measure of support for the district, he had to mobilize that support and provide a public forum in which members of the school community could express "how they felt about their children's education and the attacks to which we have been subjected." In speaking in the collective "we" he implicitly drew the wider community of parents into the circle as objects of the women's charges and consequently allies of the district. In early November he distributed a memorandum to parents announcing a Superintendent's Colloquium. Provocatively titled "Ending the 'Witch Hunt,'" the meeting was to be held at the high school later that month. He closed the memo by expressing the hope that the event would correct "the distortions and inaccuracies" that had been circulated about the district.[81]

THE COMMUNITY RESPONDS AND REACTS

These were the events that brought more than nine hundred parents and residents of the Bedford Central School District to make a public appeal to "stop the witch hunt." Circulated by two mothers and published in local newspapers, the message expressed anger at the recent attacks against the district and urged "all who are concerned" to participate in the superintendent's open forum. These were also the events that brought a crowd estimated at more than one thousand people to pack the high school auditorium beyond capacity that November evening. Attendance at the forum was limited to school staff and residents of the school district; local clergy and members of the press were also invited to attend. On hand were camera crews from nearly every news station, in addition to PBS, along with reporters from every area newspaper.

In his opening remarks, the superintendent described the earlier forum organized by DiBari and DiNozzi as "the most manipulated public event" he had attended "in 27 years of public education."[82] He then went on explicitly but with a hint of sarcasm to defend the various books, practices, and programs under attack. As described by a local news reporter, "In a manner which at times resembled a stand-up comic," Dennis went down the list of accusations.[83] One by one he displayed on an overhead projector the covers of books the women found objectionable: *Bridge to Terabithia* by Katherine Patterson, *My Side of the Mountain* by Jean Craighead George, *Changes* by Anthony Browne. Students who obviously were familiar with the titles laughed in disbelief as each one appeared on the screen. He also took the opportunity to defend the district's use of the Yale Decision-Making Program, a target of attack, which he described as teaching adolescents how to "make good decisions" and to "develop healthy coping strategies" for stress.

MaryAnn DiBari followed Dennis to the podium. He had waived the speakers' three-minute time limit and allowed her the fifteen minutes she had requested. Facing a hostile audience, some of them wearing witch hats or horns, she addressed the crowd in a steady and deliberate voice. She tried to assure them that AASOC was "not engaged in censorship." "We burn no books and restrict no one other than our own children from reading anything in school or out of school," she said. She expressed concern for her granddaughters. For them, opting out meant either staying home from school or sitting on the library bench or even on the "punishment" bench outside the principal's office. She underscored her support for the separation of church and state and her interest in "raising the consciousness" of the community. She explained that the association and its members "look only to the fundamental right to cling to the seeds of tradition, truth, and family. . . . Moral relativism . . . is not the only answer to those of us who believe in absolutes." She also explained how she and her husband had sent six children through the Bedford public schools "without a hitch" and how she wanted the "tradition of excellence" to return "in the midst of revolutionary change."[84]

The superintendent then opened the discussion to questions and comments from the audience. For more than two hours, an almost steady stream of parents, students, and staff stood up to defend the district and its curriculum and renounce the two women who had provoked the controversy. About half of the speakers were students. One proudly informed the crowd that 75 percent of the high school and 47 percent of the middle school students had signed a student-initiated petition supporting the district, including a total of more than 920 signatures.[85] A parent who would later support the district in an amicus curiae brief in court received a standing ovation when she compared the women's accusations to Salem in 1692, Munich in 1938, and Washington in the 1950s. "When a witch hunt begins," she warned the group, "it is not only morally wrong but ultimately dangerous for good citizens to be silent."[86] Another parent said she was fearful that DiBari did not share her view of public education, which, as she described it, "is one of the vehicles through which we train ourselves to participate in a democracy. One of the things essential to that is open mindedness and respectful consideration of different points of view."[87]

The Reverend Alcorn, the local Presbyterian pastor who had sponsored the *Magic* tournament the previous year, read a letter on behalf of the Northern Westchester Clergy Association calling for confidence in the school administration and staff: "We believe that they are functioning with wisdom and sensitivity regarding the diversity of our population, and that they are astutely aware of what is appropriate and inappropriate in subject-matter in our school curriculum."[88] The district's science coordinator took exception to the accusation that the district was teaching the occult through the observation of owl pellets. He read several excerpts from letters received from doctors and professors nationwide defending the activity. One of these concluded unequivocally that "to construe this activity as part of a death curriculum or as promotion of the occult requires a distressing and pernicious combination of scientific illiteracy, fanaticism and paranoia."[89] A second-grade teacher whom the mothers had accused of promoting Hinduism held up a child's construction paper mask of an elephant and said in a tone of disbelief, "This is the Ganesha which was referred to, and I think this speaks for itself."[90]

Only a handful of parents came forward to support DiBari. One mother compared *Magic*'s math utility to using a Ouija board to learn letters. One lone student thanked her for her courage. "I'm probably going to be hated for saying this," he said, "but . . . I've seen the [*Magic*] cards and I do think they're revolting. They have definite occultic implications."[91]

Before concluding the meeting, Dennis reaffirmed his position: the authority to determine what is taught in the schools rests with the board. "They [DiBari and DiNozzi] are not the arbiters of the curriculum," he stated forcefully. He also made clear that he would not yield to parental requests for accommodation:

"I've instructed staff that they are not to go through the work or time of offering different assignments and have their classes disrupted while . . . children determine whether a particular piece of the curriculum is suitable."[92]

The colloquium once again put the Bedford schools in the media spotlight. Within the week, the *New York Times* had run two articles with provocative headlines: "Bedford Residents Defend Schools from a Satan Hunt"[93] and "Bedford's Struggle with the Devil." Local cable news stations covered the event and rebroadcast it at a later date. An editorial in the local press voiced concern that the school district's "sterling reputation . . . was being blackened by silliness" and complimented the students for "show[ing] the two moms up for what they are: pathetic reachers for a glimmer of fame."[94] A vocal minority, however, saw it differently. Several community members roundly criticized the superintendent for having responded to the women's objections by discrediting them "through the politics of public ridicule."[95]

The barbed comments hurled back and forth in the press made clear that this was more than a controversy over the alleged teaching of the occult. The reaction to the superintendent's colloquium revealed deep governance issues percolating beneath the surface of what appeared to be solely a conflict over curricular values. One outspoken critic of the district fired off a heated letter to the editor of a local newspaper:

> People who went to this presentation . . . were duped. . . . We must insist on parents' rights to question decisions made by the administration, that may adversely affect our children. . . . Certainly the heavy-handed statement by the administration that the School Board is the final arbiter (one with absolute power of determining) of the "curriculum" is only a half-truth. . . . The trustees serve as our elected representatives and are accountable to us. You mention a witch hunt. The mean and unjust treatment of these two women—two moms—who expressed legitimate concerns and were forced to endure the indignity of a kangaroo court, calls to mind the English Law by which the witches of Salem were put to death. Must critics of the Administration run a gauntlet of censure?[96]

From MaryAnn DiBari's perspective, the colloquium was "riddled with misinformation." As she would later recall:

> It wasn't two crazy ladies banning books or burning anything. It was an audience silencing two crazy ladies. That's censorship. We received life-threatening phone calls. Our children were assaulted verbally. We were alienated, isolated, ostracized, castigated, denigrated, because we had the audacity to stand up and say to this town,

"That's bad stuff." Who's the witch hunter and who's the censor? Who got shut up? Who got silenced? I have never burned a book, banned a book, or asked to change a curriculum. I asked to opt-out, which is my right. I asked to inspect and opt out and they said, "If you don't like it, take your kids and get out."[97]

As far as Bruce Dennis was concerned, the colloquium had brought closure to the matter. Several weeks later he would state with exasperation in his voice, "It's over from my perspective. I don't want to spend any more time on it. They've been renounced by their community."[98] But it was far from over for MaryAnn DiBari and Ceil DiNozzi. In the months following the colloquium, DiBari waged a running battle with school officials over opting her granddaughter out of the drug and alcohol awareness program. In response, the superintendent continued to cite state law supporting the school board's authority to determine the curriculum.[99] He even threatened that the child might "jeopardize her promotion" if she failed "to complete this part of the curriculum."[100] Like many states, New York requires school districts to offer a drug education program but there is no provision in the law, as there is for sex education, that permits parents to opt out for religious or other reasons.

DiBari would not give up, persistently opposing "DARE's transpersonal psycho-therapeutic methods," including "negative role-playing . . . and an ends-justifies-the-means philosophy that harms children." She insisted that the program takes seventeen weeks merely to prove how "available, accessible, alluring and powerful drugs are."[101] DiNozzi shared DiBari's views on DARE's methodology. To her mind, the program was inappropriate and unnecessary for her children. She was confident that they would not take drugs because "that's how they have been raised."[102]

DiNozzi also met roadblocks at the high school. She requested that her eldest son be permitted to opt out of the peer facilitation program. The program involved the use of student facilitators who worked with students in small groups under the guidance of a social worker. But the high school principal warned her that her son risked academic discipline, including expulsion, if he failed to participate in the sessions.[103] Even on those few occasions when opting out was made available to one of her children, it proved to be uncomfortable and isolating. As DiNozzi saw it, schools had turned the pathological into the norm and vice versa. School policy should allow students with specific problems to opt in to certain programs, she argued, rather than place the burden on students who show no need for help to opt out.

Objecting to programs consisting of everything from films on domestic violence to suicide education, DiNozzi became increasingly frustrated with school

officials, who "have been fed with this idea that they are there to rescue everyone in trouble."[104] She was adamant: "other parents [may] have given up their
rights to their children," but she had not. She was weary of one lesson after another trying to "desensitize the children to anything traditional." "I want my
children to be prepared for college," she said, "and it's not the social stuff that
I'm looking for; it's the academics."[105]

By the end of the school year, DiNozzi had decided to place her youngest three
sons in the local Catholic school, while allowing her eldest to remain at Fox Lane
High School. In the meantime, she and MaryAnn DiBari had engaged the services of pro bono attorneys to bring them justice. The local administrative and
political processes had failed them, as they had so many parent dissenters before: now the women would seek redress in federal court.

THE "BEDFORD PROGRAM" GOES TO COURT

Acting on the advice of William Donohue of the Catholic League for Civil
Rights, MaryAnn DiBari and Ceil DiNozzi contacted Christopher Ferrara,
president and general counsel of the American Catholic Lawyers Association.
The association, founded in 1990 and based in New Jersey, relies on a network
of Catholic lawyers around the country. According to the group's promotional
literature, its purpose is to "provide a truly Catholic response to the forces of liberalism which have converted America into a secularist regime utterly hostile to
the Kingship of Christ."[106]

Ferrara agreed to serve as lead counsel, calling upon Joseph Infranco, a New
York lawyer, to join him on the case. Infranco had been involved in several high
profile religion-based lawsuits. He had represented the plaintiffs in the early
stages of the *Lamb's Chapel* litigation.[107] There the U.S. Supreme Court unanimously held that a school district had engaged in viewpoint discrimination
when it denied the request of a religious group to use school facilities for a film
series on family values while permitting nonreligious groups to use the facilities
for similar purposes. Infranco had collaborated in several other local cases with
Pat Robertson's American Center for Law and Justice[108] and with the American Catholic Lawyers Association.[109] Having earned a reputation for challenging schools on the denial of religion-based rights, he would later be called to testify before the U.S. Commission on Civil Rights in the course of public hearings
examining the protection afforded freedom of religion and freedom of expression in the public schools. The two lawyers worked closely with DiBari, also an
attorney, to draft a complaint that encompassed a wide range of seemingly di-

verse claims under a single and novel concept—what they labeled the Bedford Program.

The new school year had barely begun when Superintendent Dennis was served with the complaint in the case of *Altman v. Bedford Central School District*.[110] Joining MaryAnn DiBari and Ceil DiNozzi and her husband were two additional parents, Victoria and Robert Altman, suing individually and on behalf of their respective children/grandchildren who had attended the Bedford schools in the previous few years. All declared that Bedford school officials had violated their sincerely held religious beliefs based in Roman Catholicism. The Bedford Program, they maintained, went beyond the "mere teaching of proper academic subjects" to include developing the "whole person."[111] They cited a catalogue of objectionable techniques, many of which defied factual belief but at the same time echoed concerns repeatedly raised within the religious conservative network and its literature. Included among their objections were the promotion of satanism and occultism, pagan religions, and "New Age spirituality"; instruction in meditation, yoga, guided imagery, and self-hypnosis, "crystal power," the use of "right-brain" and other "self-realization" techniques; psychological evaluation and treatment through self-revelation, psychodrama, role-playing, "stress management," so-called "stress thermometers," relaxation and deep breathing, blindfold walks, and encounter groups; instruction in "decision-making," in which moral issues were "reduced to a process of choosing options divorced from objective moral norms"; and transpersonal "affective" teaching methods which subjected students to "'learning' intuitively by 'sharing' [their] innermost fears, dreams, likes, dislikes, aversions, failures, insecurities and the intimate details of their personal and family lives with strangers in the classroom."[112]

The complaint continued with a detailed list of specific activities and programs, the factual details of which would later become contested at trial. Included among these were *Magic: The Gathering*, the making of clay idols of the Hindu god Ganesha, the "obsessive study of the pagan religion of the Aztecs," Aztec Day of the Dead rituals, a student-made booklet of poems by fourth graders that included the theme "How God Messed Up," daily morning and afternoon meditation exercises broadcast over the elementary school intercom system with "guided imagery" instruction, meditation as part of the sixth-grade Yale Decision-Making Program, instruction to fifth graders to observe a family member for five minutes and then report to the teacher their thoughts and feelings about that person, a requirement in the elementary school that students keep private journals containing their innermost thoughts and feelings, an attitudinal questionnaire administered in the middle school that included among its propositions, "The government of the United States is oppressive and reactionary," a "ropes course challenge program" in which blindfolded ninth graders negotiated an obstacle course that included a web of ropes while remaining absolutely silent and allegedly communicating with each other mentally—the list went on and on.[113]

The parents maintained that the district had promoted "Earth Worship and New Age Spiritism" through various activities, including an Earth Day celebration at which a poet announced that the Earth "is God," a guest speaker who lectured students on the power of crystals, a speaker who gave a "New-Age style lecture by the 'ghost' of Abraham Lincoln," and a lesson in making "worry dolls" at the district's discovery center.[114]

The complaint discussed in considerable detail the Drug Awareness Resistance Education Program, popularly known as the DARE program, a controversial approach to drug prevention that has caught the attention of the media.[115] Begun in 1983, DARE is organized and operated by local police officers who come into the schools and instruct fifth graders on drug prevention through a seventeen-lesson core curriculum developed by the Los Angeles Unified School District. Having a budget in 1996 of $750 million, of which an estimated $600 million came from federal, state, and local governments, DARE is now used in 70 percent of the nation's schools and reaches twenty-five million students.[116]

Despite its popularity, the program has fallen under severe criticism from researchers who question its long-term effectiveness, from parents who question its methods, and from civil libertarians who are uncomfortable with classrooms being turned over to uniformed police officers.[117] One series of studies found that DARE-type programs actually increase drug experimentation among suburban children. Another study found that in addition to increasing drug use, the DARE program gave students who took part in it "more tolerant views toward drugs," while failing to produce any beneficial outcomes.[118] The media's focus on DARE's alleged shortcomings has dampened some of the original enthusiasm for the program. In recent years, a number of city school districts, including Oakland, Omaha, Spokane, Burbank, and Fayetteville, North Carolina, have abandoned DARE.[119]

The parents' complaint in the Bedford case attacked several DARE techniques, some of which would become the subject of conflicting perceptions in trial testimony. As described in the complaint, DARE asks children to role-play drug pushers and drug users; uses the "DARE box" in which fifth graders are "ordered by [a] police officer to . . . [disclose] in writing their 'fears' and what they perceive to be the 'harmful' or possibly illegal activities of family members and friends"; uses "aversion therapy" techniques, including a movie shown to ten-year-olds presenting a woman "in the throes of a drug overdose"; demonstrates drug use techniques and drug paraphernalia in the classroom; and provides "sex-abuse awareness" counseling as part of the "Good Touch, Bad Touch" presentation, also conducted by police officers. As far as the DiBaris, DiNozzis, and Altmans were concerned, "DARE violates the fundamental right of parents to teach their own children, at the time they deem appropriate, about the evils of drug abuse as a violation of God's law, and not as a matter of a mere choice between options."[120]

The legal claims drew on Supreme Court precedent from *Meyer* and *Pierce* to *Yoder* and pulled selectively from an arsenal of litigation strategies used by religious conservatives in such seminal cases as *Mozert* and *Smith*. The complaint listed six causes of action, the most salient ones based in the First and Fourteenth Amendments. Like the parents in *Smith*, they relied on the establishment clause of the First Amendment, alleging that the Bedford program impermissibly promoted certain religious beliefs and practices which were inimical to their sincerely held Catholic beliefs. Yet they were careful not to raise the specter of secular humanism, which the appeals court in *Smith* had rejected. Like the Amish in *Yoder* and the Christian fundamentalist parents in *Mozert*, they argued that a public school program was burdening their free exercise rights by coercing them to commit acts forbidden by their religion but also to refrain from practices and beliefs that are a part of their religion.[121]

Reaching back to *Meyer* and *Pierce*, the plaintiffs maintained that the district had violated their Fourteenth Amendment liberty interest in "raising their children according to their religion, system of values and moral norms they deem appropriate."[122] The program, they argued, also violated the liberty interest of their children in "a religious and moral formation in the home, under the guidance of their parents, without interference by the State."[123] To round out their complaint, they raised additional claims under the New York State constitution, the federal Protection of Pupil Rights Amendment (the Hatch Amendment), and the New York Public Health Law.[124]

School officials dismissed the parents' description of the facts as gross distortion. They also believed that legal precedent was squarely on their side and that the complaint raised no credible legal claims. Represented by attorneys from Ingerman Smith, a Long Island–based law firm that specializes in education law and constitutional litigation, the district moved to dismiss the complaint.[125]

They distinguished the claims brought against them from the now-famous transcendental meditation case of *Malnak v. Maharishi Mahesh Yogi*.[126] In *Malnak*, the federal appeals court had held that the teaching of the Science of Creative Intelligence Transcendental Meditation in New Jersey public schools constituted the teaching of religion in violation of the establishment clause. In contrast, Bedford officials argued that there essentially was no evidence of religion in the district's educational program.[127] A religion, they maintained, must demonstrate a text, creed, or organized group, none of which is associated with New Age beliefs. And even if these practices were of a religious nature at some time in history, they claimed, the secular study of ancient gods and religious symbols has no current religious significance nor might an objective observer view these practices as impermissibly endorsing religion.[128] Here the district relied on several federal appeals court opinions, including *Smith*, which rejected secular humanism and the teaching of Wicca as a religion.[129]

In response to the free exercise claims, school officials predictably held fast to *Mozert*. The parents, they insisted, had to show more than the fact that their children were merely exposed to materials that offended them; they had to demonstrate that the programs and materials had a coercive effect on the practice of their religion. More fundamentally, in their view the parents' objections were not religious in the first instance but merely value-based. And even if the court should find that the concerns raised were validly grounded in religion, they argued, the particular practices were neutral toward religion and not motivated by hostility toward any one sect.[130]

As for the parents' liberty interest, school officials acknowledged that *Meyer, Pierce,* and *Yoder* supported such an interest in the upbringing of one's child but only under limited circumstances. The right did not include "the right to shield or exempt the child from exposure to texts, materials, practices or curriculum which offend the parents' sensibilities or to compel a school district to modify or adapt its curriculum to meet parental preferences."[131] They cited several recent cases, including *Immediato*, which the very same judge assigned to the Bedford case, Judge Charles Brieant, had decided at the district court level.[132] Quoting from that opinion, they warned that if the court should "require a school district to conform its instructional program to [the] moral norms or values [of particular parents]," it would "wreck havoc in the administration of schools."[133]

With the ink barely dry on their court papers, school officials found that they were not alone in defending the curriculum before the court. A group of fifteen parents held a joint press conference with PFAW announcing that the New York

City law firm of Rosenman and Colin had filed an amicus curiae brief on their behalf, adding another dimension to the litigation.[134] The parents, some of whom had spoken up at the superintendent's colloquium on *Magic: The Gathering* the previous year made clear, however, that, depending on the outcome of the litigation, their interests ultimately might be in tension with those of the district. They expressed deep fears of censorship and concerns about the potential impact on the curriculum. As several members of the group stated to the press, a court ruling against the district would threaten "the very basic idea of academic freedom," leaving behind "a curriculum that is bland, timid, the least common denominator."[135]

Their brief echoed these concerns, renouncing the apparent attempt by the DiBari, DiNozzi, and Altman families to alter the Bedford curriculum and affirmatively asserting the constitutional rights of other parents and children to a broad-based education, one that "cultivates self-reliance and integration in modern society."[136] Their vision of educational purpose or mission, reaffirming education's socializing function, stood in stark contrast with the more narrow focus on teaching "proper academic subjects" presented by the opposing side.[137] But they developed their argument even further. Citing Justice Douglas's dissent in *Yoder,* they boldly suggested that the court should protect children from the narrowness of their own parents. "A child's interest in a diverse education," they maintained, "is particularly important when that right to exposure to a wide variety of ideas conflicts with his or her parents' notion of religious and moral propriety."[138] The brief appeared to be more than a mere statement of support for the district. In fact, it sounded far more like a blueprint for another round of litigation or at least a warning to school officials and the court that if either should acquiesce to the mothers' demands, then other constitutional claims would quickly follow.

The Bedford Amici Parents, as they came to be known, would later gain statewide and national recognition for their efforts to "thwart censorship" and "support intellectual freedom."[139] In the fall of 1997, the New York State English Council, an affiliate of the National Council of Teachers of English, presented them with the first intellectual freedom award ever granted to a parent group by a statewide English teachers organization. The award obviously was more than a symbolic gesture of professional recognition. It signaled that the Bedford litigation and its surrounding circumstances were raising critical issues of national importance, becoming another flashpoint in the struggle over educational values.

REASON, RHETORIC, AND THE POWER
OF INNUENDO

In the two years leading up to the trial, while the parents and school district officials were gathering their evidence, fine-tuning their legal arguments, and repeatedly facing off in Judge Brieant's court, the lawsuit assumed a life of its own. In doing so, it triggered a series of responses and interactions among disparate elements within the Bedford school community which served as a prism for viewing the many interconnected tensions lying beneath the surface of this school system and of education in general.

MaryAnn DiBari and Ceil DiNozzi had concluded early on that the *Magic* card game was merely the "tip of the iceberg"; the same can be said of their lawsuit. Their public forum in the fall of 1995, the resulting litigation, and the surrounding media hype not only spread fear and suspicion throughout the Bedford school community, but served to mobilize and polarize several factions of parents and community leaders seemingly beyond the reach of political consensus. The more the mothers' claims and rhetoric resounded in religious fundamentalism, the more their serious educational concerns became clouded and the more resentful and angry others grew at what they viewed as a slight to their well-regarded educational system and community. The so-called Satan suit had become a public embarrassment with potentially harmful consequences. As several mothers noted and the local press warned, the litigation could impact property values, access to talented faculty, and even their children's college admission.[140] More immediately, the lawsuit apparently signaled to some community members that the Christian Coalition had targeted the Bedford schools for a religious takeover, although there was little tangible evidence of any such organized effort.

These fears became tied to the budget-cutting demands of local and statewide taxpayer groups, whose back-to-basics philosophy shared elements with the educational issues reflected in the litigation. The head of the local Taxpayers Oversight Committee admitted that it was not a particular program but a philosophy that concerned him about the schools. He put a fiscal spin on the mothers' claims, maintaining that the district should "get rid of social programs and spend more on education" and that schools "should not be wasting money on philosophical programs. If the lawsuit informs people of what's going on, then it's a good thing." Nevertheless, he too believed the mothers' forum was "too religious" and estimated that at least one-third of the 250 members of his organization were outraged over the cost of defending the district in court.[141] His view made it obvious that, despite what some individuals in the community might have thought, not all fiscal conservatives are necessarily religious conservatives. As one community member appropriately advised, one should not equate "financial responsibility with fiscal conservatism or religious fanaticism or opposition to the quality of education of our children."[142]

Much of the public debate came to focus on the school board election of May 1997 and the fear of "stealth" candidates allegedly supported by the Christian Coalition. The Satan suit lent credibility to that fear and mobilized a group of parents, many of whom were amici to the lawsuit, to formally organize a counterattack of public information and political advocacy. Calling themselves Partners in Action for Community and Education (PACE), the group spelled out in solicitation literature not only its purpose—"to respond to the growing crisis in our community"—but also its vision of education as a "comprehensive . . . experience reflective of American democratic principles."[143] Its first newsletter focused on the upcoming school board election, pointedly asking, "Who Will Control Our Schools?" The group's "Declaration of Principles" warned the community about candidates with a hidden agenda and undisclosed support or affiliation. Without naming names, it drew attention to current school board members who either breach the separation of church and state or place undue weight on fiscal needs at the expense of educational concerns.[144]

Groups such as PACE specifically targeted fiscally conservative candidates, suggesting some affiliation with the Religious Right. The perceived threat of a takeover by extreme religious elements, made palpable by the lawsuit, sent waves of fear and distrust throughout the community. Ostensibly to shed light on the key issues but more likely to produce a particular outcome in the impending board elections, the women's group of a local synagogue together with PACE and several other religious and secular organizations enlisted the cosponsorship of PFAW in an "Open Discussion" on "The Religious Right and Local School Board Elections: Fact or Fiction?" One of the cosponsors was the Bedford Presbyterian Church, whose pastor, the Reverend Alcorn, had sponsored the *Magic* tournament and who was a candidate in the upcoming school board election.[145] Flyers distributed throughout the school community ominously warned that "all over the country, school districts are being targeted for 'takeover' by religious fundamentalists. Often, candidates supported by the religious 'right' don't identify their true agenda until they gain a majority hold on the school board . . . and then it is too late."

On a dreary April evening, a standing-room-only audience packed the Mount

Kisco Library meeting room to hear Deanna Duby, an attorney with PFAW, present one horror story after another of stealth school board takeovers by religious fundamentalists supported, in some cases, by taxpayer groups. She gave examples of how the Religious Right had won majorities on school boards from Buena Vista, California, to Merrimack, New Hampshire, with resulting turmoil in the curriculum. "The schools are not made better when they are torn apart by these battles," she warned the group. "The key is to ask what the battle is really about and what the goals are and what can be done as a community to resolve this."

Duby linked local conflicts to voucher proposals nationwide. From her perspective, the overall goal of the movement is to undermine public education. Its leaders believe that if they can "create enough chaos, it will be easy to go to policy makers and say, 'We've lost public education so you have to give us a voucher system to get our kids out.'" She disclaimed any knowledge that a fundamentalist takeover might be afoot in Bedford or that stealth candidates might be lurking in the background of the upcoming board elections. Her presentation was informative and cautionary but nonetheless unsettling, even frightening. She obviously intended her tales from around the country to serve as a wakeup call to the possibility of a similar scenario unfolding in Bedford. To give immediacy to that warning, she quoted from a statement made by Ralph Reed, former executive director of the Christian Coalition, in 1992: "It's like guerilla warfare. . . . It's better to move quietly. . . . I want to be invisible. I do guerilla warfare. I paint my face and travel by night."[146]

A second speaker, unannounced in the forum's advertisements, was outgoing school board member and former chairperson Karen Akst Schecter. In a twenty-minute presentation threaded with innuendoes, she wove a web of conspiracy, discrediting several school board members and other vocal critics of the board majority and the school administration. To anyone familiar with district politics, she appeared to be targeting her remarks and accusations at the three members of a minority faction on the seven-member board, all of whom had developed a reputation as "budget-skeptics" and all of whom were present in the audience. The gathering quickly degenerated into a heated debate, fueling the fires of fear and distrust.

Two of the alleged targets, board members Camillo Santomero and Robert Frisch, heatedly objected to being "vilified" simply for having focused on finances and student test scores. The following day, the third board member, James Markowski, fired off a letter to a local newspaper calling Schecter "a kindred spirit with the plaintiffs in the 'Satanism' lawsuit," both taking "a neutral germ of fact and cultivating fantastic false allegations." For Markowski, the real issue in the upcoming school board election was not the Christian Coalition but money, above all the fiscal strain imposed by the teachers' contract which would be renegotiated in the coming year by newly elected board members.[147] For several weeks the name-calling and accusations continued in letters to the local press. As one community member observed, this was "the epitome of intolerance run amok."[148] A newspaper editorial tried to bring the debate back to civil discourse, calling the stakes in the upcoming election "too high to allow any witch-hunt to spread infection in the community" and urging "both sides to restrain their arguments to what is known and demonstrable. . . . Reason, not rhetoric, is what is needed here."[149]

Amidst all the inflammatory bravado and name-calling, the meeting in fact shed far more darkness than light over the impending school board election and cast an ever-deepening cloud over the Bedford schools. Nevertheless, in the end it proved a success for its sponsors, whose clear objective was to influence the results of the May election. Those candidates endorsed by the local taxpayers' group and by the three fiscal conservatives on the board fell in resounding defeat, while those supported by PACE and the local teachers' union, including the Reverend Alcorn, made their way onto the school board.

Judging from the political mud-slinging that continued in the press as the campaign drew to a close, fears of a religious takeover were not the sole driving force behind the election results. The cast of characters in this drama was fighting battles over educational priorities, vision, and mission, battles that had manifested themselves as budgetary concerns long before Satan had become a household word in Bedford. In fact, one could conclude that at least some of the community response elicited by the lawsuit was merely symptomatic of deeper disagreements over school governance and philosophy among board members and within the community.

JUDICIAL RELUCTANCE

While the election results spared the district any dramatic shift in control of the school board, religious or otherwise, school officials still had the lawsuit and the threat of a contentious court battle hanging over their heads. Judge Brieant, the judge assigned to the case, was a Republican long active in county politics; he had practiced law in Westchester and worked his way through various elected positions before being appointed to the federal bench in 1971 by Richard Nixon. He had a known distaste for litigants clogging up his courtroom with trivial claims and a reputation for holding attorneys' feet to the fire. He was not a new-comer to conflicts over values promoted in the schools: just two years earlier, in the *Immediato* case, he had upheld a mandatory community service requirement for high school graduation.

In sharp contrast with the Bedford claims, *Immediato* had presented no reli-gious issues. There the judge refused to recognize a Fourteenth Amendment right to have one's children opt out of programs that are contrary to the parents' secular beliefs and values. Judge Brieant's unequivocal words in *Immediato* would resonate throughout the Bedford litigation. "Plaintiff parents," he stated, "may not use this Court to interpose their own way of life or their own philos-ophy, however laudable, as a barrier to reasonable state and local regulation of the educational curriculum."[150] Echoing Chief Justice Burger's opinion in *Yo-der,* he reaffirmed that "[a] way of life, however virtuous and admirable, may not be interposed as a barrier to reasonable state regulation of education if it is based on purely secular considerations."[151] It was evident that the claim had to be rooted firmly in religion or the district's practices had to be clearly unreasonable.

As already noted, Bedford school officials had moved to dismiss the case, be-lieving that the law clearly was on their side. In ruling on the motion, Judge Brieant expressed legal and policy concerns about judicial involvement in school governance similar to those he had raised in *Immediato,* this time with more bite. Yet he still denied the motion. School officials and amici parents, attempting to place themselves within the scope of *Immediato* and to distinguish themselves from *Yoder,* characterized the claims brought against the district as secular. But each side obviously had a distinct understanding and recollection of the facts. Viewing these as "highly subjective characterizations" of what had occurred, the judge concluded that pretrial discovery was essential to provide the court with an adequate record. In a further blow to the district, the judge threw into the decisional calculus an expansive reading of religion, noting that the state need not have adopted "a full religion with rituals and doctrines" for the court ulti-mately to find that a First Amendment violation had occurred.[152]

These opening words offered a brief measure of hope and comfort to the DiBaris, DiNozzis, and Altmans. The remainder of the opinion, however, bris-tled with annoyance and sarcasm at the apparent misuse of the federal judiciary, giving both sides, but particularly the plaintiffs, cause for apprehension. He called litigation of this sort "costly, lengthy and divisive" and denied that federal judges had any expertise in educational matters. He cited the doctrine of Home Rule supporting the interests of communities in managing their own affairs.[153]

He also cited New York State Education Law, which grants local school boards control over the curriculum subject to the state commissioner's enforcement.[154]

The judge questioned the parents' failure to seek either an administrative remedy through state Education Department channels or even a political remedy in the school board electoral process. "Rather than pursue these logical avenues of relief," he chided, "it appears to this Court that the protagonists in this case, and their lawyers, like Tweedledum and Tweedledee, have 'resolved to have a battle,' and have selected the federal courts as their battlefield."[155] In an effort to avoid additional "costs, delays and rancor, as well as the waste of scarce judicial resources," he stayed the proceedings for a period of sixty days and sent the plaintiffs off to the state commissioner of education in hopes that an administrative resolution could be reached. Although the judge's order was not binding, both sides speedily complied and wrote to the state commissioner, Richard Mills, asking his involvement in a mediation process.

But the commissioner's consideration was purely discretionary. Just as the sixty-day period was drawing to a close, the state Education Department informed the attorneys and the court in writing that "action by the Commissioner would not be appropriate at this time." The letter offered several reasons for his refusal to intervene: deference to the plaintiffs' choice of forum in the federal courts in lieu of an appeal to the commissioner, the numerous issues of fact which might require substantial discovery and testimony, and the constitutional violations alleged in the complaint.[156] This sent the case back to the reluctant judge, ending a brief respite from what threatened to be a long, arduous court battle with potentially far-reaching educational and constitutional ramifications.

Over the following year, both sides busily engaged in pretrial discovery, which the judge assigned to the oversight of a magistrate. Each amassed a mound of documents to convince the court that its spin on the facts was the one the court should accept as truth. Included among these were affidavits signed by the complainants and their children, by school officials, and by three amici parents, two of whom were Catholic, who flatly denied any hint of religion or mind manipulation or practices offensive to Catholicism in the district's curriculum. One parent expressed strong objection to what he saw as "an attempt by a small group of individuals, backed by right-wing religious groups, to impose their religious values on [him] and [his] children."[157] Another expressed anger over the lawsuit having "upset innocent children and driven away competent teachers."[158] Superintendent Dennis warned the court of the "extraordinary difficulties and chaotic results" that would ensue if the court recognized a parental right to opt out of any part of the educational program that parents found offensive. It would "render any academic program totally ineffective . . . stifle any spontaneity" and leave the curriculum "sterile and devoid of diversity of opinion," he argued.[159] Yet the complainants insisted that their religious beliefs had been violated. "If non-sectarian prayers at graduation or even a moment of silence can be banned by courts," they maintained, "then so should . . . unprecedented activities . . . [that] have nothing to do with 'education.'"[160]

In an apparent attempt to extract statements supporting the parents' argument that certain programs crossed over into the realm of parental privacy, attorneys for the complainants took numerous depositions from school staff and district officials, including the district's social worker, whom they questioned about her counseling activities, and a police officer assigned to the DARE program in the Bedford schools. The district's attorneys, in turn, tried to undermine the credibility of the parents and their children, to raise serious questions as to their recollection and depiction of what had actually occurred in the Bedford schools, and to demonstrate inconsistencies between the parents' curricular objections and practices condoned in their private lives. From the DiBari, DiNozzi, and Altman children the attorneys extracted detailed facts—from their television (MTV), movie (R-rated), and video game (*Mortal Kombat*) viewing habits to the costumes (ghosts and scary clowns) they had worn on Halloween.

As yet another school year opened under the cloud of the Satan suit, both sides requested the court to grant partial summary judgment in their favor. But the documents supporting their briefs to the court left no doubt that they were still miles apart on key factual issues. Conflicting affidavits prepared by the parents' expert witness, William Coulson, and three district psychologists exemplified that distance. Each side painted a totally different picture of the DARE, peer facilitation, Yale Decision-Making, and suicide prevention counseling programs and their potential harms or benefits.[161] As noted, Coulson had testified on behalf of the plaintiffs in the *Smith* case from Alabama in the late 1980s, his critical assessment of home economics textbooks centering on parental rights. He claimed here to have a unique perspective. He had been one of the originators in the early 1960s, along with the psychologist Carl Rogers, of a technique known as "nondirective psychotherapy," or the use of discussion groups and facilitators in the schools. Both he and Rogers later repudiated these techniques as psychologically damaging and educationally inappropriate. For Coulson, the programs engaged students in a form of psychotherapy that sets aside moral absolutes while leading them to a decision that is right for them. The district psychologists refuted this characterization, insisting that the programs were not therapeutic but educational in nature.

A similar conflict arose between reports addressing the religious claims prepared for each side by experts in Catholic teaching. Does New Age thinking constitute a religion? Did the school programs and practices under challenge violate the teachings of the Catholic Church? The parents' expert was Father Charles Fiore, a Catholic priest with training in theology and philosophy who also serves on the board of several Catholic home school organizations and writes for various conservative Catholic publications. In his opinion, the district's actions were objectionable on several counts. They violated the First Commandment prohibition against worshiping "false gods," the natural rights of parents to "properly educate their children . . . [as] citizens of/with the saints and members of God's household," and the natural rights of children to the "integrity and privacy of their bodies and their minds . . . which includes the right not to be taught erroneous and/or questionable matters without the approval of their parents or guardians."

The district's expert, Daniel Maguire, a professor of moral theology from Marquette University, roundly rejected the parents' claims regarding Catholic teaching on meditation, on the study of other religions, including Hinduism, on drug education, and on satanism. He also repudiated the notion of New Age as a "discernible religion." In his view, the assessment prepared by the plaintiffs' witness on Catholic doctrine was not only outside "the realm of the scholarly [but] . . . very much in the genre of right wing paranoia."[162] The questions thus left for the court were not only which was the more credible witness but whether any one theologian or priest could speak for all Catholics and whether religious claims could be grounded in subjectively defined beliefs rather than mainstream doctrine.

Yet while the factual allegations remained broad, the parents narrowed their legal arguments—at least for purposes of partial summary judgment—and focused on the religious claims. Their attorneys apparently had concluded that, from the perspective of legal precedent, this was their strongest argument. They asked the court to rule as a matter of law on twelve activities that violated the establishment and free exercise clauses. To reinforce their case and underscore the continuing nature of the violations, they added to their original list of charges yoga instruction at the high school and another Earth Day ceremony celebrated the previous spring.[163]

When the attorneys appeared before Judge Brieant, he was still far from convinced that this case had any place in his court. He plainly was averse to ruling whether a visit by a yoga master or a field trip to a cemetery or a fantasy card game were infringing on some students' freedom of religion or promoting some religious beliefs while excluding others. He allowed the attorneys only brief arguments, expressing his continued frustration with the case. "The people who met in Philadelphia in 1789 never intended this kind of mess," he rebuked them. "Some of [the charges] look a little silly," he said. "I know practicing Christians who do yoga, and they don't feel it compromises their beliefs one little bit." But the judge was keenly aware that the stakes here were high and that the parties were in this for the long haul. He knew that even if pushed to rule on the case, his would not be the last word. "I'll give you my findings and conclusion and let you go to the Second Circuit Court of Appeals. And you can see what the Supreme Court does," he said.

Judge Brieant requested the attorneys to go into closed chambers and try to negotiate a resolution or at least narrow some of the twelve issues over which they continued to disagree before going to trial. He repeatedly offered the option of mediation, exclaiming at one point somewhat plaintively, "This case cries out for some diplomacy."[164] As a starting point, he endorsed a suggestion made by the parents' attorney that the district consider adopting guidelines developed by the Freedom Forum at Vanderbilt University addressing the role of religion in the public schools. When the lawyers emerged after nearly an hour of discussions they reported having made some progress but had no agreement in hand. The judge made one final attempt to avoid trial. He ordered them to submit within a month letters jointly detailing their progress. But as the month drew to a close and further discussion proved fruitless, the judge denied summary judgment as well as the parents' request for a preliminary injunction and ordered the attorneys to prepare for a speedy trial.[165]

EDUCATION ON TRIAL

The trial in fact took place two months later. In the meantime, Judge Brieant, eager to resolve the case, had denied the request of the parents' attorney, Christopher Ferrara, for a delay. Ferrara was engaged at the time in a high-profile Oregon case defending, on behalf of the American Catholic Lawyers Association, one of a group of antiabortion activists charged with inciting violence through a Web site called the Nuremberg Files. The activists were using the site to gather detailed information on doctors who performed abortions and who in the future might be tried for "crimes against humanity." Ferrara was preparing the appeal in Oregon when the Bedford case went to trial, so he asked James Bendell, a Washington State attorney who had argued other cases on behalf of the association, to take his place at the eleventh hour in a case that potentially could shake public education to its core.

Over the course of six days, in a trial that drew national attention for its sweeping implications, the court heard testimony on an array of practices—from Earth Day ceremonies to lessons on ancient cultures to drug awareness programs, relaxation techniques, and risk-taking exercises—that had woven their way into the fabric of the school curriculum in the names of diversity, self-awareness, and social development. The defendant in the case clearly was not just the Bedford school system but the whole of American education and especially the progressive notion of educating the whole child. According to the *New York Times,* the trial "opened a window on [educational] trends that have subtly shifted emphasis away from traditional topics like European history, grammar and physical education to offer classes on non-Western cultures, discussion groups on improving self-esteem and programs to discourage drug use."[166] As the attorneys paraded their witnesses before the court, they effectively if not intentionally dissected some of the most widely used programs and techniques developed and embraced by modern-day educators.

The trial began with testimony from several of the children whose parents had brought the charges against the district. While the point was to describe how the district had violated their religious beliefs, one by one with the help of their attorney they painted a portrait of a school system that seemed to have lost sight of its core mission. They talked about a class trip to a cemetery to make tombstone rubbings during which a student was asked to lie down on a grave and demonstrate that people were shorter in the late 1880s, a lesson in which students made images of the elephant-headed Hindu god Ganesha, an exercise led by a psychic who instructed students to close their eyes and draw with the left hand in order to use the right side of the brain, a physical education class in which a Sikh yogi wearing a turban and tunic and sitting barefoot on a prayer mat led students in yoga exercises, a drug awareness program in which students were never explicitly told that "drugs were wrong," a meditation exercise in which students were to imagine "blue liquid" filling their bodies and then slowly draining out, and a lesson on "crystal power."

Both Ceil DiNozzi and MaryAnn DiBari told the court that these various activities violated their Catholic beliefs. Father Mitchell Pacwa, a Jesuit priest, confirmed their position. When pressed by the judge on the teaching of religion for historical purposes, he responded that it all depends on whether it is being "taught at a distance" or being "glorified and admired." Testimony from the psychic revealed that she also is a minister and healer for the Life Spirit Congregational Church. The yogi, whose trademark name is the Yoga Guy and whose Web site bills him as a "motivational guru and minister," informed the court that yoga is not based in the Hindu religion, but he himself also practices numerology and is considered by some to be a spiritual healer. Nevertheless, he explained that he had been invited to the high school solely to teach stress reduction. In his testimony, Coulson maintained that psychotherapy was taking place in the DARE program, the peer facilitation program, and the ropes challenge program.

Strikingly absent from the witness stand were other students who could verify the facts as the complainants' children had remembered and recounted them. And the attorneys did not call other parents to support their claims. From the vantage point of the courtroom, it appeared that it was the three families on one side of this great philosophical and religious divide and the remainder of the Bedford community on the other. One had to wonder if there were parents in the community who sympathized with the educational concerns raised by these families but who would not come forward, refusing to sacrifice themselves or their children on the altar of religious orthodoxy.

School officials and witnesses called by the district's attorneys remembered and depicted the exact same practices in a very different light. For James Young, former principal of Pound Ridge Elementary School, visiting a cemetery and lying down on a grave is a valuable educational experience. Superintendent Dennis drew a distinction between teaching about other cultures and religions and teaching "the thing itself." Jackie Reizes, the teacher of Ganesha fame, explained that she was following the New York State curriculum in teaching about Hinduism. She flatly denied ever having instructed students to create images of the god out of clay, and several student witnesses confirmed that. Other students denied that they had ever been instructed to place crystals to their heart and "feel the power," while the instructor who had made the presentation, an amateur rock collector known as the Rock Hound, explained the activity as merely a lesson in geology. Marvin Godfried, a practicing psychotherapist, insisted that although several of the Bedford programs used techniques from psychotherapy, they were not psychotherapeutic in nature. In his view, some of the programs merely taught "personal or social intelligence" that involved knowing how to deal with other people.

A high school student explained the peer facilitation program as one in which upper-class students worked with groups of ninth graders on such issues as peer pressure and other school-related matters. On cross-examination it became evident that the student facilitators were not trained specifically on how to handle sensitive subjects like sex, drugs, and alcohol. The same student described the ropes challenge program as a means of promoting teamwork among students and teachers and denied that any of the exercises used in the program encouraged students to use mental telepathy, as the parents asserted. Students were free to opt out of any of these activities without penalty. Another student denied that students in her fifth-grade class had been instructed to make images of the Aztec god Quetzalcoatl, as the children of the complainants had testified. A student who helped organize the Earth Day ceremony, an event recognized and celebrated around the world, explained that it was intended to promote students' respect for the environment. A local police officer assigned to the Bedford schools as a DARE instructor testified as to the program's emphasis on decision making, risk assessment, peer pressure, and stress management and admitted on cross-examination that she presents the family as a source of stress to students. She also submitted that the program does not provide any psychological training to its instructors on stress or on alcohol abuse.

As the days wore on, the legal claims and even the details of the events in Bedford slowly became lost in the more general exegesis of American schooling. On the final day of the trial, PFAW issued a press release warning that "[a]s ludicrous as [the parents'] charges may be, the potential results are deadly serious. A victory for the plaintiffs . . . would lead to similar disruptions in school districts across the United States as right-wing ideologues seek to gain a veto over what other parents' children read and learn."[167] Obviously ideologues sit on the political right and the left but beneath the inflammatory rhetoric and one-sidedness of this statement, there rested a reasonable suggestion that this lawsuit could change the dynamic of educational decision making dramatically. At the close of the trial, Judge Brieant commended the attorneys for having acted in accordance with the "highest traditions of the bar" but again reminded them that he would have preferred that the issues had been resolved by a means other than the courtroom.

In their post-trial brief, the parents' attorneys drew an analogy with the information conveyed by television programs and likened the Bedford Program to the *Twilight Zone*. In closing, they emphasized the impressionability of young students and the double standard of religious influence in the schools, asking rhetorically, "If a school may not show a video of the Life of Christ, how can a teacher personally read the Life of Buddha to *elementary* school students? If a high school cannot allow a picture of a crucifixion to hang on the wall, how can it ask *elementary* school students to make an image of Lord Ganesha and hang it on the wall?" Again, they asked the court to enjoin the district from engaging in First Amendment violations and to require advance parental notification and opt-ins for the "psychological manipulation" of students.[168]

Looking objectively at the programs and practices laid open to public view in the course of the trial, one had to wonder whether the Bedford curriculum was representative of school districts nationwide. Some of the commercially developed programs like DARE are used throughout the country, whereas some of the specific practices may be idiosyncratic or specific to certain communities. Were these reasonable approaches to addressing the needs of contemporary students living in a diverse, fast-changing, and complex society or were they modern-day remnants of progressive child-centeredness "run amok"? Is a fantasy card game that uses grotesque, violent imagery and teaches children to reduce their opponents to zero an appropriate activity for an extracurricular school club? Do all ten-year-olds across the country need exposure to drug paraphernalia and the dangers of taking beer to parties if there is no evidence of a problem among their age group in their community? Are eleventh-grade students sufficiently mature and trained to facilitate discussions among ninth graders on sensitive topics that may arise under the rubric of handling peer pressure? Should schools subject adolescents to the social pressure of either engaging in risk taking, yoga-type exercises, and group discussions on socially and emotionally sensitive topics despite personal discomfort or parental disapproval, even if technically voluntary, or requesting to opt out under the disapproving gaze of their peers?

Has the Bedford curriculum or education in general succumbed to a variant of what Sen. Daniel Patrick Moynihan has coined "defining deviancy down?"[169] In other words, what traditionally was considered aberrant behavior now is treated as normal and vice versa. Rather than gear the curriculum toward the norm of students who demonstrate no need for psychologically based programs, educators have redirected it toward those who do in fact demonstrate a need. Instead of requiring this smaller group to opt in to specialized programs, schools now expect students who fall within the norm to participate or at best to bear the burden of opting out.

These hard questions kept surfacing throughout the trial, creating a subtext that gradually dominated the courtroom drama. Yet they were questions of a nonlegal nature for which a federal judge would have no conclusive answers. Reasonable minds might disagree as to at least some of them. Viewed in this light, one can sympathize with and understand Judge Brieant's apparent frustration with this case. The courtroom is an inappropriate venue for debating educational policy and practice. On one level, there was something wrong with this picture, as the saying goes. But on another, one could not lose sight of the legal claims that had brought this cast of characters into court in the first place. That was the task facing the judge—to make sense of all the conflicting testimony and to distinguish between serious constitutional violations and pedagogical excess. And while the religious claims evidently were prominent throughout this litigation, at trial they seemed to recede against the backdrop of arguable intrusions into the interest of parents in guiding their children's education. Yet converting that interest into a constitutional right is a project the federal judiciary repeatedly has avoided undertaking and one that this judge was not likely to spearhead.

Judge Brieant's ruling in fact was predictably narrow, recognizing only three of the fifteen claims made by the parents, yet rejecting the notion of any "such thing as the 'Bedford Program.'"[170] At most, he concluded, the evidence pointed to a large number of separate constitutional claims, some of them "trifling." Several, like the student poem titled "How God Messed Up," were student initiated, while others, like the alleged lesson on crystal power, failed to gain support in the evidence or were merely random acts initiated by individual teachers or others with no advance direction or authorization in district policy, as were lying down on the cemetery grave and stress reduction taught by the yogi. The judge threaded his well-crafted decision with sarcasm, referring to certain challenged practices as "terminally dumb" (lying on the grave), "humbug" (exercises on improving the function of the right hemisphere of the brain), "useless" (non-yoga meditation), and "truly bizarre" (the Earth Day celebration). At the same time, he voiced sensitivity toward local control over education, the limits of judicial expertise and authority, the tensions inherent in mass compulsory schooling, and the constraints of the Constitution as interpreted by the Second Circuit Court of Appeals and the Supreme Court of the United States. He also reaffirmed that under New York State Education Law, the local school board has the power and duty to prescribe the course of study. Parents who find aspects of the curriculum worthless or hostile to their religious beliefs should seek redress in the political process, not in the courts.

The court focused on the religion clauses, applying the coercion test to both the establishment and free exercise claims. The rationale rested on the impressionable age of the students and the question of whether the state was burdening the exercise of religious beliefs by conditioning an important benefit, that is, education, on conduct mandated or proscribed by a religious faith. In the absence of clear guidance from the Supreme Court, the court also adopted the definition of religion articulated in the case of *Malnak v. Yogi*. There the appeals court looked toward outward manifestations associated with traditional religions, including ceremonial functions, a clergy, organization and structure, and the observance of holidays.

One by one, Judge Brieant examined the programs and practices under challenge, some of them more significant than others for their widespread representation in school districts nationwide. He began with *Magic: The Gathering*, the fantasy card game that originally had set this controversy in motion. Here the court could find neither coercive pressure on students nor a message of religious endorsement. Participation was voluntary and with parental consent, while the game was offered as a mere extracurricular activity. "No reasonable person," the court stated, "could regard sponsoring this game as a teaching of religion." The court also found insufficient evidence to demonstrate that the Yoga Guy had made any effort to advance any religious concepts or ideas, and, in any event, the plaintiffs' children and others would have been permitted to opt out of the exercise. The DARE program and the peer facilitation program further withstood attack, the court finding no use of federal funds in either case that would give rise to a claim under the federal Hatch Amendment; nor was either program found to be a "health service" requiring prior parental consent under New York Public Health Law.

On the other hand, the judge did uphold three of the parents' claims. He concluded that advising students to place worry dolls under their pillow to dispel anxieties was a "rank example of teaching superstition to children of a young and impressionable age." He also found that constructing paper images of the Hindu god Ganesha not only communicated a message endorsing Lord Ganesha and the Hindu religion, but was a "subtle coercive pressure of instructing young impressionable children to make images of a god other than their own in violation of their religious beliefs."

The court took particular exception to the Earth Day celebration annually sponsored by the Fox Lane High School. The event is grounded in a New York State law of 1888, amended periodically, requiring the commemoration of Conservation Day on the last Friday in April of each year. Over the years, the day has come to be known as Earth Day. The court found, however, that the liturgy of the high school celebration far exceeded compliance with state law and in fact constituted religious worship, with participants reciting a creed intoning that "the mother of us all is Earth, the father is the Sun." The court noted that "the worship of the Earth is a recognized religion (Gaia), which has been and is now current throughout the world," while the ceremony demonstrated many of the attributes of organized religions, including gifts presented to the earth, symbolic structures similar to an altar, and a chorus of drums throughout the presentation. In the course of one particular Earth Day celebration, the teacher in charge of the event told the participants that there were too many people on this earth and that we need to do something about it. The court found this statement to be in direct conflict with the biblical command in Genesis 1 to "increase and multiply and fill the earth." The court also concluded that a tape recording interspersing prayers and invocations to the earth as "Mother of us all" and "Holy Earth Mother" that was played for a science class of twelve- and thirteen-year-olds represented various Native American creeds and was a clear example of religious teaching.

While the court allowed this narrow victory to the parents on religious grounds, it rejected their constitutional claims to family privacy, which would have granted a broader remedy beyond practices with religious overtones. Here the judge relied on the appeals court decision in the *Immediato* case, which recognized the right of parents to direct the upbringing of their children but severely limited that right to a mere reasonableness test. In other words, a court will defer to the judgment of school officials and permit a challenged practice or program to stand as long as it is reasonably related to a legitimate state interest. In the case at hand, the court found that homework assignments to observe and report on family members, instructing students to maintain journals on their intimate thoughts, and the Yale Decision-Making Program, which is designed to educate students to make informed decisions, all met the reasonableness standard.

But perhaps the most sweeping blow to the parents and the most significant victory for the school district came when Judge Brieant explicitly denied a blanket right for parents to opt their children out of objectionable activities in which First Amendment rights are not implicated. Here the court found credible and persuasive the district superintendent's warning of the administrative and educational burdens that inevitably would flow from a potentially endless number of such requests. The district's refusal to acknowledge such a general parental right, the court held, was rationally related to its educational objectives. Absent a clear violation of religious beliefs or a definitive transgression of church–state separation, parents would have no constitutional recourse to remove their children from programs or practices that they find offensive.

In the end, the court enjoined school officials from engaging in any acts similar to those struck down on religious grounds and directed the district to adopt a published policy instructing teachers and others to implement the constitutional standards discussed in the decision. The judge also allowed the plaintiffs to recover their legal fees and costs to the extent that these were attributable to the three claims on which they prevailed.

Each side immediately put its own gloss on the decision, publicly claiming victory to an eager press. For MaryAnn DiBari, the decision was "a real vindication," yet she reaffirmed her objection to the *Magic* cards, claiming that two students in Littleton, Colorado had played the game before going on a shooting spree that killed a number of high school students and a teacher. The events surrounding that incident had captured the emotional and intellectual energy of the American public in the weeks preceding the trial court decision. She restated a refrain of several years earlier when the controversy began, noting the dangers inherent in the cards: "We have to get rid of the lie that it's math . . . that it's creative or intellectual or enrichment. It's horrible." For her, academic freedom in Bedford apparently meant "freedom from academics . . . [turning] learning . . . on its head."[171] And while Superintendent Dennis was deeply disturbed that the judge had struck down three "trivial incidents" on constitutional grounds, he was also "pleased that the judge found on behalf of the district for the vast preponderance of matters."[172] PFAW, which had supported the amici parents in the case, immediately fired off a press release with the headline, "Religious Right Suffers Defeat in Bedford, NY Federal Lawsuit." Hailing the court ruling for its "message to the Religious Right: Don't use public schools as your ideological playground" and dismissing *Magic: The Gathering* as "an innocuous mathematics card game," PFAW Legal Director Elliot Mincberg also interpreted the decision as a lesson to school districts nationwide to adopt a clearly drafted policy on religion in the schools. The statement made clear that PFAW would continue to represent the amici parents if, as expected, the plaintiffs appealed the decision.

At the same time, in an effort at damage control, the superintendent quickly distributed a memorandum to staff members offering them his insights into the court's decision before the media put its spin on the day's events. He urged the staff to "rely on [their] own judgment in determining lessons and activities" and expressed his continuing concern about the "pernicious effects of self-censorship." Entreating them to "not lose heart," he officially stated that he would recommend to the school board that it appeal the decision to the Second Circuit Court of Appeals.

In his final ruling in the case, Judge Brieant set the plaintiffs' attorneys' fees at $106,856, a sum that district officials deemed too high considering that the plaintiffs had lost on twelve of their fifteen claims. At the same time, the judge found that none of the claims on which the plaintiffs had prevailed had been mooted despite the fact that the Altmans, the only one of the three families that still had a child of elementary school age, had moved out of the school district to nearby New Canaan, Connecticut, while the DiNozzi family were relocating to Delaware. According to the court, MaryAnn DiBari still maintained a personal stake in the outcome of the litigation as a resident of the district, as a taxpayer, and as legal guardian of her two school-aged granddaughters.[173] As the district set in motion the appeals process, the Satan suit, with its multifaceted constitutional claims and political high stakes, was headed toward the Supreme Court with this lone grandmother leading the struggle against what she deeply perceived as the forces of evil.

LESSONS FROM BEDFORD

The Bedford story began in the fall of 1995 with several *New York Times* articles, complete with compelling photographs, recounting "Bedford's Struggle With the Devil."[174] As the following months have turned into years, the gradual progression of that struggle has proven painful and disruptive, leaving numerous aspects of the district's educational program potentially in the hands of the federal courts. Nevertheless, significant lessons may be learned by examining the Bedford experience thus far—from the impact of this drama on the schools and community to its general implications for the substance and structure of schooling in America. The events leading up to the court's engagement further provide some perspective on the resolution of values-based conflicts and the limitations of operating in the legal mode.

At the school level, the public nature of the accusations had an immediate chilling effect on instruction. Although the mothers requested only the opportunity to opt out and technically did not censor any materials, their broad-based attack on the curriculum produced the effect of self-censorship among school personnel. Teachers were apprehensive of being held up to public scrutiny or, worse, being named as defendants in a lawsuit. On the surface it was easy to blame the mothers for this climate of fear. But on closer examination, at least some fault had to rest with the system, which apparently had not established a formalized procedure, such as a review committee, for addressing complaints about books, materials, and programs. And school officials had not adopted nationally publicized and federally endorsed guidelines on the role of religion in the schools as a guidepost for teachers and administrators. In its single-minded zeal to protect the integrity of the educational program, the district's unpreparedness, inability, and ultimate refusal to accommodate most of the mothers' requests in fact produced just the opposite effect. It opened the entire curriculum to broadside attacks, creating a spillover effect into areas totally unrelated to the specific objections that the mothers continued to raise.

At the district level, the lawsuit had a profound effect on the community, heightening existing tensions between warring factions. As events unfolded following the mothers' initial public claims of satanism and occultism, it became manifest that the Satan suit was symptomatic of deeper issues dividing the community—issues of educational and fiscal priorities and competing visions of schooling. As the many individual and group stories came to be told, the lawsuit became a metaphor for the tensions inherent in the very concept of a common school and the conflict between majoritarian democracy and pluralism.

It is tempting to speculate that perhaps things could have worked out differently, that maybe some consensus or compromise could have been reached if the key actors had tried harder to understand each other's point of view and had attempted to chart a middle course. There is a sense that more effective procedures and more open minds and sensitivities toward religious commitment could have resolved at least some of the substantive issues. Perhaps the community could have maintained a level of civil discourse if fears of a religious right takeover, whether real or imagined, had not been imprinted indelibly on their psyches by the language of the occult woven throughout the women's challenge. But then again, it was the occultic nature of the *Magic* card game that had set the controversy in motion in the first instance. The women might have received a more sympathetic hearing from a newly constituted school board if some community members had not branded, directly or by innuendo, certain back-to-basics contenders as stealth candidates for the Christian Coalition. The lawsuit and the surrounding public debate arguably contributed in some measure to the defeat of those candidates.

On an issue-by-issue basis, the women might have mobilized a measure of community support had they not drowned out their voices in the frightening rhetoric of what reasonably appeared as religious fundamentalism. Had they focused instead on a few specific programs or materials and grounded their objections in "good pedagogy," they might have elicited a more open and conciliatory response from school officials, for whom their repeated demands for accommodation became increasingly frustrating and burdensome. Their perceived religious extremism and the threat of censorship were key factors that turned this largely secular school community—Jews, Catholics, and Protestants alike—against them. Several Catholic parents were particularly troubled by the suggestion that the legal claims here were grounded in Catholic beliefs. One mother noted how she was "appalled and embarrassed" by the lawsuit. "Like the 'plaintiffs,'" she said, "I am a Catholic and attend the local Catholic church. However, I completely disagree with their allegations."[175] Several parents who had joined in the amici parents' brief also found nothing offensive or contrary to Catholicism in the district's curriculum.[176] Some community members had initially been open- minded about *Magic: The Gathering* but became alarmed by the occultic experts flown in from around the country. This apparently was more than a controversy over a card game. As one local newspaper editor observed, "The community drew the lines at book burning. Eight out of ten parents had no idea what the card game was all about. But when a list of objectionable books came out, that was a different kettle of fish."[177]

Here was a politically involved and sizeable group of parents who trusted and deferred to the educational experts in their schools and who shared a view of education that went far beyond the basics. The mothers' all-encompassing attack on the educational program threatened to undermine that trust and perspective. Their vision of schooling was far more traditional than the philosophy represented in the Bedford curriculum. As they stated in their complaint to the court, they were seeking a curriculum confined to what they considered the "proper academic subjects," one that would reinforce or at least not subvert their basic values and beliefs. On the other hand, the amici parents strongly supported the broad-based, diverse educational program that Bedford offered—an education that cultivated "self-reliance and integration in modern society" and that exposed students to a "wide variety of ideas," even though those ideas might conflict with the religious and moral values of their family. Whether their convictions exemplified those of the majority of parents in the community or simply those of a vocal, active plurality is not clear.

The distance between these views was so wide that there was no common ground for discussion between the women and school officials and their supporters. The women could not find their place in the Bedford schools absent a major philosophical and curricular redirection which the court was incapable of mandating. And although they shared elements of their educational perspective with the fiscally conservative opponents of the status quo and perhaps with other traditionally minded parents, their extreme religious conservatism placed them at the fringe of this amorphous and largely invisible political minority and precluded them from serving as their spokespersons or even publicly joining forces with them.

Why did they use religion as their sword in the first place, framing their concerns in boilerplate language drawn directly from Christian fundamentalist literature? They might have been more effective had they attacked the targeted programs as educationally inappropriate or unnecessary. The images depicted on the *Magic* cards were indeed violent, offensive, frightening, and indeed misogynist by secular standards. Even many nonreligious parents, when rationally confronted, would rail against yet more violence thrown at their children, especially violence endorsed by school officials. Undoubtedly some politically liberal parents would question the presence of police officers in the classroom introducing their ten-year-olds to the language and paraphernalia of drug abuse. What is critically necessary in the inner city, where exposure to drugs is a daily reality for children of all ages, may be inappropriate for fifth graders in a community such as Bedford.

Perhaps the yogi controversy best captures the essence of what the Bedford conflict is all about and what it represents. Most families would not find yoga or many of the other programs and practices challenged here sufficiently offensive to pursue court action. But many parents, when fully informed and on reflection, might question the appropriateness of some of those practices, not the least of which would be the introduction of the yogi, along with a psychic, risk-taking exercises, and even the use of personal journals into the curriculum. As a matter of law, these may not rise to the level of a religious violation in this or most cases or an invasion of family privacy as a general rule. Yet they do reflect a distinct educational philosophy with no claim to superiority over others. This is not to deny that the religious claims made by the parents in this case, while sincere beyond question, are outside the mainstream. Reasonable minds might even sense a strain of right wing paranoia running through the mothers' arguments. But the apparent extremism should not divert attention from significant educational and policy issues that lie just beneath the surface of this arguable constitutional conflict. The district has remained resolute against a general opting-out rule, and the district court now has validated that position. Even parents who raise purely educational complaints devoid of any hint of religious orthodoxy or extremism against any of the practices challenged here would still be fighting an uphill battle. In fact, without the religious gloss they would have no chance of judicial relief.

Did the womens' deeply held beliefs so cloud their vision that they could not see the political downside of a religiously based assault on the curriculum? Or did they consciously understand from the beginning that their concerns were so far-reaching and so out of step with the prevailing majority that they had to lay the foundation for litigation and that only a claim grounded in religion would have any chance of succeeding in court? Did they view themselves as champions of a higher cause—crusaders who would turn the law around by 180 degrees to protect the rights of religious and traditional parents all across America? Perhaps the intransigence of school officials and the limitations of the system left them no choice short of legal action. Whatever their understandings and motives, once they took their claims to federal court, they recast this multifactioned controversy into a bipolar dispute (although the amici involvement hinted at a potential third dimension). And once they articulated their objections as legal claims, they locked themselves and school officials into fixed adversarial positions and lost the opportunity for compromise.

Yet despite the deep divide between the mothers and the wider Bedford community, and despite their apparent disagreement with several widely accepted educational programs, the mothers have doggedly refused to give up on public education in the long run. They believe that somehow their differences ultimately can be resolved in court. Until she finally packed her bags and moved her family out of New York, Ceil DiNozzi had hoped to put her children in the Bedford schools again. "I pay my . . . taxes, and my children are being denied this. I have a right to be in public school."[178] Then again, perhaps what they tenaciously have clung to is not the concept of public schooling per se but rather their right to publicly supported schooling. Nevertheless, aside from dismissing them as religious fanatics, as some members of the community have done, one wonders what force would drive a pro bono criminal defense attorney and grandmother with a master's degree in Russian literature and a legal secretary and mother of four to keep pursuing their cause in the face of the harassment heaped on them and their children? In fact, not unlike other individuals who have made history in seeking redress through the courts, whether it was Linda Brown or Mary Beth Tinker and their families, these are ordinary people with extraordinary inner strength of conviction and outward concerns who place "conscience above conformity."[179]

Throughout this saga the mothers repeatedly have rebuffed accusations that they are trying to impose their values on other people's children. Like the parents in the *Mozert* textbook litigation from Tennessee, they have insisted that they merely want their children to be allowed to opt out of certain programs, materials, and activities. Yet their rhetoric, their actions, and the scope of the lawsuit itself seem to belie these assertions. Their broad-based legal attack, including establishment clause claims, and the relief they have sought from the federal courts could profoundly affect the entire Bedford curriculum and ultimately public school programs nationwide. More significantly, their public forum on the occult, their connections to a network of religious conservative experts and organizations, their television and radio interviews, and their numerous statements to the press all suggest a much larger agenda: saving America's schools from the forces of evil. If they could inform not just the Bedford community but the American public at large of the questionable and even bizarre practices promoted by professional educators, then they could set American education on a right course. It could very well be that what started out as an attempt to protect their children from an educational program they believed had spun out of control turned into a quest for systemic changes and even personal vindication.

For their lawyers, this is *planned litigation*—on a far smaller scale than the typical public interest test case but equally important. If they could move the court to develop the law in their favor, then they and other religious conservatives could take their strategy on the road and find judicial relief for other similarly aggrieved parents of faith. Even more optimistically, this could be just the case that makes it to the Supreme Court and perhaps even forges a constitutional doctrine of parental rights. Yet unlike other organized lawsuits that indeed may have an underlying motive to restructure public schooling, there has been no hint here of anything but a deep philosophical dilemma, cast in the legalities of religion and parental autonomy, over a critical need to rein in a public school curriculum that may be out of step with mainstream America.

The district court decision, although well reasoned, is not the definitive word on the Bedford curriculum. The case is now marching toward the Supreme Court bearing consequences of monumental proportion. It is technically true that a favorable Court ruling on several of the parents' claims would grant only individual relief in the form of an exemption while leaving the curriculum intact. But the practical effect could be otherwise. The curriculum-wide accommodation these parents have sought for their handful of children spread throughout the grades could prove an enormous burden to school administrators and teachers. It could open the floodgates for similar values-based claims and requests for opting out. Driven to its furthest conclusion, a large enough number of accommodations, mandated by law, could induce school officials to dramatically modify the educational program in the name of administrative efficiency, in the end diminishing the curriculum to the least common denominator for all students. Carried a step further, programmatic changes designed to conform to the religious beliefs of some members of the school community could provoke claims of censorship and religious endorsement from others. Such a reaction would place the school district in a Catch-22 situation, as the amici parents warned in their brief to the court.

But in a more realistic sense, the difficulty of proving that a teaching technique or program places a burden on religious beliefs renders it nearly impossible to obtain accommodation through court action. Moreover, given case precedent within the Second Circuit, particularly the *Immediato* decision, the likelihood of the appeals court recognizing a generalized parental liberty interest in controlling their children's education is close to nil. The same can be said of the Supreme Court in view of a developing pattern among the Justices of avoiding grand constitutional theories in favor of leaving questions of social policy and justice to political majorities.[180]

A broadly favorable ruling on the establishment clause claims could have extensive consequences. As the district court ruling on the Earth Day celebration demonstrates, a finding that the so-called Bedford Program, in whole or in significant part, promotes any religion, occult or otherwise, theoretically could demand systemwide changes in the curriculum and could directly affect the education of all children within the district and beyond. Based on the facts of this case, however, it appears highly unlikely that an appeal up the judicial ranks will elicit any more support for officially sanctioned religious endorsement than the trial court's narrow ruling allowed.

The breadth of the legal claims and the potentially far-reaching remedy, in fact, markedly distinguish this case from similar high-profile litigation of recent years. In the typical case, plaintiffs challenge a specific reading program, textbook series, library book, or educational program on the grounds that it violates their religious or secular beliefs or establishes a religion of secular humanism. Yet the courts have rebuffed these narrowly focused claims even though they seem more judicially manageable and amenable to a legal remedy. In the Bedford case, on the other hand, the claims are so numerous and disparate that disputes between the parties over the factual issues alone buried the attorneys in pretrial discovery for months, leaving a reluctant judge to ponder a remedy that might have rested anywhere on a continuum from totally meaningless to draconian. Meanwhile, as this drama slowly worked its way to trial, the children involved continued to be buffeted about as their families did daily battle with the district and its curriculum until, at least for the DiNozzis and the Altmans, it simply was no longer worth the fight. Initially, they transferred all but the oldest DiNozzi son into Catholic schools. Ultimately, by the time the judge issued his final ruling, they had relocated outside of the school district.

The psychological and educational cost to the children in such conflicts should not be underestimated. If the school permits them to opt out of a program or activity, which typically means a free study period, then they not only lose instructional time but experience the social discomfort of being set apart from their classmates. On the other hand, if the school denies them accommodation, they must endure the emotional discomfort and psychological dissonance that inevitably come with forced exposure and participation that offends the fundamental values of their family. These circumstances and effects are reminiscent of school desegregation efforts in the South, where children became "unconsenting footsoldiers" sent off to war by judges and parents "fighting to save the nation's soul."[181] The same can be said of children whose parents persistently challenge the curriculum based on deeply held beliefs.

For the DiBari, DiNozzi, and Altman children, the lawsuit itself has meant not merely the public notoriety that comes with being a plaintiff in a nationally visible case, but hours of stressful and socially embarrassing prodding by the district's attorneys as they attacked the youngsters' credibility and extracted information of a personal nature. The local press laid bare before the community some of the most detailed facts of their lives.[182] Yet what alternative is left to families caught in the vise of a system that leaves little room for diverse worldviews or even educational philosophies? As the lawsuit dragged on, these families transferred most of their children into private schools at an obvious financial burden, and two of them finally moved on. But what about poor families who lack the economic resources to take the highway, as one of the *Mozert* judges bluntly put it? For most of them, neither private nor home schooling is a reasonable option.

There is no easy resolution to the Bedford controversy, either in the law or as a matter of public policy. Yet how one frames the dispute depends on one's perspective. For the Bedford plaintiffs, the question has been whether parents have the constitutionally protected right to educate their children at public expense according to their own beliefs and values, whether religious or secular. For the amici parents and the Bedford school officials, the question has been whether a minority of parents can use the courts and the Constitution to shape education according to their own religious or secular views. Each side firmly believes it has a lock on the truth. Yet beyond a consensual core of basic skills and civic commitments which apparently are not at issue here, the dispute boils down to opinion, perspective, and preference. There simply is no universal right or wrong.

The judiciary has been reluctant to intervene in values-based disputes, has defined the parameters of religiously based claims in the most narrow of terms, and generally has rejected claims grounded in secular values. If the courts were to recognize a broad right to freedom of conscience or a liberty interest to direct the education of one's child, the inevitable result would be the judicial dismantling of public education, a decision more appropriately placed in the political arena. As the district court judge suggested, once the courts have identified the constitutional wrong, how can they fashion an appropriate remedy without crossing the bounds of judicial expertise and intruding on a firm tradition of local control over education? Both prior case law and remedial constraints have weighed heavily against the mothers here. Their free exercise claim is weakened by countervailing assertions made by other Catholics in the community and by the district's expert witness, a respected theologian. Their liberty claim opens a Pandora's box of psychosocial school practices used in many, although not all, of the nation's school districts.

For reasons founded in precedent and court legitimacy and capacity, this case may prove an empty victory at best for MaryAnn DiBari, the sole remaining plaintiff—but that depends on her immediate and ultimate goals. If the motive behind the litigation goes deeper than the facts of this particular case, then a personal defeat in court does not necessarily preclude a long-term victory in the political arena. In other words, she may lose the battle in Bedford but garner support in fighting the larger war over American educational values. The case carries enormous symbolic weight, having attracted national attention for its extreme religious claims grounded in Catholicism yet outside of mainstream Catholic beliefs, for its unique setting in a high-status metropolitan New York community, and for its sweeping attack on the curriculum. As it works its way on appeal up through the federal courts, the educational issues raised will continue to engage the media and generate debate over practices and programs that have captured the imagination of educational professionals but may have escaped the attention of parents and the general public.

For now the district can claim victory on most counts, although the trial court's detailed discussion of the Earth Day celebration should give pause to even the district's strongest defenders. But this case is unlikely to prove a zero-sum game for Bedford school officials. By the conclusion of the trial, defending the Satan suit had cost the district in excess of four hundred thousand dollars in legal fees,[183] including compensation to the plaintiffs for their litigation expenses to the extent that they prevailed. At least some Bedford taxpayers, and certainly the district's detractors, are bound to conclude that the litigation costs have diverted tax dollars away from the educational program so prized in this academically oriented community. And if the district were to lose in the end, even a final affirmation of the trial court's narrow ruling could create a public backlash in which board members and school officials would be held accountable for having drained the district's resources in defending practices and programs over whose educational merit reasonable minds might sharply disagree. Further, while the addition of three amici parents to the school board over the course of the litigation, with the Reverend Alcorn now serving as president, can be interpreted as a measure of community support for the district and its educational program, at least among the small percentage of those who vote in school board elections, it can also hold the board up to greater scrutiny and criticism.

On a more constructive note, there are signs that the events surrounding the lawsuit and the potential fallout may have proven sobering to the entire Bedford school community. In September 1997 board members adopted revised principles of board conduct, including one that directs the board president to move away from topics that have become attacks on individuals. Another principle directs them, in public discussion and with the press, to refrain from using terms that divide the board into groups or factions.[184] Over the summer of 1997, district officials responded openly to a petition signed by forty-two parents challenging the middle school sex education program (on grounds of inappropriateness and not religion) and agreed to implement a new human sexuality curriculum beginning the following fall.[185] Obviously this narrowly focused but educationally based secular challenge presented a more compelling argument for consideration than the seemingly idiosyncratic religiously based claims presented in the Satan suit. Even the local press, which has wavered between dismissal and hostility in the litigation, commended the school board's "appropriate response" to the parents' petition. "The subject is obviously delicate," the editorial stated, "and parents can legitimately wonder whether its handling under specific conditions strains the preparedness level of adolescents, without laying themselves open to charges of acting puritanical."[186]

In October 1997, the school board began an evaluation of the district's overall curriculum under the direction of a newly appointed assistant superintendent of curriculum and instruction.[187] That the renewed curricular interest and more conciliatory approach were directly related to the lawsuit, to the influence of new board members, one of whom is a member of the clergy, to a new board president, to a new individual in charge of the curriculum, or to a combination of any or all of these factors is speculative but reasonable. In the meantime, the district has dropped the Yale Decision-Making Program, one of the points of contention in the litigation, while a controversial exercise on peer pressure to engage in sex is no longer used with ninth graders in the peer facilitation program.

These changes undoubtedly have proven of some comfort to MaryAnn DiBari and Ceil DiNozzi. But given their deep qualitative differences with the district's curriculum, the faint promise of incremental change and the reality of the district court's narrow victory have left DiBari in particular not far from where she began back in 1995 in her challenge to the *Magic* card game. More significantly, it still leaves her grandchildren immersed in an educational program that is directly at odds with their family's most fundamental values and beliefs.

Valuable lessons on policy and politics can be extracted from this seemingly legal controversy. But the generalizability of the findings and conclusions depends directly on the representativeness of the context. This takes one back to where the saga began. Is Bedford typical of most school districts? It goes without saying that not every school system boasts the property values, high standardized test scores and school expenditures, and famous residents of Bedford. And although many districts find themselves in isolated or organized conflicts over the curriculum, most do not end up in court fighting charges of satanism. But underneath the surface, Bedford—with its elected school board that oversees a school budget funded significantly through the local property tax and its parent population characterized by diverse values, beliefs, and perspectives on education—from recently immigrated Latin American laborers to sophisticated, well-educated professionals, from sixties liberals and neoprogressives to fiscal and social conservatives—could be Anytown, USA. Whether district officials represent the majority of parents or merely the most vocal, active, and organized segment of the community remains uncertain, but that question is one that plagues local school politics across the country. Like school districts nationwide, Bedford has come under all the social and political forces and all the educational trends that have swept over the twentieth century. Those elements have defined the conflicts and the factions that have emerged over the past several years, not only in Bedford but across the field of education.

Perhaps the most striking lesson to be learned from Bedford is that the real devil in such struggles may be the common school itself, an outdated, one-size-fits-all approach to compulsory education set against the backdrop of an almost endless universe of programmatic options. Bedford has shown that reasonable, well-intentioned people can and will disagree on which of those options are best for their children and for their community.

Chapter 7 Education for Democratic Citizenship

The Supreme Court has repeatedly instructed the American public that the ultimate objective of publicly supported primary and secondary education is to prepare the young for democratic citizenship. One can safely assume widespread agreement on this broad, state-directed objective, although most Americans would look for a balance of individual self-fulfillment. The case law, however, reveals far less agreement over the specific skills, traits, and knowledge necessary for maintaining the democratic state. This disagreement frequently emanates from deeply held convictions, convictions grounded most often but not always in religious beliefs which conflict with the pervasively secular values of the common school.

Driving the values debate is the fundamental question of how to preserve basic freedoms in a pluralist society governed by majority consent and founded on both the liberal principle of individualism and the republican ideal of civic virtue. When we talk about education for democratic citizenship, we mean an education that instills in students those political beliefs and values that are the bedrock of a liberal democratic state. Among these are the recognition of basic rights and freedoms, the rejection of racism and other forms of discrimination as affronts to individual dignity, and the duty of all citizens to uphold institutions that embody a shared sense of justice and the rule of law.[1] To achieve these goals, we look toward an education that is both common and diverse at the same time. On the common or universal side, education must strive to achieve a strong influence on the beliefs of students regarding public matters. On the diverse or particular side, it must endeavor to maintain a principled forbearance of influence regarding private matters, avoiding the danger of imposing on children a single correct and comprehensive vision of the good life.[2]

Attempts to work through this inherent tension between commonality and diversity inevitably get caught in a tangled web of interconnected concepts drawn from America's liberal roots in the eighteenth-century Enlightenment and nourished by the spirit of twentieth-century progressivism. Prominent among these concepts are autonomy, neutrality, rationality, and tolerance. Each of these has been subject to intense scrutiny from postmodernists at one end to pre-Enlightenment religious conservatives on the other, a strange alliance indeed. Both distrust modern claims to knowledge and both trumpet the failure of the Enlightenment project and its direct descendant, liberalism. At the same time, center-left communitarians and various shades of liberals within the academy have engaged in heated and at times vituperous philosophical debate, struggling to reconcile the liberal notion of education for democratic citizenship with the needs and demands of religious minorities whose beliefs and practices defy commitment to one or more of these concepts. Much of this debate revolves around religious and particularly fundamentalist objections to the public school curriculum, which presents a most complicated case and extreme vantage point for balancing the conflicting and overlapping interests of child, parent, and society. A close examination of the competing arguments in this polemic sheds light on the ambiguities within education's liberal underpinnings and the implications for policy reform.

THE LIBERAL VIRTUES: TRUTH, MYTH, AND SPECULATION

For the past decade, two court decisions and one particular scholarly work have dominated the discussion on the limits of liberalism in accommodating religious diversity in the context of education. The underlying facts and legal claims presented in *Yoder* and *Mozert,* together with Amy Gutmann's book *Democratic Education,* have come to serve as a baseline in the debate over educational values and purposes.[3] All three have ignited and sustained a firestorm of reaction and response on the respective roles of parents and the state in educating children for citizenship. *Yoder* and *Mozert* provide a unique and extreme context with debatable judicial rationales, while *Democratic Education* has proven equally controversial in its almost unyielding commitment to core political virtues, especially its reliance on particular models of autonomy and rational deliberation. Taken together, they create a useful backdrop for examining the paradoxes of liberalism and for redefining the essential principles of education in a liberal democracy. As scholars have carefully weeded through Gutmann's arguments and the court decisions, they have left a winding trail of insights that selectively reveal the truths, myths, and speculations surrounding the liberal virtues and how they relate to parental dissent and educational values. As an exemplar of liberal thought on schooling, Gutmann's book is an appropriate place to start the discussion on the meaning of education in a pluralist society.

For Gutmann, the core value of democracy is "conscious social reproduction," and the principal aim of education is political: to cultivate in children "the virtues, knowledge, and skills necessary for political participation" in a democracy. In her view, the primary goal of education is a collective one, that is, education must meet the ends of the state. To that end, the educational process must impart to the young the core liberal virtues of autonomy, rational deliberation or critical thinking, and tolerance for differing ways of life. She grudgingly recognizes the interests of parents in teaching their children conceptions of the good life. Within the ideal of democratic education, Gutmann maintains, the family is hardly a "haven in a heartless world" but rather the appropriate object of moral scrutiny. She views political education as the mechanism for leading children to appreciate and evaluate ways of life that are contrary to those of their families.[4]

Educators, Gutmann argues, must develop in children the capacity to critically deliberate among "good lives and good societies" so that as adults they can distinguish between democratic and undemocratic ideas. In order for the state to make choice and freedom possible and meaningful, it must teach future citizens "respect for opposing points of view and ways of life." Children must "learn to *behave* not in accordance with authority," she argues, "but to *think* critically about authority if they are to live up to the democratic ideal of sharing political sovereignty as citizens."[5]

Gutmann's arguments bear directly on the current debate over the content and structure of schooling and especially on claims brought by parents for greater voice and choice in the education of their children. Her insistence on autonomy, rational deliberation, and tolerance continues to provide a political and judicial rationale for dismissing the claims of dissenting parents, as the *Mozert* opinions demonstrate. Since the original publication of her book in 1987, conflicts between religious minorities and the larger liberal cultures within which they are located have intensified, not just in the United States with respect to Christian fundamentalists but in countries such as England with growing Muslim communities. The pervasiveness of the problem and the foundational differences between secular liberal thought and the worldview of religious conservatives have invited scholars both in the United States and abroad to dissect liberalism's fundamental premises one by one within the context of education's unique tensions and purposes. Almost inevitably, Gutmann's work, including her more recent writing, plays into the discussion.

Over the past decade and a half, political philosophers from John Rawls to Stephen Macedo and William Galston have reconsidered the premises underlying what they term *comprehensive* liberalism, of which Gutmann's work is a contemporary modified version applied to education.[6] In its stead they have presented a more tempered *political,* or minimal, liberalism reconceived in various forms, all of which allow for greater social diversity (although Galston goes the furthest in this regard). They and others have refuted in varying degrees comprehensive interpretations of liberal commitments and have made diverse claims concerning the aims of education for citizenship. More recently, Gutmann has challenged the notion that political liberalism accommodates more social diversity through civic education than comprehensive liberalism, but her argument seems to miss some of the fine distinctions between the two.[7]

While not presenting a monolithic viewpoint, minimalist liberals have one critical point in common. They reject the notion of an expansive ethical doctrine or comprehensive set of *moral* commitments on the order of Mill's ideal of individuality or Kant's value of rational self-perfection and autonomy that would govern every aspect of public and private life.[8] Instead, they shift the focus to the *political* values shared by reasonable people. They struggle to reconcile these values with cultural pluralism, recognizing that within society there exists reasonable diversity of religious, philosophical, and moral beliefs as the inevitable consequence of free institutions.[9] They distinguish between the private and public spheres, recognizing that people may be bound by moral or religious commitments unrelated to choice in their personal lives even though they bracket those commitments in the public arena of politics and law. For the minimalists, the moral center of people's existence is not to be found in public space but in more private spaces. They reject the notion that we should all be integrated into a public community in which "our differences are marginal to who we are."[10] For political liberals, education in a liberal democracy should teach children to reflect on politically relevant issues but not on issues that bear on their personal lives.

Liberals give salience to the political over the cultural. Minimalist liberals, on the other hand, see a place within liberalism for cultural membership. Concepts of the self, they maintain, are not autonomously chosen but are rather embedded in a shared social context. In taking this position, they at least partially address the communitarian critique of liberal autonomy and individuality.[11] The liberal vision, communitarians argue, fails to incorporate an independent principle of community in the sense of shared practices and understandings which in turn influence how a society defines principles of justice. Communitarians reject the liberal politics of rights for a politics of the common good. Political liberalism, in its various forms, attempts to incorporate this sensitivity to culture and context, modifying but not abandoning fundamental liberal understandings of justice, toleration, and reason.

Before examining these understandings, I want to clarify the basic premise that the purpose of education is to prepare the young for active participation in a democratic society. Citizenship is undeniably an important aspect of education. As Mann and the common school reformers well understood more than a century ago, a state-centered purpose offers a politically acceptable justification for the use of tax revenues to support a vast system of universal government-funded schools. Nevertheless, overemphasizing the state's interests as the ultimate end of education could easily undercut not only liberalism's concern for autonomy but significant interests in preserving diversity and community, to which liberals effectively lay little claim. Standing alone, the notion of education for citizenship risks negating or at best minimizing the benefits that children gain from becoming self-fulfilled individuals who can choose from among various visions of the good life under the guidance of their family and cultural community. Indeed, it presents a frightening image of children as instruments for advancing political ends. When one talks about education for democratic citizenship one needs to temper the discussion by reflecting on the developmental needs of children, including their need for a culturally coherent life.

Keeping that caveat in mind, one can gain insight into the aims and purposes of common schooling and the potential for educational reform by examining core liberal commitments together with several related principles and concepts that repeatedly surface in the debate over dissent and educational values. Included among these are autonomy, neutrality, rationality, tolerance, and the notion of the examined life.

Autonomy

The question of whether autonomy or tolerance is at the center of liberal theory and whether one can exist without the other has played a key role in the contemporary debate over schooling.[12] For minimalists, autonomy in a pluralist society must give way to tolerance in order to preserve community and governmental stability.[13] Galston totally refutes autonomy as a core liberal value, arguing that liberalism is not about choice but rather about the protection of diversity. While the autonomy principle ostensibly protects the capacity for diversity, he argues, it paradoxically imposes a kind of uniformity on those who choose a way of life that does not embrace autonomy.[14] There is merit to his argument; to insist on autonomy as the driving force behind education is a form of authoritarianism and consequently illiberal in itself. Rawls, on the other hand, does not reject autonomy entirely but rather restricts it to political contexts. In our personal lives, he argues, autonomy does not accurately portray our deepest understandings. As one strives to make life worth living, one's personal identity can conceivably be so tied to particular constitutive ends that one is precluded from seeing those ends as rationally revisable. Since everyone does not accept the ideal of autonomy, then presenting it as "the only appropriate foundation for a constitutional regime," he argues, renders liberalism nothing more than another "sectarian doctrine."[15]

The bare notion of autonomy conjures up images of the rootless child untouched by choices made by others. But to saturate young children with a variety of competing visions of the good life that reaffirm those presented in the wider secular culture but negate the vision fostered by their family can undermine their autonomy by effectively forcing the choice of a life contrary to that of their parents and community. An alternative way of approaching the autonomy debate is to recognize that, regardless of whether autonomy is essential to liberalism, there are different starting points for the child's journey to that end. For some, it might be the experience of the common school. For others, it might be a particular worldview rooted in cultural or religious beliefs.[16] To be autonomous is not to be "free-floating" but to engage in a dialogue between reflectiveness and embeddedness. In order to engage in critical reflection, one must start with a prereflective set of values which when carefully considered lead one to establish goals that encompass a life of continuous character. The development of a stable worldview early in life is a precondition for this internal dialogue.[17]

Parents who seek accommodation for their dissenting views present the Lockean argument that it is exactly such autonomy that they are asserting for themselves. The conventional liberal response is that it is not the autonomy of the parent but that of the child as a future citizen that needs to be protected in order to enhance the child's participation in democratic society. From that view, these same parents are denying autonomy to their children, a danger underscored by Justice Douglas in his separate opinion in *Yoder*. This line of argument suggests that parents may not represent the best interests of their children, and, beyond that, the state may prod the child in a direction contrary to the interests of the parent.

A democratic society undoubtedly should not afford parents unfettered authority over their children. In extreme cases of child neglect or abuse or when parents deny the child a basic education in literacy, mathematical skills, and a fundamental understanding of core constitutional commitments, the state may step in to protect the interests of the child. As Rawls tells us, "Society's concern with [the] education [of children] lies in their role as future citizens, and so in such essential things as their acquiring the capacity to understand the public culture and to participate in its institutions, in their being economically independent and self-supporting members of society over a complete life, and in their developing the political virtues, all this from within a political point of view."[18]

But on the other hand, we should not presume in the ordinary course of events that the state, as represented by administrators and school board members arguably promoting the majoritarian values and preferences of the community, is most able to determine what is best for the child in all cases. Such a presumption in favor of dominant state control is highly contestable where the interests of families holding minority views are involved. A look at public policies in somewhat divergent but related contexts suggests a more balanced resolution. For example, as a society we do not deny adults a significant measure of self-governance merely because many of them harm and even kill themselves. Nor do we deny parents in general custody over their children because some parents abuse and neglect children. In both cases, we "police the extremes"—by involuntarily confining the mentally ill who show signs of posing a danger to themselves and by withdrawing or denying custody to parents who behave in ways that pose a real threat to their children. This second practice suggests a normative policy judgment and legal presumption that parents as a rule act in the best interests of their children.[19]

Aside from policy arguments questioning the consequences that flow from the autonomy ideal, the concept itself presents inherent conflicts, especially when applied to education. *Autonomy* is an ambiguous term. First of all, it is difficult if not impossible to identify the type and degree of critical reflection that fosters an acceptable level of autonomy. But there is also something paradoxical about the claim for autonomy as an aim of liberal education, which itself involves the systematic introduction to the public symbolic forms that make up a culture. And even beyond socialization, education exerts a powerful indoctrinating force whose direction is determined by a combination of school policy and teacher discretion. Once we acknowledge this reality, it would be inconsistent to regard education as an activity that expresses or nurtures a person's autonomous choice.[20]

Neutrality, Rationality, and Religion

The discussion of autonomy relates to the liberal insistence on neutrality as a prescription that political decisions be made independently of any particular vision of the good life. But neither neutrality nor other liberal virtues, including autonomy and rational deliberation, are themselves non-neutral. They all stem from partisan, dogmatic assumptions. The inherent indoctrinative function of education combined with its compulsory nature, its contemporary favored position on certain social issues beyond the core constitutional commitments, and the financial constraints on families seeking private alternatives all make this issue of particular significance to schooling.

The discrepancy between the promise and the reality of the neutrality principle hinges on the distinction between procedure and substance. The state can validly argue that schooling is procedurally neutral in that the same curriculum within a given school or program is offered to all students of similar ability regardless of such irrelevant factors as race, ethnicity, gender, or social class. Substantively, however, the curriculum is decidedly not neutral. Those in authority, acting under the forceful and almost unquestioned influence of the educational establishment, determine and design the formal and informal curriculum in accordance with their own values and pedagogical judgments, which may or may not reflect those of the community majority. The curriculum is value-laden— from the textbooks selected to the methods of teaching to extracurricular offerings and the historical figures profiled as role models—from what is included to what is excluded. Whatever is done or said in the classroom conveys an inescapable and powerful non-neutral message to children that convention and authority are behind a specific value or practice.[21]

The principle of neutrality, with its hidden nuances and inconsistencies, reflects a decided subjectivity that directly bears on the related discussion of critical thinking or rational deliberation. What is reasonable and "deserving of a
voice" is largely defined by the dominant cultural group, who view those challenging the larger culture as the "embodiment of Unreason."[22] By disqualifying
religious judgments or beliefs, for example, liberalism in effect "privilege[s] a
particular conception or range of conceptions of rationality," which seriously
undercuts liberalism's claims to neutrality and impartiality.[23] From the rafters
of postmodern deconstructionism, Stanley Fish has pointedly underscored
these internal contradictions within liberal theory. At the center of the liberal
project, he argues, "is a very particular moral agenda . . . that has managed, by
the very partisan means it claims to transcend, to grab the high moral ground,
and to grab it from a discourse—the discourse of religion—that had held it for
centuries." Yet, as Martha Nussbaum points out, a religious search for the good
is a liberty "most deserving of protecting by a liberal state."[24]

The liberal concern appears to rest at least partially on a fear that religiously
devout individuals are inclined to blindly form their opinions on public issues
based upon those of their religious leaders and not as a matter of individual reflection. This line of thinking is a throwback to the presidential campaign of
1960, during which there were widespread fears that a Roman Catholic in the
White House would more likely answer to the papacy than to individual conscience or to the public good. Political leaders of various denominations have
since demonstrated the fallacy of that blanket assumption. At the same time, the
question of public officials bracketing their religious beliefs in their public decisions has become a topic of lively debate. Such concerns, in fact, demonstrate
a suspicion of and even a hostility toward religious as compared with other
deeply held views, lending credence to Stephen Carter's observation that contemporary culture conveys a message that "people who take their religion seriously, who rely on their understanding of God for motive force in their public
and political personalities . . . [are] scary . . . [and] maybe irrational."[25] Citizens
of every stripe are influenced in their opinions by group identification, whether
it be membership in a political party, a union, a professional organization, or
any interest group. This "blind spot" toward religious believers is especially
prevalent within the academy, where "unbelievers can expound . . . crudities
about the sources of [religious] belief, of a level which any educated believer
would be excoriated for applying . . . to members of another confession.[26]

From Horace Mann to John Dewey and on to the contemporary educational
establishment, common or public schooling is believed to be the essential one

best system for realizing the ideal of education for democratic participation. The conventional wisdom tells us that public schools teach children to think critically in the sense of reaching independent conclusions. But that wisdom again is based on the mistaken belief that schooling is neutral, while the evidence indicates that education is inherently indoctrinative. What John Coons refers to as the "neutrality legend" of the common school, he says, "borrows heavily from the idiom of liberty for the sound political reason that in this culture liberty is a rich source of value energy." Yet looking back at the history of common schooling, one sees that the legend itself was borne out of "nativist folklore" in an attempt to free immigrant children from the shackles of their culture and religion.[27] School officials may believe—or at least want to believe—that they develop in students critical thinking skills that will lead them to form their own opinions. But the curriculum in fact leads students to certain school/teacher-directed opinions.

Many liberals would refute that assertion and agree with the conclusion drawn by two judges in *Mozert* that mere exposure to certain instructional materials does not require students to affirm or deny their beliefs. This position, however, overlooks the indoctrinative power that values reflected throughout the school experience may have over the formation and transformation of beliefs, values, and identities, above all in young students. In other words, while school officials may not consciously *intend* to influence values in this way, repeated exposure can have the *effect* of affirmation or denial in the minds of impressionable students, leading some of them to adopt values such as those supporting abortion rights or the theory of evolution as fact that directly contradict the beliefs espoused by their family. This argument, which the parents in *Mozert* unsuccessfully advanced, actually turns on its head the liberal view that rational thought is the best safeguard against indoctrination.[28] Indoctrination, while often quite subtle, is nonetheless powerful.

Although it seems evident that critical thinking skills are crucial to democratic participation, one cannot assume, for example, that all religiously inclined parents who challenge certain instructional programs or materials oppose rational deliberation or prefer their children to think any less critically than others. Many merely want their children, as most parents do, to reach a conclusion similar to their own regarding certain values and scientific phenomena. If by *critical thinking* one means the ability to examine information presented objectively by the teacher and to reach an independent conclusion, must that conclusion be free of parental influence? To suggest so may imply that there is one conclusion or set of conclusions that the school would find preferable—a state-imposed orthodoxy. In the context of mass compulsory education, in which the dominance of government-operated schools has an intellectual grip on the ideas presented to a captive audience of impressionable students, such an outcome preference violates the neutrality principle and even hints at totalitarianism.

One cannot assume that parents and children who reject secular teaching are incapable of rational thought simply because they ground their views of worldly phenomena in transcendental norms rather than in what is conventionally thought of as objective scientific inquiry. The suggestion that their religious orientation will impair their ability as adults to participate effectively in the democratic process or to distinguish between good and bad societies or to engage in republican deliberation is purely speculative. If what one means by rational deliberation is the ability to reflect on basic civic ideals, then, as Galston notes, this sort of civil deliberation is "compatible with unshakable personal commitments."[29] Individuals should be deemed reasonable citizens because they espouse certain shared political commitments regardless of their private commitments, religious or otherwise.

Liberalism exalts science over religion. Science is neutral, factual, and objective while religion is biased and subjective. John Dewey, for example, insisted that the scientific method is the "one sure road of access to truth" in all spheres of life. In the postmodern world, people have merely replaced the "worship of God" with the "worship of science."[30] Political liberalism, on the other hand, is not based in a comprehensive commitment to science but rather allows citizens to individually connect shared political values with their beliefs about "the truth as a whole."[31]

There are those who argue that scientifically proven ideas are not essential to democracy, which requires only a consensual understanding of social good within the bounds of constitutional norms.[32] Although this argument may be valid in the abstract, it must be tempered in practice with the responsibility of schooling to give students a common understanding of basic scientific truths or incontestable phenomena, for example, the laws of physics. Nevertheless, both democracy and republicanism depend for their sustenance on a mix of diverse views that generate civil debate and dialogue. A liberal education should try to assure that students are capable of making "all things considered" judgments rather than "accept uncritically the conventional wisdom of any discipline, including science."[33]

Religious challenges to the curriculum have in fact questioned scientific claims to intellectual authority, revealing science as its own brand of orthodoxy immersed in a cultural context with no claim to historical objectivity.[34] These arguments resonate throughout the debate over evolution versus creation science. To juxtapose religion and science in American culture confirms the similarities which provoke the intense competition between the two as models of explanation and order. Each looks to certain kinds of relations (causal versus teleological) and requires certain kinds of evidence (founded in sense perception versus religious experience or Scriptures). Each operates within its respective worldview without critically examining its basic assumptions.[35]

Reasonableness and objectivity depend in large measure on one's conceptual net. Even those who support special constraints on religion in the public square reject the epistemological attack on religion. As the legal scholar William Marshall tells us, "Just as not all non-religious postulates and mores depend on reason, not all religious principles derive from faith. . . . The belief that reason inspires moral or political truths is just that—a belief . . . [E]ven if faith can be epistemologically distinguished from reason, the conclusion that mores produced by rational discourse are superior to those derived by faith seems arbitrary at best."[36]

Cultural Coherence, Self-Esteem, and the Examined Life

The notion that education must impart the ability to deliberate critically among a range of good lives has intuitive appeal.[37] Galston unequivocally counters that "liberal freedom entails the right to live unexamined as well as examined lives." He recognizes the philosophical position that a life guided by unquestioned authority may be incompatible with individual freedom. Yet he also questions whether the state can build this conclusion into a system of public education "without throwing its weight behind a conception of the good life unrelated to the functional needs of its sociopolitical institutions and at odds with the deep beliefs of many of its loyal citizens."[38] Many strongly traditional parents, regardless of their religious attachments, firmly believe that children must be taught to respect and obey authority unquestioningly. Can the state rightly undermine this parental preference in child rearing? Is it essential to challenge authority in order to choose a life that is worth living? By whose standards?

The obeying of authority does not necessarily preclude drawing on Socratic method in questioning and examining the alternatives within the concept of a good human life. For some religious believers, however, the answer arrived at would most likely not endorse the Socratic ideal of the "scrupulously examined life."[39] Galston warns that if the liberal state attempts to prescribe a sole disputable conception of how human beings should live their lives, then "in the name of liberalism, it will betray its own deepest and most defensible principles."[40] Besides, if preparation for democratic citizenship is the primary concern, surely it is possible for children to obey authority unquestioningly in their personal lives yet acquire the necessary skills and attitudes to critically examine governmental practices and policies. The private and public postures can be distinct yet compatible without one driving the other.

This leads more specifically to the developmental needs of children and particularly their need for cultural coherence, that is, for a consistent moral code and values base that connect the school with their family and cultural community. By presenting students with a broad range of life choices, it is conceivable that schools could make young children skeptical of their family's values and conception of the good life. This was precisely the fear expressed by the parents in *Mozert,* that even if their children continued to openly "empathize" with them, they would inwardly become "alienated" from their family's religious tradition.[41] Depending on the gap between school and family, that skepticism and alienation could produce psychological dissonance and prevent the child from achieving an integrated sense of self.

One's sense of self is strongly enmeshed in the hierarchy of values that guide one's life. We draw our values from the culture or subculture in which we are raised. As the child psychiatrist Robert Coles notes in his piercingly insightful book *The Spiritual Life of Children,* "Children try to understand not only what is happening to them but why; and in doing that, they call upon the religious life they have experienced, the spiritual values they have received, as well as other sources of potential explanation."[42] For children, sharp discontinuities between their immediate cultural values and those presented in the external culture of the school can pose a serious threat to their identity. Pushing children to engage in serious reflection on ethical alternatives could leave them feeling "confused, demeaned or frightened" if their own ethical convictions are not yet securely established.[43] To sever young children from their family roots before they have achieved a stable self-image could prove to be "bad medicine," over all for children from minority homes.[44] In the *Smith* case, in which religious parents challenged textbooks as teaching a religion of secular humanism, one parent reported that he had "more than once seen his children in tears over the conflict between the religious values they learned at home and the moral relativism dogmatically taught in the schools."[45] Of course, this is not to suggest that publicly supported schools should accommodate religious beliefs that undermine our basic political commitments.

Research on contextual dissonance reveals that children reared in a religious context in which their family religion differs from the predominant religion in the surrounding community are likely to exhibit low self-esteem, anxiety, and depression. In fact, a combination of religious dissonance and schooling may produce stark negative effects as compared with other socially dissonant contexts, particularly in view of the specific characteristics of religious affiliation and compulsory education. Religious group membership is clear and unequivocal, the identifying factor is socially salient, and it is evaluated differentially in the larger society. At the same time, the institutional authority of the school and the teacher affords the message conveyed a distinct air of credibility. When children from families with deeply religious views that depart from those of the community majority are encouraged to challenge or question the values of their family and community, credibility can border on coercion.[46] Looking at the problem in reverse, one finds recent studies revealing a similar positive relation between self-esteem and religiosity. One study conducted among Catholic junior high school students in Canada found higher levels of self-esteem in both Catholic and public school students who took part actively in religion, while an earlier cross-cultural study across twelve middle-class high school samples including the United States, the Yucatan, Puerto Rico, Spain, and Germany resulted in similar findings.[47]

It is incontestable that children need to be connected to and not forcefully disconnected from the nurture and support of their family and culture. Children need more than education for civic competence. They need a "moral and sentimental" education, the type of education provided in most cultures by small social units with strong emotional ties.[48] They need what James Coleman and Thomas Hoffer have referred to as the "social capital" embodied in relationships with their parents and other family members.[49] Our primary bonds to family and religion as well as others' views of us, whether real or imagined, play a pivotal role in the process of defining ourselves.[50] We are not merely individuals standing at some "epistemic distance" from the many options that life presents but rather members of communities, "characters in ongoing stories."[51] As Alasdair MacIntyre puts its, "I can only answer the question 'What am I to do' [or 'what am I to think?'] if I can answer the prior question 'Of what story or stories do I find myself a part?'"[52]

Strong ties to the family, the church, and the community not only help individuals shape a personal identity, but also further the ends of democracy. These "mediating structures" of our "personal and communal existence" form a network of intimate, expressive, and associational institutions intervening between the individual and the state. Political observers have long regarded these constituent parts of civil society as critically essential to democracy.[53] These are the "value-generating" and "value-maintaining" agencies of society. They locate the child "in his or her little estate, the family, which itself [is] nested within a wider, overlapping framework of sustaining and supporting civic institutions," including the church and the school.[54]

In recent years, both minimalist liberals and communitarians have embraced the importance of associational commitments and attachments in maintaining a stable civic order. Macedo suggests that liberals "should plan for citizen virtue by accommodating and . . . promoting an active and pluralistic pattern of group life." Among the citizen virtues that further the ends of liberal self-government, according to Rawls, are what he refers to as the "cooperative virtues," that is, "the virtue of reasonableness and a sense of fairness, a spirit of compromise and a readiness to meet others halfway."[55] In that sense, political liberals find themselves sharing common ground with communitarians, for whom associational institutions are the "seedbeds of civic virtue" that form human character, competence, and capacity for citizenship. Separate schools that support family values, particularly in the early years, may constitute an especially solid groundwork for cultivating the "psychological precursors" of rationality and reasonableness that characterize the "fully virtuous citizen."[56]

At this point, however, I wish to take a step back and ask what Nomi Stolzenberg poses as the critical question in this discussion: "What rights, and whose rights are violated by . . . estrangement of children from parents . . . from the cultural tradition into which they were born?" Stolzenberg points out that while the parents in *Mozert* repeatedly warned of the danger that their children would be brainwashed by exposure to the offensive materials, the interest that they most specifically claimed was their exclusive right to control the upbringing of their children.[57] But just as parents enjoy only qualified authority to shape their children's civic education within the bounds of basic skills, cultural literacy, and constitutional commitments, they do not have absolute authority in choosing *any* vision of the good life for their child. Contrary to what at least some parental rights advocates might argue, parental autonomy is not an end in itself but rather the means to the end of developing the child. This is not to deny that most parental decisions benefit the child and that most parents are at least as good if not better judges, as compared with state officials, of what is an appropriate education for their children. Courts and legislatures have rightly afforded parents a presumption of good faith and competence. While that presumption must remain rebuttable by strong and convincing evidence to the contrary, it is only a presumption, not an absolute principle.

Children, for example, arguably have the right to an education that includes an understanding of ethical diversity, something that the *Mozert* parents unequivocally opposed. Exposure to diversity in some degree is necessary for teaching the basic civic virtue of tolerance.[58] This problem can be approached from the perspective of timing and sensitivity on the part of school officials. One compromise strategy that has been suggested is to limit separate schooling to the early years followed by common schooling for the remainder of the educational program to create later on the dialogic context necessary for engaging in critical reflection on public issues.[59] Although this Solomon-like approach may have broader appeal, it carries the questionable assumption that religious commitments per se preclude critical thinking or that diverse ideas cannot be presented in the separate school context.

Of course, there is a long distance between merely exposing children to diverse points of view on public issues or teaching tolerance of diverse religious beliefs, on the one hand, and encouraging them to choose among alternatives in their personal lives, on the other. There is also a lack of realism in the liberal argument that the school of necessity must provide the context for the examined life in the sense of presenting children with a wide range of options from which they can freely chose. Secular culture is dominant, pervasive, and unavoidable. Even children from religious homes can hardly escape popular culture's bombardment of images depicting alternative avenues to the good life. Television presents them with a wide range of life choices, some completely foreign and even antithetical to those reflected in their home and community. And as every parent is painfully aware, peer influence is a powerful force in shaping children's cultural knowledge and values. Children would have to live in a bubble to be immune from other ways of human flourishing. Even the Amish, judging from their rates of defection, have proven not to be that isolated.

Tolerance

It seems intuitive not only that tolerance, especially religious tolerance, would arouse little controversy in a liberal society, but also that it should prove essential to the success of democratic education in a society that values pluralism. But here again, moving from the conceptual to the practical presents definitional hurdles. Like other liberal virtues, tolerance admits of ambiguities and inconsistencies. Just as autonomy, despite its grounding in individuality and the promise of freedom, can lead in fact to homogenization and the negation of differences when applied absolutely, tolerance as a core liberal value presents an analogous paradox. In fact, the tolerance that autonomy-based liberalism justifies seems to apply only to those worldviews that value autonomy. As Macedo points out, "Religious communities that value simplicity and withdrawal from the modern world, such as Old Order Amish, or the fundamentalist communities committed to honoring the literal and inerrant truth of the revealed word of God, may fail to win full protection from a toleration guided by the promotion of individual autonomy."[60] Extricated from the autonomy ideal, true tolerance requires accommodation of other points of view or at least a willingness to live with them, including opposing views whose commitments preclude tolerance.[61] Tolerance requires us to be tolerant even of the intolerant.

Tolerance as a central liberal virtue guiding public policy is often misunderstood, overstated, and expected to deliver more than any reasonable definition would permit. In theory, liberal tolerance promises too much, while, in practice, it delivers too little, stacking the deck as it does against those who refuse to sign on to the whole liberal agenda and most patently against "ascetic, totalistic, and otherworldly" religions.[62] Looked at from a practical perspective, a less robust definition may prove more suitable to the ends of liberal democracy. In that sense, tolerance need not require that one pretend to afford all beliefs, values, cultures, and ideas equal worth and standing;[63] nor need it require that one respect those beliefs, values, cultures, and ideas. We would all prefer our views to be respected rather than merely "endured," yet those who "self-consciously tolerate" opposing views or visions of the good life are not likely to offer those views or visions "equal concern and respect."[64] Taken together, these requirements ask too much.

This is not to confuse respect for another's views with the mutual respect between and among individuals regardless of race, ethnicity, religion, or gender, which, as Rawls tells us, is an essential precondition to a just and stable order. Individuals can demonstrate mutual respect for each other without demonstrating "equal regard" for each other's beliefs.[65] But neither does tolerance mean indifference toward the views of others, which would ask too little. Tolerance "comes into play . . . between a ceiling of harm that rules out forbearance and a threshold of concern that makes someone else's behavior [one's own] business."[66] This tentative but shared political culture of forbearance despite our differences is what creates the possibility of a constitutional consensus.

In the context of minority dissent, tolerance is a two-way street between minority and majority perspectives and beliefs. It suggests both mutuality and non-coercion. Each side must refrain from coercing or intruding on the other, although neither is required to adopt the other's views or convictions as one's own. A useful example is a situation in which even though we might consider each other's religious beliefs absurd, we nevertheless demonstrate public reasonableness by the fact that we do not impose our religious beliefs by political means but rather join in acknowledging the political authority of reasons we can share.[67]

The argument can be made that parents who seek individualized accommodation by opting their children out of an offensive program or materials, in fact, are demonstrating tolerance for the views of others by not asking officials to eliminate the program or materials from the school. What they ask in return is that the school community demonstrate similar tolerance toward their views. This sense of mutuality often eludes communities caught in values conflicts. For example, there were those in the Bedford school community who publicly decried the notion of showing "tolerance toward the intolerant." Yet parents object to their children being exposed to materials that offend their religious beliefs not necessarily because they have a "reflexive intolerance" to the presentation of diverse views per se but because they do not want their children corrupted by premature or improperly mediated perspectives that run counter to their own.[68] As *Yoder* demonstrates, the harm that some parents may fear is that exposure to views antithetical to their religious or moral beliefs may lead their impressionable children to adopt "false beliefs" and act in conformity with those beliefs, committing "moral error."[69] For religious conservatives in New York City, for example, the distribution of condoms in the public schools without a parental opt-out provision could have caused their children to act in violation of a basic tenet of their faith that requires sexual abstinence outside of marriage.

This is not to deny that some religious parents, as the facts in *Mozert* suggest, may object to an idea of religious tolerance that recognizes religious diversity. For example, one of the selections challenged by the *Mozert* parents was *The Diary of Anne Frank,* in which Anne explains to her friend Peter Van Doan what religion means to her: "I don't mean you have to be Orthodox . . . or believe in heaven or hell and purgatory and things. . . . I just mean some religion . . . it doesn't matter what. Just to believe in something!" From the parents' viewpoint, this passage was objectionable because it encouraged tolerance for religious views contrary to their own.[70] Here Judge Lively offered the notion of civil toleration which democratic education rightly demands and the bounds of which the school officials had not transgressed. "When asked to comment on a reading assignment," the judge noted, "a student would be free to give the Biblical interpretation of the material or to interpret it from a different value base."[71] Nevertheless, we cannot assume that all parents who raise religious or philosophical objections to the curriculum are as extreme or out of the mainstream in their views as the parents in *Mozert*. It is too easy to fall into the common predilection of painting all seriously religious people into a fundamentalist corner of one description or another. Many parents with moderate but sincerely held religious convictions can easily live within the bounds of an education for democratic citizenship that neither lays claim to a comprehensive truth nor marginalizes their religiously based view of truth.

THE LIMITS OF ACCOMMODATION

The discussion of tolerance leads directly to the responsibility of the state in accommodating minority views, whether based in secular or religious beliefs. Nowhere is this issue of more critical importance than in the realm of public education, where the notion of tolerance itself seems to collide head-on with the homogenizing purposes of the common school as originally envisioned and as it functions in contemporary society. As the school population continues to expand to include various non-Judeo-Christian religions and non-Western cultures, pleas for tolerance beyond a live-and-let-live notion will inevitably escalate into demands for affirmative state accommodation. Claims made by Christian conservatives with their attendant high-profile litigation have set the theoretical and political groundwork for moving into the accommodationist mode.

The arguments advanced by minimalist liberal scholars make a strong case for greater accommodation of dissenting views within public schooling. And while courts are reluctant to recognize accommodation as a constitutional right either as a liberty interest under the Fourteenth Amendment or as a free exercise right under the First Amendment, the political and pedagogical bases for denying any and all accommodations to dissenting parents are increasingly losing ground. But the problem contains subtle complexities that get overlooked in the adversarial mode of legal action. Weighed in the balance are the individual interest in accommodation set against countervailing interests of the school, the society, and the community.

Let us assume that the primary aim of education is to promote democratic citizenship with due consideration for the developmental needs of the child. Even setting aside the question of a constitutional right, the interests of the parent and child are limited by conflicting administrative and legal concerns. In considering the claims of dissenting parents, one should not lose sight of sound pedagogy and the constitutional rights of the wider school community. Included among the interests commonly raised in opposition to accommodation are those of the school in maintaining administrative efficiency and a coherent curriculum, the interests of society in assuring that future citizens obtain the necessary skills and virtues for democratic participation, and the interests of the majority of students to an education free of censorship and religious coercion. Each of these interests assumes a distinct cast when considered in the context of the various approaches to accommodation that parents have presented before school officials and courts. Included among these are removing offensive material, granting an exemption through a partial opt-out with or without alternative instruction, and providing equal treatment. Implicit in each of these are legal and administrative problems that must be addressed in the specifics and not in the abstract.

Removal versus Exemption

As the fears expressed by the amici parents in the Bedford case demonstrate, if schools yielded to dissenting demands by totally removing objectionable materials from the curriculum, such action would create a climate of censorship potentially in violation of the free speech rights of other students. While the Supreme Court has reaffirmed the authority of school officials over the curriculum, that authority ends at the point where materials are removed for politically or religiously motivated reasons. Courts have proven unsympathetic to demands for book removal even when the materials have gone beyond value inconsistency but are blatantly offensive. As one federal appeals court cautioned in rejecting a claim that certain books contained racially derogatory terms, the threat of future litigation inevitably would lead many school districts to "buy their peace" by avoiding the use of books or other materials that could arguably cause harm to any group of students.[72] Removal for religious reasons would create a public perception or, in the words of the Supreme Court, send a message that school officials were favoring or endorsing one religion or set of beliefs over others in violation of the establishment clause. It might also generate similar requests from others and eventually eviscerate the curriculum of any meaningful content in an endless downward race toward the least offensive denominator, leaving in its wake an educational program that is bland at best and morally rudderless at worst. On this note, Justice Jackson's warning rings even truer today than it did a half century ago. If we eliminated everything found objectionable or inconsistent with the increasingly vast array of religious doctrines now represented in the schools, we would "leave public education in shreds."[73]

More modest accommodation in the form of a partial opting-out could prove administratively problematic or not, depending on the circumstances. If schools exempted children from classes, programs, or materials that their parents found offensive and perhaps even provided alternative instruction as the *Mozert* parents had requested, they might risk fragmenting the curriculum and sacrificing the cohesiveness that a sound educational program, integrated across subject areas, should strive to attain. The degree of fragmentation is a function of the subject matter, the breadth of the request, and the pervasiveness and parameters of parental discontent within the school. For example, permitting parents to opt their children out of a comprehensive language arts curriculum that is central to the instructional program in the elementary grades arguably may undermine the school's overall educational objectives to a greater degree than opting out of community service or physical education or the use of a particular library book. If only one family or several families seek a particular accommodation, this situation presents a far smaller burden on the school than the more extreme case in which a number of families each seeks an individualized exemption from different programs or materials.

Admittedly, accommodation in the form of differentiated education is widely used in other contexts. Over the past three decades, public schools have become accustomed to the concept of difference. Federal and state mandates require schools to accommodate vast numbers of students, including the handicapped, linguistic minorities, and the educationally disadvantaged, with special instructional needs. Students identified for remedial and special instruction frequently are part of what conventionally are called pull-out programs: they leave their regular classroom for a segment of the school day for small-group or individualized instruction. The school typically receives at least partial funding from federal or state sources for each student. As anyone familiar with this approach will attest, a major weakness in these programs is that they do in fact fragment the curriculum from both the individual student's and the school's perspective. Although the intent is to provide supplementary instruction while the student remains in the core curriculum, the reality is that students inevitably lose core instruction during their absence from the regular classroom.

Yet despite their disadvantages, such programs also carry advantages to both the student and the school. Individualized instruction for part of the school day is a mechanism for keeping students with different needs in the educational mainstream, and this, it is believed, benefits both the children whose needs are addressed and the remainder of the school population. A similar argument can be made for children whose family values conflict with those represented in specific aspects of the curriculum. In response to those naysayers who worry about the cultural isolation and potential balkanization caused by private education and home schooling, accommodation may dissuade at least some families from exiting the public schools and thereby preserve the diversity of views that strengthens the educational experience for all.

Undoubtedly the right to opt out needs to be circumscribed for administrative and pedagogical purposes. But where should schools draw the line? What would happen to the overall instructional program if a school were confronted with an onslaught of opt-out requests, each demanding an idiosyncratic form of accommodation? And opting out combined with alternative instruction poses an even greater financial and staffing burden on the school. How many reading programs can one school reasonably implement at one time? How can one judge whether the school is delivering the same or a superior quality of education to dissenters as to the larger school population? If accommodation translates into individualized or small-group instruction for part of the school day, are children whose minority beliefs are recognized being treated more favorably than those remaining in classrooms of twenty to thirty students? If so, then accommodation grounded in religious claims could raise establishment clause concerns. Requests for accommodation could also become an administrative nightmare, unless standards are established to guide the exercise of official discretion.

One can examine the question of standards as a matter of constitutional limits or as a matter of sound public policy. Either way, once a school establishes guidelines by policy or practice, it is locked into applying them consistently or runs the risk of coming under constitutional charges of procedural unfairness or perhaps even of favoring some dissenters over others based on the religious or secular nature of their objections. One solution, at least in determining eligibility for an individualized or group exemption, is to follow the narrow standards set forth in *Yoder* under the First Amendment free exercise clause. There the Court focused on the Amish's insularity from the larger society, the centrality of the objection to their religious beliefs, and the impact of the exemption on the child's education for citizenship and self-sufficiency. But as case law has proven, these standards are so narrow that they exclude a vast majority of claims such as those advanced by the parents in *Mozert,* who, according to the appeals court, did not have to abandon their beliefs to comply with the law but could instead have attended private schools or engaged in home schooling.

Given the Court's emphasis on the group characteristics of the Amish, the *Yoder* standards expressly exclude nonreligious claims and may even exclude individual spiritual claims not founded in group-based beliefs. The centrality factor likewise places school officials, and subsequently the courts, in the questionable position of making discretionary value judgments about the relative importance of certain beliefs to the continued exercise of the claimant's faith. Such governmental scrutiny of religion creates problems under the establishment clause. Here again the school would send a message to the larger community that it is endorsing one religion over others or religion over nonreligion.

The distinction the Court made in *Yoder* between religious beliefs on the one hand and philosophical and other secular beliefs on the other, along with the fine line drawing that it necessitates, raises the same concerns as the centrality factor, calling upon school officials and ultimately the courts to define what is a bona fide religious objection and what is merely secular. The distinction also relates to what has become a matter of scholarly debate as to whether religion is special in the constitutional hierarchy of rights or whether the accommodation of only religious objections violates the neutrality principle by privileging religious beliefs over secular values and thereby denying both sets of beliefs "equal constitutional dignity."[74] Of course as a matter of policy, school districts can ignore the legal distinction between religious and nonreligious claims and grant accommodations to all values-based claims equally, establishing other criteria that are applied consistently. The problem is finding other criteria that would prove fair and acceptable to all but not overly burdensome administratively.

This brings the discussion to a final but overarching issue raised too infrequently in the context of accommodation. Parental discretion and deference are not unlimited. At times they must yield to the state's interest, repeatedly reaffirmed by the Supreme Court, in providing children with the essential skills for participation in democratic citizenship. Just as the child is not the "mere creature of the state," neither is it the mere extension of its parents. A theory of schooling that places the developmental needs of the child at the center of family autonomy must also carve out a role for the child's voice in acquiescing to requests for accommodation made by the parent. Fixing the boundaries of that role is a delicate matter, as it involves state intervention, either administratively or judicially, into the child–parent relationship. The Supreme Court has held this relationship to be almost sacrosanct, to be disrupted only in extreme instances of real or threatened palpable harm to the child.

But just as child abuse and neglect, the most common justifications for state intervention, result in serious physical and emotional harm, so to some children the social ostracism and psychological pain of being singled out as different from other students—not to mention the limitations placed upon the child's options as an adult—can be equally troubling. Here is where the child's voice comes into play. Obviously, such factors as the child's age and maturity level and the nature of the specific program, practice, or materials from which exemption is sought are fundamental to setting the bounds of the child's expressed preference for remaining in the educational mainstream. If we look at the problem from the child's perspective alone, children need the connection with family and cultural community in order to form a coherent identity. At the same time, children of certain maturity and capacity have a very narrowly defined claim to have their own wishes taken into account, even if they conflict with those of their parents. The bottom line is the democratic goal of citizen participation, which requires that children have universal access to an education of adequate quality and substance. The question here becomes how far above that line the state should go to accommodate the specific preferences of the child.

Any discussion of potential child–parent conflict in the context of educational accommodation inevitably leads back to *Yoder* and the appropriate official and judicial role in addressing and resolving such conflicts, whether real or speculative. Justice White's opinion in *Yoder* proves quite helpful here. Although he concurred in the judgment of the Court, he tried to strike a more equitable balance among the various interests at stake while tipping the scales a bit toward the developmental and educational needs of the child. On the issue of parent-child conflict, he charted a middle course between the dismissiveness of the majority and the extreme and potentially harmful child-centeredness of Justice Douglas's partial dissent, which continues to receive accolades from child rights advocates a quarter of a century later. Justice White rightly suggested that the Court should at least have considered the interests of the children independent of those of their parents, which the majority had failed to do. Justice Douglas, on the other hand, went much further. He would have required the trial court to affirmatively elicit the children's views. He maintained that the record was incomplete without the testimony of all the children involved as to their agreement or disagreement over leaving school two years prior to the age required under the state compulsory education statute.

The truth was that not one of the children had indicated any displeasure with their parents' request for accommodation. One child in fact had testified at trial that she agreed with her parents' decision. Given that factual background, Justice Douglas's opinion raises the question as to whether in cases in which there is no evidence of a child-parent conflict, the court—or for that matter school officials—should prevail upon children to search within themselves for some seed of disagreement with their parents' values and preferences. For either to do so completely ignores the psychological and emotional needs of children to maintain a stable relationship with their parents and cultural community and forces children publicly to either disavow them or confront and announce their own helplessness in the face of parental authority. The case would have been different had the children, aged fourteen and fifteen, voluntarily expressed dissatisfaction with their parents' decision to withdraw them from formal schooling, assuming they had also demonstrated sufficient maturity to articulate their own developmental needs.

Absent any such conflict or apparent discontent, *Yoder* was rightly decided despite its narrow rationale centering on the unique group characteristics of the Amish. Having completed schooling through the eighth grade, the children had achieved the basic literacy and computational skills and knowledge of civic culture necessary to function effectively in a democratic society. There was no evidence that the parents were limiting their children's potential choices for the future, as the defection rate among the Amish affirms. In that case, the Court was correct in denying the state the right to impose its own vision of a better way of life over the parents' preferences.[75]

Yoder affords legal and political scholars a real-world context in which to examine the child-parent-state conflict and other aspects of parental accommodation. Its underlying facts, however, are not representative of most accommodation cases, which typically arise in the context of a request for exemption from an express program, practice, or materials. In that sense both *Mozert* and to a lesser extent the Bedford case, with its almost systemwide claims, are more paradigmatic. How should a child-parent conflict be resolved under those circumstances? Suppose the children in *Mozert* had wanted to continue the reading program that their parents found so harmful to their religious beliefs. Admittedly the state, acting through school officials, should weigh the preferences notably of mature children who have reached the teen years. The case here, however, involved elementary school children, and the materials at issue were a reading program. It could be argued that the children did not have the capacity to make a decision independent of their parents. Furthermore, what the parents were requesting in the form of an alternative program would not have irreparably harmed the children's life opportunities.

If one puts aside issues of administrative inconvenience and curriculum fragmentation and focuses on a hypothetical child-parent conflict over educational materials or programs, as a general rule the state should defer to the parents' interest in providing the child with an education whose values are consonant with those of the home, so long as it lies within the parameters of education for citizenship and precludes values that are inimical to the public welfare. Again, age, maturity, and context may create exceptions to the rule. Suppose, for example, that the Bedford children, contrary to the request of their parents, had voiced an objection to opting out of the drug awareness program. Here is a case in which children of approximately ten years of age choose to remain in a state-mandated course with clear social purposes (although the choice of the particular program is left to the discretion of the local district) over the religiously based objections of their parents. If the state's interests are significant, the state mandate has been reached by broad political consensus as a matter of public policy, and the child is of sufficient maturity (which may or may not be true of a ten-year-old) and has voluntarily articulated his or her own development needs, then school officials should not defer to a parental request for complete exemption from the required instruction. On the other had, if parents request not a total exemption from the state mandate but merely alternative instructional materials, then school officials should attempt to grant that request regardless of the child's age, maturity level, or preference.

But the point of this discussion is largely academic. It is rare for children to express opposition to or displeasure with an opting-out request made by their parents. Typically, children from deeply religious homes are so immersed in their culture and community that they readily comprehend the importance of their parents' values and beliefs. This is not to deny that they may also feel constrained by their parents' authority or, much worse, fear parental reprisals for raising objections. Whatever their motivation, to repeatedly acquiesce in their parents' request for exemption even in the face of taunts and ostracism from their classmates takes a strong, resilient, committed child. From all the evidence gathered in the Bedford case, there can be little doubt that the children of the challengers have a sincere commitment to the cause undertaken by their parents; yet they undoubtedly have paid a heavy emotional and social price for that commitment. At the same time, the weight and inevitability of that price neither command nor sanction school administrators or courts to go on a fishing expedition, as Justice Douglas suggested in *Yoder,* to find conflict within the family to support the state's position. School officials and judges should defer to parental requests when administratively feasible, taking into account the immediate and future developmental needs of the child in assessing the appropriateness of accommodation. When the child is sufficiently mature and clearly articulates those needs, then the state has a clearer picture from which to exercise its discretion.

A recent case from Virginia places these complex questions in bold relief, providing the exceptional set of facts for which Justice Douglas's controversial opinion has been searching all these years. His passionate appeal for the rights of the hypothetical Amish child who "may want to be a pianist or an astronaut or an oceanographer" became animated in the opinion of a juvenile court judge upholding the right of sixteen-year-old Jennifer Sengpiehl to attend her local public high school rather than continue to be schooled at home as her parents demanded. As she explained to the local press, home schooling would prepare her to be "a homemaker, cooking and taking care of babies," while public school would provide her with the science classes she needs to attend medical school and with greater social interaction with other teenagers. In the words of Justice Douglas, this young woman desired to be "master of her own destiny" rather than remain "harnessed" to her parents' way of life.[76] But her parents saw it differently. Represented by the Home School Legal Defense Association, they argued that the court had "stripped [them] of all [their] rights." They wondered how a judge could make that determination when there was "no evidence whatever that their choices [were] wrong." They too wanted what was best for their child, but they wanted it to be their decision.[77] This may have presented the ideal test case in which age, maturity, and context created the "compelling circumstances" exception to the general rule that the state should defer to the parents' wishes.

Equal Treatment of Religious Speech

A form of accommodation that has gained increasing political and legal support and has proven far less administratively burdensome and somewhat less legally problematic is the concept of equal treatment or access as it relates to religious expression. In recent years, both Congress and the federal courts have recognized the concept of religious speech as viewpoint and in doing so have expanded the right to private or individual religious expression on school grounds on an equal basis with nonreligious perspectives. Against this changing backdrop of legal rights, religious, educational, and other public interest groups have reached a fragile consensus on the role of religion in the schools in response to the judiciary's newly evolved perspective. It is now widely accepted that public schools should incorporate into the curriculum the role that religion has played historically, politically, and culturally over the centuries. The place of student religious speech, however, presents a more complex issue to resolve.

Secondary school students may organize student-led religious group meetings, similar to those sponsored by any other student organization, on school grounds during the school day as part of the extracurricular program. The Equal

Access Act of 1984 established this right as a matter of federal statutory law. Students may also distribute religious literature on school grounds subject to reasonable time, place, and manner regulations that are equally applicable to distributions of a nonreligious nature. Students may express a religious perspective on an otherwise secular topic in the course of the curriculum. Nevertheless, school officials must still exercise caution in establishing parameters for the expression of religious views or risk running afoul of the establishment clause.[78] Factors to consider include the degree of state official involvement or direction, the age of the students, the context in which the speech takes place, and whether the religious expression demands a response from a captive audience.

The legal right of students to express a religious viewpoint in the school setting is circumscribed by the bounds of coercion and endorsement within the establishment clause. Coercion turns on whether the speech imposes governmental pressure upon students to support or participate in religion or a religious activity, while endorsement turns on whether the speech conveys a message of government support making some students feel like political insiders and others political outsiders to the school community. For example, it may be permissible for students to express their religious views during nonclass hours—such as lunchtime in the cafeteria or in the school yard and hallways—if other students are permitted to express nonreligious views on similar topics. The question inevitably arises, however, as to whether religious speech by students in the course of classroom activities, while students are constructively captive, may have a proselytizing effect on other students. That question demands a contextual and nuanced analysis.

On the one hand, students should be able to express a religious viewpoint in the course of classroom discussion and in their written work. To exclude religious perspectives from the public school setting not only demonstrates hostility toward religion but also undermines the purposes of democratic education in a pluralist society. On the other hand, unlike political speech, which demands broad constitutional protection even in the school setting, religious speech can neither coerce others to accept the views expressed nor give the appearance of having been authoritatively approved by the school. If it does, it would impermissibly stretch the bounds of civil toleration. The context and manner must plainly convey the message that the school maintains a neutral position toward what is essentially private speech.

The Supreme Court has noted the unique character of public education and the "heightened concerns for protecting freedom of conscience from subtle coercive pressure in the . . . public schools."[79] To be sure, some of the dangers of coercion progressively decrease as one moves up the grades from elementary through middle and high school, particularly with regard to the private speech of individual students as opposed to school-sponsored speech. Older students are more secure in their ideas. And while middle and high school students may respond to peer pressure when it comes to fashion, speech, and other external-ities, they are less likely to do so when it comes to embracing religious beliefs. An isolated expression of religion by an individual or group of classmates is un-likely to have a coercive effect on other students.

Nevertheless, group as compared with individual expression of religious views may under some circumstances assume a coercive cast. Even if the speech does not induce nonadherents to change their beliefs, it may cause them to seriously question either those beliefs or their own position within the school. The harm, as Justice Sandra Day O'Connor has noted, is that group religious expression creates a dichotomy between insiders and outsiders within the political com-munity of the school.[80] As the plaintiff in *Lee v. Weisman* stated after the Court struck down a nondenominational school-sponsored prayer, "When I am forced to participate in a ritual . . . it's an attempt to make me different from what I am—to change my identity to make me conform."[81] Of course, student par-ticipation in a prayer or benediction, which indeed is ritualistic, in the context of a symbolically meaningful school-sponsored group activity—for example, graduation exercises—differs materially from merely listening to another stu-dent express religious views on an otherwise secular topic. The element of coer-cion is far more real in the first case than in the second.

In fact, the constitutionality of devotional exercises has become a hotly con-tested issue in school districts nationwide. The most frequently litigated prac-tice has been prayer at graduation ceremonies. Some courts have rejected any semblance of prayer outright.[82] At least one federal appeals court, however, in the latest round of litigation testing the constitutionality of an Alabama law en-acted in 1993, has given a ringing endorsement to a wide range of nonsectarian, nonproselytizing student-initiated prayer activities, including prayer at assem-blies and athletic events, and prayer at high school graduations.[83] Several other courts have drawn a similar line between officially sponsored and student-initi-ated activities that are nonproselytizing and nonsectarian.[84] Yet these seem to be distinctions without an appreciable difference. What exactly is a nonsectar-ian prayer? Would sincere Satan worshipers be granted equal treatment and ac-cess? How would school officials determine whether or not a prayer is prosely-tizing or not? By its intent or its effect or both? As demonstrated by what evidence? Whether it be student-led prayer over the intercom at the beginning of the school day or prayer over a loudspeaker at a school football game or prayers at high school ceremonies, even where students of all faiths or beliefs are granted equal access, it cannot be denied that invocations, whether denominationally identifiable or not, to a transcendental being or spiritual force are fundamentally more coercive in effect than other forms of religious expression. Practices of this nature have both the intent and the effect of creating an atmosphere of solemnity in which participants are expected to make some visible gesture of affirmation or sign of acknowledgment—bowing one's head or standing—which is substantially different from merely listening passively to another student's expression from a religious perspective. To consider any devotional exercises otherwise would distort the neutrality principle of the establishment clause beyond recognition.

But even in the context of student expression, the danger of coercion or endorsement could arise under extreme circumstances. For example, religious speech with a particular viewpoint may so dominate the range of ideas expressed that a formal policy of equal treatment is transformed into a vehicle for coercion or a demonstration of government favoritism. Suppose that students espousing the beliefs of a Protestant denomination represent an overwhelming majority of the student population in a school in which the minority is composed of small, disparate groups of Mormons, Jews, Muslims, and other non-Christians. While it may be permissible in this context for one or several students to present independent reports on the life of Christ to fulfill a course requirement, a similar presentation made by a sizeable group of Christian students who represent the dominant religious view in the school may have the effect of coercing nonbelievers to at least publicly assent to those views in order to be accepted by the dominant group. It might also send a message of school endorsement, thereby causing non-Christians to feel like outsiders to the school community. These dangers could cross over the establishment clause threshold.

A similar distinction can be drawn between an independent research project or oral presentation on a religious theme that merely represents the expression of personal views and a student survey of religious views among the student body. The independent project or presentation may arguably further the school's educational mission by exposing students to a variety of age-appropriate private speech. The survey, on the other hand, may cause some students to engage in religious soul-searching and to question their own family-directed religious beliefs. Now it is true that student discomfort alone does not justify restricting the speech of others in the school setting, as the strict constitutional limits placed on hate speech regulations have proven. However, religious speech is unique among First Amendment expressive rights in that it is the only form of speech subject to the constraints of another provision within the Constitution, namely, the establishment clause. School officials must be aware of these competing interests as they walk the fine line between free speech and non-establishment. The spate of federal court litigation that this issue has generated in recent years confirms both the importance of religious expression to students of faith and the difficulties that schools are experiencing in drawing constitutional lines.

Each time we turn a corner on the religious speech road we encounter another "What if?" This apparent indeterminacy is the inevitable consequence of the indoctrinative force of schooling for democratic citizenship within a culture that values both pluralism and government neutrality toward religion. As school officials now struggle to put into operation the recently legitimized and evolving doctrine of religious speech and to work through the many factual permutations in the real world of school policy and administration, they often fall into the thicket of litigation, leaving the federal courts to design a doctrinal road map step-by-step.

In spite of these drawbacks, accommodation in the sense of equal treatment of religious expression, within judicious limits, may in fact have a salutary and stabilizing effect on public schools. As is true of other forms of accommodation, it could very well be that the more public schools succeed in taking minority concerns and religiously inspired ideas seriously, the less motivated disaffected parents may be to seek options outside public schooling. For some parents at least, voice within the public school system may dull the passion for choice among alternatives outside the system.

Chapter 8 Re-Envisioning
Common Education

Values-based educational claims have met minimal success in the courts. The judiciary has vacillated between incredulity and hostility in addressing parental challenges, leaving any hope for meaningful resolution to local administrative discretion and state legislative reform. Yet the underlying significance and potential implications of the problem seem to have eluded most state and local officials. Unless named as defendants in a lawsuit, they tend to dismiss such conflicts as isolated eruptions unrelated to larger issues of school governance and educational purposes. The most visible movement on this front has come from private organizations that have begun to chart a tentative middle course on the national level. That effort has initiated a slow and perhaps all too quiet national dialogue which has, in the least, infused the key issues with a conciliative symbolic force whose real effect will be tested over time.

Nevertheless, this thin consensus, largely driven by recent Supreme Court decisions and the fear among liberals of Republican proposals for a constitutional school prayer amendment, has reached only several points of contention in the educational values dilemma, most notably religious expression and teaching about religion. These points have been relatively easy to mitigate when viewed against the vast backdrop of curricular conflicts for which the Court has offered little guidance. Moreover, the agreement itself is merely aspirational and lacks any mechanism for enforcement at the local level. And despite presidential endorsement, the prodding of the federal Department of Education, and attention in the educational press, public hearings held in 1998 by the U.S. Commission on Civil Rights reveal that many school officials have remained unaware of or indifferent to what should have proven to be a first step toward respecting the importance of religious and other minority views in the public schools.

To accept the concept of private, non-school-sponsored religious speech demands a change in attitude, albeit a significant change given historical separationist views throughout the educational mainstream. In contrast, questions addressing the curriculum, which by its nature is school sponsored, not only demand attitudinal changes and institutional acquiescence but further suggest affirmative steps toward broader substantive and perhaps even structural reform. School officials and educational leaders have proven particularly resistant to moving in that direction. This carries the discussion back to the fundamental question posed at the beginning: In a pluralist society that recognizes rights to freedom of conscience and belief, and also prohibits government endorsement of or interference with religion, how can education promote a national identity while at the same time preserving community and individual interests? How can it reconcile society's conflicting demands of commonality and diversity? On the side of commonality, education must develop shared values, principles, and political commitments to promote stability, coherence, and justice for free and equal citizenship. On the side of diversity, it must recognize legitimate demands of pluralism and encourage understanding and tolerance.[1]

Two approaches to resolving this seemingly irresolvable dilemma within the traditions of liberal democracy suggest themselves, one within the current system and the other more transformative in nature. Both recognize, in differing degrees, the contradictions in American democratic ideals and the need to develop mechanisms for balancing common and conflicting interests. Both reject the competing assumptions that dominate the rhetoric and distort the debate over educational values, that is, that interests must always converge in the common school or that they will always conflict in separate schooling.[2] The truth lies somewhere in between these two extremes. Democracy demands and educational governance should recognize that we share certain core beliefs. At the same time, liberalism respects the rights of individuals and groups to disagree at the wide margins.

The first approach returns to the question of accommodation within the current framework of state-operated and -funded schools, but this time with a specific view toward underlying values. Here the focus is on the local level; the aim is to construct a political framework for the exercise of official discretion to accommodate diverse views within the existing public school structure. The second approach explores the concept of family choice through various strategies, some more politically charged than others, that challenge the existing governmental monopoly over schooling. The most far-reaching and visionary of these demands a statewide commitment to structural reform and a dramatic rethinking of educational governance at the state and local levels.

Both approaches build on certain fundamental premises. Both recognize that society publicly funds education for two primary purposes: national definition and national perpetuation. These collective purposes depend upon a common core of values embodied in our public aspirations, culture, and traditions that bind the citizens together despite their peripheral differences. Both acknowledge the distinction between diversity, which emphasizes the individual's social identity in one or another cultural group, and pluralism, which focuses on variant expressions and interpretations of a common American civic idea.[3] And both recognize, despite assertions to the contrary from the multicultural and values clarification camps, that this common civic idea is embodied in ascertainable core values and commitments that can be inculcated through the pervasive indoctrinative and socializing process that we call education. While our traditions draw on the contributions of our multicultural past (and present), we are not a nation of diverse, disconnected cultures. We share a certain "cultural tradition," along with its history, ideals, and symbols, that holds us together in our diversity.[4]

The next premise is that, given existing limitations of government funding for alternatives to the common school, public schools should maintain a position of neutrality toward religion, neither directly inculcating religious values per se nor denying their existence and their fundamental role in the moral and psychological lives of certain students. Denial by silence or omission effectively is a form of repression. And finally, both approaches build on the concept of community, not only in the geographic and political connotation of the neighborhood school but also in the philosophical and cultural meaning of individuals who embrace common goals and purposes. Schools play a crucial role in articulating community values, and rightly so as long as those values do not conflict with the core values and commitments that give us common purpose as a nation. Communitarians tell us that communities "congeal" around schools, which at their best, "communicate a form of life, a *paideia*, through which we grow up in a morally and intellectually intelligible world."[5] The relation between the community and the school looms large in any meaningful examination of parental dissent, educational values, and pluralism.

The discussion turns on the distinction between *education* and *schooling*, both *common* and *separate*. The key concerns here cover not only the questions of funding and control which typically drive this debate but also what is taught, to whom, and the resulting "institutional ethos." The objective is to replace the concept of common schooling with the more expansive notion of common education, one that aims to achieve a set of educational outcomes—virtues, abilities, and knowledge—that are democratically desirable for all while at the same time acknowledging both the diverse convictions that thrive within a pluralistic society and the diverse educational applications that flow from those convictions.[6] Two alternative paths are offered to achieve that goal. The first represents a moderate, partial conception of common schooling and the second a moderate conception of separate schooling. Each aims to preserve an overriding commitment to a core of common education while accommodating uncommon values.

COMMON SCHOOLING AND THE BALANCING OF VALUES

Accommodation, most typically in the form of a partial opting out, is the mechanism currently available to parents whose values clash with those reflected in the school curriculum. While it generally is assumed that the dominant values of the school represent those of the local political majority, the reality is that at times schools speak more directly for the educational establishment and/or a visible and vocal minority within the community than for the numerical majority. Yet regardless of how deep the conflicts run or how pervasive the discontent might be, at the heart of accommodation lie values and sharp disagreements over values. These disagreements raise a host of thorny questions that demand more detailed examination than the superficial attention generally afforded them. Should school officials submit to parental demands challenging core values that define us as a nation? What about local values that help define the community and give it moral and social coherence, a shared sense of the good life? The distinction between these two definitional levels, the national and the local, is crucial to understanding the limits and potential of accommodation.

But before developing the concept of values any further, a brief detour by point of clarification needs to be made. The concept of core values must not be confused with the concept of nationally defined subject area standards, the latter being the topic of intense debate within and beyond educational circles. Standards present specific pedagogical goals based on implicit or explicit underlying values. For example, the controversial *Goals 2000: Educate America Act* fashioned by the Bush and Clinton administrations establishes a list of core indicators against which states are compared to each other and to national performance.[7] Included among these indicators are reading and mathematics achievement, a children's health index, the sale of drugs at school, and student and teacher victimization. Proposals to adopt national standards as a nationwide requirement or benchmark for measuring state performance inevitably evoke criticism from the political right to the left. For conservatives, national mandates impermissibly intrude into state and community control over education; for libertarians, they violate individual rights to freedom of conscience.

As contrasted with the level of specificity found in standards, values are "abstract idealizations." And unlike uniform curriculum standards that are imposed by an outside authority such as the state or federal government, common values ideally should emerge through deliberation on policy choices establishing the shared identities and self-definition that enable community members to engage in yet further debate and discussion.[8]

In searching for common values here, I am not suggesting a didactic approach wherein values are examined as a discrete part of the curriculum, the approach taken by the now-much-maligned values clarification movement and espoused by some modern-day advocates of character education. On the contrary, for values to be meaningful they should infuse the entire school experience. And they should be "ontologically deep," that is, they should constitute "the dominant forms of being" of those involved in the educational enterprise.[9] As Diane Ravitch aptly points out, schools possess powerful resources for developing character: "Science, properly taught, teaches children the values that are embedded in scientific inquiry. . . . Literature is a potent vehicle for questions of social and personal values. . . . History provides limitless prospects for the study of values and ethics."[10] Yet regardless of the instructional approach, any attempt to identify a core of shared values inevitably runs the risk of being criticized as no more than an abstract, subjective, feel-good "bag of virtues," a "normative illusion akin to magical thinking."[11] There is indeed some merit to that contention. Nevertheless, as a practical matter, in order to effectively balance the interests of accommodation against the fundamental purposes of democratic education, there must first exist an identifiable bottom line of essential commonalities below which idiosyncratic views cannot fall.

Although not intended to be exhaustive, a listing of those values or, more specifically, virtues that bind us together as a nation might include a mix of such incontestable moral values or character traits as honesty, integrity, responsibility, delayed gratification, self-control, and respect for authority combined with social values like concern for the environment and more fundamental political principles generally imparted through what we call civic education. Encompassed by the latter are justice and fairness, freedom of conscience and belief, freedom of expression, political and religious tolerance, and equality in the sense of equal dignity for all. These shared political commitments draw from several sources, including our common history and folklore. More specifically, they derive from legal norms established in the federal Constitution as interpreted by the Supreme Court, from federal statutes with supporting administrative regulations, and from executive orders. Taken together, these legal pronouncements represent a statement of national consensus. Their relative force and their lexical ordering come into bold relief in the distinction between negative rights—that is, the right to be free from government interference in choosing particularized visions of the good life—and the affirmative constitutional protections implicated by government funding of private alternatives to public schools.

The Supreme Court has used a similar approach to defining national public policy through positive sources of law as evidence of the nation's commitment to the principle of racial equality. Three cases that specifically address prohibitions against race discrimination and the countervailing constitutional rights of religious and associational freedom come to mind. In *Bob Jones University v. United States,* the Court upheld a federal policy that denied tax-exempt status to a private religiously affiliated university and a high school on the grounds that their racially discriminatory policies did not render them institutions organized for "charitable" purposes under federal tax law. Here the Court drew on a quarter-century history beginning with *Brown v. Board of Education* followed by an "unbroken line of cases" and "myriad Acts of Congress and Executive Orders" to establish that "racial discrimination in education violates a most fundamental national public policy." The Court unequivocally stated that "there can no longer be any doubt that . . . [such] discrimination violates deeply and widely accepted views of elementary justice" that override the exercise of sincerely held religious beliefs.[12]

The Court cited to an earlier case, *Norwood v. Harrison,* which had struck down the state loan of textbooks to private schools that engage in racial discrimination, noting that "discriminatory treatment exerts a pervasive influence on the entire educational enterprise." In *Norwood* the Court affirmed the nation's prior commitment to racial equality over other constitutional protections. While "invidious private discrimination may be characterized as a form of exercising freedom of association protected by the First Amendment," the Court stated, "it has never been accorded affirmative constitutional protections." The Court also stressed the "limited scope of *Pierce* which simply affirmed the right of private schools to exist and operate."[13] Several years later in *Runyon v. McCrary* the Court found further affirmation for the priority afforded racial equality and the antidiscrimination principle in a federal Reconstruction Era statute that prohibited racial discrimination in the making of contracts. Searching the legislative history of the statute, the Court found that it prohibited private schools from denying admission to students based on their race. Applying the statute to private schools, the Court held, did not infringe on the parents' rights to privacy or freedom of association or on the parental right recognized in *Meyer, Pierce, Yoder,* and *Norwood* to direct the upbringing and education of their children.[14]

The equality principle offers highly useful insights into the nuances and potential stumbling blocks that definitional attempts at shared values inevitably present. The most consistent justification for equality as a moral precept has rested on the belief of *humans qua humans,* a belief inherited from various sources spanning the centuries—from the Stoics, who based their egalitarian principles on the natural equality of humans as rational beings with an equal capacity for virtue, to the New Testament doctrine of equality of all souls in the sight of God, to the Declaration of Independence proclamation that "all men are created Equal" and that they are "endowed by their Creator with certain inalienable Rights."[15] This historical exaltation has evolved into an antidiscrimination principle that transcends culture. Yet beyond race and possibly gender, the philosophical and political consensus that private individuals and government officials should treat others with equal dignity and respect has not translated into universal political agreement on the degree to which formal equality in the sense of equal treatment should be recognized as a legally enforceable right. Neither has it engendered widespread agreement on whether the government should take affirmative steps to achieve substantive equality in the sense of equal results for certain groups in society.

Few Americans, nevertheless, would deny that racial equality in its formal version is a principle upon which majority consensus reflected in legal doctrine does in fact exist. Those who disagree would be looked upon with disfavor and even scorn. The Supreme Court has articulated the most exacting level of judicial scrutiny for examining governmental classifications based on race under the Fourteenth Amendment equal protection clause. Racial classifications must be narrowly tailored to promote a compelling government interest. As the Supreme Court emphasized in *Bob Jones,* Congress has enacted a comprehensive body of statutory law prohibiting racial discrimination in a vast array of human endeavors, including education, employment, and public accommodations. These laws are supported by administrative regulations issued and enforced by various federal agencies. Most fundamentally, racial equality stands unique among our political commitments in our having fought a civil war to bring that commitment to reality.

The same cannot be said of gender equality, the national consensus on equality for women being more culturally complex and less clearly defined. Here the distinction between cultural values such as equality and social norms becomes clearly apparent. Norms realize values, that is, they identify and generate rules of conduct for specific situations and contexts. Conflict arises when we attempt to create a new norm under the rubric of a generally accepted value in order to meet changed social conditions that threaten to restructure society in a profound way.[16] With regard to women's rights, most Americans save for an unenlightened minority support an antidiscrimination principle in the sense of equal treatment, at least in the public sphere. This principle could properly be placed within our common core values of constitutional commitments. Numerous federal statutes and regulations promoting gender equality in education and employment have granted equal access to schools and colleges, coursework, athletics, counseling, and job opportunities to millions of women over the past three decades with minimal exceptions drawn for conflicting religious beliefs. The Supreme Court has identified an exacting level of judicial scrutiny under the Fourteenth Amendment equal protection clause for government actions that classify individuals on the basis of gender, although admittedly a somewhat lower standard than that applied to racial classifications. The Court, most recently in *United States v. Virginia* striking down the all-male admissions policy of the Virginia Military Institute, reaffirmed that gender classifications are permissible only when they are based on an "exceedingly persuasive justification."[17]

But gender equality, unlike racial equality or even equality for the disabled, also raises controversial issues of role models and lifestyle choices which bear on privacy as well as religious concerns. Here one finds wavering support for, but only ambiguous evidence of a national consensus to replace traditional gender-specific roles for men and women with gender-neutral roles. Material proof of the culture's ambivalence toward complete gender neutrality can be found in gender role distinctions that continue to characterize the development and marketing of children's toys and video games as well as the gendered role models presented in children's television programming, despite more than a quarter century of court decisions and federal statutes promoting gender equality. Cultural disagreements over the distinction between women as professionals in traditional male-dominated careers and women as homemakers and caretakers, and the various societal implications that flow from the continuum of options between these two poles, continue to percolate beneath a thin and misleading surface of national agreement.

Gender equality provokes visceral reactions and exceptionally lively debate from within the organized conservative religious network. Many religious as well as some social conservatives see the traditional dichotomy between male and female spheres as critical to the preservation of family life. What mainstream culture considers the subordination of women, for religious conservatives has much to do with cultural and religious reproduction. From their perspective, men historically have been the "agents of assimilation" and women the "transmitters of tradition." Some cultural minorities, including a growing population of Muslims, worry whether their fundamental beliefs can be sustained once women enter the public sphere of public schooling, in which the moral and cultural messages depart so dramatically from those of their subgroup. For them, toleration implies "a right to cultural reproduction."[18]

Disagreement on the issue of gender roles has arisen in the context of the curriculum and the role models that textbooks and other instructional materials present, notably of women but also of men. In the *Mozert* case, for example, the parents objected to a reading exercise depicting a boy making toast while a girl reads to him on the grounds that it "denigrates the differences between the sexes" affirmed in the Bible. Others, including the publisher and school officials, would argue to the contrary that the exercise seeks to eliminate gender differences in basic liberties and opportunities while parents still retain the right to teach their children that boys should not have fun cooking because that is what the Bible says.[19] In view of these disparate perspectives, this aspect of the gender equality principle may work more effectively as a value determined by local consensus rather than as a national commitment.

There is even less evidence of national consensus over homosexual rights. The Supreme Court has been unwilling to extend privacy rights under the Constitution to homosexual acts;[20] and there are no federal statutory or administrative protections for homosexuals. California and several other states as well as some municipalities, including Los Angeles and New York, have enacted antidiscrimination statutes protecting homosexuals, but these are manifestations not of national but of state and local consensus. In making these distinctions among groups, my intent is not to deny or weaken the antidiscrimination force of equality in terms of respecting the equal dignity of all individuals regardless of personal characteristics. Certainly homosexuals fall under that umbrella of protections. To hold otherwise would betray our basic commitment to the equality ideal. Neither am I suggesting that public schools should never incorporate nontraditional lifestyles into the curriculum. Rather the definition of "contested cultural norms" such as the acceptability or relative value afforded alternative as compared with traditional lifestyles based on sexual orientation should be left to community discretion.[21] As in the question of gender roles, the direction of that discretion should be determined by a locally based process of reasoned deliberation and dialogue whereby community members, including parents, students and educators, and members of the clergy jointly define those local values upon which they can agree for inclusion in the curriculum.[22]

The fragility of any consensus on contested cultural norms such as homosexual rights and the political difficulties in gaining support on more than a local level became manifest in the events preceding and following the adoption in 1992 by popular referendum of an amendment to the Colorado state constitution. The amendment prohibited local and state government and any of its agencies from granting protected status on the basis of homosexual, lesbian, or bisexual orientation.[23] Its adoption was a direct response to ordinances previously enacted in several cities banning such discrimination in housing, education, employment, public accommodations, and health and welfare services. The amendment effectively repealed these local ordinances. The controversy eventually came full circle when the Supreme Court ruled that the amendment violated the equal protection clause of the Fourteenth Amendment. But the Court avoided making a sweeping pronouncement on homosexual rights and instead grounded its decision in political process. According to the Court majority, laws of this nature and scope that disqualify a class of persons identified by a single trait from the right to seek protection from the law are "unprecedented in our jurisprudence" and "not within our constitutional tradition."[24]

Despite these sharp disagreements, all discussion of contested cultural norms should not be considered off-limits in the public schools, as long as the subject is presented within the bounds of age-appropriateness. Without such dialogue among the students' "primary moral languages," not only will the common culture become too thin (which is already becoming manifest in the drive to avoid controversy), but students will fail to develop the understanding of views with which they disagree. That understanding is essential for democratic engagement. In fact, at least some and perhaps even many members of cultural and religious minority groups who challenge the secularist bias of the public schools would welcome such an inclusive policy. Parent dissenters do not necessarily want the curriculum to privilege their views over others but merely to include their perspectives along with others. In some cases, they merely want the curriculum to reflect an appropriate range of moral perspectives on nonconsensual issues without falling into the trap of moral relativism.[25] Of course, the precise limits of appropriateness could themselves become controversial. And those who view certain questions as moral absolutes might take exception to any discussion as a demonstration of validation.

Even an inclusive process of local deliberation will not satisfy those in the community whose beliefs, whether religious or philosophical, compel them to take an unyielding position. That fact became evident in the controversy in New York City in the early 1990s over condom distribution in the schools. It was manifest in the objections raised by the parents in *Mozert*. It has crystallized in many but not all of the concerns raised by the claimants in the Bedford case, in which worldviews are so far apart that there seems to be no common ground for agreement or compromise.

As a matter of policy, should school officials accommodate parents like the Bedford mothers who challenge noncore values based on either religious or philosophical grounds? For example, what about parents who espouse a modern-day view of women's role but reside in a community where the schools have infused the curriculum with a more traditional perspective? Or those who want their children to learn respect and affirmation and not merely tolerance for gays and lesbians where the community majority opposes that position? Or parents who object to family life programs? Do their concerns merit accommodation? Aside from the constitutional merits of their claims and the arguable incursions on family privacy, if the objection is based on a noncore local value, which by definition is peripheral and discretionary on the part of local officials, then the school should make every effort to accommodate the parents within the bounds of reasonable administrative capabilities and sound pedagogy. The justification for accommodation becomes even more compelling when the challenged instruction or materials do not merely expose children to ideas that their parents find offensive or disagreeable but could potentially induce children to engage in behavior that has serious social, psychological, or physical consequences, as in the case of condom distribution.

For families who fall outside the community consensus, the school can offer an exemption from the program or materials entirely, as some districts have done with regard to AIDS and sex education and often under mandate of state law. Another option would be to offer the children alternative instruction or materials, as school officials had originally allowed in the *Mozert* case. The appropriateness of each of these alternatives hinges on the particular program or practice challenged and the underlying value opposed. Assuming the objection is directed at a noncore value, the closer the program is to basic skill development like reading or mathematics, the greater the school's interest in providing alternative instruction and not complete exemption. Conversely, the closer the program is to matters traditionally addressed within the family like sex education and drug awareness, the greater the family's interest in obtaining a complete exemption as opposed to alternative instruction. If the objection, on the other hand, is related to a core value like racial equality or religious toleration, then clearly school officials should have no obligation to provide accommodation, and, in fact, it would be wrong for them to do so. Core values are so central to the preservation of democratic government and so basic to the constitutional enterprise that they do not lend themselves to governmental exemption.

On this specific point, Amy Gutmann is correct. She offers the example of the *Mozert* parents, who objected to a passage describing a central idea of the Renaissance as "a belief in the dignity and worth of human beings," on the grounds that such a belief is incompatible with their religious convictions. They also disputed a short story that described a Catholic Indian settlement in New Mexico. For the parents, the story constituted teaching Catholicism, while the school board drew the widely accepted distinction between teaching religion and teaching about religion. As Gutmann concedes, schools may not teach particular values such as Catholic doctrine, but they should teach public values such as religious tolerance, which demands an understanding of diverse ways of life and human dignity, both of which are essential to democratic citizenship.[26]

Another alternative would be to remove the offensive materials altogether from the curriculum. But as *Smith* and other cases demonstrate, federal courts are justifiably reluctant to extract religious and moral implications from materials and practices that the wider culture generally accepts as secular. The broad range of practices and programs challenged in the Bedford case, from a popular fantasy card game alleged to teach mathematical skills to relaxation techniques and yoga, presents a serious challenge to the court. One such practice that is almost universally recognized as secular in American culture is the celebration of Halloween. Yet religious conservatives have challenged school Halloween parties and decorations, which, they argue, promote witchcraft (as a religion) in violation of the establishment clause of the First Amendment. Courts have correctly denied the right to accommodation in these cases.[27] How can anyone conceivably interpret a Halloween celebration or the representation of witches in that context as an official endorsement of religion when the holiday has no contemporary religious significance throughout American culture?

The establishment clause is used not only as a sword by oppositionist parents, however, but also as a shield by school officials. Officials rightly retort that if they yield to pressure or the threat of litigation and remove materials or discontinue practices specifically to accommodate the religious views of any segment of the school population, they risk promoting or endorsing religion. If they do so in response to politically or religiously motivated opposition to the ideas expressed and not based on legitimate pedagogical concerns, they also raise the specter of censorship, which may violate the free speech rights of other students, who arguably have a right to receive information. Strong Supreme Court precedent and a string of lower court decisions compel schools to err on the side of church-state separation and free speech.

UNCOMMON SCHOOLS IN A LIBERAL
DEMOCRACY

As the discussion up to this point illustrates, accommodation within the current system is fraught with legal, administrative, and political problems. As a practical matter, accommodating individual or minority group family values through partial opting out can satisfy those parents whose concerns are narrow and specifically focused on a discrete program, practice, or set of materials. But for those with more pervasive religious or philosophical disagreements with the curriculum, it permits at most a resolution at the margins, leaving parents and children, as the Bedford case so poignantly demonstrates, at the sufferance of school authorities overwhelmed by the administrative implications of broadscale accommodation. Constrained by the very purposes of common schooling itself, this modest approach fails to resolve the layers of conceptual, constitutional, and governance conflicts that emerge from attempts to unfold and resolve the educational values question.

The prevailing system of individualized discretionary accommodations also falls short on fulfilling the promise of *Pierce v. Society of Sisters.* There the Supreme Court, three quarters of a century ago, affirmed the right of parents to direct the education of their children. At the same time, the Court recognized the authority of the state to reasonably require studies that are essential to citizenship and to prohibit the teaching of anything that is "manifestly inimical" to the public welfare. The *Pierce* decision is a studied lesson in compromise, a careful and reasoned balancing of conflicting pressures that lend meaning to the contemporary debate. As the legal scholar Mark Yudof describes that compromise,

> The state may promulgate its messages in the public school, while parents are *free to choose* schools with different orientations. The state must tolerate private education, but need not fund it. The state may make some demands of private schools to satisfy compulsory schooling laws, but those demands may not be so excessive as to turn private schools into public schools managed and funded by the private sector. The integrity of the communications and socialization processes in private schools and families remains intact, while the state's interest in producing informed, educated and productive citizens is not sacrificed.[28]

Pierce essentially grants parents an abstract constitutional right, a freedom to choose private schooling at their own expense for their children. But as the ever-worsening plight of inner-city poor children dramatically has proven, that right rings hollow for many parents whose lack of economic resources places a severe burden on their ability to exercise choice in the marketplace of private schools. Without that ability, parents are disempowered within the debate over value formation and realistic efforts at community building. As Stephen Arons has pointed out, the result is "freedom of choice" for those of economic means and "compulsory socialization" for everyone else.[29]

But the widening gap between the haves and have nots is not the only factor contributing to the unraveling of *Pierce's* delicate compromise between the rights of parents and the needs of democratic society. An essential element implicit within that compromise has all but disappeared from the American scene. No longer can we assume that common residence brings with it a commonality of values and worldviews. The notion of the neighborhood school as an outgrowth of a functional community is becoming a thing of the past. As a result, many communities have lost a values consensus that traditionally would have been transmitted through public schooling.

Many school districts now serve culturally and religiously diverse populations. This diversity stems in part from a new demographic profile wherein the exigencies of a rapidly changing job market, the vagaries of a globalized economy, and the phenomena of corporate downsizing and political unrest abroad now periodically and unexpectedly transport families around the country and around the world. As a result, communities have become less stable and more fluid; no longer are they necessarily composed of families with multigenerational roots.[30] Diversity, above all in the larger cities, also stems from increased immigration, which has brought a far wider range of cultures and religious beliefs than any experienced since the beginning of the Republic. Unlike the first great wave of immigrants, who came largely from western Europe beginning in the mid-nineteenth century, most recent immigrants come from Mexico, Latin America, Korea, Vietnam, India, Pakistan, and eastern Europe. The consequence of these changing patterns is that it has become increasingly more difficult to draw on a common European or Western tradition as a source of collective identity. Added to the profound effects of demographic shifts is the pervasive presence of the media and advanced telecommunications, particularly the Internet, which have replaced the face-to-face talk that used to nourish community life. This phenomenon has become a powerful influence on young people, enabling them to pick and choose from among a broad menu of values and lifestyles that compete with those of their family and community.

These dramatic transformations have painted a social and cultural landscape that differs markedly from the one facing the common school reformers or even the progressives that followed them. Some of the old assumptions and understandings about education, schooling, and society no longer hold true. The issues raised in the contemporary debate over the substance and structure of education unmistakably indicate that the time has come to fine-tune the *Pierce* compromise, reexamine educational governance, and seriously consider alternative models that give families a meaningful voice and therefore choice in the education of their children.

The Rising Tide of Family Choice

In the policy arena, public debates on values and choice typically occur in parallel fashion, although their interconnection is almost self-evident. In fact, the two discussions intersect on an overt level only occasionally and peripherally, most often in the fears of choice opponents who charge that choice initiatives are merely a smokescreen for religious conservatives to dismantle common schooling and retreat into their own isolated worlds with government funds. Those fears are now becoming eclipsed by the organized efforts of inner-city minority parents and political and religious leaders who have embraced school choice as a mechanism for saving poor children from the apparent failure of inner-city schools. Choice is no longer just a liberty issue; it has become a salient equality issue.[31] Once considered a heresy against the creed of the common school, family choice proposals are now gaining increased support from across the political spectrum and promise or threaten (depending upon one's viewpoint) to change the face of educational governance in America. As the debate over family choice broadens, proposals for incrementally restructuring educational governance in this country may offer the most effective means for balancing the individual, community, and societal interests inherent in the values debate.

Educational choice has only recently moved into the mainstream of public policy, capturing the serious attention of a growing number of public officials and scholars.[32] The choice concept, however, has been percolating beneath school reform debates for years, having undergone a dramatic transformation ever since the economist Milton Friedman introduced his free market proposal more than three decades ago.[33] Friedman's idea of a pure voucher scheme would have granted a government subsidy to every elementary and secondary school student equal to average per pupil expenditures. His system would have been unregulated; the school could have charged whatever the market could bear. Inefficiently run schools would have lost out in the competition generated by educational options.

In the early 1970s social reformers such as Christopher Jencks and his colleagues at Harvard and John Coons and Stephen Sugarman, originally known for their groundbreaking work on state school finance reform, took the voucher idea in a new direction.[34] On the heels of the Great Society programs and judicial struggles to racially integrate the schools, these researchers looked to vouchers as a means to advance education for the poor. Unlike Friedman, who believed that family choice would equalize the social and private costs of child rearing, Coons and Sugarman grounded their model in the belief that the family has special knowledge and understanding of the child and therefore can make the most informed decisions concerning the child's education. It is within this context that school choice is now garnering more broad-based political favor, notably from African American political and educational leaders and clergy in urban areas. Combined with growing support for the concept of educational scholarships for the poor, a wave of state and local initiatives designed to free public schools from burdensome regulations is leading the country slowly but steadily toward the possibility of reconfiguring schooling as we now know it.

There are several permutations on the choice theme.[35] Beginning in the 1970s, many urban school districts expanded options beyond the neighborhood school, offering flexible enrollment combined with a broad range of specialized educational programs. Some of these initiatives grew out of court-ordered desegregation plans in which "magnet" schools of high academic quality were a mechanism for attracting a racially mixed student body. Many of these programs were funded under the federal Emergency School Aid Act, which was repealed in 1981 and reestablished in 1985 as the Magnet Schools Assistance Program. In fiscal year 1999, the federal Department of Education appropriated over one hundred million dollars for magnet school assistance. More recent programs, while still mindful of racial integration goals, have focused more directly on providing educational options to families residing in large urban school systems. One of the most successful models for racially integrating schools while granting families greater voice in the education of their children is the controlled choice program developed in Cambridge, Massachusetts, and later adopted by the Fall River, Massachusetts, and White Plains, New York, school districts. In Cambridge, for example, 91 percent of all students from kindergarten to grade eight have gained admission to a school of their choice. The success of that effort can be attributed in part to a highly effective parent information system, an essential feature of any choice program.[36] This concept of public school choice has attracted support from participating parents, politicians, and teachers' unions, the latter being the strongest opponents of other choice models.

Lying a step beyond public school choice programs on the scale of political acceptability is the concept of the charter school.[37] Charter schools are essentially a compromise between a more expansive voucher program and the current system. Their driving purpose is to create an alternative within government-funded schools that improves student learning and achievement and increases educational options for parents, students, and teachers within a performance-based—as opposed to the prevailing rule-based—accountability system. They vary somewhat from state to state depending upon their authorizing legislation, which in turn depends on the political and demographic characteristics of the state. But they tend to share key elements. Structurally they are autonomous public institutions established under a contract between a group that manages a school and a public sponsoring authority that oversees it. The contractor might be a group of parents or teachers, a labor union, a college or a university, or other nonprofit organization. The sponsor might be a school board, a state education department, a state university campus, or a government agency. Each state's governing statute establishes the maximum number of charters that can be issued throughout the state, with the possibility of increasing that number by legislative act.

Charter schools are technically public schools that are exempt from many of the burdensome state regulations and local rules that tend to inhibit flexible management within conventional public education. They are funded exclusively through public funds, receiving for each student enrolled an amount somewhat equivalent to the average per pupil expenditure in the school district or state. They exclude sectarian schools from participation. If oversubscribed, they generally select students by lottery, although some states permit admission on a first-come, first-served basis. Depending on the state legislation, existing private schools may or may not be permitted to convert to charter status. If they do, they must forego selective admissions criteria and, if religiously affiliated in their prior existence, eliminate any teaching of religion during the school day. They are accountable to their clients, who readily can abandon them, and to the public entity that originally granted them their charter. If they fail to meet agreed-upon standards of performance, as measured by standardized test scores or student retention rates, for example, the sponsoring agency can revoke their charter and effectively close them down.

The first charter school opened in Minnesota in 1992. To date, thirty-six states, many of them including the nation's largest cities, and the District of Columbia have enacted charter legislation, New York, Oklahoma, and Oregon being the most recent. By the 1999 school year, there were more than 1,500 charter schools serving more than 350 million students throughout the country. At the federal level, the Department of Education awarded more than one hundred million dollars during fiscal year 1999 to help pay for charter school planning, design, and start-up costs. Yet despite their potential for promoting educational pluralism and efficiency and giving parents and teachers greater ownership over the educational program with relatively few bureaucratic constraints, charter school proposals have met roadblocks in a number of state legislatures. The strongest opposition has come from teachers' unions and other public school advocates, who raise concerns about the hiring of noncertified teachers, lack of accountability, loosening of curricular requirements, selective admissions standards, and the education of students with special needs. Obviously, accountability standards and access in particular demand serious attention, and only experience will prove the ability of alternative charter models to address those issues adequately.

Charter school laws give credence to the maxim "The devil is in the details." Massachusetts, for example, is considered by charter proponents to have one of the nation's strongest charter laws primarily because it places almost exclusive decision-making power in the state Secretary of Education, a gubernatorial appointee, while removing local school districts from the approval process. Georgia's charter legislation, on the other hand, is far more restrictive. Charter schools must be approved by the local school board and the state board of education and organized by existing public school staff and faculty, two-thirds of which must agree on the conversion. While this structure lends itself to greater local accountability, it also places charter schools at the unfettered discretion of the local school establishment, which can easily place unreasonable and self-serving obstacles in the path of successful school design, student selection, and management.

The New York charter school law grants schools blanket exemptions from state and local mandates operating on public schools except for laws relating to health and safety, civil rights, and student assessment. It requires charter schools to establish an academic program at least as rigorous as that of other public schools and to participate in standardized tests administered to public school students. Schools must comply with the terms of a five-year performance-based charter, are required to publish a school report card annually, and must give preferential admission to at risk students. They may hire up to 30 percent or five uncertified teachers, whichever is the lesser number, and are free from mandated union representation at 10 schools regardless of size and at an additional 90 if a school's average enrollment remains under 250 for the first year.

The U.S. Department of Education is nearing the end of a four-year study on charter schools. The annual reports that have emerged from that effort have provided a useful documentation of the concept as it is evolving over time. One of the criticisms commonly leveled against charter schools is that they will pull white and economically advantaged students from traditionally public schools. Data indicate otherwise. In 1997–98 in a study of twenty-four charter states, 37 percent of charter school students were eligible for free or reduced-price school meals as compared with 38 percent of students in all public schools in the same states. In fourteen states, charter schools served a considerably higher percentage of minority students than the public schools as a whole. Charter schools also seemed to benefit from smallness of scale, with a median enrollment of 132 students as compared with 486 students in the regular public schools. The department further has found a consistently high demand for charter schools, with seven out of ten maintaining a waiting list.[38]

According to a *Wall Street Journal/NBC News* poll conducted in 1997, respondents favored public school choice 73 percent to 25 percent. But, as the *Wall Street Journal* pointed out, "The real battleground is over extending choice to private schools using taxpayer dollars" with the "hot-button topic" being religion. About 23 percent of schools across the nation are private, but nearly 79 percent of these are religiously affiliated.[39]

A third choice strategy, using the system of state income taxation in the form of tax deductions or tax credits, includes private secular and religious schools within its net. In Minnesota, for example, the legislature in 1997 approved a tax deduction for middle-income families and a tax credit of up to $1,000 a year for low-income families. The legislature has since increased the deduction to $1,625 per student in grades kindergarten through six and to $2,500 for students in grades seven through twelve and expanded the credit by $200 to $350 for families with household incomes of $29,000 a year or less. Parents can use the deduction and credit to offset the cost of private school tuition or ancillary costs incurred in the public schools. The State of Arizona has more directly provided aid for private schools through the allowance of a state tax credit of up to $500 for those who donate to school tuition organizations. The Supreme Court of Arizona, in a case that was carefully watched by both sides of the choice debate, upheld the law under both the state and federal constitutions, seeing "little difference in the levels of choice available to parents" between the Arizona tax credit and the Minnesota tax deduction upheld by the U.S. Supreme Court more than two decades ago.[40]

The most controversial choice measure by far has been the educational voucher concept. For almost three decades, the debate over vouchers has vacillated between Friedman's free market and the Coons and Sugarman equality models. The mild enthusiasm for vouchers generated in the 1970s became dampened in the wake of a failed attempt to implement a voucher system in the federally funded Alum Rock, California, experiment carried out under the direction of Christopher Jencks. Not only did school districts reject the plan, but the intended beneficiaries—the nation's poor and racial and ethnic minorities—never rallied around it.[41] During the 1980s, the Reagan administration and Republicans in Congress placed the voucher concept back on the table for national discussion. But it became too closely identified with Christian conservatives and the extreme Right to garner serious political attention, much less support. John Chubb and Terry Moe's book *Politics, Markets and America's Schools* (1990),[42] however, redirected and invigorated the debate. Looking at vouchers from the economic angle, their basic thesis was that market-driven schools lead to higher achievement. But their free market model with only minimal restrictions soon gave way again to the more politically palatable equality concept in both public and privately sponsored programs.

Throughout the 1990s, fueled by the perceived bankruptcy of inner-city schools, political and scholarly interest in seeking alternatives to public schooling began to spread across the disciplines. By that time, it was becoming increasingly evident that court-ordered desegregation, federally funded remedial programs, and efforts to reform state financing systems had failed to fulfill their promise to equalize educational opportunities across the economic and racial divide. From there an alliance began to be forged between the political right and the left, one that engaged business leaders, advocates for the poor, and more recently African American ministers in a joint effort to build on the success of religiously affiliated inner-city schools to provide quality education through private schooling.

Aside from limited initiatives in Vermont and Maine and a newly adopted Florida plan for children in failing public schools, to date only Milwaukee and Cleveland have functioning public voucher programs. Both serve children from low-income families. The inclusion of religious schools has subjected both programs to constitutional challenge, placing the publicly funded voucher concept in a state of suspended animation. Meanwhile, private philanthropy has generated a far more ambitious and successful experiment in family choice, converting the educational voucher into scholarships for poor children in cities across the nation. By 1998, more than thirteen thousand students in more than thirty cities, including Dayton, Indianapolis, Milwaukee, New York City, San Antonio, and Washington, D.C., participated, in privately funded scholarship programs that permit inner-city schoolchildren to attend the private school of their choice.[43] Those figures increased dramatically the following year when the Wall Street financier Theodore Forstmann and Wal-Mart heir John Walton, with $100 million and matching funds, offered another forty thousand scholarships to low-income families.

Reports on the success of choice programs are inconclusive and controversial.

A study conducted by researchers at Indiana University on the Cleveland voucher program found positive achievement results in language skills but no significant differences in reading, science, mathematics, or social studies among voucher students attending established private schools as compared with their public school counterparts. The study also found negative results among those attending schools established specifically to serve the voucher program.[44] A similar report on the Milwaukee voucher program, finding no significant differences in achievement but high attrition rates, has come under serious methodological attack.[45] The Harvard political scientist Paul Peterson, who has challenged the results of both the Cleveland and Milwaukee studies and has overseen the assessment of the private voucher program in New York City, notes that compared with conventional public schools, choice schools tend to demonstrate higher parental and teacher satisfaction, lower student mobility, and higher student achievement.[46] His analysis of the Cleveland program at the conclusion of the second year reveals that parents participating in the voucher program tended to be more satisfied with their children's schools than those whose children remained in the city's public schools; in addition, children attending two schools established specifically for voucher students had made better than average gains that were maintained through the second year.[47]

Yet the problem of selection bias continues to cloud positive findings in the world of school choice. Research has indicated that private schools do in fact attract families that are more knowledgeable about their options and "have faith in the power of education in the intellectual and status marketplace."[48] Critics of choice maintain that even the adjustment for family characteristics, including education background and income, cannot fully correct for the fact that families who exercise choice when offered tend to be more involved in their child's education, which undoubtedly has a positive effect on the child's academic performance. The many privately organized school choice experiments around the country may offer the opportunity to circumvent the selection bias problem in assessing program outcomes. These programs typically are limited to inner-city children selected for participation from a lottery.

In New York City, for example, entering student test scores in 1997 indicated that choice applicants were neither the most high performing students nor the most advantaged. Only 26 percent performed at grade level in reading and 18 percent in math, far below the reported 55 percent for elementary students citywide. The average annual family income was below ten thousand dollars, and 60 percent received public assistance.[49] Even more significantly, the randomized selection process creates an arguably homogeneous sample from which researchers can compare the achievement of those selected and those not selected over time. Preliminary findings at the conclusion of the first year proved promising. Students taking part in the choice program out-performed a control group by 2 percentile points in math and 2.2 percentile points in reading, the widest differences showing in the upper grades. With the control group composed of students who had applied but were not accepted through random selection, this carefully designed four-year evaluation project can potentially yield informative findings on school choice and performance.[50]

Until such longitudinal research findings provide more definitive answers, the jury is out on the academic success of choice programs. Nevertheless, they remain the preferred model for poor parents in the inner city. A poll conducted in 1997 by the Joint Center for Political and Economic Studies found that 75 percent of African Americans with annual incomes of less than fifteen thousand dollars advocate voucher plans, while only 50 percent of those earning more than thirty-five thousand dollars favor them. A survey conducted by the Public Policy Forum among Ohio and Wisconsin taxpayers that same year yielded similar positive responses in the two states with publicly supported voucher programs. Seventy-six percent of those surveyed supported school choice, and 53 percent supported expanding the program to all children regardless of family income. Eighty-three percent supported the inclusion of religious schools. A poll conducted in June 1999 by the Gallup Organization for Phi Beta Kappa reveals support among Americans in general for voucher plans, including those that involve religious schools. According to those findings, 51 percent favored the use of taxpayer money to permit parents to send their children to any school, up from 43 percent in 1996. Groups most likely to favor a partial tuition proposal included nonwhites (68 percent) and eighteen- to twenty-nine-year-olds (60 percent).[51] These figures have proven ominous for traditional voucher opponents, who are watching their support base for public schooling erode.

The Legal and Policy Critique

The various voucher proposals now pending in state legislatures and in Congress indicate that educational choice is steadily gaining momentum. Yet as the conflicting reports on student achievement demonstrate, the concept is still wide open to political and pedagogical debate. Throughout the 1990s, proponents of the voucher concept have been repeatedly rebuffed at the polls, voters in California, Oregon, Washington, and Colorado overwhelmingly rejecting direct ballot initiatives for private school choice. Organized groups on the political left, most notably PFAW, have mounted a campaign to discredit the voucher concept as a "mean-spirited hoax" and a "naked grab for money by groups like the Christian Coalition." And despite growing support for vouchers among African American religious leaders and inner-city parents nationwide, the National Association for the Advancement of Colored People has joined forces with PFAW in unequivocally rejecting voucher programs as a "pernicious, steal-from-the-poor-and-give-to-the-rich scheme."[52] Opponents, including the National Education Association, the American Federation of Teachers, the American Civil Liberties Union, and Americans United for Separation of Church and State perceive vouchers as a threat to the public school system and a diversion of tax dollars to private and most significantly religious schools, raising the specter of the establishment clause and various state constitutional prohibitions against public funding of religious educational institutions.

The federal constitutional argument may have been more plausible in the past. In recent years, the Supreme Court repeatedly has reaffirmed the neutrality principle while moving incrementally, with few digressions, toward greater accommodation of religious beliefs. In a series of cases beginning in the early 1980s, the Court has held that the following programs or practices do not violate the establishment clause: a state educational tax deduction allowed to parents of public and nonpublic school children, including students attending religious schools; a state vocational rehabilitation program awarding assistance payments to a blind student engaged in religious studies at a Christian college; the provision of a sign-language interpreter under the federal Individuals with Disabilities Education Act to a deaf student attending a religious school; the provision of funding by a state university to a student organization that published a newspaper with a Christian point of view; and a federally funded program offering supplemental remedial instruction on a neutral basis to disadvantaged students attending religious schools.[53] According to the Court, the key features in each of these cases were that, first, government financial assistance was not made directly to a religious group or institution but rather indirectly through private individual decisions; and second, the aid was made available to a broad class of beneficiaries for both religious and secular activities.

The 1998 school year proved a crucial period for the legal permissibility of family choice programs nationwide. In addition to the Arizona decision upholding a tax credit scheme, the courts of Wisconsin, Ohio, Maine, and Vermont delivered important but conflicting messages on school vouchers. The Wisconsin Supreme Court in 1998 upheld Milwaukee's publicly funded school voucher program, which permits low-income students to attend private schools, including schools that are religiously affiliated.[54] The program served more than six thousand children in 1998–99. The Wisconsin court based its decision on both the federal and state constitutions. On the federal claim, the court applied what has come to be known as the "*Lemon* test,"[55] interpreting prior Supreme Court decisions as having established the principle that state educational assistance programs that provide aid to both sectarian and nonsectarian schools do not have the primary effect of advancing religion if they are neutral with regard to religion and distribute aid on the basis of private choices of individual parents. The U..S Supreme Court declined in an eight to one vote to review the case, letting stand the decision of the Wisconsin high court.

In June 1999, the Ohio Supreme Court reached a similar conclusion regarding the state and federal constitutions, although it invalidated the Cleveland voucher program based on a technical violation of the state constitution's "one-subject" rule for legislative bills. The state legislature subsequently reinstated the voucher program in a manner that avoided the procedural defect. Voucher opponents immediately mounted another round of litigation on constitutional grounds. The Ohio decision brought the number to three high state courts whose rulings suggested that the U.S. Supreme Court had shifted since the early 1980s to permit neutral, indirect government aid that benefits religious schools through the private decisions of parents. On the other side of the constitutional ledger, however, the supreme courts of Vermont and Maine and a federal appellate court in a separate Maine case conveyed a different perspective in refusing to require local communities to reimburse parents who send their children to religious schools. These cases all address a long-standing practice popularly known as tuitioning in which towns that do not operate their own high school pay the tuition of students to attend public high schools in neighboring towns or nonreligious private schools. The Vermont court was unique among this group in deciding the case solely on state constitutional grounds. However, the Maine high court made clear that inclusion of religious schools would violate the establishment clause of the federal Constitution and that their exclusion would not violate the parents' free exercise rights. The federal appeals court pointedly stated that "the Supreme Court has never permitted broad sponsorship of religious schools. . . . Approving direct payments of tuition by the state to sectarian schools represents a quantum leap that we are unwilling to take."[56] The U.S. Supreme Court declined to review both Maine decisions.

The Maine cases did not present the ideal context for a final showdown over vouchers, addressing as they did an almost unique version of the voucher concept practiced for decades in Maine and Vermont as compared with a newer wave of school choice models in the form of "scholarships" for low-income students and tuition tax credits. Nevertheless, with the growing number of government programs granting direct and indirect aid to religiously affiliated schools, it is only a matter of time before the Court will agree to bring final resolution to the constitutionality of school vouchers. And judging from recent trends in the Court's thinking and an evolving majority consensus among the Justices, federal constitutional impediments to the voucher concept may be lifted in the not-too-distant future.

Setting aside the legal arguments, voucher opponents voice additional political and policy concerns. They argue that choice programs are likely to foster racial segregation and economic stratification in the schools, marginalize religious and cultural minorities even further from the mainstream, undermine education's mission to prepare young people for democratic citizenship, and breed fraud and waste in a proliferation of poorly managed and educationally inadequate private and charter schools. They also suggest that the accountability that comes with state funding would create overregulation of private schools, which in turn would erode their distinctive nature and even threaten the religious integrity of sectarian schools.[57] Several scholarly studies have validated popular images of religious schools as damaging to society and to children, restricting their basic liberties, stifling their emotional development, and instilling dogmatic and intolerant attitudes.[58]

Yet research has proven otherwise. In 1992, the U.S. Department of Education sponsored the National Educational Longitudinal Study, which surveyed a national sample of twelfth graders along with parents, teachers, and administrators. Data drawn from that study reveal that private school students are significantly more likely to be in racially integrated classrooms than their public school counterparts. As compared with public schools, private schools tend to engage in less tracking and ability grouping, which improves student diversity in the classroom. Private school students also tend to demonstrate more racial tolerance, to exhibit less racial conflict, and to more readily form cross-racial friendships than students in the public schools.[59] These findings confirm those of earlier studies which also indicated greater racial integration and more positive educational outcomes for minorities in private schools than for their public school counterparts.[60] While critics argue that these positive effects might result more from student selectivity and organizational features than from the privateness of the school, the fact remains that private schooling per se does not produce the damaging social results that some critics of family choice ascribe to it.

Oppositionist arguments directed at isolation, balkanization, and the dangers to democratic participation demand particular attention because these prove to be the most politically compelling. If, in fact, America is in imminent danger of losing its shared cultural order to the "corrosive forces" of individualism, privatization, and cultural polarization, as cultural commentators warn, then the dismantling of the public school system will only accelerate that process—or so the argument goes.[61] To refute these claims one need only look to the vast system of American Catholic schools as an example of separate schools whose core mission turns on developing in students an ethic of social justice and concern for others. More than three decades ago in their study of Catholic school graduates, Andrew Greeley and Peter Rossi challenged the assumption that religious subcultures, or "ghettos," were harmful to society. To the contrary, their findings indicated that what they termed the "ghetto path" (Catholic school attendance and majority of Catholic friends at age seventeen) as compared with the "assimilationist path" (non–Catholic school attendance and less than majority Catholic friends at age seventeen) promoted not only achievement but also greater tolerance. Individuals in this group scored lower on the anti-civil-liberties and anti-Semitism scale than a comparable group of Catholics who had not attended Catholic schools. A consistency between the religious orientation (or values) of one's school and one's friends (cultural community) during adolescence also appeared to have a positive effect on educational level and occupational success. The authors speculated that such subcultures may give a person "a relatively secure social location and a fairly clear answer to the difficult question, 'Who am I?'"[62]

More recent research on Catholic schools offers further evidence that separate schools do not necessarily pose a threat to society but in fact may develop a sense of civic duty in their students. In their comprehensive study of Catholic schooling in the United States, Anthony Bryk, Valerie Lee, and Peter Holland found that "beliefs about the dignity of each person and a shared responsibility for advancing a just and caring society" are fundamental to Catholic education. They suggest that the sense of community instilled by such separate schools may actually encourage the same social commitment that we seek in common schools. "Although the common school ideal inspired the formation of American public education for over one hundred years," they maintain, "it is now the Catholic school that focuses our attention on fostering human cooperation in the pursuit of the common good. While the Catholic school, like the Catholic church itself, has become increasingly public, the public schools have become increasingly private, turning away from the basic social and political purposes that once lent them the title of 'common schools.'"[63]

Survey data from the U.S. Department of Education support these findings that private schooling does not necessarily lead to social isolation. In a study of 9,393 parents of school-age children, researchers found that Catholic, Protestant, and nonreligious private and home schooling parents are, in fact, consistently more involved in a wide range of civic activities than are families of public school children.[64] These examples demonstrate that separate schooling need not necessarily represent the intent or the effect of withdrawal from public life or social fragmentation. For parents, the intent may simply be to educate one's child within the framework of a community in which social morality is meaningful, while the institutional effect might foster civic virtue. For many religiously affiliated schools, the intent encompasses both objectives as mutually supportive. A clear manifestation of this synergy comes through in the five educational goals articulated by a highly regarded religious school in San Francisco: developing in its students a "personal and active faith in God," a "deep respect for intellectual values," and a "social awareness which implies action," while at the same time "building community as a Christian value" and "fostering personal growth in an atmosphere of wise freedom." These goals undeniably promote the ends of democratic citizenship and in a more conscious and pervasive way than most public schools can admit.[65] Undoubtedly, there exist many non-Christian religious schools with a similar focus. The problem for the state is to distinguish between the larger number of sponsoring groups whose aim is to coexist with the majority and those on the fringe whose aim is to deny even the possibility of public discourse.[66]

As Sugarman has pointed out, rather than question the desirability of choice itself, criticisms merely affirm the safeguards that must be built into a choice plan, including guaranteed access to all students, parent outreach and information programs, and consumer protections.[67] I would add to these a system of performance standards and a mechanism for assuring that students are afforded the skills, character traits, and knowledge that foster democratic citizenship. And if religious schools were to lose their distinction by compromising their religious values and mission in order to benefit from government funding, that loss would be a matter of institutional choice rather than government imposition. Admittedly, some religious schools would continue to refuse government aid, even indirect aid through a voucher program, in order to preserve their distinctly religious values.

Choice proposals, particularly the voucher concept but to a more limited extent charter schools as well, fly in the face of the common school emphasis on homogeneity and government control. Depending on one's perspective, that apparent inconsistency is either a positive or a negative. Only thoughtfully designed programs supporting randomized research efforts will ultimately vindicate the educational merits of choice programs. But the value of family choice cannot rest solely on academic achievement. The value of family choice rests firmly in family values. A structured program of common education within a pluralistic system of common and separate schools with high accountability would also free the discussion on educational values from conventional attempts to resolve values-based conflicts through a patchwork of forced accommodations that sometimes create more problems than they solve. While proposals of this nature are highly controversial, they are gaining increased interest in the public policy arena, especially in urban areas, and may well shape the future of educational reform in this country.

Values Within a Structured Choice Model

With the family choice movement gaining increased momentum, a multitiered framework appears to be evolving incrementally. That framework serves as a useful base for more fully developing an educationally sound and legally permissible model of structured choice, including both common and separate schools under the umbrella of government support. The proposed model would include a mix of three formats of government-supported schools operating under state education statutes: publicly funded and controlled public schools in their current form under the auspices of local school boards, some or all of which may introduce family choice strategies within the geographical bounds of a state-established school district; public charter schools funded directly by government and managed by outside groups under the sponsorship of a legislatively designated governmental entity; and private choice schools, including religiously affiliated institutions, funded through voucher payments provided by the state to parents who demonstrate economic need. Under this third model, the state may grant scholarships in the form of tuition vouchers that could be redeemed at participating private schools if accepted as full tuition payment. An alternate approach might provide vouchers to parents on a sliding scale of need, varying inversely with family income, with the result that those at the extreme low end of the economic continuum might pay no tuition while others might pay differential amounts between a partial voucher and the full tuition cost. Private schools choosing not to opt into the structured choice program or deemed ineligible on the basis of state requirements would continue to exist under private funding.

The primary objective of the proposed model is to balance both common and diverse values in a structured system that promotes the ends of a pluralist democracy. Created under state legislation, the system would impose standards and offer incentives in order to promote a critical core of common education in civic knowledge and attitudes to all students despite separate schooling. Even private choice schools partially funded through government tuition subsidies to parents would be prohibited from teaching or acting in any way that undermines the nation's overarching commitment to racial equality or political commitments to gender equality (within the reasonable bounds of religious beliefs), to religious tolerance, and to basic justice. The state enabling legislation would prohibit participating schools from advocating unlawful behavior or promoting the inferiority of either sex. It would also require both public and private choice schools to develop fair procedures that meet minimal standards for addressing academic and disciplinary problems and to apply them consistently.

Schools could establish admissions criteria within certain limitations. Specialized schools for the educationally challenged and the educationally gifted, including students with particular talents in art or music, for example, could exist provided that students attend these schools voluntarily and provided that a comprehensive school with an open admissions policy exists within a reasonable geographic distance as a meaningful alternative. The state would establish an administrative procedure for addressing substantial violations and determining a school's continued participation in the choice program.

Schools receiving federal funds would continue to be bound by civil rights requirements attached to those funds, including prohibitions against racial, ethnic, gender, and handicap discrimination. For schools considered public schools—that is, those that are directly funded through government sources and operated under government sponsorship, including public school choice and charter schools—such principles as racial and gender equality in the sense of equal treatment as well as religious freedom and freedom of expression are already enforceable as a matter of constitutional law under the First and Fourteenth Amendments.

However, private choice schools that receive indirect state aid through tuition subsidies awarded to families would not be considered "state actors" for constitutional purposes. Such a designation would subject them to federal claims brought by students and employees under a complete array of constitutional provisions, including specific guarantees of due process in disciplinary matters and freedom of speech, for example. The practical result would be a direct impact on behavior and dress codes, the student press, personnel matters, admissions policies, the curriculum, and extracurricular offerings. An extension of state action doctrine that imposed not only such broadly defined constitutional norms as racial equality, religious tolerance, and fairness but the full body of Supreme Court decisions interpreting these norms would serve as a disincentive for private schools to participate in the program, would defeat the underlying intent of family choice, and could potentially obliterate the distinction between public and private schools. For almost two decades, the Supreme Court has been disinclined to impose constitutional liability on private action and specifically on private schools, even in the case of almost exclusive government funding and extensive government regulation (at least where the regulation was unrelated to the specific decisions challenged).[68]

But if private choice schools were free of constitutional constraints, then what would prevent hate groups such as the Ku Klux Klan, the Aryan Nation, and the Nation of Islam from operating schools under government sponsorship? This is a frequently raised and understandable concern among even some cautious supporters of school choice. The response lies in strong legal precedent drawing from Supreme Court decisions over the past three decades. State aid to private schools that discriminate on the basis of race creates legally enforceable limitations on both the school and the state. On the one hand, the school risks having its tax-exempt status denied under the principle laid down in *Bob Jones University v. United States*. The school would not be considered a charitable institution under the Internal Revenue Code. The school would also be found in violation of federal law granting individuals the freedom to enter into and enforce contracts free of racial discrimination, as the Court made clear in *Runyon v. McCrary*.

On the other hand, the state would be subject to constitutional claims under the Fourteenth Amendment equal protection clause. As the Court noted in *Norwood v. Harrison*, the state cannot grant aid, direct or indirect, to schools that discriminate on the basis of race. In fact, as Laurence Tribe has noted, racially discriminatory private schools are probably the one exception to the Court's seeming endorsement of the proposition that individuals' private choices eliminate any "impermissible effects" of state programs that aid religiously affiliated schools.[69] The state, therefore, has a compelling interest in establishing and enforcing an antidiscrimination policy that prohibits racial discrimination in private choice schools. That prohibition should be written expressly into state law.

Even if the law made it practically impossible for private choice schools to discriminate against students and teachers on the basis of race, can they freely engage in gender discrimination? If such schools receive federal funds for any of their programs or activities, they are subject to Title IX prohibitions covering gender discrimination in admissions, counseling, athletics, and course offerings with certain exceptions for religiously affiliated institutions. But can they insulate themselves from legal liability by refusing federal funds? The answer here lies in the fine and not-so-fine distinctions between and among race and gender equality as political and constitutional commitments. The schools themselves would not be subject to the constraints of the Fourteenth Amendment equal protection clause because they would not be state actors. Nor is the Supreme Court certain to extend the *Bob Jones University* ruling and deny tax exemptions to private educational institutions that engage in gender discrimination. In that decision, the Court affirmed the uniqueness of racial equality as a firmly established national policy. But that does not necessarily permit private choice schools to engage in gender discrimination with impunity, leaving students and teachers without a legal remedy. It may be possible to extend *Norwood v. Harrison* with somewhat less bite and, depending on the policy in question, hold the state constitutionally accountable on the grounds of funding gender discrimination.

In the Virginia Military Institute case, the Court did not rule out all gender classifications but made clear that only those supported by an "exceedingly persuasive justification" can withstand constitutional scrutiny. Gender classifications are permissible, the Court stated, "where they advance the full development of the talent and capacities of our nation's people," but not where they are used "to create or perpetuate the legal, social, and economic inferiority of women."[70] For example, the Court left open the door to single-sex education under certain conditions, explicitly recognizing "the mission of some single-sex schools to 'dissipate, rather than perpetuate, traditional classifications.'"[71] While the issue of publicly funded single-sex schools has become the subject of intense debate, it appears that the VMI decision would not preclude government funding of private schools that deny admission to men or women or that separate them for sports activities. "Separate but equal" voluntarily entered into in the context of single-sex schools is distinguishable from the legally sanctioned and mandated racially segregated schools outlawed in *Brown v. Board of Education* almost a half century ago. Besides, at least some religious groups, for example, Muslims and Orthodox Jews, could argue that separation of the sexes is required by the tenets of their religion, thereby providing an "exceedingly persuasive justification." Invoking *Yoder,* they could contend that to deny them state aid would violate their free exercise rights under the First Amendment.[72]

Other forms of gender discrimination may render state aid to private choice schools impermissible. For example, differential admissions standards for males and females, differential salaries for equally qualified male and female teachers, denial of certain course offerings to members of one sex or the other, or dramatically unequal or inequitable allocations of resources for male and female sports activities may all trigger denial or withdrawal of state aid either to avoid or in response to constitutional claims against the state. It would depend on how loosely the courts were to interpret "the exceedingly persuasive justification" standard when applied especially to curricular offerings. Programmatic questions not only bear on fiscal priorities and capabilities (for example, the revenue raised from boys' football as compared with girls' soccer teams), but may also infringe on religiously and culturally sensitive lifestyle issues and appropriate gender roles.

As experience in other countries has taught, public funding for private schools generally brings with it government regulation, and understandably so. The public has an interest in assuring that its tax monies are expended on programs that do not undermine public ends. At the same time, governments are attempting to maintain a certain level of academic quality for all schools and to protect the consumer interests of families. In fact, in most cases, there is a direct correlation between the level of funding and the degree of regulation.[73] For the same reasons, a system of structured family choice in the United States would of necessity have to temper the inducement of government subsidies with certain institutional requirements, some of which already exist in many states and others that might prove a disincentive to some private schools and families.

For all segments of the structured choice model, state legislation supported by state Department of Education standards should define not only health, safety, and enrollment, all of which are now common throughout the states, but also academic compliance along with an enforcement mechanism. The notion of academic standards would shift the focus from a rule-based or school inputs model to a performance-based model assessing the quality of the educational program on the basis of student outputs. The state could monitor student performance in public and private choice schools through standardized tests in math and reading skills administered annually or at benchmark periods. This state-mandated assessment program would assure that schools provide what the Court in the *Pierce* decision referred to as the "basic essentials" of an adequate and effective educational program that prepares students for participation in a liberal democracy. If schools failed to meet an established level of student performance, the state could place them on probation and ultimately deem them ineligible for participation in the choice program. The state could also publish an annual report card on both public and private choice schools to provide full information to parents on the level of compliance with state performance standards.

A strong argument can be made, however, that education for democratic citizenship demands more than basic skill development: it must include a civic education component to assure that students develop an understanding of and commitment to fundamental political principles. This brings the discussion to the regulation of content areas, which would prove more politically and perhaps legally problematic. In *Meyer v. Nebraska,* the Supreme Court in dicta reaffirmed the authority of the state to "prescribe a curriculum for institutions which it supports."[74] However, for the state to exercise control over the curriculum directly or indirectly presents the danger of government overreaching into community and parental discretion. More than seven decades ago in *Farrington v. Tokushige,* the Supreme Court cautioned against state regulations that are so invasive and all-encompassing as to obliterate the distinction between public and private schools, although within the proposed model completely private schools would continue to exist as an option.[75]

There could also be an "unconstitutional conditions" problem lurking in a requirement that a sectarian school carry the state's values message and not just meet its narrower academic requirements as a condition to receiving the benefit of even indirect government aid. In this case, it can be argued that the government would be offering the benefit on the condition that the school as an institution as well as the parents and children waive their right to freedom of expression or the free exercise of religion unless the government's interest in developing the knowledge and traits necessary for democratic participation can prove sufficiently compelling. In any event, even if the state's requirement on curricular content passed constitutional scrutiny, as a practical matter the school's failure to meet the condition would prove difficult to enforce.[76]

But as the Court stated in *Pierce,* the state has an interest in ensuring that even private schools not teach anything "inimical to the general welfare" and that they in fact reinforce core political principles.[77] How can the state give meaning to that interest without running afoul of the Constitution? One solution might be for the state to require participating choice schools to follow loosely drafted curricular standards, particularly in history and civic education, that can be covered in any sequence of topics over the course of the elementary, middle, and secondary school grades. This limited requirement would permit schools to supplement the curriculum and would still afford them broad discretion over the remainder of the overall instructional program. As a complementary approach, the state might offer schools a financial incentive, similar to textbook loan programs that currently exist in seventeen states, to select textbooks in subjects such as history or science from a state-approved list that offers options within each subject area. Private choice schools would take part in the textbook program on a voluntary basis while the cost-free element would serve as an inducement. The state should make every effort to develop a list that represents a range of political perspectives and educational philosophies but still reflects core democratic principles. The list should be developed by a broadly representative statewide committee composed of educators, parents, and other community leaders, including the clergy. Similar committees or commissions addressing such highly charged public issues as physician-assisted suicide, AIDS education, the death penalty, and reproductive technologies have now become commonplace at the state level. The aim here is to offer families choice within a framework of a common civic culture.

Each choice school, whether public or private, could define and apply noncore values and contestable principles according to the philosophy of its school community. In this way, the concept of the community would no longer be defined by geography, as under the prevailing neighborhood school system, but by the individual families that have voluntarily chosen to establish and sustain it. The school therefore would represent a cultural community in the true sense. To promote choice across the economic spectrum, the state would provide transportation within a reasonable radius to students attending all three categories of publicly supported schools. It would also establish an effective parent information system completely detached from the public schools to assure that even less educationally aware families receive complete and objective information about their options for educating their children within the public and private sectors.

Undoubtedly, some private schools would choose not to participate in this loosely structured but decidedly regulated three-tiered system of state-supported choice schools, either because they oppose government regulation in principle as some Christian fundamentalist schools have argued in court over the years, because they consider state standards burdensome, or because they reject a core value such as religious tolerance. They would maintain their current status, and, except for those who engage in racial discrimination, they would continue to receive whatever funds are available to them under state programs, including student transportation and textbook loans administered under a combination of state mandates and local implementation. This might still prove the education of choice for many families for whom conventional public schooling presents the most severe clash in worldviews. Others might choose among the government options available to them with a greater likelihood of finding a school that is largely, if not totally, compatible with their values.

FORGING MIDDLE GROUND

Public school choice, charter schools, and private needs-based school tuition subsidies ultimately support the concept of family choice as a means to improve the quality of the educational program and thereby enhance student performance regardless of family economic circumstances. Taken together, they promise to provide greater equality of opportunity for the educationally and economically disadvantaged, who now are held hostage to a public school monopoly that has failed to meet their needs despite massive infusions of local, state, and federal funding over the past three decades. They also remove the wealth factor as the primary basis upon which parents now effectively can choose for their children loosely regulated private educational alternatives under a system which excludes from government support and government scrutiny even schools whose educational perspectives undermine core democratic values. In fact, it is not unreasonable to speculate that the inducement of government funding will diminish the numbers of schools falling into the last category. As public schools operated by government decrease, the system will impel an increased number of formerly private and essentially unregulated schools to provide equal opportunity and an education that adequately prepares students for democratic citizenship.

The proposed three-tiered model of common and separate schooling further offers a political remedy to the legal limitation placed on opting out in the wake of *Yoder*, extending family choice to members of less well-established religious communities and even to those with individual commitments of a religious or nonreligious nature.[78] By applying a set of objective academic standards to individually assess the fitness and commitment of each school to prepare students for citizenship in a liberal democracy, the proposed model frees reform efforts from the weighty negative assumptions typically ascribed to religious schools and religious families. While some religious schools undoubtedly will find at least some of their basic beliefs and values to be incompatible with the aims of democratic citizenship and will choose to remain independent of even indirect government support, history has proven that others are effective in promoting these objectives.

This pluralistic model resolves several of the problems that arise in the more modest accommodationist approach to conflicts over curriculum values. It permits parents to choose, from a variety of alternatives, the school that best reinforces their own value preferences, whether religious or philosophical, and their own approach to education, whether traditional or progressive, and the whole continuum in between. One could reasonably predict that releasing families from the constraints of the neighborhood school would consequently reduce litigation and disengage a reluctant judiciary from determining educational policy. It also promises to avert the community turmoil and the educational uncertainty that litigation of this nature inevitably engenders, as the Bedford case has demonstrated.

A constrained and structured choice model, in fact, attempts to promote community well-being. Here the community is not necessarily defined by residence but by a shared sense of purpose. It is a social construct through which families can coalesce in groups to establish and sustain institutions of education built on a shared worldview, provided they adhere to core political commitments, the value of civil toleration, and specified academic performance standards. As Coleman and Hoffer suggested, choice presents the possibility of replicating the academic success now found among religious and particularly among Catholic schools by creating schools that are an outgrowth of a functional community centered on shared values and educational purposes consciously designed through active family participation.[79]

This model would ideally recognize true cultural pluralism for individuals and groups across the political and economic spectrum: for at least some religious conservatives who contest the pervasively secular nature of public schooling, for multiculturalists who challenge what they perceive as a pervasively Eurocentric curriculum, for traditionalists such as the mothers in Bedford who prefer an education that focuses on the basics without the psychosocial programs and approaches that have been added to the curriculum in recent decades, and for others who embrace or reject such controversial perspectives as homosexual lifestyles and abortion rights. By offering options to the economically disadvantaged, structured family choice inherently promotes the core value of equality, permitting poor parents the discretion to direct the education of their children now available only to those of greater economic means.[80]

The suggested approach also responds to concerns raised by African American parents that forced busing to achieve racial balance in the schools erodes community ties and results in feelings of inferiority among students. These sentiments suggest an interpretation of equal educational opportunity under *Brown v. Board of Education* that looks not necessarily to a racially integrated school but to an academically strong education in the school of one's choice.

That interpretation also reflects more recent Supreme Court decisions wherein the Justices have deferred both to local and state school authorities and to the private choices of parents in measuring progress toward racial equality in the schools.[81] Finally, a structured family choice model promotes the value of religious tolerance by permitting the participation of religiously affiliated schools that agree to advance certain core political principles and comply with educational standards imposed by the state to assure that children in their charge are receiving an adequate education for democratic citizenship.

A varied model of government-supported and -regulated schooling permits each school to develop a comprehensive curriculum, including core and selected noncore values, that reflects a "coherent moral-cultural perspective." This pluralistic approach averts the value dilution that inevitably results when schools strain to be neutral and secular by relying solely on those "low-doctrine" values that have gained minimal acceptance.[82] As the philosopher Eamonn Callan warns us, common schools attached to such a minimalist conception offer an education that is "badly distorted. [B]y excluding all except the lowest common denominator of acceptable learning, a mistaken view of even that small common ground is apt to become embedded in the hidden curriculum."[83] In the rush toward acceptability and stability, we lose the strength of our commonality.

A pluralistic approach to schooling further precludes the curricular fragmentation arguably created by opting-out provisions. On a more human level, it may also prevent the psychological and emotional fragmentation of students whose religious and moral values still must be left at the schoolhouse door despite national efforts to create a more open and receptive environment. It affords children a coherent, robust moral education, reinforces their emotional ties to their family and community, and spares them the cultural dissonance often created when the messages conveyed in school directly clash with those conveyed in the home. At the same time, by prohibiting all government-subsidized schools, whether public or private, from conveying a message or engaging in any activities that are inconsistent with core political commitments, the proposed model suggests political and legal safeguards to preserve those democratic principles which bind us together as a nation.

This approach attempts to distill from the school choice debate those features that hold the most promise for meeting the competing demands of political unity and pluralism while at the same time advancing equal opportunity and preserving educational quality. Over the years, others have advanced many of these ideas, not the least of which were proposed two decades ago by Coons and

Sugarman in their California model.[84] The proposal here continues that ongoing discussion in the context of current legal and political understandings and with an eye toward balancing common and diverse values. It is not offered as the definitive word on school choice or as a cure-all for the ills surrounding value conflicts or the academic failure of urban schools. In attempting to change the deeply entrenched status quo, the issue cannot be whether the approach satisfies some ideal but rather what imperfections society is willing to accept and what tradeoffs it is inclined to make in promoting divergent interests.[85] In fact, a number of critical details remain to be worked out, the most thorny being admissions standards, the education of children with special needs, and the place of religious instruction, whether voluntary and discrete or mandatory and pervasive, in religiously affiliated choice schools. Nevertheless, in promoting family choice, the model serves as an initial framework for guiding policy discourse toward a more effective and stable resolution of values-based curricular conflicts and more general differences in educational philosophies.

This proposal, in fact, is a relatively modest one that attempts to balance competing demands for family choice and democratic citizenship. It maintains the essential features of *common education* while rejecting the notion of *common schooling* as the norm. It does not eliminate public schooling, as a pure voucher scheme would, nor does it give parents carte blanche over the education of their children. Rather, it complements the current system with parallel public and private choice alternatives that meet certain standards for preserving our core political and constitutional commitments.

Despite alarming assertions to the contrary, programs that support family choice are not likely to sound the death knell for common education or for public schooling. Both will continue to flourish, transformed and improved, within a system that allows for meaningful educational options. In fact, at least for the foreseeable future most families undoubtedly will remain in the conventional neighborhood school by choice, particularly outside the inner city. If anything, such schools may become more academically attractive in response to the increased competition. But if permitted to evolve gradually over time through thoughtfully designed programs, educational choice inevitably will sound the death knell for the common school as a government monopoly over education.

Conclusion

The concept of common schooling is built on a shared vision of education. It is also built on shared values and a common civic purpose which each succeeding generation conveys to the next. The cultural conflicts that have arisen over the past several decades raise the question of how we may remain true to this principle of regeneration without allowing our history necessarily to bind our destiny.

Conflicts over educational values are indeed controversial, politically divisive, and difficult to resolve administratively or judicially. They cut to the core of the common school concept and lay bare its questionable assumptions and political weaknesses. Dissenting parents rarely gain even a small measure of the control over their children's education that they seek. Nevertheless, their struggle to wrest education from the hands of a bureaucracy that they perceive as dangerous at worst and insensitive at best goes on unabated. And while mainstream America may oppose their underlying beliefs and question their ultimate goals, their claims reveal sobering truths about American pluralism, democratic education, and the limits of constitutionalism.

American society obviously has not remained static since the early days of the common school movement, and neither has the field of knowledge that informs educational policy and practice. Concepts of individual rights and liberties, the rise of the administrative state, and the expanded role of government in regulating schooling were far from the consciousness of the common school reformers, much less the constitutional framers of the previous century. Sociological and psychological advancements in teaching and learning theory have provided professional educators with an understanding of education and child development unforeseen in the mid-1800s. Progressive notions of educating the whole child, the increasing American emphasis on emotional well-being, the breakdown of the family, and the pressing social needs of the underclass have dramatically expanded the roles of schooling and professional educators well beyond imparting the basic skills, knowledge, and civic values necessary to participate in a democratic society.

At the same time, high literacy rates generated largely through compulsory schooling, together with the rapid expansion of mass media throughout the twentieth century and the technological explosion of recent decades, have left parents far more knowledgeable and capable of advocating on behalf of their children's educational interests. These developments have also helped create and disseminate a common culture, exposing children to values and lifestyles beyond and often contrary to those presented in their home and immediate community. Social and political transformations of the past four decades, from the civil rights and women's movements of the sixties, to the religious revivalism and political mobilization of the seventies and eighties, to the racial and ethnic backlash, religious conciliation, and public school failures of the nineties, have further altered the context for examining the purpose, process, and substance of education in America.

As American society has become transformed over the course of this century, minority groups, including religious minorities, have fought to gain political and legal recognition of their views. That diversity and political activism have struck at the heart of the common school and the concept of educating for homogeneity, revealing a critical distinction between education and schooling, both common and separate. Religious dissenters in particular have struggled to wrest their children from the clutches of neoprogressive practices and a continuing child-saving philosophy left over from a century ago. In doing so, they have articulated their claims in the language of parental rights and underscored the complexities of childhood and parenting. On close examination, however, children and parents need not be considered in opposition to each other or as totally distinct and disconnected rights holders but rather as mutually dependent and supportive members of the family unit whose collective and individual interests should be addressed within an educational system that affords families greater voice and control over the education of their children.

Values-based conflicts over the curriculum also reveal the need for a political resolution to what is frequently cast as a legal wrong. Over the years, the Supreme Court has developed two lines of arguments, sometimes presented in the same cases, that converge and collide in the context of disputes over the school curriculum. On the one hand, the Court in broad dicta has upheld the rights of parents to direct the education of their children and has even affirmed broad rights to freedom of conscience on the part of public school students. On the other hand, the Court has upheld the authority of local school officials to determine the curriculum and to develop in students the essential skills necessary for democratic citizenship. The apparent irreconcilability of these two positions stems in part from the Court's keen awareness of its own legitimacy and limited institutional capacity and the dramatic consequences that would flow from a definitive bow to the liberty interests of parents and their children. The ambiguities inherent in Court decisions over the years have left lower courts struggling to balance the individual and collective interests at stake, leaving parental dissenters essentially without a legal remedy.

In view of constitutional and institutional constraints, the Court is unlikely to reach the core of the parental decision-making question but will continue at best to nibble away at the edges. Given that reality, the problem is fast intensifying into a political one revolving around family choice, particularly in the form of charter schools and government tuition grants to private school students. Here the connection between values-based conflicts and proposals to restructure education seems almost self-evident. But the discussion at this point unfortunately becomes immobilized by fears concerning the dismantling of public education and the dangers of privatization. It also becomes mired in comprehensive liberal notions of autonomy, misconceptions of rational deliberation and tolerance, and overstated stereotypes regarding parents and their educational aspirations for their children.

As values-based conflicts so clearly demonstrate, education is essentially a process of indoctrination and socialization. That process has played a key role in developing and preserving a national identity and a sense of national purpose. While the common school concept may have proven significant and perhaps even essential to that cause through the early years of nation building, a curiously diverse group of advocates for family choice—from religious conservatives, to libertarians, to inner-city minorities and their clergy—are now joining forces in an effort to regain a meaningful voice for families in the education of their children that was lost more than a century ago in the common school movement.

Throughout the decades, the hard questions raised in several controversial court cases have generated much discussion and debate in academic circles and in the popular press. In recent years, the parents' rights movement has pushed that debate into the halls of state legislatures and the Congress. Yet despite scores of articles, books, media debates, and legislative hearings, the public discussion of educational values appears to be caught in a time warp, fixated on a system of education that was originally designed more than a century ago to promote the cultural assimilation and industrialization purposes of a young and uncertain nation at the onset of a grand experiment. In the intervening years, those political and economic goals have become modified and rearticulated to accommodate the progressive notion of educating future citizens for democratic participation. Thus the ghosts of Horace Mann and John Dewey continue to hover over us as we enter yet another century.

The escalating controversy now played out with increasing frequency in courts and legislatures, despite or perhaps because of repeated bows to the status quo, may be a signal to consciously unpack, carefully examine, and selectively unload this historical baggage. The events surrounding the Bedford litigation confirm that observation, attesting to the fact that disputes over educational values are merely symptomatic of broader disagreements over educational purposes and mission. The sharper those disagreements, the more they defy resolution within the current one-size-fits-all system. The time has come to sort through the myths, misunderstandings, and prevailing orthodoxy surrounding education for democratic citizenship.

The family choice movement is gaining momentum, spurred on by a Supreme Court reluctant to affirm parental rights but more inclined to lift the constitutional impediment that significantly constricts government aid to parents whose children attend religiously affiliated schools. Given that political backdrop, policymakers and educators are coming under increased pressure to move beyond political ideology and thoughtfully consider alternative models that preserve our basic political commitments while at the same time permitting educational communities to coalesce around shared values and reasonable visions of the good life. In doing so, we can hope to find *via media,* a middle ground with several diverging paths, where the ideological poles in the current debate over values and educational purpose can peacefully carry through a common undertaking of democratic education that respects both the *pluribus* and the *unum* in our civic culture.

This is an undeniably daunting task but one that is worth the effort. It demands boldness of spirit, openness of mind, and a deep resolve to foster a common civic culture and national identity to succeeding generations of native- and foreign-born students in an accessible pluralistic system of common and separate schooling. Whether America can successfully regenerate and self-perpetuate without the cohesive force of a government monopoly over schooling remains to be seen. This could be the nation's grand experiment for the new millennium.

Notes

CHAPTER 1. INTRODUCTION

1. The term as originally used referred to the dispute between Protestants and Catholics at the end of the nineteenth century over the religious content of public education in Germany. *See* James Davison Hunter, *Culture Wars: The Struggle to Define America* (New York: Basic, 1991), xii.

2. John Davison Hunter, *Before the Shooting Begins: Searching for Democracy in America's Culture War* (New York: Free Press, 1994), 31.

3. Karen Diegmuller, "Fighting Back," *Education Week*, 16 November 1994, 32.

4. Leslea Newman, *Heather Has Two Mommies* (Boston: Alyson Publications, 1989).

5. Laurie Ann Lattimore, "The Herdahl Family's Hurdle," *Liberty* (May/June 1996): 17–21. In *Herdahl v. Potontoc County School District*, 964 F.Supp. 1113 (N.D. Miss. 1997), the federal court struck down the practice of daily prayer over the school intercom, classroom prayers, and the Bible history class as violating the establishment clause of the First Amendment.

6. Richard John Neuhaus, *The Naked Public Square: Religion and Democracy in America* (Grand Rapids: Eerdmans), 1984.

7. Ronald F. Thiemann, *Religion in Public Life: A Dilemma for Democracy* (Washington, D.C.: Georgetown University Press, 1996), 3.

8. Peter Applebome, "Prayer in Public Schools? It's Nothing New for Many," *New York Times*, 22 November 1994, A1.

9. Christian Coalition, *Contract with the American Family* (Nashville: Moorings, 1995), xi, xiii.

10. Lynn Schnaiberg, "Staying Home from School," *Education Week,* 12 June 1996, 24, 25.

11. Brian D. Ray, *Strengths of Their Own: Home Schoolers Across America* (Salem, Ore.: National Home Education Research Institute, 1997), 1.

12. Maralee Mayberry, J. Gary Knowles, Brian Ray, and Stacy Marlow, *Home Schooling: Parents as Educators* (Thousand Oaks, Calif.: Corwin Press, 1995), 39.

13. James Carper, "The Christian Day School Movement, 1960–1982," *Educational Forum* 17 (1983): 135–49, 139.

14. Alan Peshkin, *God's Choice: The Total World of a Fundamentalist Christian School* (Chicago: University of Chicago Press, 1986), 258–59; Eugene F. Provenzano, Jr., *Religious Fundamentalism and American Education* (Albany: State University of New York, 1990), 90. For a discussion of the "total institution" concept, *see* Charles A. McEwen, "Continuities in a Study of Total and Nontotal Institutions," *Annual Review of Sociology* 6 (1980): 143–85.

15. James C. Carper and Jack Layman, "Black-Flight Academies: The New Christian Day Schools," *Educational Forum* 61 (Winter 1997): 114–21. 114.

16. News Release, "Catholic Schools Week Prompts Celebration of National Enrollment Increase, Educators Say Values and Character Count" (Washington, D.C.: National Catholic Educational Association, December 18, 1998).

17. *See* Charles Leslie Glenn, Jr., *The Myth of the Common School* (Amherst: University of Massachusetts Press, 1988), 10.

18. John E. Coons and Stephen D. Sugarman, *Education by Choice: The Case for Family Control* (Berkeley: University of California Press, 1978).

19. Arthur M. Schlesinger, *The Vital Center* (Boston: Houghton Mifflin, 1949). For a contemporary discussion, *see* Arthur M. Schlesinger, *The Disuniting of America* (New York: W. W. Norton, 1991).

CHAPTER 2. THE COMMON SCHOOL: PAST AS PROLOGUE

1. Benjamin Barber, *An Aristocracy of One: The Politics of Education and the Future of America* (New York: Ballantine, 1992), 42.

2. Some state constitutions, for example, Article 11, §1 of the New York State Constitution, mandate merely a system of "free public schools," while others, for example, Article VIII, §4 of the New Jersey Constitution, call for "a thorough and efficient system of free public schools." Still others, for example, Article IX, §1 of the Washington Constitution, mandate a stronger commitment, defining "the paramount duty of the state to make ample provision for the education of all children . . . without distinction or preference on account of race, color, or sex."

3. For a discussion of the federal role in education, *see* Diane Ravitch, *The Troubled Crusade* (New York: Basic, 1983); Rosemary C. Salomone, *Equal Education Under Law* (New York: St. Martin's Press, 1986).

4. Lawrence A. Cremin, *The Genius of Education,* Horace Mann Lecture, 1965 (Pittsburgh: University of Pittsburgh Press, 1965), 2.

5. Lorraine Smith Pangle and Thomas L. Pangle, *The Learning of Liberty: The Educational Ideas of the American Founders* (Lawrence: University Press of Kansas, 1993), 58.

6. Quoted in Lawrence A. Cremin, *American Education: The Colonial Experience, 1607–1783* (New York: Harper and Row, 1970), 181.

7. Thomas Jefferson, "A Bill for the More General Diffusion of Knowledge," in *Crusade Against Ignorance: Thomas Jefferson on Education,* ed. Gordon C. Lee (New York: Teachers College Press, 1961), 85–92.

8. Robert M. Taylor, Jr., ed., *The Northwest Ordinance of 1787: A Bicentennial Handbook* (Bloomington: Indiana Historical Society, 1987), 81.

9. David Tyack, Thomas James, and Aaron Benavot, *Law and the Shaping of Public Education, 1785–1954* (Madison: University of Wisconsin Press, 1987), 55.

10. Frederick M. Binder, *The Age of the Common School* (New York: John Wiley, 1974), 24; Clarence J. Karier, *The Individual, Society, and Education: A History of American Ideas* (Urbana: University of Illinois Press, 1986), 224.

11. Lawrence A. Cremin, "Horace Mann's Legacy," in *The Republic and the School: Horace Mann on the Education of Free Man,* ed. Lawrence A. Cremin (New York: Teachers College Press, 1957), 8.

12. Lawrence A. Cremin, *The American Common School: An Historical Conception* (New York: Teachers College, Bureau of Publications, 1951), 44–47.

13. David Tyack and Elizabeth Hansot, *Managers of Virtue: Public School Leadership in America* (New York: Basic, 1982), 20.

14. Cremin, *The Republic and the School,* 19.

15. Carl F. Kaestle, *Pillars of the Republic: Common Schools and American Society, 1780–1860* (New York: Hill and Wang, 1983), 116.

16. Horace Mann, "Twelfth Annual Report," in Cremin, *The Republic and the School,* 106.

17. Charles Leslie Glenn, Jr., *The Myth of the Common School* (Amherst: University of Massachusetts Press, 1988), 166.

18. Warren A. Nord, *Religion and American Education: Rethinking a National Dilemma* (Chapel Hill: University of North Carolina Press, 1995), 72.

19. Mann, "Twelfth Annual Report," in Cremin, *The Republic and the School,* 101–02.

20. Jeffrey E. Mirel, "'Between God and the Youth of Our City:' Conflicts over Religion and Education in Detroit, 1842–1949," *Urban Education* 22, 2 (July 1987): 203–26, 206.

21. Michael W. Kirst, *Who Controls the Schools? American Values in Conflict* (New York: W. H. Freeman, 1984), 28.

22. John Westerhoff, *McGuffey and His Readers* (Nashville: Abingdon, 1978), 103–04.

23. Ruth Miller Elson, *Guardians of Tradition: American Schoolbooks of the Nineteenth Century* (Lincoln: University of Nebraska Press, 1964), 338–39.

24. Mann, "Twelfth Annual Report," in Cremin, *The Republic and the School,* 97.

25. Carl F. Kaestle, "Moral Education and Common Schools in America: A Historian's View," *Journal of Moral Education* 13 (May 1984): 101–11, 107–08.

26. Joel Spring, "The Evolving Political Structure of American Schooling," in *The Public School Monopoly,* ed. Robert B. Everhart and Clarence J. Karier (Cambridge, Mass.: Ballinger, 1982), 84.

27. David Tyack, "Preserving the Republic by Educating Republicans," in *Diversity and Its*

Discontents, ed. Neil J. Smelser and Jeffrey C. Alexander (Princeton: Princeton University Press, 1999), 63–83, 65.

28. Barbara Finkelstein, "Exploring Community in Urban Educational History," in *Schools in Cities: Consensus and Conflict in American Educational History,* ed. Donald K. Goodenow and Diane Ravitch (New York: Holmes and Meier, 1983), 309; Jane Addams, "Immigrants and Their Children," in *Twenty Years of Hull House* (New York: New American Library, 1981), 169–85; Mann, "Twelfth Annual Report (1848)," in *The Republic and the School,* 87.

29. Carl Kaestle and Maris Vinovskis, *Urbanization and the History of Education: An Analysis of the Determinants of School Attendance in New York State in 1845* (Madison: University of Wisconsin Center for Demographics and Ecology, Working Paper 73–31, 1974), cited in Samuel Bowles and Herbert Gintis, *Schooling in Capitalist America* (New York: Basic, 1976), 175.

30. David Tyack, *The One Best System: A History of American Urban Education* (Cambridge: Harvard University Press, 1974), 69.

31. Kaestle, *Pillars of the Republic,* 166.

32. During the 1830s, 600,000 Catholics migrated to the United States, followed by 1,700,000 in the 1840s and 2,600,000 more in the 1850s. Of these, 43 percent were from Ireland, 26 percent from Germany, 17 percent from England, Scotland, and Wales, and the remainder from Italy and eastern Europe. By the late 1880s, the number of Catholics in the United States had reached more than 6 million. John Davison Hunter, *The Culture Wars: The Struggle to Define America* (New York: Basic Books, 1991), 69.

33. Robert Michaelsen, *Piety in the Public School* (New York: Macmillan, 1970), 89–90; Francis Michael Perko, *A Time to Favor Zion: A Case Study of Religion as a Force in American Educational Development, 1830–1870,* Ph.D. diss., Stanford University, June 1981 (Ann Arbor: University Microfilms International, 1981), 128–35.

34. Lloyd P. Jorgenson, *The State and the Non-Public School, 1825–1925* (Columbia: University of Missouri Press, 1987), 76.

35. Michaelson, *Piety in the Public School,* 87.

36. Hunter, *Culture Wars,* 200.

37. Elson, *Guardians of Tradition,* 47–51.

38. Kaestle, *Pillars of the Republic,* 168.

39. Diane Ravitch, *The Great School Wars: New York City, 1805–1973* (New York: Basic Books, 1974), 48, 53.

40. Kaestle, *Pillars of the Republic,* 169.

41. John Higham, *Strangers in the Land: Patterns of American Nativism, 1860–1925* (New Brunswick: Rutgers University Press, 1955), 4.

42. Jorgenson, *The State and the Non-Public School,* 29, 107.

43. New York State Constitution, Article XI, §3. For a discussion of similar state constitutional amendments enacted throughout this period to prevent aid to religiously affiliated schools, *see* Joseph P. Viteritti, "Blaine's Wake: School Choice, the First Amendment, and State Constitutional Law," *Harvard Journal of Law and Public Policy* 21 (1998), 657–718.

44. James Clarkson, "General Grant's Des Moines Speech," *Century Magazine* 55 (March 1898): 788, cited in Tyack and Hansot, *Managers of Virtue,* 77.

45. "Pronouncement of the Plenary Council of Baltimore, 1884," cited in Michaelson, *Piety in the Public School,* 124; Vincent P. Lannie, *Public Money and Parochial Education* (Cleveland: Case Western University Press), 257–58.

46. Kaestle, "Moral Education and Common Schools in America," 101, 105.

47. Charles L. Glenn, "'Molding' Citizens," in *Democracy and the Renewal of Public Education,* ed. Richard John Neuhaus (Grand Rapids: Eerdmans, 1987), 25, 53.

48. Lannie, *Public Money and Parochial Education,* 62.

49. Ravitch, *The Great School Wars,* 61–62.

50. David B. Tyack, "Ways of Seeing: An Essay on the History of Compulsory Schooling," *Harvard Educational Review* 46 (3) (August 1976): 355–89, 360.

51. Ralph Henry Gabriel, *The Course of American Democratic Thought: An Intellectual History Since 1815* (New York: Ronald Press, 1949), 176.

52. John A. Nietz, "Why the Longevity of the McGuffey Readers?" *History of Education Quarterly* 4 (June 1964): 119–25, 123.

53. John H. Westerhoff III, *McGuffey and His Readers: Piety, Morality, and Education in Nineteenth-Century America* (Nashville: Abingdon, 1978), 104–05.

54. Mirel, "Between God and the Youth of Our City," 224.

55. Martin S. Dworkin, "John Dewey: A Centennial Review," in *Dewey on Education,* ed. Martin S. Dworkin (New York: Teachers College Press, 1959), 9.

56. Arthur Zilversmit, *Changing Schools: Progressive Education Theory and Practice, 1930–1960* (Chicago: University of Chicago Press, 1993), 17.

57. Michaelsen, *Piety in the Public School,* 257.

58. Tyack, James, and Benavot, *Law and the Shaping of Public Education,* 170.

59. William G. Ross, *Forging New Freedoms: Nativism, Education, and the Constitution, 1917–1927* (Lincoln: University of Nebraska Press, 1994), 61.

60. John Dewey, "My Pegadogic Creed," reprinted in *The Philosophy of John Dewey,* ed. John J. McDermott (Chicago: University of Chicago Press, 1973, 1981), 443.

61. Toni Marie Massaro, *Constitutional Literacy* (Durham: Duke University Press, 1993), 25–26.

62. John Dewey, *Democracy and Education* (New York: Free Press, 1916), 152–53.

63. Dewey, "My Pedagogic Creed," 446.

64. National Education Association, *Report of the Committee of Ten on Secondary School Studies* (Washington, D.C.: U.S. Government Printing Office, 1983); *Cardinal Principles of Secondary Education: A Report of the Commission on the Reorganization of Secondary Education, Appointed by the National Education Association,* bulletin no. 35, ed. C. D. Kingsley (Washington, D.C.: U.S. Government Printing Office, 1983).

65. Michaelson, *Piety in the Public School,* 144, 146–48.

66. Kaestle, "Moral Education and Common Schools in America," 105.

67. Alan Freeman and Betty Mensch, "Religion as Science/Science as Religion: Constitutional Law and the Fundamentalist Challenge," *Tikkun* 2, 5 (1987): 64–69, 67 (paraphrasing Dewey's essay, "Religion in Our Schools").

68. George S. Counts, *Dare the Schools Build a New Social Order?* (New York: John Day, 1932), 6, 13–26, 10–12.

69. Ravitch, *The Troubled Crusade,* 63.

70. Ibid., 65.

71. University of the State of New York, State Education Department, *Fifty-Second Annual Report of the Education Department* (Albany: State University of New York, 1958), cited in Zilversmit, *Changing Schools,* 97.

72. Bernard Iddings Bell, *Crisis in Education* (New York: McGraw-Hill, 1949); Lawrence A. Cremin, *The Transformation of the School—Progressivism in American Education 1876– 1957* (New York: Vintage, 1961), 339–40.

73. Ravitch, *The Troubled Crusade,* 75, discussing Albert Lynd, *Quackery in the Public Schools* (Boston: Little, Brown, 1950), 19–20, 42, 75; Robert M. Hutchins, *The Conflict of Education in a Democratic Society* (New York: Harper, 1953), 19–20, 42.

74. Arthur Bestor, *Educational Wastelands: The Retreat from Learning in our Public Schools* (Urbana: University of Illinois Press, 1953), 14, 64–65, 47.

75. "The New Mood," *Time,* 3 March 1958, 39–40; Theodore Shultz, "Investment in Human Capital," *American Economic Review* 51, 1 (1961): 1–17, 13; Mann, "Fifth Annual Report," in Cremin, *The Republic and the School,* 53; Cremin, *The Transformation of the School,* 348; Samuel Bowles and Herbert Gintis, *Schooling in Capitalist America* (New York: Basic Books, 1974), 181; *Alliance for Academic Achievement: Building the Value-Based Community* (Chicago: Academic Development Institute, 1990), 21.

76. American Association of School Administrators, *American School Curriculum, Thirty-first Yearbook* (Washington, D.C., 1953), 57–70, cited in Zilversmit, *Changing Schools,* 119.

77. Charles Silberman, *Crisis in the Classroom* (New York: Random House, 1970), 111–57.

78. Bowles and Gintis, *Schooling in Capitalist America,* 181.

79. For a comprehensive discussion of the differentiated curriculum in the high school, *see* David Angus and Jeffrey Mirel, "Rhetoric and Reality: The High School Curriculum," in *Learning from the Past,* ed. Diane Ravitch and Maris A. Vinovskis (Baltimore: Johns Hopkins University Press, 1995), 319.

80. Cremin, *The Transformation of the School,* 353.

81. Diane Ravitch, *The Schools We Deserve* (New York: Basic Books, 1985), 84.

82. Frances FitzGerald, *America Revised: History Schoolbooks in the Twentieth Century* (Boston: Little, Brown, 1979), 191.

83. Sidney B. Simon, Leland W. Howe, and Howard Kirschenbaum, *Values Clarification: A Handbook of Practical Strategies for Teachers and Students* (New York: Hart, 1972), 16.

84. Stephen Bates, "A Textbook of Virtues," *New York Times* (Education Life), 8 January 1995, 16–19, 43–46, 18.

85. Simon et al., *Values Clarification: A Handbook of Practical Strategies for Teachers and Students,* 18.

86. Peter F. Carbone, Jr., "Introduction," in *Value Theory and Education,* ed. Peter F. Carbone (Malabar, Fla.: Robert F. Krieger, 1987), 6–7; Philip Selznik, *The Moral Commonwealth: Social Theory and the Promise of Community* (Berkeley: University of California Press, 1992), 16.

87. Bates, "A Textbook of Virtues," 18.

88. Stephen Arons, *Compelling Belief: The Culture of American Schooling* (New York: McGraw-Hill, 1983), 5–7.

89. Jacques S. Benninga, "Moral and Character Education in the Elementary School: An Introduction," in *Moral, Character, and Civic Education in the Elementary School,* ed. Jacques S. Benninga (New York: Teachers College Press, 1991), 3–20, 15.

90. Lawrence Kohlberg, *The Philosophy of Moral Development: Moral Stages and the Idea of Justice* (San Francisco: Harper and Row, 1981), 296–97.

91. "Why Public Schools Fail: A Three-Part Special Report on the Crisis of Confidence in the American Public School," *Newsweek,* 20 April 1981, 62–65; "The Bright Flight," *Newsweek,* 20 April 1981, 66–73; James S. Coleman, Thomas Hoffer, and Sally B. Kilgore, *High School Achievement: Public, Catholic, and Private Schools Compared* (New York: Basic Books, 1982); Andrew M. Greeley, *Catholic High Schools and Minority Students* (New Brunswick, N.J.: Transaction Books, 1982).

92. National Commission on Excellence in Education, *A Nation at Risk: The Imperative for Educational Reform* (Washington, D.C.: U.S. Government Printing Office, 1983), 5.

93. FitzGerald, *America Revised,* 192–94.

94. Muriel Cohen, "New Right Tries Shaping US Education," *Boston Globe,* 29 November 1982, 1, 12. *See* Joan Dellatorre, *What Johnny Shouldn't Read* (New Haven: Yale University Press, 1992).

95. Kaestle, "Moral Education and Common Schools in America," 107.

96. Martin S. Dworkin, "John Dewey: A Centennial Review," in *Dewey on Education* (New York: Teachers College Press, 1959), 10, citing "Progressive Education and the Science of Education," in John Dewey, *Progressive Education* (New York: John Dewey Society, 1928), 5:197–204.

97. Ravitch, *The Troubled Crusade,* 47, 59, quoting John Dewey, *Experience and Education* (New York: Collier, 1963, orig. pub. 1938), 21–30, 64–65.

98. Cremin, *The Transformation of the School,* 348.

99. Selznick, *The Moral Commonwealth,* 15.

100. For an insightful critique of contemporary liberalism and the erosion of community, *see* Michael J. Sandel, *Democracy's Discontent: America in Search of a Public Philosophy* (Cambridge: Harvard University Press, 1996).

101. James S. Coleman, "Changes in the Family and Implications for the Common School," *University of Chicago Legal Forum* (1991): 153–70, 158–59; William Bennett, "Moral Literacy and the Formation of Character," *NASSP Bulletin* 72 (1988): 29–34.

102. Robert Bellah, Richard Madsen, William M. Sullivan, Ann Swidler, and Steven M. Tipton, *Habits of the Heart* (New York: Harper and Row, 1985), vi, 282.

103. Peter Schmidt, "Despite Controversy, Consensus Grows on the Need to Teach Values in Schools," *Education Week,* 7 February 1990, 1, 10.

104. Thomas Lickona, *Educating for Character* (New York: Bantam Books, 1991), 49.

105. *Getting By: What American Teenagers Really Think About Their Schools* (New York: Public Agenda, 1997), 42.

106. *1996 Report Card on American Integrity* (Marina del Rey, Calif.: Josephson Institute of Ethics, 1996), 21.

107. Steve Farkas and Jean Johnson, *Kids These Days: What Americans Really Think About the Next Generation* (New York: Public Agenda, 1997), 8.

108. Jack Frymier, Luvern Cunningham, Willlard Duckett, Bruce Gansneder, Frances Link,

June Rimmer, and James Scholz, *Values on Which We Agree* (Bloomington, Ind.: Phi Delta Kappa International, September 1995), 29.

109. Metropolitan Life Survey of the American Teacher, 1996, *Students Voice Their Opinions On: Learning about Values and Principles in School,* pt. 3 (New York: Louis Harris), 4.

110. Jean Johnson and John Immerwahr, *First Things First: What Americans Expect from the Public Schools* (New York: Public Agenda, 1994), 24; "The Moral Child," (Culture and Ideas), *U.S. News and World Report,* 3 June 1996, 52–59.

111. Members of the partnership include the American Association of School Administrators, the American Federation of Teachers, the National Association of Secondary School Principals, the National Education Association, and the National School Boards Association. According to its mission statement, the purpose of the partnership is to develop "civic virtue and moral character in American youth for a more compassionate and responsible society."

112. Included among the approximately one hundred organizations that now compose the Character Counts Coalition are the YMCA, the American Association of Retired Persons, La Raza, the Little League, and the Urban League. Among its council of advisors, the organization has boasted former secretary of education William Bennett and Marian Wright Edelman, president and founder of the Children's Defense Fund.

113. *Preparing Students for the 21st Century* (Annapolis Junction, Md.: American Association of School Administrators, 1996).

114. The Improving America's Schools Act of 1994, Pub. L. No. 103–382, §10103 authorized up to ten grants of as much as one million dollars each to state agencies to join in a partnership with at least one local school district in implementing a character education pilot project. More than $22.5 million have since been awarded to twenty-eight states.

115. *See* Millicent Lawton, "Values Education: A Moral Obligation or Dilemma?" *Education Week,* 17 May 1995, 1; "State of the Union Address," *New York Times,* 24 January 1996, A14.

116. *See* e.g., Indiana Statutes Annotated §20–10.1–4-4 (Burns 1995) ("Each public and non-public school teacher, employed in the regular courses of the first twelve (12) grades, shall present his instruction with special emphasis on honesty, morality, courtesy, obedience to law, respect for the national flag, the constitutions of the United States and Indiana, respect for parents and the home, the dignity and necessity of honest labor and other lessons of a steadying influence, which tend to promote and develop an upright and desirable citizenry"); "'Character' Office Opens," *Education Week,* 20 November 1997, 4.

117. Susan Douglas Franzosa, "Authoring the Educated Self: Educational Autobiography and Resistance," *Educational Theory* 42 (Fall 1992): 395–412, 397–98.

118. For a thorough discussion among leaders in moral development with varying perspectives on the hidden curriculum, *see The Hidden Curriculum and Moral Education,* ed. Henry Giroux and David Purpel (Berkeley: McCutchan, 1983).

119. Mark G. Yudof, *When Government Speaks* (Berkeley: University of California Press, 1983), 213.

120. Arons, *Compelling Belief,* 205–07.

121. Walter A. Kamiat, Note "State Indoctrination and the Protection of Non-State Voices

in the Schools: Justifying a Prohibition of School Library Censorship," *Stanford Law Review* 35 (1983): 497–535, 502.

122. Robert D. Kamenshine, "The First Amendment's Implied Political Establishment Clause," *California Law Review* 67 (1979): 1104–53, 1134.

123. Michael W. McConnell, "Multiculturalism, Majoritarianism, and Educational Choice: What Does Our Constitutional Tradition Have to Say?" *University of Chicago Legal Forum* (1991): 123–51, 142.

124. Nadine Strossen, "'Secular Humanism' and 'Scientific Creationism': Proposed Standards for Reviewing Curricular Decisions Affecting Students' Religious Freedom," *Ohio State Law Journal* 47 (1986): 333–407, 375–76.

125. Joseph Tussman, *Education and Mind* (New York: Oxford University Press, 1977), 85.

126. Bruce C. Hafen, "Developing Student Expression Through Institutional Authority: Public Schools as Mediating Structures," *Ohio State Law Journal* 48 (1987): 663–731, 670.

127. Malcolm Stewart, "The First Amendment, the Public Schools, and the Inculcation of Community Values," *Journal of Law and Education* 18 (1989), 23–92, 29.

128. Lawrence A. Cremin, *Public Education* (New York: Basic Books, 1976), 69.

CHAPTER 3. FROM CHILDREN'S RIGHTS TO PARENTS' RIGHTS

1. Philippe Ariès, *Centuries of Childhood: A Social History of Family Life* (New York: Alfred A. Knopf, 1962).

2. David Nicholas, "Childhood in Medieval Europe," in *Children in Historical and Comparative Perspective,* ed. Joseph M. Hawes and N. Ray Hiner (New York: Greenwood Press, 1991), 31; Ralph A. Houlbrooke, *The English Family, 1450–1700* (London: Longman, 1984), 143–38.

3. Ariès, *Centuries of Childhood*, 253.

4. Anne Yarbrough, "Apprentices as Adolescents in Sixteenth Century Bristol," *Journal of Social History* 13 (Fall 1979): 67–81.

5. J. H. Plumb, "Children: The Victims of Time," in *The Light of History,* ed. J. H. Plumb (Boston: Houghton Mifflin, 1973), 158–59.

6. Ivy Pinchbeck and Margaret Hewitt, *Children in English Society* (London: Routledge and Kegan Paul, 1973), 2:348.

7. John Locke, *Two Treatises on Government* (1690), ed. Peter Laslett (Cambridge: Cambridge University Press, 1963), 347–48.

8. Ibid., 350, 352, 402. According to Locke, individuals relinquish a part of their naturally possessed reason to the state at some historical juncture in order to protect their liberty and property. However, the state's authority to act is limited by the terms of this agreement. Ibid., 398.

9. Melinda A. Roberts, "Parent and Child in Conflict: Between Liberty and Responsibility," *Notre Dame Journal of Law, Ethics & Public Policy* 10 (1996): 485–542, 507.

10. William Blackstone, *Commentaries on the Laws of England,* bk. 1 (Oxford: Clarendon Press, 1765), 440–41, 434–38, 440–41.

11. Jean-Jacques Rousseau, *The Social Contract of Principles of Political Right* (1762), trans. and ed. Charles M. Sherover (New York: New American Library, 1974), 7.

12. Jean-Jacques Rousseau, *The Emile* (1762), ed. and trans. William Boyd (New York: Teachers College, 1965), 18, 38–39, 40–42.

13. Ibid., 40.

14. Arlene Skolnick, "The Limits of Childhood: Conceptions of Child Development and Social Context," *Law and Contemporary Problems* 39 (Summer 1975): 39–77, 45.

15. John Stuart Mill, *On Liberty* (1859), ed. Currin V. Shields (Indianapolis: Bobbs-Merril Educational Publishing, 1956), 13.

16. Ibid., 128–29.

17. Chancellor James Kent, *Commentaries on American Law*, 4 vols. (New York: O. Halstead, 1826–30), quoted in Grace Abbott, *The Child and the State*, vol. 1, *Legal Status in the Family, Apprenticeship, and Child Labor* (Chicago: University of Chicago Press, 1949), 49–52.

18. Joseph M. Hawes, *The Children's Rights Movement: A History of Advocacy and Protection* (Boston: Twayne Publishers, 1991), 1–7. For a particularly compelling example of state intervention with a decidedly moralistic tone, *see* Joseph M. Hawes, *Children in Urban Society: Juvenile Deliquency in the Nineteenth Century* (New York: Oxford University Press, 1971), 97–98, recounting the story of selectmen in Watertown, Massachusetts, in 1737 ordering the town clerk to post a notice informing certain families believed to be guilty of "negligence and indulgence" that they should "take care to put out and dispose of their children to such families where they may be taken good care of." Failure to do so would cause the selectmen to take similar action.

19. Alexis de Tocqueville, *Democracy in America* (1835), ed. Phillip Bradley (New York: Vintage, 1945), 2:202.

20. Hamilton Cravens, "Child Saving in Modern America 1870s-1990s," in *Children at Risk in America: History, Concepts, and Public Policy*, ed. Roberta Wollons (Albany: State University of New York Press, 1993), 3–31, 5.

21. Christopher Lasch, *Haven in a Heartless World: The Family Besieged* (New York: Basic Books, 1977), 13.

22. Hawes, *The Children's Rights Movement*, 15–25.

23. Lasch, *Haven in a Heartless World*, 13.

24. F. Raymond Marks, "Detours on the Road to Maturity: A View of the Legal Conception of Growing Up and Letting Go," *Law and Contemporary Problems* 39 (1975): 78–92, 88.

25. Hawes, *The Children's Rights Movement*, 51.

26. Selwyn K. Troen, "Technological Development and Adolescence: The Early Twentieth Century," *Journal of Early Adolescence* 5, 4 (1985): 429–39.

27. George Randall, *History of the Common School of the State of New York* (New York: Ivison, Blakeman, Taylor, 1871), 221, cited in Edwin G. West, *Education and the State: A Study in Political Economy*, 3d ed. (Indianapolis: Liberty Fund, 1994), 308.

28. Stuart N. Hart, "From Property to Person Status: Historical Perspective on Children's Rights," *American Psychologist* 46, 1 (January 1991): 53–59, 55.

29. Minot J. Savage, "The Rights of Children," *Arena Magazine* (1892): 8–16, 13.

30. Anthony M. Platt, *The Child Savers* (Chicago: University of Chicago Press, 1969), 139.

31. Lasch, *Haven in a Heartless World*, 15; Martha Minow, "Rights for the Next Generation:

A Feminist Approach to Children's Rights," *Harvard Women's Law Journal* 9 (1986): 1–24, 10.

32. Platt, *The Child Savers*, 145.

33. Willard Gaylin, Ira Glasser, Steven Marcus, and David J. Rothman, *Doing Good: The Limits of Benevolence* (New York: Pantheon, 1976), 72–75.

34. Rochelle Beck, "The White House Conferences on Children: An Historical Perspective," *Harvard Educational Review* 43, 4 (November 1973): 653–68, 657.

35. Gaylin et al., *Doing Good: The Limits of Benevolence*, 72.

36. *Brown v. Board of Education*, 347 U.S. 483 (1954).

37. Hendrik Hartog, "The Constitution of Aspiration and 'The Rights That Belong to Us All,'" *Journal of American History* 74 (1987): 1013–43, 1031.

38. United Nations, General Assembly Resolution 1386 (XIV), November 20, 1959, published in the *Official Records of the General Assembly, Fourteenth Session, Supplement No. 16* (1960), 19. While the Universal Declaration of Human Rights, adopted by the General Assembly in 1948, had implicitly included the freedoms and rights of children, it was believed that the special needs of children justified a separate document. "The Declaration of the Rights of the Child," in *The Children's Rights Movement: Overcoming the Oppression of Young People*, ed. Beatrice Gross and Ronald Gross (New York: Anchor Press/Doubleday, 1977), 333–39, 335.

39. Rosalind Ekman Ladd, "Some Theoretical Issues," in *Children's Rights Re-visioned*, ed. Rosalind Ekman Ladd (Belmont, Calif.: Wadsworth, 1996), 10–59, 12.

40. Minow, "Rights for the Next Generation," 9.

41. *White House Conference on Children, Report to the President* (1970), 423–42.

42. Beck, *The White House Conference*, 662–63.

43. Mary Kohler, "The Rights of Children: An Unexplored Constituency," *Social Policy* (March/April 1971): 36–43. (Mary Kohler chaired the Forum on the Rights of Children at the White House Conference on Children in 1970).

44. Henry H. Foster and Doris Jonas Freed, "A Bill of Rights for Children," *Family Law Quarterly* 6 (1972): 343–75, 347.

45. John Holt, *Escape from Childhood* (New York: E. P. Dutton, 1974), 18.

46. Richard Farson, *Birthrights* (New York: Macmillan, 1974).

47. Skolnik, "The Limits of Childhood," 76, quoting from an unpublished book review of Holt and Farson by D. Baumrind, "Children's Rights-Adult Responsibilities" (1974).

48. "An Interview with Marian Wright Edelman," *Harvard Educational Review* 44, 1 (February 1974): 65–73, 67.

49. Peter B. Edelman, "Children's Rights Coming to the Fore," *New York Times*, 15 January 1975, 71.

50. Hillary Rodham, "Children Under the Law," *Harvard Educational Review* 43, 4 (November 1973): 487–514, 506–07.

51. Bill Kovach, "New Unity to Fight for Child Rights," *New York Times*, 23 May 1973, 16.

52. Barbara Campbell, "Children's Rights Drive Centered in Courtroom," *New York Times*, 31 October 1976, 26.

53. "Children's Rights: The Latest Crusade," *Time*, 25 December 1972, 41.

54. *In re Gault*, 387 U.S. 1, 27, 28 (1971).

55. *Tinker v. Des Moines Independent Community School District,* 393 U.S. 503 (1969).

56. *Goss v. Lopez,* 419 U.S. 565, 582–83 (1975).

57. *Planned Parenthood v. Danforth,* 428 U.S. 52 (1976).

58. *Carey v. Population Services International,* 431 U.S. 678, 693 n.15 (1977).

59. *Bellotti v. Baird,* 443 U.S. 622 (1979).

60. *Ingraham v. Wright,* 430 U.S. 651 (1977).

61. *New Jersey v. T.L.O.,* 469 U.S. 325 (1985); *Board of Education, Island Trees Union Free School District v. Pico,* 457 U.S. 853, 870 (1982); *Hazelwood School District v. Kuhlmeier,* 484 U.S. 260, 273 (1988).

62. *Schall v. Martin,* 467 U.S. 253, 265 (1984).

63. *Parham v. J.R.,* 442 U.S. 584, 602. (1979).

64. *H.L. v. Matheson,* 450 U.S. 398, 410 (1981).

65. Justin Witkin, "A Time for Change: Reevaluating the Constitutional Status of Minors," *Florida Law Review* 47 (1995): 113–46, 124.

66. Michael S. Wald, "Children's Rights: A Framework for Analysis," *University of California, Davis Law Review* 12 (1979): 255–82, 282.

67. John E. Coons and Robert H. Mnookin, "Towards a Theory of Children's Rights," in *The Child and the Courts,* ed. John E. Coons and Robert H. Mnookin (Toronto: Carswell, 1978), 391–98, 392.

68. Joseph Goldstein, Anna Freud, and Albert J. Solnit, *Beyond the Best Interests of the Child,* 2d ed. (New York: Free Press, 1979), 7.

69. Laura M. Purdy, *In Their Best Interest: The Case Against Equal Rights for Children* (Ithaca: Cornell University Press, 1992), 138.

70. Wald, "Children's Rights: A Framework for Analysis," 275.

71. John E. Coons, Robert H. Mnookin, and Stephen D. Sugarman, "Puzzling Over Children's Rights," *Brigham Young University Law Review* (1991): 307–50, 348–49.

72. Kenneth J. Karst, "The Freedom of Intimate Association," *Yale Law Journal* 89 (1980): 624–92, 635, citing Lasch, *Haven in a Heartless World.*

73. Robert Burt, "Children as Victims," in *Children's Rights,* ed. Patricia A. Vardin and Ilene N. Brody (New York: Teachers College Press, 1979), 37–52, 51.

74. Rena K. Uviller, "Children versus Parents: Perplexing Policy Questions for the ACLU," in *Having Children: Philosophical and Legal Reflections on Parenthood,* ed. Onora O'Neill and William Ruddick (New York: Oxford University Press, 1979), 214–20, 219.

75. Martha Minow and Mary Lyndon Shanley, "Relational Rights and Responsibilities: Revisioning the Family in Liberal Political Theory and Law," *Hypatia* 11, 1 (Winter 1996): 4–29, 5.

76. *See,* e.g., Joan Tronto, *Moral Boundaries: A Political Argument for an Ethic of Care* (New York: Routledge, 1993).

77. Carol Gilligan, *In a Different Voice: Psychological Theory and Women's Development* (Cambridge: Harvard University Press, 1982).

78. Minow, "Rights for the Next Generation," 15.

79. Martha Minow, "What Ever Happened to Children's Rights?" *Minnesota Law Review* 80 (1995): 267–98, 295.

80. Martha Minow, *Making All the Difference* (Ithaca: Cornell University Press, 1990), 283.

81. *See*, e.g., MaryAnn Glendon, *Rights Talk: The Impoverishment of Political Discourse* (New York: Free Press, 1991).
82. Minow, "Rights for the Next Generation," 17–19, citing *Yoder v. Wisconsin,* 406 U.S. 205 (1972).
83. Minow, *Making All the Difference,* 297.
84. Bruce C. Hafen, "Children's Liberation and the New Egalitarianism: Some Reservations About Abandoning Youth to Their 'Rights,'" *Brigham Young University Law Review* (1976): 605–58, 650; Robert Mnookin, "The Enigma of Children's Interests," in *In the Interests of Children: Advocacy, Law Reform, and Public Policy,* ed. Robert Mnookin, Robert Burt, et al. (Cambridge: Program on Negotiation at Harvard Law School, 1985), 16.
85. Martha Minow, "Interpreting Rights: An Essay for Robert Cover," *Yale Law Journal* 96 (1987): 1882–85.
86. Minow, "Rights for the Next Generation," 14, 19.
87. Wendy Ann Fitzgerald, "Maturity, Difference and Mystery: Children's Perspectives and the Law," *Arizona Law Review* 36 (1994): 11–111, 19; Barbara Bennett Woodhouse, "Out of Children's Needs, Children's Rights: The Child's Voice in Defining Family," *Brigham Young University Journal of Public Law* 8 (1994): 321–41, 323; Theresa Glennon and Robert G. Schwartz, "Foreword—Looking Back, Looking Ahead: The Evolution of Children's Rights," *Temple Law Review* 68 (1995): 1557–72, 1564–65.
88. Tom D. Campbell, "The Rights of the Minor: As Person, As Child, As Juvenile, as Future Adult," in *Children, Rights and the Law,* ed. Philip Alston, Stephen Parker, and John Seymour (Oxford: Clarendon Press, 1992), 1–23, 21.
89. Onora O'Neil, "Children's Rights and Children's Lives," in *Children, Rights and the Law,* ed. Alston, Parker, and Seymour, 24–42, 24–25.
90. Katherine T. Bartlett, "Re-expressing Parenthood," *Yale Law Journal* 98 (1988): 293–340, 296.
91. Shelley Burt, "In Defense of *Yoder:* Parental Authority and the Public Schools," in *Nomos, Political Order,* ed. Ian Shapiro and Russell Hardin (New York: New York University Press, 1996), 412–37, 422, 425.
92. Woodhouse, "'Out of Children's Needs,'" 333–39; Barbara Bennett Woodhouse, "Hatching the Egg: A Child-Centered Perspective on Parents' Rights," *Cardozo Law Review* 14 (1993): 1747–1865, 1755.
93. The phrase "lone rights bearer" is borrowed from Glendon, *Rights Talk,* 47–75, where she discusses the image of the rights bearer in American political discourse as a "self-determining, unencumbered individual" without any social dimension or supports.
94. Barbara Bennett Woodhouse, "A Public Role in the Private Family: The Parental Rights and Responsibilities Act and the Politics of Child Protection and Education," *Ohio State Law Journal* 57 (1996): 393–430, 395.
95. Ferdinand Schoeman, "Rights of Children, Rights of Parents, and the Moral Basis of the Family," *Ethics* 91 (October 1980): 6–19, 6. A less authoritarian version of the parental rights approach suggests a constitutionally protected associational right to maintain the parental relationship and that this right should be balanced against the child's asserted interest. *See* David Fisher, "Parental Rights and the Right to Intimate Association," *Hastings Law Journal* 48 (January 1997): 399–433.

96. Hafen, "Children's Liberation and the New Egalitarianism," 654, 648.

97. Bruce D. Hafen, "The Constitutional Status of Marriage, Kinship and Sexual Privacy—Balancing the Individual and Social Interests," *Michigan Law Review* 81 (1983): 463–574, 468.

98. Dana Mack, *The Assault on Parenthood: How Our Culture Undermines the Family* (New York: Simon and Schuster, 1997), 25.

99. Hearings Before the Oversight and Investigations Subcommittee of the House Economic and Educational Opportunities Committee, *Parents, Schools and Values,* December 5 and 6, 1995.

100. Christian Coalition, *Contract with the American Family* (Nashville: Moorings, 1995), xii.

101. The White House, Office of the Press Secretary, Press Release, February 10, 1995.

102. Among the organizations supporting the convention are a number of religious groups and churches, including Catholic Charities USA, Episcopal Peace Fellowship, Greek Orthodox Church of North and South America, Lutheran World Relief, Mennonite Central Committee, National Council of Churches of Christ in the USA, Presbyterian Church USA, Unitarian Universalist Service Committee, United Church of Christ Office for Church in Society, and United Methodist Church General Board of Global Ministeries.

103. Hafen, "Children's Liberation," 344–51.

104. Woodhouse, "Out of Children's Needs," 331.

105. *Tinker v. Des Moines Independent Community School District,* 393 U.S. 503 (1969); *Hazelwood School District v. Kuhlmeier,* 484 U.S. 260 (1988).

106. *Wisconsin v. Yoder,* 406 U.S. 205 (1972).

107. *San Antonio Independent School District v. Rodriguez,* 411 U.S. 1 (1973) (holding that education is not a fundamental right guaranteed under the federal Constitution).

108. For a comparison of the convention and United States law, *see Children's Rights in America,* ed. Cynthia Price Cohen and Howard A. Davidson (Chicago: American Bar Association, Center on Children and the Law, 1990).

109. Lawrence Stenzel II, "Federal-State Implications of the Convention," in *Children's Rights in America,* ed. Cohen and Davidson, 57–83, 58–62.

110. Glendon, *Rights Talk,* 99.

111. Susan Kilbourne, "Placing the Convention on the Rights of the Child in an American Context," *Human Rights* 26, 2 (Spring 1999): 27–31, 29.

112. American Bar Association Project on the U.N. Convention on the Rights of the Child, "State Education Law Compared to the U.N. Convention on the Rights of the Child," *Georgetown Journal on Fighting Poverty* 5, 2 (Summer 1998): 241–49, 245.

113. For a comprehensive discussion of empowerment rights provided in the convention and the negotiations leading up to their adoption, *see* Lawrence A. LeBlanc, *The Convention on the Rights of the Child: United Nations Lawmaking on Human Rights* (Lincoln: University of Nebraska Press, 1995), 157–82.

114. S.R. 133, 104th Cong., 1st Sess. (1995).

115. *Contract with the American Family,* 50. For a discussion of opposition to and support for the convention, *see* Susan Kilbourne, "U.S. Failure to Ratify the U.N. Convention on

the Rights of the Child: Playing Politics with Children's Rights," *Transnational Law and Contemporary Problems* 6 (Fall 1996): 437–61.

116. Sanford J. Fox, *Report on the United Nations Convention on the Rights of the Child,* American Bar Association Working Group on the United Nations Convention on the Rights of the Child, June 1993, 16.

117. *Meyer v. Nebraska,* 262 U.S. 390 (1923); *Pierce v. Society of Sisters,* 268 U.S. 510 (1925).

118. *Prince v. Massachusetts,* 321 U.S. 158, 166 (1944); *Ginsburg v. New York,* 390 U.S. 629, 639 (1968); *Moore v. East Cleveland,* 431 U.S. 494, 499 (1977); *Stanley v. Illinois,* 405 U.S. 645, 651 (1972). For a discussion of supporting case law, *see Commentary on Protections Which Should Be Afforded Parental Rights and Responsibilities,* American Center for Law and Justice, Washington, D.C. (undated).

119. Hearings Before the Subcommittee on Administrative Oversight and the Courts of the Senate Judiciary Committee, Parental Rights and Responsibilities Act of 1995, December 5, 1995 (testimony of Rep. Steve Largent).

120. H.R. 1946, 104th Cong., 1st Sess. (1995); S. 984, 104th Cong., 1st Sess. (1995).

121. Hearings Before the Subcommittee on Administrative Oversight (testimony of Sen. Charles E. Grassley).

122. Hearings Before the Subcommittee on Administrative Oversight (testimony of Margaret F. Brinig, professor of law, George Mason University).

123. Hearings Before the Subcommittee on Administrative Oversight (testimony of Sammy J. Quintana, National School Boards Association).

124. Peter Applebome, "An Array of Opponents Do Battle Over 'Parental Rights' Legislation," *New York Times,* 1 May 1996, A1 (quoting August W. Steinhilber, former general counsel, National School Boards Association).

125. *The Parental Rights Amendment to State Constitutions* (Arlington: Of the People, 1995).

126. *See* Drew Lindsey, "Telling Tales out of School," *Education Week,* 14 February 1996, 27.

CHAPTER 4. THE SUPREME COURT AS SCHOOLMASTER

1. *Meyer v. Nebraska,* 262 U.S. 390 (1923).

2. *Brief and Argument of State of Nebraska, Defendant in Error, Meyer v. Nebraska,* No. 325, United States Supreme Court, October Term, 1922, 50.

3. William G. Ross, *Forging New Freedoms: Nativism, Education, and the Constitution 1917–1927* (Lincoln: University of Nebraska Press, 1994), 61, 44.

4. William G. Ross, "A Judicial Janus: *Meyer v. Nebraska* in Historical Perspective," *University of Cincinnati Law Review* 57 (1988): 125–204, 145–46.

5. 187 N.W. 927 (Neb. 1922) (*McKelvie II*). Pending Meyer's appeal of his conviction, the Nebraska Supreme Court in *Nebraska District Evangelical Lutheran Synod v. McKelvie* (*McKelvie I*), 174 N.W. 531 (Neb. 1919) upheld the constitutionality of the Siman Act in such a way that it severely weakened its operation. The state legislature repealed the Siman Act and enacted in its place the Norval Act, which specifically prohibited instruction in a foreign language to children below the completion of the eighth grade "in all schools and at all times." The Nebraska Supreme Court upheld the constitutionality of

the Norval Act in *McKelvie II.* The only issue argued before the Nebraska Supreme Court in *Meyer* was the sufficiency of the evidence for Meyer's conviction and the imposition of the twenty-five-dollar fine. The federal constitutional question was raised on a motion for a rehearing which the Nebraska Court denied and later on appeal to the U.S. Supreme Court. *Brief and Argument of State of Nebraska, Defendant in Error, Meyer v. Nebraska,* 4–7, 10–11.

6. *Oral Argument of Arthur F. Mullen, in Behalf of Plaintiffs-in-Error, Meyer v. Nebraska and Nebraska District of Evangelical Lutheran Synod of Missouri,* 6–8, reprinted in *Landmark Briefs and Arguments of the Supreme Court of the United States: Constitutional Law,* ed. Philip B. Kurland and Gerhard Casper (Arlington: University Publications of America, 1975), 21:767–69.

7. *Brief and Argument of State of Nebraska,* 13–15.

8. The second opinion in *Bartels v. Iowa,* 262 U.S. 404 (1923) reversed decisions from the supreme courts of Iowa, Ohio, and Nebraska on the authority of *Meyer.*

9. *Meyer v. Nebraska,* 262 U.S. at 402–03.

10. Ibid., 400–01.

11. A detailed discussion of William Guthrie and his influence on the Court's decision in *Meyer* is contained in Barbara Bennett Woodhouse, "'Who Owns the Child?': *Meyer* and *Pierce* and the Child as Property," *William and Mary Law Review* 33 (Summer 1992): 995–1122, 1070–80.

12. *Pierce v. Society of Sisters,* 268 U.S. 510 (1925).

13. David B. Tyack, "The Perils of Pluralism: The Background of the *Pierce* Case," *American Historical Review* 74 (1968): 74–98, 79.

14. *Brief for Appellee, Pierce v. Society of Sisters,* No. 583, United States Supreme Court, October Term, 1924, Appendix A, 95–98.

15. Tyack, "The Perils of Pluralism," 87–90.

16. *Brief for Appellee, Pierce v. Society of Sisters,* 74–75, 81, 85.

17. *Brief for Appellant,* Isaac H. Winkle, Attorney General of the State of Oregon, *Pierce v. Society of Sisters,* No. 583, United States Supreme Court, October Term, 1924, 72.

18. *Pierce,* 268 U.S. at 535–36.

19. Ibid., 534, emphasis added.

20. "Can the Supreme Court Guarantee Toleration?," *New Republic* 43 (June 17, 1925), 85–87.

21. Tyack, "The Perils of Pluralism," 98.

22. *Moore v. City of East Cleveland,* 431 U.S. 494, 500–01 (1977); *Santosky v. Kramer,* 455 U.S. 745, 753 (1982); *Planned Parenthood v. Casey,* 505 U.S. 833, 834 (1992); *Tinker v. Des Moines Independent Communty School District,* 393 U.S. 503, 506 (1969).

23. *Planned Parenthood of Pennsylvania v. Casey,* 505 U.S. at 851, 849.

24. *M.L.B. v. S.L.J,* 519 U.S. 102 (1996), quoting *Santosky v. Kramer,* 455 U.S. at 774. (Rehnquist, J., dissenting). In *M.L.B.,* Justice Ginsburg, writing for the majority, held that a Mississippi statute that required a parent, whose parental rights had been terminated, to pay in advance record preparation fees incident to her appeal violated the due process and equal protection clauses of the Fourteenth Amendment.

25. Laurence H. Tribe, *American Constitutional Law,* 2d ed. (Mineola, N.Y.: Foundation Press), 1318–19.
26. *Farrington v. Tokushige,* 273 U.S. 284, 298 (1927).
27. *Wisconsin v. Yoder,* 406 U.S. 205 (1972).
28. In *Griswold v. Connecticut,* 381 U.S. 479 (1965) the Court held that for the state to punish someone for providing married persons with contraceptives and information on their use would constitute an invasion of privacy, although the Justices could not agree on a specific provision within the Constitution wherein the right could be found. However, *Griswold* marked the beginning of the Court's modern-day revival of substantive due process leading up to a series of abortion cases beginning with *Roe v. Wade,* 410 U.S. 113 (1973).
29. *Cantwell v. Connecticut,* 310 U.S. 296 (1940); *Sherbert v. Verner,* 374 U.S. 398 (1963).
30. *Employment Division, Department of Human Resources of Oregon v. Smith,* 494 U.S. 872 (1990).
31. For a detailed account of the *Yoder* litigation, *see* William Bentley Ball, *Mere Creatures of the State?: A View from the Courtroom* (Notre Dame: Crisis Books, 1994).
32. *Wisconsin V. Yoder,* 182 N.W. 2d 539 (1971).
33. *Brief for Respondents in Opposition to Petition for a Writ of Certiorari to the Supreme Court of the State of Wisconsin, Wisconsin v. Yoder,* No. 70–110, October Term, 1970, 8–9.
34. *Yoder,* 406 U.S. at 208–09 n.3.
35. Letters to and from the Wisconsin Superintendent of Public Instruction, cited in *Brief for Respondents,* 46.
36. Ball, *Mere Creatures of the State,* 61.
37. *Yoder,* 406 U.S. at 210–12.
38. Ball, *Mere Creatures of the State,* 69.
39. For a discussion of the Burger Court's concern for the preservation of community, *see* Robert Douglas Chesler, "Imagery of Community, Ideology of Authority: The Moral Reasoning of Chief Justice Burger," *Harvard Civil Rights–Civil Liberties Law Review* 18 (1983): 457–82, 458.
40. *Yoder,* 406 U.S. at 218 n.9.
41. Mark Tushnet, *Red, White, and Blue: A Critical Analysis of Constitutional Law* (Cambridge: Harvard University Press, 1988), 274.
42. *Yoder,* 406 U.S. at 226, 222, 218.
43. Ibid., 231.
44. *Brown v. Board of Education,* 347 U.S. 483 (1954).
45. *Brief for Petitioner, Wisconsin v. Yoder,* No. 70–110, United States Supreme Court, October Term, 1971, 18.
46. *Brown,* 347 U.S. at 493.
47. Martha Minow, "Pluralisms," *Connecticut Law Review* 21 (1989): 965–77, 969.
48. *Yoder,* 406 U.S. at 232.
49. Ibid., 233–34, 215–16, emphasis added.
50. In both *United States v. Seeger,* 380 U.S. 163; 174 (1965) and *Welsh v. United States,* 398 U.S.

333 (1970), the Court recognized, for purposes of the Universal Military Service and Training Act, an individual's "sincere religious beliefs" even though not theistic in nature as long as they were based on some faith to which all else was subordinate or ultimately dependent upon.

51. *Yoder,* 406 U.S. at 235–36.

52. Tribe, *American Constitutional Law,* 1181 n. 21.

53. *Yoder,* 406 U.S. at 246 (Douglas, J., concurring in part and dissenting in part).

54. Jeff Spinner, *The Boundaries of Citizenship* (Baltimore: Johns Hopkins University Press, 1994), 98.

55. *Yoder,* 406 U.S. at 216.

56. Ibid., 235, 236 n. 23.

57. Ibid., 213.

58. *Yoder,* 406 U.S. at 241 (White, J., concurring).

59. Ibid., 242 n.1 (Douglas, J., concurring in part and dissenting in part). Justice Douglas here compared *Yoder* with *Prince v. Massachusetts,* 321 U.S. 158 (1944), in which the Court directly addressed the narrow issue of the religious liberty of a Jehovah's Witness who was convicted of having violated a state child labor law by permitting her nine-year-old niece to distribute religious literature on the streets. In both cases, the children had "no effective alternate means to vindicate their rights." The Court in *Prince* thereby implicitly considered the religious freedom of the child in sharp contrast with the majority approach in *Yoder.*

60. Ibid., 245 n.3, 245–46.

61. Robert A. Burt, "Developing Constitutional Rights of, in, and for Children," *Law and Contemporary Problems* 39 (Summer 1975): 118–43, 130.

62. Minow, "Pluralisms," 970.

63. *West Virginia Board of Education v. Barnette,* 319 U.S. 624 (1943).

64. Ibid., 642, 631–32 n. 12.

65. Ibid., 641, 642, 637.

66. *Wooley v. Maynard,* 430 U.S. 705, 714–15 (1977).

67. David B. Gaebler, "First Amendment Protection Against Government Compelled Expression and Association," *Boston College Law Review* 23 (1982): 995–1023, 1004–05.

68. Stephen Arons, *Compelling Belief* (New York: McGraw-Hill, 1983), 209.

69. Stephen Arons, "The Separation of School and State: *Pierce* Reconsidered," *Harvard Educational Review* 46, 1 (February 1976): 76–104, 88 n.39, 89 n.1.

70. Stephen G. Gilles, "On Educating Children: A Parentalist Manifesto," *University of Chicago Law Review* 63 (Summer 1996): 937–1034, 1021, 1013 n. 276.

71. *Tinker v. Des Moines Independent School District,* 393 U.S. 503, 506, 511 (1969).

72. *Engel v. Vitale,* 370 U.S. 421 (1962); *School District of Abington Township v. Schempp,* 374 U.S. 203 (1963); *Stone v. Graham,* 449 U.S. 39 (1980); *Wallace v. Jaffree,* 472 U.S. 38 (1985); *Edwards v. Aguillard,* 482 U.S. 578 (1987); *Lee v. Weisman,* 505 U.S. 577 (1992).

73. Michael McConnell argues that the combined commitment to values inculcation and secularism has translated into a public school system constitutionally committed to inculcating a "secularist morality." *See* Michael W. McConnell, "Multiculturalism, Ma-

joritarianism, and Educational Choice: What Does Our Constitutional Tradition Have to Say?" *University of Chicago Legal Forum* (1991): 123–151, 141.

74. *Keyes v. School District No. 1*, 413 U.S. 189, 246 (1973) (Powell, J., concurring in part and dissenting in part); *San Antonio Independent School District v. Rodriguez*, 411 U.S. 1, 51–52 n. 108 (1973); *Milliken v. Bradley*, 418 U.S. 717, 741–42 (1974).

75. *Board of Education, Island Trees Union Free School District No. 26 v. Pico*, 457 U.S. 853 (1982); *Bethel School District v. Fraser*, 478 U.S. 675 (1986).

76. *Pico*, 457 U.S. at 864; *Fraser*, 478 U.S. at 681.

77. *Pico*, 457 U.S. at 864, quoting *Ambach v. Norwick*, 422 U.S. 68, 76–77 (1979); *Fraser*, 478 U.S. at 683; *Edwards v. Aguillard*, 482 U.S. 578, 584 (1987), quoting *Illinois ex rel. McCollum v. Board of Education*, 333 U.S. 203, 231 (1948).

78. *Fraser*, 478 U.S. at 681.

CHAPTER 5. VOICES OF DISSENT

1. Rousas John Rushdoony, *The Messianic Character of American Education* (Nutley, N.J.: Craig Press, 1968), 309, 31.

2. John S. Detweiler, 'The Religious Right's Battle Plan in the 'Civil War of Values,'" *Public Relations Review* 18, 3 (1992): 247–55, 248.

3. Lee Epstein, *Conservatives in Court* (Knoxville: University of Tennessee Press, 1985), 134–35.

4. Ralph C. Chandler, "The Wicked Shall Not Bear Rule: The Fundamentalist Heritage of the New Christian Right," in *New Christian Politics*, ed. David G. Bromley and Anson Shupe (Macon: Mercer University Press, 1984), 202. *See also* Dinesh D'Souza, *Falwell: Before the Millennium* (Chicago: Regnery Gateway, 1984), 23.

5. *Scopes v. Tennessee*, 289 S.W. 363 (Tenn. 1927) (upholding a state law making it a crime to teach evolution theory in public schools).

6. John Davison Hunter, *Evangelicalism: The Coming Generation* (Chicago: University of Chicago Press, 1987), 163.

7. For a comparison between deliberative and dedicated cultures, *see* Robert Justin Lipkin, "Liberalism and the Possibility of Multi-Cultural Constitutionalism: The Distinction Between Deliberative and Dedicated Cultures," *University of Richmond Law Review* 29 (1995): 1263–1325. *See also* Warren A. Nord, *Religion and American Education: Rethinking a National Dilemma.* (Chapel Hill: University of North Carolina Press, 1995), 50–55.

8. Barbara B. Gaddy, T. William Hall, and Robert J. Marzano, *Resolving Our Conflicts Over Religion and Values* (San Francisco: Jossey-Bass, 1996), 135–49.

9. Nord, *Religion and American Education*, 55.

10. Charles M. Sennott, "Christian Right Woos Catholics, Ralph Reed Makes Pitch to 400 Prospects at Boston Hotel," *Boston Globe*, 10 December 1995, 41; Laurie Goldstein, "Catholics Prove Hard to Convert to the Politics of Coalition," *Washington Post*, 2 September 1996, A1.

11. Richard John Neuhaus, "What the Fundamentalists Want," *Commentary* (May 1985): 41–46, 45–46.

12. *Roe v. Wade*, 410 U.S. 113 (1973).

13. D'Souza, *Falwell: Before the Millennium*, 96, 112–13, 100, 13.

14. *See*, e.g., *Attacks on the Freedom to Learn: 1996 Report* (Washington, D.C.: People for the American Way, 1996). The credibility of PFAW's data came under scrutiny in 1996 when a former staff member published an article suggesting that the group's "startling censorship numbers . . . are cooked." Marc Herman, "Giving the People What They Want," *Salon Magazine*, 23 July 1997 <http:www.salonmagazine.com/media/media960723. html>. For a response by Matthew Freeman, PFAW's research director, see "Censorship and Sensibility" (letter), *Harpers* (January 1997):6–7.

15. *See*, e.g., *Teaching Fear: The Religious Right's Campaign Against Sexuality Education* (Washington, D.C.: People for the American Way, June 1994); *Winning Through Reason, Not Fear: Meeting the Challenge of the Religious Right* (Washington, D.C.: People for the American Way, Fall 1994); *A Turn to the Right: A Guide to the Religious Right Influence in the 103rd/104th Congress* (Washington, D.C.: People for the American Way, 1995).

16. For a discussion of the "anti-pietist" alliance, *see* Allen D. Hertzke, *Representing God in Washington: The Role of Religious Lobbies in the American Polity* (Knoxville: University of Tennessee Press, 1988), 185–87.

17. *See* Carol Weisbrod, "Family, Church, and State: An Essay on Constitutionalism and Religious Authority," *Journal of Family Law* 26 (1987–88): 741–70, 747, for this distinction between models of interaction adopted by religious subgroups toward legal rules in trying to reconcile conflicts in their overlapping authority over the family.

18. Tim LaHaye, *The Battle for the Mind* (Old Tappan, N.J.: Fleming H. Revell, 1980); Tim LaHaye, *The Battle for the Public Schools* (Old Tappan, N.J.: Fleming H. Revell, 1983). For a more historical critique of secularism in American society written during the same period, *see* James Hitchcock, *What Is Secular Humanism?* (Ann Arbor: Servant Books, 1982).

19. LaHaye, *The Battle for the Mind*, 135–40.

20. LaHaye, *The Battle for the Public Schools*, 258, 71.

21. *School District of Abington Township v. Schempp*, 374 U.S. 203 (1963).

22. *Lee v. Weisman*, 505 U.S. 577 (1992).

23. For a discussion of the difficulties in developing a legal definition of religion, *see* Jesse H. Choper, "Defining 'Religion' in the First Amendment," *University of Illinois Law Review* (1982): 579–613, 597–601; George C. Freeman, "The Misguided Search for the Constitutional Definition of Religion," *Georgetown Law Journal* 71 (1983): 1519–65.

24. Paul J. Toscano, *Invisible Religion in the Public Schools: Secularism, Neutrality, and the Supreme Court* (Bountiful, Utah: Horizon Publishers, 1990), 31–40.

25. *United States v. Seeger*, 380 U.S. 163, 184 (1965).

26. *Welsh v. United States*, 398 U.S. 333, 339–40 (1970) and *United States v. Seeger* both granted conscientious objector status to nontheists under the Military Selective Service Act of 1948, current version at 50 U.S.C. §456(j) (1994).

27. Richard John Neuhaus, *The Naked Public Square* (Grand Rapids: Eerdmans, 1984), 80.

28. *Yoder v. Wisconsin*, 406 U.S. 204, 219 (1972).

29. Military Selective Service Act, current version at 50 U.S.C. §456(j) (1994).

30. *Malnak v. Yogi*, 592 F.2d 197, 207–10 (3d Cir. 1979) (Adams, J., concurring).

31. *Africa v. Commonwealth of Pennsylvania*, 662 F.2d 1025, 1032–34 (3d Cir. 1981).

32. *United States v. Ballard,* 322 U.S. 78 (1944); *Thomas v. Review Board,* 450 U.S. 707 (1981); *Hobbie v. Unemployment Appeals Commission of Florida,* 480 U.S. 136 (1987); *Frazee v. Illinois Department of Employment Security,* 489 U.S. 829 (1989).

33. *New Humanist* (May-June 1933), reprinted in *Humanist Manifesto I and II* (Buffalo: Prometheus Books, 1973).

34. *Torcaso v. Watkins,* 367 U.S. 488, 495 n. 11 (1961).

35. *School District of Abington Township v. Schempp,* 374 U.S. 203, 225 (1963).

36. *Smith v. Board of School Commissioners,* 827 F.2d 684 (11th Cir. 1987).

37. *Board of Education, Island Trees Union Free School District No. 26 v. Pico,* 457 U.S. 853 (1982).

38. Joan Dellafattore, *What Johnny Shouldn't Read: Textbook Censorship in America* (New Haven: Yale University Press, 1992), 80–84.

39. *Attacks on the Freedom to Learn 1986–87* (Washington, D.C.: People for the American Way, 1987), 3.

40. Rosemary C. Salomone, "From *Widmar* to *Mergens:* The Winding Road of First Amendment Analysis," *Hastings Constitutional Law Quarterly* 18 (1991): 295–323, 299–301.

41. *Smith,* 827 F.2d at 690, 692, 694.

42. Glenn Ruffenbach, "Critics Try to Cast a Bad Spell on Harcourt," *Wall Street Journal,* 16 November 1990, B1.

43. Louise Adler and Kip Tellez, "Curriculum Challenge from the Religious Right: The *Impressions* Reading Series," *Urban Education* 152, 2 (1992): 153–73, 160–61.

44. Donna Harrington-Lueker, "Book Battles," *American School Board Journal* (February 1991): 18–21, 37, 19.

45. *Fleischfresser v. Directors of School 200,* 15 F.3d 680 (7th Cir. 1994); *Brown v. Woodland Joint Unified School District,* 27 F.3d 1373 (9th Cir. 1994).

46. John Ankerberg and Craig Branch, *Thieves of Innocence* (Eugene: Harvest House Publishers, 1993), 21. Other books within this genre that discuss the dangers of New Age thinking and particularly the impact of the movement on public schools include Eric Buehrer, *The New Age Masquerade* (Brentwood, Tenn.: Wolgemuth and Hyatt, 1990); Randall N. Baer, *Inside the New Age Nightmare* (Lafayette, La.: Huntington House, 1989); Mitch Pacwa, S.J., *Catholics and the New Age* (Ann Arbor: Servant Publications, 1992); Berit Kjos, *Brave New Schools* (Eugene: Harvest House Publishers, 1995); Kathi Hudson, *Reinventing America's Schools,* vol. 1 (Costa Mesa, Calif.: Citizens for Excellence in Education, revised 1993).

47. Ankerberg and Branch, *Thieves of Innocence,* 26.

48. *Alvarado v. City of San Jose,* 94 F.3d 1223, 1229, 1227 (9th Cir. 1996). The court denied a claim that a sculpture representing Quetzalcoatl, the Plumed Serpent of Aztec mythology, designated to be placed in a public park represented a religious figure in violation of the establishment clause.

49. In *Epperson v. Arkansas,* 393 U.S. 97, 106 (1968), the Court invalidated a state statute that made it unlawful for teachers in state schools to teach the theory of human evolution on the ground that such a prohibition would have a religious purpose in violation of the establishment clause.

50. *See Concerned Citizens for Parental Rights v. San Mateo County Board of Education,* 124

Cal. Rptr. 68 (Cal. Ct. App. 1975), *appeal dismissed,* 425 U.S. 908 (1976); *Smith v. Ricci,* 446 A. 2d 501 (N.J. 1982), *appeal dismissed sub. nom. Smith v. Brandt,* 459 U.S. 962 (1982).

51. *See Ware v. Valley Stream High School District,* 550 N.E.2d 420 (N.Y. 1989), in which the religious group known as the Brethren sought an exemption from the state's mandatory AIDS education program.

52. *Mozert v. Hawkins County Board of Education,* 827 F.2d 1058 (6th Cir. 1987), *cert. denied,* 484 U.S. 1066 (1988). In addition to this final decision by the Sixth Circuit Court of Appeals, four other published opinions comprise the body of the *Mozert* litigation, all bearing the name *Mozert v. Hawkins County Public Schools:* 579 F.Supp. 1051 (E.D. Tenn. 1984); 582 F.2d 201 (E.D. Tenn. 1984); 765 F.2d 75 (6th Cir. 1985); 647 F.Supp. 1194 (E.D. Tenn. 1986). For a sensitive and thoughtful discussion of the parents' claims and the underlying legal and philosophical issues in the litigation, *see* Nomi Maya Stolzenberg, "'He Drew a Circle That Shut Me Out:' Assimilation, Indoctrination, and the Paradox of a Liberal Education," *Harvard Law Review* 106 (1993): 581–667.

53. Stephen Bates, *Battleground: One Mother's Crusade, the Religious Right, and the Struggle for Control of Our Classrooms* (New York: Poseidon Press, 1993), 213.

54. *Mozert,* 647 F.Supp. at 1199.

55. Stolzenberg, "He Drew a Circle That Shut Me Out," 611.

56. Bates, *Battleground,* 207–08.

57. Eammon Callan, *Creating Citizens: Political Education and Liberal Democracy* (New York: Oxford University Press, 1997), 160.

58. *Mozert,* 647 F.Supp. at 1200, 1201–03.

59. Kirsten Goldberg, "Textbook Decision Fuels Debate on Role of Religion in Schools, Rights of Parents," *Education Week,* 5 November 1986, 1, 19.

60. *Mozert,* 827 F.2d at 1070, 1064, 1067 (Lively, J.).

61. Ibid., 1066 (quoting *West Virginia State Board of Education v. Barnette,* 319 U.S. 624, 633 (1938)), 1068–69.

62. *Mozert,* 827 F.2d at 1072 (Kennedy, J., concurring) (quoting *Illinois ex rel. McCollum v. Board of Education,* 333 U.S. 203, 216 (1948) (Frankfurter, J., concurring)).

63. *Mozert,* 827 F.2d at 1071.

64. Stolzenberg, "He Drew a Circle That Shut Me Out," 641.

65. *Mozert,* 827 F.2d at 1071 (quoting *Bethel School District No. 403 v. Fraser,* 478 U.S. 675, 681 (1986)).

66. *Mozert,* 827 F.2d at 1074, 1076 (Boggs, J., concurring).

67. Ibid., 1076–77, 1080 n. 9.

68. Ibid., 1080, 1079–80, 1074.

69. Bates, *Battleground,* 306 (quoting Michael Farris, attorney, Concerned Women for America, from People for the American Way transcript of 1987 CWA Convention).

70. Jeff Spinner, *The Boundaries of Citizenship: Race, Ethnicity, and Nationality in the Liberal State* (Baltimore: Johns Hopkins University Press, 1994), 106–07.

71. *Alfonso v. Fernandez,* 606 N.Y.S. 2d 259, 265, 266, 268 (A.D. 2 Dept. 1993), *appeal dismissed without opinion,* 637 N.E. 2d 279 (1994). The court also decided the case on statutory grounds, concluding that condom availability was not an educational service but

rather a health service under the state Public Health Law, which requires parental consent for the medical treatment of minors. Ibid., 263.

72. *Curtis v. School Committee of Falmouth*, 652 N.E. 2d 580, 585–86, 587 (Mass. 1995), *cert. denied*, 516 U.S. 1067 (1996).

73. *Brown v. Hot, Sexy and Safer Productions, Inc.*, 68 F.3d 525, 533–34 (1st Cir. 1995), *cert. denied*, 516 U.S. 1159 (1996).

74. Ibid., 534, n. 6 (quoting *Alfonso* at 266).

75. In *Steirer v. Bethlehem Area School District*, 97 F.2d 989 (3d Cir. 1993), *cert. denied*, 510 U.S. 824 (1993), the federal appeals court ruled that a mandatory community service requirement for graduation did not compel students to express a belief in altruism in violation of the First Amendment nor did it constitute involuntary servitude in violation of the Thirteenth Amendment.

76. *Immediato v. Rye Neck School District*, 73 F.3d 454, 461 (2d Cir. 1996), *cert. denied*, 519 U.S. 813 (1996).

77. Ibid., 461, citing *Murphy v. Arkansas*, 852 F.2d 1039 (8th Cir. 1988), and *Cornwell v. State Board of Education*, 428 F.2d 471 (4th Cir. 1970) (adopting per curiam the full opinion in *Cornwell v. State Board of Education*, 314 F.Supp. 340 (D.Md. 1969), *cert. denied*, 400 U.S. 942 (1970). A third case not cited by the court is *People v. Bennett*, 501 N.W. 2d 106 (Mich. 1993), in which the Michigan Supreme Court held that absent a claim based on religious beliefs, parents do not have a fundamental right to home-school their children, and home schooling may be subject to reasonable regulations.

78. Lynn Schnaiberg, "Staying Home from School," *Education Week*, 12 June 1996, 24–32.

79. *Engle v. Vitale*, 370 U.S. 421 (1962); *School District of Abington Township v. Schempp*, 374 U.S. 203 (1963); *Stone v. Graham*, 449 U.S. 39 (1980); *Wallace v. Jaffree*, 472 U.S. 38 (1985); *Edwards v. Aguillard*, 482 U.S. 578 (1987); *Lee v. Weisman*, 505 U.S. 577 (1992).

80. Kenneth M. Dolbeare and Phillip E. Hammond, *The School Prayer Decisions* (Chicago: University of Chicago Press, 1971), documented widespread violations of the Court's school prayer decisions in five communities within a midwestern state in the late 1960s. Similar violations were reported throughout North Carolina in *Religion in North Carolina Public Schools* (Washington, D.C.: People for the American Way, 1983).

81. *Duran ex rel. Duran v. Nitsche*, 780 F.Supp. 1048 (E.D. Pa. 1991); *DeNoyer v. Livonia Public Schools*, 799 F.Supp. 744 (E.D. Mich. 1992); *Settle v. Dickson County School Board*, 53 F.3d 152 (6th Cir. 1995), *cert. denied*, 516 U.S. 989 (1996).

82. Equal Access Act of 1984, 20 U.S.C. §§4071–74 (1997). For a discussion of the compromise struck among mainline Christian denominations, evangelicals, and fundamentalists on the Equal Access Act, *see* Allen D. Hertzke, *Representing God in Washington*, 175–93.

83. *Board of Education of the Westside Community Schools v. Mergens*, 496 U.S. 226, 250 (1990).

84. *Hazelwood School District v. Kuhlmeier*, 484 U.S. 260, 270–71 (1988).

85. *Lamb's Chapel v. Center Moriches Union Free School District*, 508 U.S. 384 (1993); *Rosenberger v. Rector and Visitors of University of Virginia*, 515 U.S. 819, 831 (1995).

86. "The Williamsburg Charter," reprinted in *Articles of Faith, Articles of Peace*, ed. John Davison Hunter and Os Guinness (Washington, D.C.: Brookings Institution, 1990), 125–45, 128.

87. *Religion in the Public Schools: Guidelines for a Growing and Changing Phenomenon* (New York: Anti-Defamation League, 1992).

88. *Finding Common Ground: A First Amendment Guide to Religion and Public Education* (Nashville: Freedom Forum First Amendment Center, 1994), 1.3, 5.4–5.7.

89. *A Shared Vision: Religious Liberty in the Twenty-First Century,* reprinted in *Liberty* (March/April 1995), 18–21.

90. Mark Walsh, "Truce Sought in School Wars Over Religion," *Education Week,* 29 March 1995, 1, 10. The six principles included religious liberty for all, the meaning of citizenship, public schools for all citizens, religious liberty and public schools, the relation between parents and schools, and conduct of public disputes.

91. *Religion in the Public Schools: A Joint Statement of Current Law* (New York: American Jewish Congress, April 1995) covers student prayers, graduation prayer and baccalaureates, official participation or encouragement of religious liberty, teaching about religion, distribution of religious literature, religious persuasion versus religious harassment, the Equal Access Act, religious holidays, excusal from religiously objectionable lessons, teaching values, student garb, and released time for religious instruction.

92. "Text of President Clinton's Memorandum on Religion in Schools," *New York Times,* 13 July 1995, B10; Letter from Richard W. Riley, U.S. Secretary of Education, to Superintendents of Schools (August 10, 1995).

93. Editorial, "Nihilism, Religion and the President," *Wall Street Journal,* 14 July 1995, A12.

94. *The Cry for Renewal: Let the Voices Be Heard,* reprinted in *Liberty* (July/August 1995), 12–14.

95. Larry Witham, "Panel Hears Views on Religion's Role in School: Students' Rights of 'Free Exercise' in the Spotlight," *Washington Times,* 21 May 1998, A2; Mark Walsh, "Panel Examining Student Religious Expression," *Education Week,* 27 May 1998, 18.

CHAPTER 6. STRUGGLING WITH SATAN

1. "A Message to the Public: 'Stop the Witch Hunt,'" *Patent Trader,* 16 November 1995, A15.

2. Debra West, "Forget Beverly Hills; The Lure Is Bedford," *New York Times,* 15 May 1997, B1; Alex Shoumatoff, "And So to Bedford," *Vanity Fair,* February 1999, 152–68.

3. During the 1997–98 school year, the per pupil expenditure in the Bedford Central School District was $15,937 with a median teacher salary at $75,299. *The State of Learning: A Report to the Governor and the Legislature on the Educational Status of the State's Schools,* tables 2, 3 (Albany: State Education Department, April 1999).

4. During the 1997–98 school year, the percentage of students in the Bedford Central School District scoring above the state reference point (SRP) in statewide tests administered under the Pupil Evaluation Program as compared with the total public school population statewide was 96 percent in grade 3 reading (84 percent statewide), 100 percent in grade 3 math (96 percent statewide), 100 percent in grade 5 writing (93 percent statewide), 90 percent in grade 6 reading (84 percent statewide), and 97 percent in grade 6 math (96 percent statewide). Ibid., table 5.

5. Although the Bedford community is best known for its wealthy weekenders residing in Bedford Village and Pound Ridge, the full-time population of the Bedford Central

School District is more diverse. The district covers sixty square miles, includes five elementary schools (Bedford Village, Bedford Hills, Mount Kisco, Pound Ridge, and West Patent), one middle school, one comprehensive high school, and one alternative high school. The socioeconomics throughout the school district vary from Pound Ridge, for example, at the high end with an average annual income of $91,918, Bureau of the Census, U.S. Department of Commerce, 1990 CP-2-34, *1990 Census of Population: Social and Economic Characteristics-New York* (1990), 39, and a median price of residential property of $464,000, Bureau of the Census, U.S. Department of Commerce, 1990 CH-1-34, *1990 Census of Housing: General Housing Characteristics-New York* (1990), 967, to Mt. Kisco, with a more diverse population, including a recently arrived Latin American community, where the average annual income is $42,910, *Census of Population*, 37, and the median price of residential property is $249,000, *Census of Housing*, 957. During the 1997–98 school year, the total school population was 3,416, with a minority enrollment of 18.7 percent (7.3 percent black and 11.4 percent Hispanic). *The State of Learning*, table 1 (April 1999), 22.

6. "Agreement Form" sent home to parents by fourth-grade teacher (on file with author).

7. Notice sent home to parents by Sue Clark, mother of Pound Ridge Elementary School student, reprinted in Alan Raphael, "Schools Super Decks Cards," *Pound Ridge Review,* 6 April 1995, 26.

8. *Magic: The Gathering Pocket Players Guide* (Renton, Wash.: Wizards of the Coast, 1995), 4.

9. Chris Cooke, "Mystical Card Game Sweeps the Board," *Sunday Times* (London), section 2, 15 October 1995, 8.

10. Steve Jackson, "The Game Page: West Coast Wizards Make Million Dollar Magic," *Daily Telegraph,* 3 June 1995, 31. In 1996 players had the opportunity to turn professional, with one million dollars in prizes offered in the annual *Magic: The Gathering* Pro Tour, a series of five regional tournaments. Cards have reportedly traded for as much as two hundred dollars. Steve Jackson, "It's Magic . . . the Pro Gathering," *Daily Telegraph,* 2 June 1995, 33.

11. Jackson, "West Coast Wizards Make Million Dollar Magic," 31.

12. *Magic: The Gathering Pocket Players Guide,* 49-51.

13. Alan Raphael, "Ending the 'Witch Hunt,'" *Towne Crier,* November 1995, A13.

14. Raphael, "Schools Super Decks Cards," 3 April 1995, at 1.

15. Ibid., quoting Karen Akst Schecter, president of Bedford Central School District Board of Education; Minutes of the Bedford Central School District Board of Education Meeting, April 19, 1995, quoting Karen Akst Schecter, school board president.

16. Evan Brandt, "Bedford Parents Spooked by 'Magic' Card Game," *Patent Trader,* 6 April 1995, A5, quoting Dr. Bruce Dennis, superintendent of schools, Bedford Central School District.

17. Evan Brandt, "'Magic' is Back in Bedford Schools," *Patent Trader,* 27 April 1995, A11.

18. MaryAnn DiBari, interview with author, Pound Ridge, N.Y., December 7, 1995.

19. Kate Stone Lombardi, "Bedford's Struggle with the Devil," *New York Times,* Westchester Weekly, 26 November 1995, 1.

20. "Bedford Residents Defend Schools from a Satan Hunt," *New York Times,* 22 November 1995, B5.

21. Daniel Corn, "The Devil and Mr. G.," *The Nation,* 10 July 1995, 41.
22. Dr. George Hogben, interview with author, Rye, N.Y., July 17, 1996.
23. Brandt, "Bedford Parents Spooked by 'Magic' Card Game," A1.
24. Steven J. Stark, "Is It Satanic or Just Plain Fun? Fantasy Card Game Debated," *Reporter Dispatch,* 7 April 1995, A1.
25. Letter from Dr. Bruce Dennis, superintendent of schools, Bedford Central School District, to Parents, April 24, 1995 (on file with author).
26. Stark, "Is It Satan or Just Plain Fun?," 7 April 1995, 1A.
27. Letter from the Reverend Bernard J. Bush to Ceil DiNozzi, April 4, 1995 (on file with author).
28. Open letter from MaryAnn DiBari to Bruce Dennis, superintendent of schools, Bedford Central School District, April 13, 1995 (on file with author).
29. Letter from Bruce Dennis, superintendent of schools, Bedford Central School District, to MaryAnn DiBari, April 13, 1995 (on file with author).
30. Editorial, "Innocent Fun?" *Pound Ridge Review,* 6 April 1995, 4.
31. Brandt, "Bedford Parents Spooked by 'Magic' Card Game," A5, quoting Scott Turnbull, owner of Starbase in Mt. Kisco.
32. Letter from John C. O'Brien to Dr. Bruce Dennis, superintendent of schools, Bedford Central School, reprinted in John C. O'Brien, "Parents Don't Need Morality Censors," *Pound Ridge Review,* 6 April 1995, 5.
33. Stark, "Is It Satanic or Just Plain Fun?" 1A.
34. Reverend Paul Alcorn, interview with author, Bedford, N.Y., December 15, 1995.
35. Raphael, "Schools Super Decks Cards," 1.
36. Letter from Flemming G. Graae, M.D., to Bruce Dennis, superintendent of schools, Bedford Central School District, April 13, 1995 (on file with author); Christopher M. Bogart, "Magic: The Gathering, An Assessment of the Potential Effects to Child Development," 1997, unpublished report (on file with author); letter from Paulina F. Kernberg, M.D., Director of Child and Adolescent Psychiatry, the New York–Cornell Medical Center Westchester Division, to Bruce Dennis, April 19, 1995, delivered by facsimile (on file with author).
37. James Markowski, school board member, Bedford Central School District, telephone interview with author, March 9, 1997.
38. Public forum doctrine is a framework developed by the Supreme Court for analyzing the right of public access to governmental property for expressive purposes. The court weighs the public's as against the government's interest in limiting the use of its property. The doctrine divides governmental property into three categories: the traditional public forum (streets, parks, sidewalks), the designated or limited public forum, and the nonpublic forum. The reference here is to the designated public forum which is created when government, by policy or practice, purposefully opens property for use by the general public, for use by certain speakers, or for the discussion of certain topics. In such a forum, government cannot regulate the content of speech absent a compelling governmental interest. For an explanation of public forum doctrine, *see, Perry Education Association v. Perry,* 460 U.S. 37, 45–46 (1983); *Cornelius v. NAACP Legal Defense and Educational Fund, Inc.,* 473 U.S. 788, 802–03 (1985).

39. Minutes of the Bedford Central School District Board of Education Meeting, April 19, 1995, quoting school board member James Markowski (on file with author).

40. Stark, "Is It Satanic or Just Plain Fun?" 1A.

41. Minutes, noting remarks of school board member Herb Nieburg concerning *Magic.*

42. Ibid., summarizing statement of parent Miles Leeds.

43. Ibid., recording statement of parent Frank Bevilacqua.

44. *Magic: The Gathering* Parent Consent Form (on file with author).

45. Letter from MaryAnn DiBari to Bruce Dennis, superintendent of schools, Bedford Central School District, April 20, 1995 (on file with author).

46. Letter from Bruce Dennis, superintendent of schools, Bedford Central School District, to MaryAnn DiBari, April 25, 1995 (on file with author).

47. Steven J. Stark, "Card-Game Opposition 'Not Conceding Defeat,'" *Reporter Dispatch,* 23 April 1995, 3A.

48. Letter from MaryAnn DiBari to Bruce Dennis, superintendent of schools, Bedford Central School District, May 1, 1995; letter from Bruce Dennis to MaryAnn DiBari, May 9, 1995) (letters on file with author).

49. Stark, "Card-Game Opposition 'Not Conceding Defeat,'" 3A.

50. Steven J. Stark, "Christian Coalition Surveys School Candidates on 'Magic,'" *Reporter Dispatch,* 23 April 1995, 3A.

51. 20 U.S.C. §1232(h)(b)(Supp. 1998). The implementing regulations appear in 34 C.F.R. §98.1 *et seq.* (1998).

52. Phyllis Schlafly, ed., *Child Abuse in the Classroom* (Alton, Ill.: Pere Marquette Press, 1984), Appendix B, 440–41.

53. For a discussion of the use of the Hatch Amendment by the Religious Right with specific reference to the "stretch technique," *see,* Janet L. Jones, "Targets of the Right," *American School Board Journal* 180 (1993): 26–29, 27.

54. Schlafly, *Abuse in the Classroom,* 21, 13, 24.

55. *Congressional Record,* §1389-01, 99th Congress, First Session, February 19, 1985, remarks by Sen. Orin Hatch.

56. Form letter Re: Pupil Rights Amendment to James Alloy, principal, Fox Lane Middle School; James Young, principal, Pound Ridge Elementary School; Bruce Dennis, superintendent of schools, Bedford Central School District, May 31, 1995 (on file with author).

57. James Young, principal, Pound Ridge Elementary School, interview with author, Pound Ridge, N.Y., May 31, 1996.

58. Rebekah Denn, "Group Plans Seminar on Occult Influences," *Gannett Suburban Newspapers,* September 15, 1995, 3A.

59. Letter from Linda Osborne Blood to Ceil DiNozzi and MaryAnn DiBari, October 1995 (on file with author).

60. Letter from John Cardinal O'Connor, archbishop of New York, to Ceil DiNozzi, June 7, 1995 (on file with author).

61. Corn, "The Devil and Mr. G," 41.

62. Tamara Collins, research analyst, Catholic League for Religious and Civil Rights, telephone interview with author, August 7, 1998.

63. *See,* e.g., Paul Vitz, *Censorship: Evidence of Bias in Children's Textbooks* (Ann Arbor: Ser-

vant Publications, 1986); Paul Vitz, "A Study of Religion and Traditional Values in Public School Textbooks," in *Democracy and the Renewal of Public Education*, ed. Richard John Neuhaus (Grand Rapids: Eerdmans, 1987), 116-40. For a discussion of Vitz's involvement in the *Mozert* litigation, *see* Stephen Bates, *Battleground: One Mother's Crusade, the Religious Right, and the Struggle for Control of Our Classrooms* (New York: Poseidon Press, 1993), 207, 244–45.

64. Letter from Dr. Paul Vitz, Professor of Psychology, New York University, to MaryAnn DiBari, June 16, 1995 (copy on file with author).

65. Letter from Monsignor Dermot R. Brennan, vicar, Vicarate of Northern Westchester and Putnam County, Archdiocese of New York, to MaryAnn DiBari, July 29, 1995 (copy on file with author).

66. Letter from the Reverend George Mather, Pastor, Sherman Oaks Lutheran Church and Children's Center, to Ceil DiNozzi, August 29, 1995 (on file with author).

67. Kate Stone Lombardi, "Sides Drawn in Satanism Suit," *New York Times*, Westchester Weekly, 30 March 1997, 1.

68. Rebekah Denn, "A Battle of Beliefs in Bedford," *Reporter Dispatch*, 20 October 1995, 1A.

69. Rebekah Denn, "Forum Accuses Schools of Supporting Satanic Forces," *Reporter Dispatch*, 30 September 1995, 1A.

70. Wendy Holibaugh, chairwoman, Westchester Chapter of the Christian Coalition, telephone interview with author, December 5, 1995.

71. Martha DePhillips, "'Magic' Game Rebuked by Speakers," *Patent Trader*, October 5, 1995, A1.

72. Denn, "A Battle of Beliefs in Bedford," 1A.

73. Ibid.

74. Karen Shaviv, letter to the editor, *Patent Trader*, 5 October 1995, A17.

75. Fred Schlottman, letter to the editor, *Patent Trader*, 5 October 1995, A17.

76. Editorial, "Accusing Schools of Voodoo Is Vile Attack on District," *Reporter Dispatch*, 29 September 1995, at A10.

77. Raphael, "Ending the "Witch Hunt," A13; Denn, "Forum Accuses Schools of Supporting Satanic Forces," A1.

78. Denn, "A Battle of Beliefs in Bedford," A1.

79. Roz Udow, director for education and public affairs, National Coalition Against Censorship, telephone interview with author, July 3, 1997.

80. Memorandum from Bruce Dennis, superintendent of schools, Bedford Central School District, to All Teachers and Principals, October 10, 1995 (on file with author).

81. Memorandum from Bruce Dennis, superintendent of schools, Bedford Central School District, to All Parents of the Bedford Central School District, November 9, 1997 (on file with author).

82. Videotape, Superintendent's Colloquium, "Stop the Witch Hunt," November 20, 1995 (on file with author).

83. Felix Carroll, "Crowd Tells Critics: 'Schools Are Satan-Free,'" *Record Review*, 24 November 1995, 1.

84. Videotape, recording statement of MaryAnn DiBari.

85. Ibid., recording statement of Josh Katzman, senior, Fox Lane High School.

86. Ibid., recording statement of Rosa Portell.

87. Ibid., recording statement of Maria Fish.

88. Ibid., quoting from letter of Rabbi David Greenberg, president, Northern Westchester Clergy Association, read by the Rev. Paul Alcorn, pastor, Bedford Presbyterian Church.

89. Ibid., recording statement of Dr. Arthur Eisenkraft, science coordinator, Bedford Central School District, reading statement of Joseph McInerny, director of Biological Sciences Curriculum.

90. Ibid., recording statement of Jackie Reizes, second-grade teacher, Pound Ridge Elementary School.

91. Ibid., recording statement of Clem Bottino, student, Fox Lane High School.

92. Ibid., recording statement of Bruce Dennis, superintendent of schools, Bedford Central School District.

93. "Bedford Residents Defend Schools from a Satan Hunt," *New York Times,* 27 November 1995, B5; Lombardi, "Bedford's Struggle with the Devil," 1.

94. Editorial, "Satan Scotched Again," *Patent Trader,* 22 November 1995, A14.

95. *See,* e.g., David A. Stallman, letter to the editor, *Record-Review,* 1 December 1995, 8.

96. Joseph Whalen, letter to the editor, *Record-Review,* 1 December 1995, 8.

97. MaryAnn DiBari, interview with author, Pound Ridge, N.Y., July 30, 1996.

98. Bruce Dennis, superintendent of schools, Bedford Central School District, interview with author, Bedford, N.Y., December 7, 1995.

99. The superintendent was applying a decision of the New York State commissioner of education in the case of *In re DeWand,* 21 Educ. Dept. Rep. 455 (1982), in which the commissioner applied New York State Education Law §1709(3), (McKinney 1998) which provides: "The said board of education of every union free school district shall have power, and it shall be its duty: . . . . To prescribe the course of study in which the pupils of the schools shall be graded and classified."

100. Letter from Bruce Dennis, superintendent of schools, Bedford Central School District, to MaryAnn DiBari, January 12, 1996 (on file with author).

101. Letter from MaryAnn DiBari to Bruce Dennis, superintendent of schools, Bedford Central School District, January 22, 1996 (on file with author).

102. Lombardi, "Bedford's Struggle with the Devil," at 1.

103. Ceil DiNozzi, interview with author, Stamford, Conn., February 17, 1997.

104. Lombardi, "Sides Drawn in Satanism Suit," at 1.

105. Ceil DiNozzi, interview with author, Stamford, Conn., February 17, 1997.

106. Letter from Christopher A. Ferrara, president and general counsel, American Catholic Lawyers Association, to Fellow Catholics, Season of Lent, 1996, explaining purposes and pending cases in which the association was involved and soliciting donations.

107. *Lamb's Chapel v. Center Moriches Union Free School District,* 770 F.Supp. 91 (E.D.N.Y.), aff'd, 959 F.2d 381 (2d Cir. 1992), rev'd, 508 U.S. 384 (1993).

108. In *Hsu v. Roslyn Free School District No. 3,* 885 F.2d 839 (2d Cir. 1996), a student religious group successfully challenged a school policy prohibiting the group from requiring that its leaders be professed Christians. The appellate court ruled that the policy violated the students' implicit right to expressive association under the Equal Access Act, 20 U.S.C. §§4071–75 (Supp. 1998).

109. In *Gheta v. Nassau Community College,* 33 F.Supp. 2d 179 (E.D.N.Y. 1999), the trial court held that a course entitled "Family Living and Human Sexuality" did not violate the establishment clause of the Constitution.

110. *Altman v. Bedford Central School District,* No. 96 Civ. 07791 (S.D.N.Y. filed Oct. 15, 1996).

111. *Altman* Complaint, 6–7.

112. Ibid., 7–8.

113. Ibid., 12–22.

114. Ibid., 23–24.

115. NBC presented an informative discussion on the controversy surrounding the DARE Program on *Dateline on NBC, Truth or . . . DARE,* NBC television broadcast, February 21, 1997 (copy of videotape on file with author).

116. Stephen Glass, "Don't You D.A.R.E.," *New Republic,* 3 March 1997, 18–28, 19.

117. *See,* e.g., Earl Wysong and David W. Wright, "A Decade of DARE: Efficacy, Politics and Drug Education," *Sociological Focus* 28 (August 1995): 283–311 (concluding from a seven-year study that DARE is not effective over the long term in preventing or reducing adolescent drug use); Richard R. Clayton, Anne M. Cattarello, and Bryan M. Johnstone, "The Effectiveness of Drug Abuse Resistance Education (Project DARE): 5-Year Follow-Up Results," *Preventive Medicine* 25 (1996): 307–18 (confirming the results of short-term studies that the original DARE curriculum has no sustained effects on adolescent drug use); Donald D. Lyman et al., "Project DARE: No Effects at 10-Year Follow-up," *Journal of Consulting and Clinical Psychology* 67, 4 (1999): 590–93 (following up on Clayton et al. sample through age twenty and finding few differences in drug use, drug attitudes, or self-esteem between groups receiving DARE and standard drug-education program).

118. Dennis P. Rosenbaum, Robert L. Flewelling, Susan L. Bailey, Chris L. Ringwalt, and Deanna L. Wilkinson, "Cops in the Classroom: A Longitudinal Evaluation of Drug Abuse Resistance Education (DARE)," *Journal of Research in Crime and Delinquency* 31 (1994): 3–31; E. Supaya Silvia, Judy Thorne, and Christene A. Tashjian, *School-Based Drug Prevention Programs: A Longitudinal Study in Selected Districts* (Research Triangle Park, N.C.: Research Triangle Institute, 1997).

119. Dirk Johnson, "Second Thoughts on Cops in the Class," *New York Times,* 26 September 1998, 3.

120. *Altman* Complaint, 25–26.

121. The parents also claimed that the Bedford Program violated the Religious Freedom Restoration Act, which the Supreme Court subsequently declared unconstitutional in *City of Boerne v. Flores,* 521 U.S. 507 (1997).

122. U.S. CONST. amend XIV, §1 provides: "No state shall make or enforce any law which shall abridge the privileges or immunities of citizens of the United States; nor shall any State deprive any person of life, liberty, or property, without due process of law."

123. *Altman* Complaint, 31–32.

124. N.Y.S. CONST. art.1 §3 provides: "The free exercise and enjoyment of religious profession and worship, without discrimination or preference, shall forever be allowed in this state to all mankind; and no person shall be rendered incompetent to be a witness on ac-

count of his opinions on religious belief; but the liberty of conscience hereby secured shall not be so construed as to excuse acts of licentiousness, or justify practices inconsistent with the peace and safety of the state." The parents further maintained that aspects of the Bedford Program that involved psychological testing, examination, counseling, and treatment of students as defined by the federal Protection of Pupil Rights Amendment also constituted a "health service," for which parental consent would be required under §2404 of the New York State Public Health Law, which provides: "Any person who is eighteen years or older, or is the parent of a child or has married, may give effective consent for medical, dental, health and hospital services for himself or herself, and the consent of no other person shall be necessary."

125. Defendants' Notice of Motion to Dismiss, *Altman* (No. 96 Civ. 07791).

126. *Malnak v. Maharishi Mahesh Yogi,* 592 F.2d 197 (3d Cir. 1979). The defendants relied particularly on a separate concurring opinion by Judge Adams presenting the essential indicia of a religious belief which subsequently were summarized in a majority opinion in *Africa v. Commonwealth of Pennsylvania,* 662 F.2d 1025, 1032 (3d Cir. 1981) as follows: "First, a religion addresses fundamental and ultimate questions having to do with deep and imponderable matters. Second, a religion is comprehensive in nature; it consists of a belief-system as opposed to an isolated teaching. Third, a religion often can be recognized by the presence of certain formal external signs."

127. Defendants' Memorandum of Law, 15–17.

128. They relied on *Alvarado v. City of San Jose,* 94 F.3d 1223 (9th Cir. 1996), in which the Ninth Circuit Court of Appeals held that New Age did not constitute a discernable religion for purposes of the establishment clause and that a twenty-five-foot-high representation of the ancient Aztec deity Quetzalcoatal in a public park had no current religious significance. To refute the parents' endorsement argument, school officials cited Justice O'Connor's concurring opinion in *Wallace v. Jaffree,* 472 U.S. 38 (1985), in which she first suggested what has come to be known as the "endorsement test," under which the establishment clause is violated when government "sends a message to nonadherents that they are outsiders, not full members of the political community, and an accompanying message to adherents that they are insiders, favorable members of the community" based on the perception of the "objective observer." Defendants' Memorandum of Law, 76.

129. *Fleischfresser v. Directors of School District 200,* 15 F.3d 680 (7th Cir. 1994); *Brown v. Joint Unified School District,* 27 F.3d 1373 (9th Cir. 1994).

130. Defendants' Memorandum of Law, 35, citing *Mozert v. Hawkins County Board of Education,* 827 F.2d 1058 (6th Cir. 1987), *cert. denied,* 484 U.S. 1066 (1988).

131. Ibid. A decision from the Ninth Circuit Court of Appeals presents an opposing view. In *Peterson v. Minidoka County School District No. 331,* 118 F.3d 1351 (9th Cir. 1997), the court held that the Fourteenth Amendment's guarantee of liberty encompasses the liberty of parents to determine the education of their children in the context of home schooling. The court also ruled that the First Amendment's guarantee of free exercise of religion protects acts rooted in religious beliefs as those beliefs are perceived by the believers and is not limited solely to those requirements mandated by a church.

132. *Immediato v. Rye Neck School District,* 873 F.Supp. 852 (S.D.N.Y. 1995), *aff'd,* 73 F.3d 454

(2d Cir. 1996), *cert. denied,* 519 U.S. 813 (1996) (upholding a mandatory community service requirement for high school graduation); *Brown v. Hot, Sexy and Safer Productions, Inc.,* 68 F.3d 525 (1st Cir. 1995), *cert. denied.,* U.S. (1996) (rejecting parental privacy right to dictate the public school curriculum in conformity with value-based objections).

133. Defendants' Memorandum, 52, citing the district court opinion in *Immediato v. Rye Neck School District,* 873 F.Supp. 846, 852 (S.D.N.Y. 1995) (opinion of Judge Brieant).

134. Included among the amici parents were Reverend Paul Alcorn, Shodie Alcorn, Rose-Ellen Raccanelli, Dr. Jed Berman, Marty-Ann Kerner, Rosa Portell, Fred Schlottman, Neil Ginsburg, Paula Kumar, Susan McCarthy, and Nancy Stein.

135. Tracey A. Barger, "Satanism Suit Draws National Attention," *Patent Trader,* 20 March 1997, 1, quoting Rose-Ellen Raccanelli and Rosa Portell.

136. Amici Parents' Memorandum of Law in Support of Defendants' Motion to Dismiss, 24, *Altman v. Bedford Central School District,* No. 96 Civ. 07791 (S.D.N.Y. filed Mar. 17, 1997).

137. *Altman* Complaint, 7.

138. Amici Parents' Memorandum of Law, 25, citing *Wisconsin v. Yoder,* 406 U.S. 205, 241–46 (1972) (Douglas, J., dissenting in part).

139. Amy Kelley, "Teachers Fete Parents for Defense of District," *Patent Trader,* 30 October 1997, A9.

140. Editorial, "The Writing on the Wall," *Patent Trader,* 17 April 1997, A22.

141. Richard Hallinan, Taxpayers Oversight Committee, telephone interview with author, March 7, 1997.

142. Steven P. Rivers, M.D., former chairman, Mandated Programs Subcommittee, Citizens Budget Advisory Committee, letter to the editor, *Patent Trader,* 8 May 1997, A19.

143. Partners in Action for Community Education, *Membership Brochure* (on file with author).

144. Partners in Action for Community Education, "Who Will Control Our Schools?" *The P.A.C.E.,* February 1997.

145. Other cosponsors of the event were the Westchester Coalition for Democracy (a nonpartisan, multi-issue coalition of thirty-four organizations dedicated to upholding democracy and the constitutional rights of all people), the Sisterhood of Bet Torah Synagogue, the Mt. Kisco Presbyterian Church, Jewish Women International, and Congregation B'nai Yisrael.

146. Deanna Duby, attorney, People for the American Way, Remarks at Open Discussion on "The Religious Right and Local School Boards: Fact or Fiction?" Mt. Kisco Public Library, April 8, 1997 (notes on file with author).

147. James J. Markowski, letter to the editor, *Patent Trader,* 10 April 1997, A22.

148. Richard Hallinan, letter to the editor, *Patent Trader,* 17 April, 1997, A20.

149. Editorial, "The Writing on the Wall," A22.

150. *Immediato,* 873 F.Supp. at 853–53.

151. *Yoder,* 406 U.S. at 215.

152. Memorandum & Order, 7, *Altman v. Bedford Central School District,* No. 96 Civ. 07791 (S.D.N.Y. July 23, 1997) (order denying in part defendants' motion to dismiss).

153. Ibid., 8–9 ("The goal of local Home Rule is to allow communities to develop rules and

regulations for the management—or mismanagement—of their own affairs, through forms of majority rule existing by the very nature of a republican form of government. An individual . . . [who] disagrees with a particular policy or rule . . . must abide by the general law while attempting to persuade others in the community to revise the rule, or to elect new local representatives who will do so.")

154. New York Education Law §1709(3) (McKinney 1998) provides that, "The said board of education of every union free school district shall have power, and it shall be its duty . . . [t]o prescribe the course of study by which the pupils of the schools shall be graded and classified."

155. Memorandum & Order, 11.

156. Letter from Kathy A. Ahearn, counsel and deputy for legal affairs, State Education Department, to Christopher A. Ferrara and Lawrence W. Reich, September 18, 1997 (on file with author).

157. Affidavit of Fred Schlottmann, October 2, 1998.

158. Affidavit of Marty-Ann Koerner, October 2, 1998.

159. Affidavit of Bruce Dennis, superintendent of schools, August 18, 1998.

160. Affidavit of Cecile D. DiNozzi, Joseph M. DiNozzi, and MaryAnn DiBari, August 21, 1998.

161. Declarations of William R. Coulson, Donald Carone, Kevin Crowley, and David Friedman.

162. Summary of Statement of Father Charles C. Fiore, April 23, 1998; Report of Daniel C. Maguire, S.T.D., professor of moral theology, Marquette University, May 5, 1998.

163. Plaintiffs' Memorandum of Law in Support of Motion for Partial Summary Judgment or, in the Alternative, a Preliminary Injunction, *Altman v. Bedford Central School District et al.*, No. 96 Civ. 07791 (S.D.N.Y. filed August 14, 1998).

164. Transcript of Hearing on Motions for Partial Summary Judgment, November 13, 1998.

165. Memorandum and Order, 5, *Altman v. Bedford Central School District*, No. 96 Civ. 07791 (S.D.N.Y. December 22, 1998) (order denying motions for partial summary judgment and plaintiffs' motion for preliminary injunction).

166. Joe Berger, "In Court, Students Describe Classes as Affront to Faith," *New York Times*, 23 February 1999, B5.

167. Press Release, "PFAW Statement on Bedford Lawsuit," People for the American Way, March 4, 1999.

168. Plaintiffs' Closing Argument, 19 (filed March 29, 1999).

169. Daniel Patrick Moynihan, "Defining Deviancy Down," *American Scholar* 62 (Winter 1993): 17–30.

170. *Altman v. Bedford Central School District*, 45 F.Supp. 368 (S.D.N.Y. 1999).

171. Emma Bladen, "Appeals Await in Decision's Wake," 26.

172. Paul Zielbauer, "Judge Rules School Curriculum Crossed Church-State Line," *New York Times*, 22 May 1999, B1.

173. Memorandum and Order, *Altman v. Bedford Central School District*, No. 96, Civ. 07791 (S.D.N.Y. July 23, 1999).

174. Lombardi, "Bedford's Struggle with the Devil," 1, 11, and "Bedford Residents Defend Schools from Satan Hunt," B5.

175. Kathleen Mora, letter to the editor, *Patent Trader*, 27 March 1997, A21.

176. Affidavit of Paula Kumar, *Altman v. Bedford Central School District et al.*, No. 96 Civ. 07791, September 30, 1998; Affidavit of Fred Schlottmann, October 2, 1998.

177. Evan Brandt, executive editor, *Patent Trader*, interview with author, Cross River, N.Y., February 2, 1997.

178. Lombardi, "Sides Drawn in Satanism Suit," at 1.

179. For an excellent portrait of the faces behind a group of high-profile Supreme Court decisions, *see* Peter Irons, *The Courage of Their Convictions* (New York: Penguin, 1988), 410–11.

180. For a well-reasoned argument supporting this position, *see* Cass Sunstein, *One Case at a Time: Judicial Minimalism on the Supreme Court* (Cambridge: Harvard University Press, 1999).

181. Robert H. Mnookin, "Test Case Litigation on Behalf of Children," in *In the Interest of Children*, ed. Robert H. Mnookin (Cambridge: Program on Negotiation at Harvard Law School, 1996), 10.

182. Emma Bladen, "'Satan Suit' Child is Ghost for Halloween," *Record-Review*, 12 December 1997, 1; Tracey A. Barger, "Testimony in Satan Lawsuit Prompts 'Disbelief,'" *Patent Trader*, 12 December 1997, A1.

183. Emma Bladen, "Judge Puts Satan Suit Bill at $107K," *Record-Review*, July 30, 1999, 1.

184. Emma Bladen, "School Board Spells Out the Public Meeting Rules," *Record-Review*, 9 September 1997, 12.

185. Emma Bladen, "Sex Education: Change Coming," *Record-Review*, 1 August 1997, 1.

186. Editorial, "Boiling Pot," *Patent Trader*, 7 August 1997, A14.

187. Emma Bladen, "School Board Set to Examine Curriculum," *Record-Review*, 17 October 1997, 11.

CHAPTER 7. EDUCATION FOR DEMOCRATIC CITIZENSHIP

1. Mark Halstead, "Voluntary Apartheid? Problems of Schooling for Religious and Other Minorities in Democratic States," in *Democratic Education in a Democratic State*, ed. Yale Tamir (Oxford: Blackwell Publishers, 1995), 99–114, 111.

2. Terence McLaughlin, "Liberalism, Education and the Common School," *Journal of Philosophy of Education* 29, 2 (1995): 239–55, 241.

3. Amy Gutmann, *Democratic Education* (Princeton: Princeton University Press, 1987).

4. Ibid., 287, 290, 30.

5. Ibid., 44, 30–31, 51.

6. John Rawls, *Political Liberalism* (New York: Columbia University Press, 1993); Stephen Macedo, *Liberal Virtues: Citizenship, Virtue, and Community in Liberal Constitutionalism* (Oxford: Clarendon Press, 1990); Stephen Macedo, "Liberal Civic Education and Religious Fundamentalism: The Case of God v. John Rawls?" *Ethics* 105 (April 1995): 468–96; William A. Galston, *Liberal Purposes* (New York: Cambridge University Press, 1991); William A. Galston, "Two Concepts of Liberalism," *Ethics* 105 (April 1995): 516–34.

7. Amy Gutmann, "Civic Education and Social Diversity," *Ethics* 105 (April 1995): 557–79.

8. Macedo, "Liberal Civic Education and Religious Fundamentalism," 474.

9. Rawls, *Political Liberalism,* 4.
10. Kenneth A. Strike, "On the Construction of Public Speech: Pluralism and Public Reason," *Educational Theory* 44, 1 (Winter 1944): 1–26, 24.
11. Michael J. Sandel, *Liberalism and the Limits of Justice* (Cambridge: Harvard University Press, 1982), 52–55. For a more recent discussion of communitarian thought, *see* Michael J. Sandel, *Democracy's Discontent: America in Search of a Public Philosophy* (Cambridge: Harvard University Press, 1996).
12. William Kymlicka argues that the most defensible liberal theory is based on autonomy, without which tolerance in the sense of individual conscience and not just collective worship cannot exist. *See* William Kymlicka, *Multicultural Citizenship* (Oxford: Clarendon Press, 1995), 158–65.
13. For other versions of political liberalism that reject autonomy as a core liberal value, *see* J. Donald Moon, *Constructing Community: Moral Pluralisms and Tragic Conflicts* (Princeton: Princeton University Press, 1993) and Charles E. Larmore, *Patterns of Moral Complexity* (Cambridge: Cambridge University Press, 1987).
14. Galston, "Two Concepts of Liberalism," 523.
15. John Rawls, "Justice as Fairness: Political Not Metaphysical," in *Philosophy and Public Affairs* 14 (1985): 223–51, 246.
16. Terence H. McLaughlin, "The Ethics of Separate Schools," in *Ethics, Ethnicity and Education,* ed. Mal Leichester and Monica Taylor (London: Kogan Page, 1993), 114–36, 123.
17. Deborah Fitzmaurice, "Liberal Neutrality, Traditional Minorities, and Education," in *Liberalism, Multiculturalism, and Toleration,* ed. John Horton (New York: St. Martin's Press, 1993), 50–69, 68.
18. Rawls, *Political Liberalism,* 200.
19. Stephen G. Gilles, "On Educating Children: A Parentalist Manifesto," *University of Chicago Law Review* 63 (Summer 1996): 937–1034, 964.
20. Brian Crittendon, "Autonomy as an Aim of Education," in *Ethics and Educational Policy,* ed. Kenneth A. Strike and Kieran Egan (London: Routledge and Kegan Paul, 1978), 105–44, 106.
21. Suzanna Sherry, "Responsible Republicanism: Educating for Citizenship," *University of Chicago Law Review* 62 (1995): 131–208, 158.
22. Kenneth L. Karst, "Boundaries and Reasons: Freedom of Expression and Subordination of Groups," *University of Illinois Law Review* (1990): 95–149, 108.
23. Michael J. Perry, Comment on "The Limits of Rationality and the Place of Religious Conviction: Protecting Animals and the Environment," *William and Mary Law Review* 27 (1986): 1067–73, 1068.
24. Stanley Fish, "Liberalism Doesn't Exist," *Duke Law Journal* (1987): 997–1001, 1000; Martha C. Nussbaum, "A Plea for Difficulty," in *Is Multiculturalism Bad for Women?,* ed. Joshua Cohen, Michael Howard, and Martha Nussbaum (Princeton: Princeton University Press, 1999), 105–14, 107.
25. Stephen L. Carter, *The Culture of Disbelief* (New York: Basic, 1993), 24.
26. Charles Taylor, "Comments and Replies," *Inquiry* 34 (1991): 237–55, 242.
27. John E. Coons, "Intellectual Liberty and the Schools," *Journal of Law, Ethics and Public Policy* 1 (1985): 496–533, 522.

28. Nomi Maya Stolzenberg, "'He Drew a Circle That Shut Me Out': Assimilation, Indoctrination, and the Paradox of a Liberal Education," *Harvard Law Review* 106 (1992): 581–667, 613.

29. Galston, *Liberal Purposes,* 253.

30. Frederick M. Gedicks and Roger Hendrix, *Choosing the Dream: The Future of Religion in American Public Life* (Westport, Conn.: Greenwood, 1991), 115–31.

31. Macedo, "Liberal Civic Education and Religious Fundamentalism," 481.

32. Mark Fischer, "The Sacred and the Secular: An Examination of the 'Wall of Separation' and Its Impact on the Religious World View," *University of Pittsburgh Law Review* 54 (1992): 325–50.

33. Warren A. Nord and Charles C. Haynes, *Taking Religion Seriously Across the Curriculum* (Nashville: First Amendment Center, 1998), 158.

34. Alan Freeman and Betty Mensch, "Religion as Science/Science as Religion: Constitutional Law and the Fundamentalist Challenge," *Tikkun* 2, 5 (1987): 64–71, 66–69 (quoting the evolution scientist Stephen Jay Gould).

35. Warren A. Nord, *Religion and American Education: Rethinking a National Dilemma* (Chapel Hill: University of North Carolina Press, 1995), 181–82.

36. William P. Marshall, "The Other Side of Religion," *Hastings Law Journal* 44 (1993): 843–63, 846–47.

37. Suzanna Sherry, drawing on our republican roots, develops a theory of republican citizenship and maintains that it is not in the public interest to educate children to lead unexamined lives. She maintains that "without the ability to think critically . . . [r]epublican deliberation will be impossible because there will be neither the capacity to deliberate nor anything about which to deliberate." *See* Sherry, "Responsible Republicanism: Educating for Citizenship," 172. Bruce Ackerman takes a similar position, arguing that, "a system of liberal education provides children with a sense of the very different lives that could be theirs." *See* Bruce Ackerman, *Social Justice in the Liberal State* (New Haven: Yale University Press, 1980), 139.

38. Galston, *Liberal Purposes,* 254.

39. Eamonn Callan, "Rejoinder: Pluralism and Moral Polarization," *Canadian Journal of Education* 20, 3 (1995): 315–32.

40. Galston, *Liberal Purposes,* 256.

41. Stolzenberg, "'He Drew a Circle That Shut Me Out,'" 609.

42. Robert Coles, *The Spiritual Life of Children* (Boston: Houghton Mifflin, 1990), 100.

43. Eamonn Callan, *Creating Citizens: Political Education and Liberal Democracy* (Oxford: Oxford University Press), 158.

44. John E. Coons and Stephen D. Sugarman, *Education by Choice: The Case for Family Control* (Berkeley: University of California Press, 1978), 84.

45. Freeman and Mensch, "Religion as Science/Science as Religion," 64.

46. Morris Rosenberg, "The Dissonant Religious Context and Emotional Disturbance," in *Religion, Culture, and Society,* ed. Louis Schneider (New York: Wiley, 1964), 549–59, 559.

47. Christopher Bagley and Kanka Mallick, "Self-Esteem and Religiosity: A Comparison of 13- to 15-Year-Old Students in Catholic and Public Junior High Schools," *Canadian Journal of Education* 22, 1 (1997): 89–92; Christopher B. Smith, Andrew J. Weigert, and Dar-

win L. Thomas, "Self-Esteem and Religiosity: An Analysis of Catholic Adolescents from Five Cultures," *Journal for the Scientific Study of Religion* 18, 1 (1979): 51–60.

48. Shelley Burtt, "In Defense of *Yoder:* Parental Authority and the Public Schools," in *Nomos,* ed. Ian Shapiro and Russell Hardin (New York: New York University Press, 1996), 413–47, 428.

49. James S. Coleman and Thomas Hoffer, *Public and Private High Schools* (New York: Basic, 1987), 223.

50. Kenneth L. Karst, *Belonging to America* (New Haven: Yale University Press, 1989), 21–22.

51. Nord, *Religion and American Education,* 202.

52. Nord, quoting Alasdair MacIntyre, *After Virtue* (South Bend: Notre Dame University Press, 1981), 201.

53. Richard John Neuhaus, *The Naked Public Square* (Grand Rapids: Eerdmans, 1984), 28; Galston, "Two Concepts of Liberalism," 531; Peter L. Berger and Richard John Neuhaus, *To Empower People: The Role of Mediating Structures in Public Policy* (Washington, D.C.: American Enterprise Institute for Public Policy Research, 1977), 2–6.

54. Jean Bethke Elshtain, *Democracy on Trial* (New York: Basic Books, 1995), 6.

55. Stephen Macedo, "Community, Diversity, and Civic Education: Toward a Liberal Political Science of Group Life," *Social Philosophy and Policy* 13, 1 (1996): 240–68, 261; Rawls, *Political Liberalism,* 163.

56. Mary Ann Glendon, *Rights Talk: The Impoverishment of Political Discourse* (New York: Free Press, 1991), 109; Eamonn Callan, "Common Schools for Common Education," *Canadian Journal of Education* 20, 3 (1995): 251–71, 252.

57. Stolzenberg, "'He Drew a Circle That Shut Me Out,'" 609.

58. Macedo, "Liberal Civic Education and Religious Fundamentalism," 485.

59. Callan, *Creating Citizens,* 182; Fitzmaurice, "Liberal Neutrality, Traditional Minorities and Education," 68.

60. Steven Macedo, "Toleration and Fundamentalism," in *A Companion to Contemporary Political Philosophy,* ed. Robert E. Goodin and Philip Pettit (Oxford: Basil Blackwell, 1993), 622–28, 624.

61. Martha Minow, "Putting Up and Putting Down: Tolerance Reconsidered," in *Comparative Constitutional Federalism,* ed. Mark Tushnet (New York: Greenwood Press, 1990), 77–113, 77.

62. Macedo, "Toleration and Fundamentalism," 625.

63. Mark Holmes, *Educational Policy for the Pluralist Society* (Washington, D.C.: Falmer Press, 1992), 95.

64. Sanford Levinson, "Some Reflections on Multiculturalism, 'Equal Concern and Respect,' and the Establishment Clause of the First Amendment," *University of Richmond Law Review* 27 (1993): 989–1021, 1019.

65. Stephen Macedo, "Liberal Civic Education and Its Limits," *Canadian Journal of Education* 20, 3 (1995): 305–13, 312.

66. George P. Fletcher, "The Instability of Tolerance," in *Tolerance: An Elusive Virtue,* ed. David Heyd (Princeton: Princeton University Press, 1996), 158–72, 158.

67. Macedo, "Liberal Civic Education and Religious Fundamentalism," 474.

68. Shelley Burtt, "Religious Parents, Secular Schools: A Liberal Defense of an Illiberal Education," *Review of Politics* 51 (Winter 1994): 51–70, 65–66.

69. John H. Garvey, "Cover Your Ears," *Case Western Reserve Law Review* 43 (1993):761–71, 766.

70. *Mozert v. Hawkins County Public Schools*, 582 F.Supp. at 202. For a discussion of the specific claims made by the plaintiffs in *Mozert* and supported by their expert witnesses, *see* Joan DelFattore, *What Johnny Shouldn't Read: Textbook Censorship in America* (New Haven: Yale University Press, 1992), 61–75.

71. *Mozert*, 827 F.2d at 1069.

72. *Monteiro v. Tempe Union High School District*, 158 F.3d 1022, 1029 (9th Cir. 1998).

73. *McCollum v. Board of Education of School District No. 7, Champaign County, Illinois*, 333 U.S. 203 (1948) (Jackson, J., concurring).

74. William Marshall maintains that religious belief "cannot and should not be segregated from its political effect" and that favoring religious ideas runs counter to both establishment clause concerns as to the religious domination over the political process and free speech concerns as to the need for equality in the marketplace of ideas. *See* William P. Marshall, "The Case Against the Constitutionally Compelled Free Exercise Exemption," *Case Western Reserve Law Review* 40 (1989–90): 357–412, 393–94. Christopher Eisgruber and Lawrence Sager argue similarly that religious beliefs should be afforded equal regard rather then greater privilege in constitutional law. *See* Christopher L. Eisgruber and Lawrence G. Sager, "The Vulnerability of Conscience: The Constitutional Basis for Protecting Religious Conduct," *University of Chicago Law Review* 61 (1994): 1245–1315, 1283.

75. Burtt, "In Defense of *Yoder*," 432.

76. *Yoder v. Wisconsin*, 406 U.S. at 244–45.

77. *In re Jennifer Sengpiehl*, CJ 98–34 (Circuit County Court, Loudoun, Virginia, 1998); Shannon Sollinger, "Court Overrules Parents' Decision," *Loudoun Times-Mirror*, 11 November 1998, A11.

78. For carefully drafted and thoughtful guidelines on incorporating religious views throughout the curriculum and accommodating religious speech, *see* Nord and Haynes, *Taking Religion Seriously Across the Curriculum.*

79. *Lee v. Weisman*, 505 U.S. 577, 586 (1992).

80. *Lynch v. Donnelly*, 465 U.S. 668, 688 (1984) (O'Connor, J. concurring).

81. Nadine Strossen, "A Discussion of Religion's Role in the Classroom," *William and Mary Bill of Rights Journal*, 4 (1995): 607–68, 624.

82. *Harris v. Joint School Dist. No. 241*, 241 F.3d 447 (9th Cir. 1994); *vacated and remanded*, 515 U.S. 1154 (1995); *vacated and dismissed as moot*, 62 F.3d 1233 (9th Cir. 1995) (rejecting prayer at graduation ceremony where speakers and program content were selected exclusively by majority of seniors); *ACLU v. Black Horse Pike Regional Bd. of Educ.*, 84 F.3d 1471 (3d Cir. 1996) (rejecting practice of permitting senior class to vote on whether they preferred "prayer, a moment of reflection, or nothing at all" at high school commencement ceremony).

83. *Chandler v. James*, 180 F.3d 1254 (11th Cir. 1999).

84. *Jones v. Clear Creek Ind. School Dist.*, 977 F.2d 963 (5th Cir. 1992) (*Jones II*); *Doe v. Santa Fe Ind. School Dist.*, 171 F.3d 1013 (5th Cir. 1999) (reaffirming the nonsectarian and nonproselytizing criteria of *Jones II* as crucial).

CHAPTER 8. RE-ENVISIONING COMMON EDUCATION

1. Terence H. McLaughlin, "Liberalism, Education and the Common School," *Journal of Philosophy of Education* 29, 2 (1995): 239–55, 239.

2. Jane J. Mansbridge, *Beyond Adversary Democracy* (Chicago: University of Chicago Press, 1980), 300–01.

3. James W. Ceaser and Patrick J. McGuinn, "Civic Education Reconsidered," *Public Interest* (Fall 1988): 84–103, 93.

4. Diane Ravitch, "Multiculturalism: E Pluribus Plures," *American Scholar* 59 (1990): 337–54, 340.

5. Amitai Etzioni, *The Spirit of Community* (New York: Crown, 1993), 135; Robert Bellah, Richard Madsen, William M. Sullivan, Ann Seidler, and Steven M. Tipton, *Habits of the Heart: Individualism and Commitment in American Life* (New York: Harper and Row, 1985).

6. The distinction between education and schooling is taken from Eamonn Callan, *Creating Citizens: Political Education and Liberal Democracy* (Oxford: Oxford University Press, 1997), 163, 165–66.

7. *See* National Education Goals Panel, *The National Education Goals Report: Building a Nation of Learners* (Washington, D.C.: U.S. Government Printing Office, 1994). For a critique of that initiative and the general concept of national curriculum standards as violating freedom of conscience, *see* Stephen Arons, *Short Route to Chaos: Conscience, Community, and the Reconstitution of American Schools* (Amherst: University of Massachusetts Press, 1997).

8. Pierre Schlag, "Values," *Yale Journal of Law and Humanities* 6 (1994): 219–32, 220–21; Suzanna Sherry, "Responsible Republicanism: Educating for Citizenship," *University of Chicago Press* 62 (1995): 131–208, 177.

9. Pierre Schlag, *Laying Down the Law: Mysticism, Fetishism, and the American Legal Mind* (New York: New York University Press, 1996), 51.

10. Diane Ravitch, *The Schools We Deserve* (New York: Basic Books, 1984), 22–23.

11. Schlag, *Laying Down the Law,* 51.

12. *Bob Jones University v. United States,* 461 U.S. 574, 593, 604 (1983).

13. *Norwood v. Harrison,* 413 U.S. 455, 469–70, 462 (1973).

14. *Runyon v. McCrary,* 427 U.S. 160, 177 (1976).

15. Rosemary C. Salomone, *Equal Education Under Law* (New York: St. Martin's Press, 1986), 17, citing "Equality, Moral and Social," in *The Encyclopedia of Philosophy,* ed. Paul Edwards (New York: Macmillan, 1972), 39.

16. Jeffrey C. Alexander and Neil J. Smelser, "Introduction: The Ideological Discourse of Cultural Discontent," in *Diversity and Its Discontents,* ed. Neil J. Smelser and Jeffrey C. Alexander (Princeton: Princeton University Press, 1999), 11.

17. *Virginia v. United States,* 518 U.S. 515, 545 (1996).

18. Michael Walzer, *On Tolerance* (New Haven: Yale University Press, 1997), 65. For diverse views on religious group rights and gender equality, *see Is Multiculturalism Bad for Women?,* ed. Joshua Cohen, Michael Howard, and Martha Nussbaum (Princeton: Princeton University Press, 1999).

19. Amy Gutmann and Dennis Thompson, *Democracy and Disagreement* (Cambridge: Harvard University Press, 1996), 66–67.

20. In *Bowers v. Hardwick,* 478 U.S. 186 (1986), the Court upheld a Georgia statute making it a criminal offense to engage in sodomy, but the Court discussed the law only as it applied to homosexuals, even though on its face the law did not distinguish between homosexuals and heterosexuals.

21. Sherry, "Responsible Republicanism," 172.

22. Michael Rebell offers a cogent argument that communities should engage in pluralistic dialogue to determine curricular values. *See* Michael Rebell, "Schools, Values, and the Courts," *Yale Law and Policy Review* 7 (1989): 275–342, 338–42.

23. Colorado Constitution, art. II, §30B (St. Paul: West, 1999).

24. *Romer v. Evans,* 517 U.S. 620, 633 (1996).

25. McLaughlin, "Liberalism, Education and the Common School," 250.

26. Gutmann and Thompson, *Democracy and Disagreement,* 63–68.

27. In *Guyer v. School Board of Alachua County,* 634 So.2d 806 (1st Dist. Fla. 1994), the court rejected a claim that the depiction of witches, cauldrons, and brooms in public school decorations as part of a Halloween celebration were religious symbols and therefore had the effect of endorsing or promoting a religion in violation of the establishment clause.

28. Mark Yudof, *When Government Speaks* (Berkeley: University of California Press, 1982), 230 (emphasis added).

29. Stephen Arons, "Educational Choice as a Civil Rights Strategy," in *Public Values, Public Schools,* ed. Neal E. Devins (New York: Falmer, 1989), 63–87, 74.

30. For a discussion of how communal activities in America have declined dramatically over the past quarter of a century, *see* Robert D. Putnam, "Bowling Alone: Democracy in America at the End of the Twentieth Century," *Journal of Democracy* 6 (1995): 65–78.

31. Joseph P. Viteritti, *Choosing Equality* (Washington, D.C.: Brookings Institution, 1999).

32. In recent years, a number of scholars writing in the liberal tradition, including William Galston, Suzanna Sherry, and Toni Marie Massaro, have affirmatively supported the concept of school choice and particularly education vouchers. More recently, Amy Gutmann has endorsed subsidizing private schools where the public schools fail to provide an adequate civic education. Amy Gutmann, *Democratic Education,* 2d ed. (Princeton: Princeton University Press, 1999), 301.

33. Milton Friedman, *Capitalism and Freedom* (Chicago: University of Chicago Press, 1962).

34. Christopher Jencks, *Education Vouchers: A Report on Financing Elementary Education by Grants to Parents* (Cambridge, Mass.: Center for the Study of Public Policy, 1970); John E. Coons and Stephen D. Sugarman, *Education by Choice: The Case for Family Control* (Berkeley: University of California Press, 1978).

35. For an overview of school choice nationwide, *see* Dorothy B. Hanks, *School Choice Programs: What's Happening in the States* (Washington, D.C.: Heritage Foundation, 1997).

36. Peter W. Cookson, Jr., *School Choice: The Struggle for the Soul of American Education* (New Haven: Yale University Press, 1994), 55–64.

37. For a discussion of the charter school model of choice, *see* Ted Kolderie, *Beyond Choice to the New Public School: Withdrawing the Exclusive Franchise in Public Education* (Washington, D.C.: Progressive Policy Institute, 1990).

38. *The State of Charter Schools: Third Year Report* (Washington, D.C.: U.S. Department of Education, 1998).

39. Theresa Walker, "Opinions Are Mixed on School Choice," *Wall Street Journal*, 14 March 1997, R4.

40. *Kotterman v. Killian*, 972 P.2d 606 (Ariz. 1999), *cert. denied*, 68 U.S.L.W. 3232 (U.S. Oct. 4, 1999).

41. Salomone, *Equal Education under Law*, 187–89.

42. John E. Chubb and Terry M. Moe, *Politics, Markets, and Schools* (Washington, D.C.: Brookings Institution, 1990). For a thoughtful critique of the market metaphor as a guide to educational policy, *see* Jeffrey R. Henig, *Rethinking School Choice: Limits of the Market Metaphor* (Princeton: Princeton University Press, 1994). For a comparison of the pure charter and voucher models, *see* Bryan S. Hassel, "The Case for Charter Schools," in *Learning from School Choice*, ed. Paul E. Peterson and Bryan C. Hassel (Washington, D.C.: Brookings Institution, 1998), 33–51.

43. Paul E. Peterson, "School Choice: A Report Card," in *Learning from School Choice*, ed. Peterson and Hassel, 3–32, 8.

44. Kim K. Metcalf et al., *Evaluation of the Cleveland Scholarship Program: Second-Year Report (1997–98)* (Bloomington: Indiana Center for Evaluation, Indiana University, November 1998).

45. *See* Paul Peterson, "A Critique of the Witte Evaluation of Milwaukee's School Choice Program," Center for American Political Studies, Harvard University, Occasional Paper 95–2 (February 1995), critiquing John F. Witte, "Who Benefits from the Milwaukee Choice Program?" in *Who Chooses? Who Loses?: Culture, Institutions and the Unequal Effects of School Choice*, ed. Richard Elmore and Bruce Fuller with Gary Orfield (New York: Teachers College, 1996), 118–37.

46. Peterson, "School Choice: A Report Card," 17–23.

47. Paul E. Peterson, William J. Howell, and Jay P. Greene, *An Evaluation of the Cleveland Voucher Program After Two Years* (Cambridge: Harvard University Program on Education Policy and Governance, June 1999).

48. Cookson, *School Choice*, 82.

49. Paul E. Peterson, "Top Ten Questions Asked About School Choice," paper presented to the Conference on Education Policy, Brookings Institution, Washington, D.C. (May 1998), 31.

50. Paul Peterson, David Meyers, and William G. Howell, *An Evaluation of the New York City School Choice Scholarship Program: The First Year* (Cambridge: Harvard University Program in Education and Governance, 1998).

51. *School Choice Accountability: A Consensus of Views in Ohio and Wisconsin* (Washington, D.C.: Public Policy Forum, February 1998), 13–14; Lowell C. Rose and Alec M. Gallup, "The 31st Annual Phi Delta Kappa/Gallup Poll of the Public's Attitudes Toward the Public Schools," *Phi Delta Kappan* (September 1999): 42–56, 53.

52. Mark Walsh, "Nationwide Campaign Targets Private School Vouchers," *Education Week*, 9 April 1997, 13.

53. *Mueller v. Allen*, 463 U.S. 388 (1983); *Witters v. Washington Department of Services for the Blind*, 474 U.S. 481 (1986); *Zobrest v. Catalina Foothills School District*, 509 U.S. 1 (1993);

Rosenberger v. Rector and Visitors of the University of Virginia, 515 U.S. 819 (1995); *Agostini v. Felton*, 117 S.Ct. 1997 (1997).

54. *Jackson v. Benson*, 578 N.W.2d 602 (Wis. 1998), *cert. denied*, 119 S.Ct. 466 (1998).

55. *Lemon v. Kurtzman*, 403 U.S. 602 (1971).

56. *Simmons-Harris v. Goff*, 711 N.E.2d (Ohio, 1999); *Simmons-Harris v. Zelman*, 54 F.Supp.2d 725 (N.D.Ohio 1999)(granting preliminary injunction); *Chittendon Town School Dist, v. Vermont Dep't of Educ.*, No. 97-275, 1999 WL 37844 (Vermont June 11, 1999); *Bagley v. Raymond School Dep't*, 728 A.2d 127 (Me. 1999), *cert. denied*, 68 U.S.L.W. 3105 (U.S. Oct. 12, 1999); *Strout v. Albanese*, 178 F.3d 57 (1st Cir. 1999), *cert. denied*, 68 U.S.L.W. 3129 (U.S. Oct. 12, 1999).

57. Steven Green offers a well-formulated argument opposing public aid to religiously affiliated schools from a policy and establishment clause perspective in Steven K. Green, "The Legal Argument Against Private School Choice," *University of Cincinnati Law Review* 62 (1993): 37–73.

58. Alan Peshkin, *God's Choice: The Total World of a Fundamentalist Christian School* (Chicago: University of Chicago Press, 1986); Susan Rose, *Keeping Them Out of the Hands of Satan: Evangelical Schooling in America* (New York: Routledge, 1988); James G. Dwyer, *Religious Schools v. Children's Rights* (Ithaca: Cornell University Press, 1998).

59. Jay P. Greene, "Civic Values in Public and Private Schools," in *Learning from School Choice*, ed. Peterson and Hassel, 83–106, 92–100.

60. Andrew M. Greeley, *Catholic Schools and Minority Students* (New Brunswick: Transaction, 1982); James Coleman and Thomas Hoffer, *Public and Private High Schools* (New York: Basic Books, 1987); Anthony S. Bryk, Valerie E. Lee, and Peter B. Holland, *Catholic Schools and the Common Good* (Cambridge: Harvard University Press, 1993).

61. Christian Smith and David Sikkink, "Is Private School Privatizing?" *First Things* (April 1999), 55–59, 55.

62. Andrew M. Greeley and Peter H. Rossi, *The Education of Catholic Americans* (Chicago: Aldine, 1966), 152–54.

63. Bryk, Lee, and Holland, *Catholic Schools and the Common Good*, 312, 11.

64. Smith and Sikkink, "Is Private School Privatizing?" 56–57.

65. *Convent of the Sacred Heart Elementary School*, Bulletin (San Francisco).

66. Christopher Richter, "Separation and Equality: An Argument for Religious Schools within the Public System," *Ottawa Law Review* 28 (1996–97): 1–44, 34.

67. Stephen D. Sugarman, "Using Private Schools to Promote Public Values," *University of Chicago Legal Forum* (1991): 171–210, 178–81.

68. *Rendell-Baker v. Kohn*, 457 U.S. 830 (1982).

69. Laurence H. Tribe, *American Constitutional Law*, 2d ed. (Mineola, N.Y.: Foundation Press, 1988), 1223 n. 57.

70. *United States v. Virginia*, 518 U.S. at 534 (1996).

71. Ibid., 534 n. 7, citing "Brief for Twenty-six Private Women's Colleges as *Amicus Curiae*," 5.

72. For a discussion of the legal issues surrounding Single-Sex schools, *see* Rosemary C. Salomone, "Single-Sex Schooling: Law, Policy, and Research," in *Brookings Papers on Edu-*

cation Policy 1999, ed. Diane Ravitch (Washington, D.C.: Brookings Institution Press, 1999), 231–97.

73. *Lessons from Other Countries About Private School Aid* (Washington, D.C.: Center on Education Policy, 1999).

74. *Meyer v. Nebraska,* 262 U.S. 390, 403 (1923).

75. *Farrington v. Tokushige,* 273 U.S. 284 (1927). For a more recent court decision reaffirming the same principle, *see State v. Whisner,* 351 N.E. 2d 750 (Ohio 1976).

76. For a discussion of various approaches to the unconstitutional conditions problem, *see* Kathleen M. Sullivan, "Unconstitutional Conditions," *Harvard Law Review* 102 (1989): 1413–1506.

77. *Pierce v. Society of Sisters,* 268 U.S. 510, 536 (1925).

78. Harry Brighouse, "The Egalitarian Virtues of Educational Vouchers," *Journal of Philosophy* 28, 2 (1994): 211–19.

79. Coleman and Hoffer, *Public and Private High Schools,* 214–15.

80. Sugarman, "Using Private Schools to Promote Public Values," 171–210.

81. *Board of Education of Oklahoma City Public Schools v. Dowell,* 498 U.S. 237 (1991); *Freeman v. Pitts,* 503 U.S. 467 (1992).

82. Mark Holmes, "The Place of Religion in Public Education," *Interchange* 24, 3 (1993): 205–23, 221.

83. Callan, *Creating Citizens,* 170–71.

84. For a more recent detailed school choice model that tilts toward the poor and includes a critique of other contemporary proposals, *see* John E. Coons and Stephen D. Sugarman, *Scholarships for Children* (Berkeley: Institute of Governmental Studies Press, University of California, 1992).

85. Stephen D. Sugarman and David Kirp, "Rethinking Collective Responsibility for Education," *Law and Contemporary Problems* 39 (Summer 1975): 144–225, 225.

Index